Ethical and Legal Issues for Mental Health Professionals: A Comprehensive Handbook of Principles and Standards

Ethical and Legal Issues for Mental Health Professionals: A Comprehensive Handbook of Principles and Standards has been co-published simultaneously as *Journal of Aggression, Maltreatment & Trauma*, Volume 11, Numbers 1/2 and 3 2005.

Ethical and Legal Issues for Mental Health Professionals: A Comprehensive Handbook of Principles and Standards

Steven F. Bucky, PhD
Joanne E. Callan, PhD
George Stricker, PhD
Editors

Ethical and Legal Issues for Mental Health Professionals: A Comprehensive Handbook of Principles and Standards has been co-published simultaneously as *Journal of Aggression, Maltreatment & Trauma*, Volume 11, Numbers 1/2 and 3 2005.

Routledge
Taylor & Francis Group
NEW YORK AND LONDON

First published by
The Haworth Press, Inc.
10 Alice Street
Binghamton, N Y 13904-1580

This edition published 2011 by Routledge

Routledge
Taylor & Francis Group
711 Third Avenue
New York, NY 10017

Routledge
Taylor & Francis Group
2 Park Square, Milton Park
Abingdon, Oxon OX14 4RN

Ethical and Legal Issues for Mental Health Professionals: A Comprehensive Handbook of Principles and Standards has been co-published simultaneously as *Journal of Aggression, Maltreatment & Trauma*, Volume 11, Numbers 1/2 and 3 2005.

The development, preparation, and publication of this work has been undertaken with great care. However, the publisher, employees, editors, and agents of The Haworth Press and all imprints of The Haworth Press, Inc., including The Haworth Medical Press® and The Pharmaceutical Products Press®, are not responsible for any errors contained herein or for consequences that may ensue from use of materials or information contained in this work. Opinions expressed by the author(s) are not necessarily those of The Haworth Press, Inc.

Cover design by Marylouise E. Doyle

Library of Congress Cataloging-in-Publication Data

Ethical and legal issues for mental health professionals: a comprehensive handbook of principles and standards /Steven F. Bucky, Joanne E. Callan, George Stricker, editors.
     p. cm.
     "Handbook of Principles and Standards has been co-published simultaneously as Journal of Aggression, Maltreatment & Trauma, Volume 11, Numbers 1/2 and 3 2005."
     Includes bibliographical references and index.
     ISBN-13: 978-0-7890-2729-0 (hc. : alk. paper)
     ISBN-10: 0-7890-2729-1 (hc. : alk. paper)
     ISBN 13: 978-0-7890-2730-6 (pbk. : alk. paper)
     ISBN 10: 0-7890-2730-5 (pbk. : alk. paper)
     1. Mental health personnel–Professional ethics–United States 2. Mental Health Personnel–Legal status, laws, etc.–United States. I. Bucky, Steven F. II. Callan, Joanne E. III. Stricker, George. IV. Journal of aggression, maltreatment & trauma.

RC455.2.E8E82 2005
174.2–dc22
                                               2005006603

Ethical and Legal Issues for Mental Health Professionals: A Comprehensive Handbook of Principles and Standards

CONTENTS

ABOUT THE EDITORS

Steven F. Bucky, PhD, received his doctorate in Clinical Psychology at the University of Cincinnati in 1970. Since 1972, he has been at the California School of Professional Psychology at Alliant International University in San Diego as Full Professor, the Director of Professional Training and Chair of the Ethics Committee and has taught the advanced Ethics course. Dr. Bucky is also in private practice that focuses on children, adolescents and families, substance abuse, forensics, and the assessment and treatment of professional and college athletes. In addition, Dr. Bucky is currently the President and Chairman of the Board of the McAlister Institute (a group of twenty programs focusing on the drug and alcohol treatment of women, their children, and adolescents). From 1972-1978, he was responsible for the evaluation of all of the U.S. Navy's Alcoholism and Drug Treatment Programs worldwide.

Dr. Bucky has 48 published papers, has made 65 presentations at professional conferences, and was the editor of a book entitled *The Impact of Alcoholism* (Hazelden, Inc., 1978). Dr. Bucky is a member of numerous professional organizations, including the American Psychological Association (Fellow) and the San Diego Psychological Association (Fellow) and has received the Silver Psi Award from the California Psychological Association (CPA). Dr. Bucky was President of CPA, was on CPA's Board of Directors, and was a member of CPA's Ethics Committee from 1990-1997. Dr. Bucky has been a consultant to the U.S. Attorney's office, the District Attorney's office, the Attorney General's office, California's Medical Board, the Board of Psychology, and the Board of Behavioral Sciences.

Joanne E. Callan, PhD, is Professor in the Clinical Psychology doctoral programs of the California School of Professional Psychology, at Alliant International University (San Diego, CA). In addition, she holds an Associate Clinical Professor appointment in the Department of Psychiatry, University of California San Diego, and is a Training and Supervising Analyst at the San Diego Psychoanalytic Society and Institute. Formerly the Executive Director of the American Psychological Association's Education Directorate, she continues to consult with education programs, from pre-school through higher education, in addition to her private practice in clinical psychology and psychoanalysis.

George Stricker, PhD, is Distinguished Research Professor of Psychology in the Derner Institute, Adelphi University. He received a PhD in Clinical Psychology at the University of Rochester in 1960 and an honorary PsyD from the Illinois School of Professional Psychology, Meadows Campus, in 1997. He received the American Psychological Association Award for Distinguished Contribution to Applied Psychology in 1990, the American Psychological Association Award for Distinguished Career Contributions to Education and Training in Psychology in 1995, the National Council of Schools and Programs of Professional Psychology Award for Distinguished Contribution to Education and Professional Psychology in 1998, the Allen V. Williams, Jr. Memorial Award from the New York State Psychological Association in 1999, and the Florence Halpern Award for Distinguished Professional Contributions in Clinical Psychology from the Society of Clinical Psychology (Division 12) in 2002. Dr. Stricker is the author or editor of approximately 20 books, 30 book chapters, and more than 100 journal articles.

ABOUT THE CONTRIBUTORS

Megan E. Callan, JD, received her law degree from the University of San Diego School of Law. She is the author of "The More the Not Marry-er: In Search of a Policy Behind Eligibility for California Domestic Partnerships," 40, *San Diego Law Review* 427 (Winter 2003). Currently, she serves as law clerk to the United States District Judge W. Royal Furgeson in San Antonio, Texas.

O. Brandt Caudill, Jr., JD, has been representing mental health professionals in civil and administrative litigation for over 20 years. Mr. Caudill has a BA in Psychology from Michigan State University and a JD from Georgetown University Law Center. Mr. Caudill is a member of the firm Callahan, McCune, and Willis, APC.

Charles Clark, PhD, specializes in forensic psychology and psychotherapy. He maintains a private practice in Ann Arbor, Michigan.

Clark R. Clipson, PhD, is an assessment psychologist in private practice, specializing in forensic and neuropsychological evaluations. He is also an adjunct faculty member at the California School of Professional Psychology in San Diego, where he taught professional ethics for ten years.

Solomon M. Fulero, JD, PhD, is both an attorney and a psychologist. He received his doctoral and law degrees from the University of Oregon, both in 1979. He is Professor of Psychology at Sinclair College in Dayton, Ohio, and Clinical Professor of Psychiatry at Wright State University, also in Dayton, Ohio.

Ronald Gandolfo, PhD, ABPP, holds a Diplomate in Clinical Psychology awarded by the American Board of Professional Psychology. He is a professor at the California School of Professional Psychology at Alliant International University, Fresno, where he has taught professional and ethics courses for 30 years. He has chaired ethics committees for professional associations and the California School of Professional Psychology. He has been in independent practice in clinical and forensic psychology for 25 years.

Muriel Golub, PhD, obtained her doctorate in Clinical Psychology in 1975 from United States International University in San Diego, CA. Dr. Golub worked at Family Services in Orange County, CA, and is currently in independent clinical practice. In addition, Dr. Golub was Chair of the California Psychological Association's Ethics Committee from 1987-1999.

Alan I. Kaplan, JD, is an attorney who concentrates in the representation of psychologists and other health care professionals who are accused of misconduct in license revocation, government audits, and other administrative proceedings. He is a graduate of Cornell University and the Loyola School of Law, and has practiced in Los Angeles since 1979. He serves as general counsel to three analytic institutes and two psychological associations in Southern California, and has given presentations throughout the state on various aspects of risk management for health care professionals.

Rodney L. Lowman, PhD, is Interim Provost and Vice President for Academic Affairs at Alliant International University. His writings on ethics include *The Ethical Practice of Psychology in Organizations* (American Psychological Association, 1998). Dr. Lowman received his PhD in psychology (specializing in Industrial-Organizational and Clinical Psychology) from Michigan State University in 1979. He is a Fellow of the American Psychological Association in two divisions (13 and 14).

Thomas McGee, PhD, ABPP, is Professor Emeritus of the California School of Professional Psychology at Alliant International University in San Diego, California. He is a diplomate in clinical psychology and group psychology, and has spent many years directing and supervising in psychology training programs.

Julian Meltzoff, PhD, received his doctorate in psychology from the University of Pennsylvania in 1950. He was Chief of the Psychology Service in several Veteran's Administration Hospitals and Outpatient Clinics until 1977. He then served as Professor and Director of Research at the California School of Professional Psychology, San Diego, until 1997. Dr. Meltzoff is the author of three books: *The Day Treatment Center: Principles, Application and Evaluation* (with R. L. Blumenthal; Charles C. Thomas, 1966); *Research in Psychotherapy* (with M. Kornreich; Aldine de Gruyter, 1970); and *Critical Thinking About Research: Psychology and Related Fields* (American Psychological Association, 1998). He has a fourth book in process. He has written numerous scientific journal articles, book chapters, and reviews.

David Mills, PhD, obtained his doctorate in Clinical Psychology in 1964 from Michigan State University. He held a faculty position at the University of Maryland from 1969-1974, and served as the Administrative Officer for the American Psychological Association's Ethics Office from 1974-1981. Dr. Mills is presently retired.

Thomas F. Nagy, PhD, received his doctorate from the University of Illinois, and is a former member of the APA ethics committee and chair of the task force that revised the 1992 edition of the psychology ethics code. He has an independent clinical practice in Palo Alto, California, and is a national consultant to mental health professionals and consumers in matters of ethics and professional practice. He is also a staff psychologist in the School of Medicine at Stanford University's Department of Psychiatry and Behavioral Sciences (Center for Integrative Medicine) and serves on the voluntary clinical faculty as well, teaching an ethics seminar for the postdoctoral students. He authored *Ethics in Plain English: An Illustrative Casebook for Psychologists* (American Psychological Association, 1999).

Natalie Shavit, LLB, PsyD, is a recent graduate of the California School of Professional Psychology in San Diego, California. She also holds a law degree from the University of New South Wales in Australia.

Simone Simone, PhD, received her doctorate from Kent State University. She is currently in private practice in Gulfport, Mississippi.

Erica H. Wise, PhD, received her doctorate in Clinical Psychology in 1980 from Southern Illinois University at Carbondale after completing her internship in the Department of Psychiatry at the University of North Carolina at Chapel Hill. In addition to her part-time private practice, she has worked in the Student Health Service at UNC-Chapel Hill and is currently a Clinical Associate Professor and Director of the Training Clinic in the Department of Psychology at UNC-CH. She was a member of the APA Ethics Committee from 1990-1993 and a member of the APA Committee on Professional Practice and Standards from 2000-2002. She is currently Chair of the North Carolina Psychology Board and has been a member since 1993.

Acknowledgments

I would like to take this opportunity to express my sincere appreciation and thank the co-editors, Dr. Joanne Callan and Dr. George Stricker, who were involved in the development, organization, writing, and editing of this manuscript; and to our exceptional editing assistants: Jennifer Zellner, MS, Julie Alley, MA, and Mary Miller, MA, who worked hard with professionalism, enthusiasm, and competence.

I would also like to thank my family, including my sons: Scott, Keith and Rob; my daughters-in-law Marvelynn and Jennifer; my grandchildren Brooklynn, Madison, Joshua and Braden; and a special thanks to my loving wife and best friend of 36 years, Marilyn, who has been unconditionally accepting and supportive of my professional responsibilities and whose guidance and support have been invaluable in the development of this manuscript and the success of my career.

Steven F. Bucky, PhD

Foreword

Ethical and legal issues in the mental health field have become much more important in clinical as well as in forensic practice in recent years. Therefore, it has become imperative that mental health professionals be familiar with the various legal and ethical requirements of their respective professions, not only to avoid malpractice lawsuits or licensing board complaints, but also to ensure that they are providing the highest quality service. Most of the professional associations involved in mental health, such as the American Psychological Association, the National Association of Social Workers, the American Psychiatric Association, the American Association of Marriage and Family Therapists, and the National Board of Certified Counselors, have revised their respective ethical codes in recent years to deal with changes in technology, clinical practice, and legislation. Many states have passed various laws and statutes specifically dealing with some aspect of mental health practice, and most graduate training programs provide specific courses in ethical practice. In addition, many states now require continuing education for licensed mental health practitioners, and some require annual updates in ethics as part of such continuing education.

Thus, keeping current with the issues has received more attention in recent years, and the various malpractice insurance companies usually offer and recommend specific workshops in risk management that include current ethical practices. Even with all of these requirements and

[Haworth co-indexing entry note]: "Foreword." Geffner, Robert. Co-published simultaneously in *Journal of Aggression, Maltreatment & Trauma* (The Haworth Maltreatment & Trauma Press, an imprint of The Haworth Press, Inc.) Vol. 11, No. 1/2, 2005, pp. xxix-xxx and Vol. 11, No. 3, 2005, pp. xxvii-xxviii; and: *Ethical and Legal Issues for Mental Health Professionals: A Comprehensive Handbook of Principles and Standards* (ed: Steven F. Bucky, Joanne E. Callan, and George Stricker) The Haworth Maltreatment & Trauma Press, an imprint of The Haworth Press, Inc., 2005, pp. xxiii-xxiv. Single or multiple copies of this article are available for a fee from The Haworth Document Delivery Service [1-800-HAWORTH, 9:00 a.m. - 5:00 p.m. (EST). E-mail address: docdelivery@haworthpress.com].

Available online at http://www.haworthpress.com/web/JAMT
xxiii

changes, there are still numerous ethical complaints against mental health professionals that are filed each year with licensing boards. In this day and age, people have become much more skeptical about the practice of mental health, the reliability and validity of various clinical techniques, and the role of mental health experts in court cases. In the past, the main complaint involved sexual interaction between clinician and client. Now, many complaints involve some aspect of a child custody case, with allegations of unethical evaluations, reports, conclusions, recommendations, or testimony in court. There is a "battle of the mental health experts" much more frequently in many forensic criminal, civil, and family court cases. The perception by the public as well as the legal community is often that many mental health professionals are not as ethical as they should be, or as they would like to be perceived. Instead of practitioners being ethical and responding from a serious scientific base, the mental health field may be perceived as more "soft science" and vague. When the mental health professions do not police themselves by requiring a strict adherence to ethical standards, the field is compromised.

In order to be able to practice in an ethical manner, it then becomes mandatory that those in the mental health fields understand and keep current with the guidelines and principles, especially in light of the recent revisions and increasing complexity of the laws, statutes, and ethical codes. The present comprehensive handbook is one way to help mental health professionals accomplish this. Drs. Bucky, Callan, and Stricker have done an excellent job of compiling an impressive list of authors and contributors for this volume. This volume incorporates and examines best practices in a thorough but readable manner. Key issues, from practice standards to confidentiality to competence, are discussed. This book should be required reading for all mental health professionals.

I am pleased that the editors have chosen the Haworth Maltreatment & Trauma Press to publish their important work. In addition, this volume will be one of a series concerning ethical practice. We will be following this handbook with two more volumes that deal with specific aspects of ethical practice, including forensic mental health. The editors are to be commended for such important contributions to the field and practice of mental health.

Robert Geffner, PhD, ABPN
Senior Editor, Journal of Aggression, Maltreatment & Trauma
Editor-in-Chief, Haworth Maltreatment & Trauma Press

INTRODUCTION

Ethics Law and Licensing

George Stricker
Steven F. Bucky

SUMMARY. Ethics, law, and licensing are overlapping but different dimensions by which professional conduct is regulated. Ethics refers to a professional code of conduct. Law refers to a relevant body of statutes. Licensing refers to permission to practice a profession granted by a relevant jurisdiction. Similarities and differences among these sources of authority and regulation are described, and the articles contained within this volume are discussed. *[Article copies available for a fee from The Haworth Document Delivery Service: 1-800-HAWORTH. E-mail address: <docdelivery@haworthpress.com> Website: <http://www.HaworthPress.com> © 2005 by The Haworth Press, Inc. All rights reserved.]*

KEYWORDS. Ethics, law, licensing, regulation

Address correspondence to: George Stricker, PhD, The Derner Institute, Adelphi University, Garden City, NY 11530 (E-mail: stricker@adelphi.edu).

[Haworth co-indexing entry note]: "Ethics Law and Licensing." Stricker, George, and Steven F. Bucky. Co-published simultaneously in *Journal of Aggression, Maltreatment & Trauma* (The Haworth Maltreatment & Trauma Press, an imprint of The Haworth Press, Inc.) Vol. 11, No. 1/2, 2005, pp. 1-10; and: *Ethical and Legal Issues for Mental Health Professionals: A Comprehensive Handbook of Principles and Standards* (ed: Steven F. Bucky, Joanne E. Callan, and George Stricker) The Haworth Maltreatment & Trauma Press, an imprint of The Haworth Press, Inc., 2005, pp. 1-10. Single or multiple copies of this article are available for a fee from The Haworth Document Delivery Service [1-800-HAWORTH, 9:00 a.m. - 5:00 p.m. (EST). E-mail address: docdelivery@haworthpress.com].

Digital Object Identifier: 10.1300/J146v011n01_01

Students and colleagues frequently call me with what they see as ethical dilemmas, often introducing their question by stating "I have an ethics question for you." More often than not, the question is not primarily an ethical question, but one that more properly belongs in the legal realm. It is not unusual for "ethics" to be used as a generic term for any conundrum that has a moral dimension, and so it embraces ethics, morality, law, politics, and clinical judgment. However, for a solution to be found to the problem that has been posed, it is important to differentiate these areas, for different contexts lead to different solutions. This article, an introduction to a handbook of ethics and law, seeks to clarify some of these distinctions, so that the reader who is faced with a problem will know whether to seek the answer with an ethicist, an attorney, or a State licensing authority.

For the purposes of this article, ethics will be used to refer to a code of conduct that governs the behavior of a group of professionals; there is a much broader literature concerning ethics as a branch of philosophy, and this leads to distinctions worthy of an entire text. However, regardless of whether one feels a philosophical kinship with utilitarianism, categorical imperatives, or more contemporary approaches to human rights, each profession's ethics code explicates a set of rules that are intended to guide members of that profession. Law is used in its broadest sense, and refers to a set of statutes, whether municipal, state, or federal, that govern the conduct of all people under the jurisdiction of that statutory code. Licensing is the prerogative of the states, and will refer to the rules of whatever authority has granted the license to practice to the particular individual who raises the question under consideration. There are several areas we may consider, and each has different implications for these three sources of authority. Let us now review each of these areas.

SOURCE

The source of a professional code of ethics always is internal. Each profession generates its own code of conduct, and does so in the interest of self-governance. The source of both legal and licensing authority always is external to the profession. The various regulations and statutes serve to impose restrictions on the conduct of a professional in the interest of the general public. It probably is accurate to suggest that one measure of the adequacy of a professional code of conduct is the extent to which the public feels protected. When the code gives the appearance of supporting guild interests, there is a vacuum created that leads to external regulations being placed on the actions of the professional.

TARGET

There is a marked difference in who is subject to the various sets of regulations created by the authorities being considered in this chapter. A code of ethics only applies to the members of an organization that promulgates such a code. Thus, the American Psychological Association (APA), for example, has a well-developed code of ethics, but it only is applicable to APA members. A psychologist who is not an APA member has no reason, other than internal, to follow the dictates of that code, and cannot be judged by APA according to the strictures of that code. A law applies to all people who live in the relevant jurisdiction, and can be applied to anyone, regardless of their citizenship. A licensing law, however, only applies to those who have been issued a license, and a person who practices as a psychotherapist (most frequently this is an unlicensed title) without a license cannot be prosecuted for failing to adhere to regulations devised to govern the conduct of licensed professionals in that jurisdiction. Thus, a person who is licensed and is a member of a professional organization will be regulated by three sometimes contradictory authorities, whereas an unlicensed practitioner who does not join a professional organization only will be subject to the laws of the governing jurisdiction. Does this suggest that a practitioner would be wise to avoid professional membership and licensing? Not at all, because there are many benefits that accrue from such membership and licensure, but the price of those benefits is the need to adhere to their respective codes of conduct.

MAXIMUM PENALTY

If an individual has been accused of a violation of the relevant code, and has been judged and found to be in violation, what consequence can follow? For a professional code of ethics, which only applies to members, the maximum penalty is expulsion of membership. At first glance, this may seem like a relatively small penalty, as it also relieves the ex-member of any further obligation to follow the code that has been violated. However, there is a much greater weight to this penalty than meets the eye. First, there is the obvious loss of professional affiliation, with all the benefits that brings. More concretely, the loss of membership often is accompanied by notifications, so that colleagues become aware of the action, as do other associations to which the member may belong, licensing authorities, and groups such as the National Register and the American Board of Professional Psychology. Each of these groups and organizations may then initiate their own actions, so that the initial loss of professional membership may be followed by a cascade of other losses. Even for those individuals who are not fazed by this set of losses and disaffiliations, the ethics action of a membership organization must be reported to a malpractice carrier, and the subsequent rise in premium, or loss of coverage, provides an additional and substantial penalty to the offender.

The violation of a legal requirement, because it applies to everyone residing in the relevant jurisdiction, carries the penalty specified by the statute. This can range from a fine to a term in jail, and this action, too, is reportable to other governing authorities. Thus, malpractice insurance, for example, can be compromised by legal as well as by ethical transgressions. Finally, the violation of a licensing law can lead to the loss of the license that had been awarded. Similar to the violation of a professional code of conduct, such a violation only can lead to the loss of the credential (membership or license) that subjected the person to that code. However, similar to the violation of a professional code of conduct, the penalty is far more severe than it initially may appear to be. The loss of a license, in and of itself, can inhibit the ability of the individual to practice. Beyond that, it is a public judgment, and other consequences follow. The loss of license in psychology is reported to a bank of disciplinary data that is maintained by the Association of State and Provincial Psychology Boards, and this, in turn, is available to other organizations as well. A great many of the cases heard by the APA Ethics Committee come to the attention of that Committee after a decision has been rendered by a state licensing board. Here too, malpractice insurance consequences also follow from licensing disciplinary actions. In each case, whether the discipline is through ethics, law, or licensing, there is the possibility that civil actions will be filed by the aggrieved individual, and the definitive action of a duly constituted authority cannot help but be consequential in the hearing of that civil case.

LOCUS OF AUTHORITY

A professional code of ethics, because it is developed by a national organization, has a national scope. Every member of the association, regardless of where they reside, is subject to the same code. However, a law only is binding in the jurisdiction where it has been promulgated. In rare cases, professional activities are subject to federal laws, or to laws of local municipalities. However, in most cases, the relevant statutes governing the behavior of professionals are statewide. This is similar to licensing, which is a state activity, and which only applies in the state where the license is issued.

The important consequence of this distinction is that every member of a professional organization is subject to a single, defining code of ethical conduct. However, appropriate legal behavior for the professional varies from state to state. As an example, professional conduct, ethically, is bound everywhere by an obligation to maintain confidentiality, but certain exceptions that mandate reports vary from state to state. The need to report child abuse is present in every state, but the criteria for child abuse and the process for reporting differ. In other areas, such as spousal or elder abuse, these are subject to mandated reporting in some states but not in others. Professionals can move from region to region and always be clear about the nature of ethical conduct, but it is incumbent upon them to be familiar with local regulations and statutes, because even crossing a border into a neighboring state can lead to a different obligation for professional conduct.

This difference between the national scope of ethics and the local scope of law and license, along with the different aspects of these three sets of governing codes, leads to the difficult dilemma that occurs when behavior is prescribed by one set of codes and proscribed by another. An example of this occurs in the clash between confidentiality and mandated reporting. Most codes of ethics will allow law to supersede ethical obligation, and not force the professional to violate the law in order to behave ethically. However, it ultimately is the judgment of the professional to determine any individual course of action, as long as there is a clear recognition that behavior outside any of the codes may lead to predictable consequences.

REVIEWERS

A professional who is charged with ethical misconduct is entitled to a hearing by a committee of peers (often including a public member as well as a group of co-professionals). This hearing is often in the form of a paper, rather than an in-person, review, and it will be governed by the rules and regulations of the organization. It can lead to a variety of decisions, ranging from dismissal of charges to expulsion from the organization, with various intermediate reprimands possible. If the charge is made on the basis of legal transgression, the hearing and decision will be made by a judge or a jury. The hearing will be in person and it will be guided by laws of evidence with all due process protections provided. The decision can either be not guilty to guilty. An alleged violation of a licensing law also will be heard by a group of peers, with some public participation, and it also is governed by local regulations. The decision can range from a dismissal of charges to a loss of license, with some intermediate disciplinary actions possible. Thus, the process and protections, and the range of decisions, is closer in an ethical hearing and a licensure review than either is to a court of law. It is only in a court of law that the defendant can be guaranteed due process rights and the rules of evidence.

OPENNESS OF PROCESS

On this dimension also, an ethical procedure is closer to a licensing action than it is to a courtroom. The ethical hearing is a closed event, and the results are only made public to the extent that the committee chooses to do so, and then often to a limited set of recipients. Expulsions are public actions, but any lesser penalty may not be available to anyone other than the parties to the charges. On the contrary, a legal action takes place in an open courtroom, and the records of that proceeding, unless they are sealed, become a matter of public record. The licensing hearing, like the ethics hearing, is closed, and the results may be very limited in their availability to the general public. It may be this secrecy that surrounds the action, which serves to protect a professional who might have been wrongly accused, that contributes to the public perception of a guild action that requires supplementation by public and externally imposed laws.

To this point, dilemmas have been approached by separating the ethical, legal, and licensing ramifications that they have, and the direction to look for solutions. However, many dilemmas do not fall into any of these categories. They are professional concerns that may be solved by a knowledge of simple etiquette, good judgment, and political finesse. The professional is well advised to be thoroughly familiar with the relevant code of ethical conduct and with all applicable licensing laws and regulations, but this alone will not guarantee a correct solution to the dilemmas that are faced. There is no substitute for wisdom and sound judgment, and these often cannot be codified or enforced. Instead, they rely on the integrity of the professional, as does so much of sound professional behavior.

GENERAL ETHICAL PRINCIPLES

The first section of this volume deals with general ethical principles associated with the mental health professions. Commencing, Callan and Callan's article reviews the basic approaches and issues in ethical and moral philosophy and principles. Their review provides a foundation for understanding ethics in mental health. Following this general overview of ethics and moral philosophy, subsequent articles in this section address general principles and standards associated with ethical principles and codes of conduct in the mental health professions. A general focus is on the analysis of legal and ethical issues critical to the practice of mental health professionals.

The principle of competence in mental health as presented by Nagy is viewed not only as a construct but also as an ongoing process. He stresses the critical importance of professional competence, noting that it constitutes the very bedrock of research, teaching, and clinical practice in the mental health field. In addition to exploring competence in the many roles that mental health professionals fill, fundamental and general concepts bearing on competence are discussed.

Mills highlights that the principle of integrity is critical to the mental health profession, declaring that both professional and personal integrity is the foundation of all mental health professionals' functioning. He focuses on issues of accuracy, honesty, fairness, and respect for others as necessary ingredients to professional behavior.

Lowman expands this exploration in his first article, addressing ethical issues associated with the concept of professional and scientific responsibility as related to the principle of integrity. He focuses on integrity as an aspirational standard. Differences between aspirational and enforceable ethical standards are reviewed and case examples and illustrations are provided. Similarly, Lowman's second article examines the nature and application of the aspirational principle addressing respect for peoples' rights and dignity. Again, he discusses issues about aspirational versus enforceable standards and provides case examples and illustrations.

Clark also discusses issues of aspirational standards in his article, addressing a fundamental principle of psychology: concern for the welfare of others. He explains that unlike so much else in professional ethics codes that involve injunctions of what not to do, or which attempts to limit the self-serving tendencies of professionals, this general principle is essentially positive, pointing to the need to approach others and to consider their welfare first.

Wise analyzes mental health professionals' responsibilities toward positively impacting the broader society or culture in which they live and work within the context of mental health professionals' codes of conduct. She considers the role of mental health professionals in changing society and associated implications.

CONFIDENTIALITY, PRIVILEGE, CONSENT, AND PROTECTION

The second section of this volume explores aspects of confidentiality, privilege, consent, and protection critical to the mental health professions. Articles in this section begin to address the practical application and associated clinical procedures involved in implementing the general ethical standards discussed in the preceding section. Golub's article examines mental health professionals' responsibility regarding informed consent and the components to be reviewed with clients as early as possible. Recent changes that have given patients greater autonomy in the treatment process are also presented.

Another significant responsibility of mental health professionals, the area of protecting privacy and confidentiality, is explored by Caudill and Kaplan. Their article discusses the confidentiality of communications between therapist and patient and the scope of, and exceptions to, the privilege preventing such communications from being disclosed.

Kaplan expands the exploration of issues surrounding confidentiality and disclosure in his article, addressing the ownership of privilege applying to any confidential communications between those persons defined by statute as able to form a confidential psychotherapist-patient relationship.

An important consideration when examining confidentiality in the mental health professions is the "duty to protect" doctrine. Simone and Fulero detail the California Supreme Court's *Tarasoff I* and *Tarasoff II* cases and the confidentiality rulings emerging from these decisions. Associated key concepts and legal issues are analyzed.

GENERAL ETHICAL STANDARDS IN PRACTICE CHAPTERS

The third section of this volume examines general ethical standards in the practice of delivery of service. Clipson explores the area of professional ethics relating to multiple relationships and the potential for misuse of mental health professionals' influence. In his article, he reviews the important dynamics of multiple relationships and boundary violations, while also providing a model for assisting mental health professionals in avoiding exploitive or harmful dual relationships.

Shavit expands this discussion in her article, focusing on dual relationships of a sexual nature including both sexual contacts while treatment is in progress and after its termination. The profiles of both mental health professionals and patients likely to be involved as well as clinical, legal, and professional issues and consequences are included. Gandolfo examines issues related to bartering arrangements in the context of providing professional mental health services. The risks associated with significant conflict of interest and the potential for exploitation of the client are analyzed.

Caudill examines the requirements and implementation of maintaining patient records in the mental health arena, stressing that records are an important source of protection for professionals. He provides guidelines for documentation that will help professionals avoid future ethical and legal problems.

Kaplan then discusses issues surrounding how mental health professionals handle referrals and fees with respect to professional ethics. The relationship between the mental health professional and the referral source is explored; the potential risks and consequences involved in this process are also included.

ETHICS IN TEACHING, TRAINING, AND RESEARCH CHAPTERS

The fourth section of this volume explores ethical considerations in the realms of teaching, training, and research. McGee provides a discussion regarding ethical and legal considerations that relate to the training of mental health professionals. A training program that emphasizes a proactive approach to identifying and resolving potential ethical and legal problems, and their close connection with clinical issues, is described. Callan and Bucky lend to this area by discussing the teaching of ethics to mental health professionals using the California School of Professional Psychology at San Diego (Alliant International University) as a model.

Meltzoff follows with an overview of the history of efforts to protect human subjects in research. He discusses the establishment of international, national, organizational, and institutional procedures designed to protect human participants. A detailed summary of the principal ethical codes for research and frequently encountered ethical issues are presented.

The last article in this section highlights ethical themes in publication. Meltzoff addresses the provenance of ideas, problems with joint authorship, plagiarism, and the practice of duplicate submission of material for publication. Confidentiality and privacy matters and the protection of human subjects in publication of research and clinical case studies are also discussed. The article further examines biases in literature reviews, and in the biased selection of one's best results for publication, intentional misinterpretation of data and the slanting of discussion, summary, and conclusions. Finally, the article deals with ethical problems that can arise in the publication of sponsored research and the ethical responsibilities of editors and readers.

GENERAL ETHICAL PRINCIPLES

An Historical Overview
of Basic Approaches and Issues
in Ethical and Moral Philosophy and Principles:
A Foundation for Understanding Ethics
in Psychology

Joanne E. Callan
Megan E. Callan

SUMMARY. This article provides a condensed history of ethics development for the purpose of exposing psychologists and other mental health professionals to ethical and moral bases upon which modern psychologi-

Address correspondence to: Joanne E. Callan, 9180 Brown Deer Road, San Diego, CA 92121.

[Haworth co-indexing entry note]: "An Historical Overview of Basic Approaches and Issues in Ethical and Moral Philosophy and Principles: A Foundation for Understanding Ethics in Psychology." Callan, Joanne E., and Megan E. Callan. Co-published simultaneously in *Journal of Aggression, Maltreatment & Trauma* (The Haworth Maltreatment & Trauma Press, an imprint of The Haworth Press, Inc.) Vol. 11, No. 1/2, 2005, pp. 11-26; and: *Ethical and Legal Issues for Mental Health Professionals: A Comprehensive Handbook of Principles and Standards* (ed: Steven F. Bucky, Joanne E. Callan, and George Stricker) The Haworth Maltreatment & Trauma Press, an imprint of The Haworth Press, Inc., 2005, pp. 11-26. Single or multiple copies of this article are available for a fee from The Haworth Document Delivery Service [1-800-HAWORTH, 9:00 a.m. - 5:00 p.m. (EST). E-mail address: docdelivery@haworthpress.com].

Available online at http://www.haworthpress.com/web/JAMT
Digital Object Identifier: 10.1300/J146v11n01_02

cal ethics are founded. In addition, it focuses on contemporary theories, with an emphasis on professional ethics. *[Article copies available for a fee from The Haworth Document Delivery Service: 1-800-HAWORTH. E-mail address: <docdelivery@haworthpress.com> Website: <http://www.HaworthPress.com> © 2005 by The Haworth Press, Inc. All rights reserved.]*

KEYWORDS. Ethical and moral philosophy and principles, ethics in psychology

The first section of this article presents a condensed history of ethics development, noting basic foundations and major contributors from early civilizations to the present time, as a context for better understanding the relevance and application of ethics in psychology. The overview is provided to expose psychologists to ethical and moral bases upon which modern psychological ethics are founded. As hard and fast rules do not entirely comprise professional ethics, effective ethics education requires ongoing dialogue about the essential nature and implications of ethics. Put another way, to appreciate ethics and then regulate professional activities and behaviors through informed self-scrutiny, psychologists must have a working knowledge of the fundamentals of ethics. Arguably, it is only with such a foundation that they will be able to address the myriad complexities and nuances of ethical issues likely to arise in their professional lives.

BASIC DEFINITION AND IDEAS

Although ethics theorists often debate the distinction between ethics and philosophy, it serves purposes here to consider ethics as a branch of philosophy tied closely to morals. Indeed, ethics is often referred to as moral philosophy. The connection between the two involves both judgment and values (Steininger, Jewell, & Garcia, 1984). As such, ethics are seen generally as dealing with what is right and wrong, defined by Webster as "A principle of right or good behavior"; "A system of moral principles or values"; and "The study of the general nature of morals . . ." (p. 445). The principles of morality, including both the science of the good and the nature of the right are viewed by Rowe (1993) as the search for a rational understanding of human conduct and by Lewy (1985) as the theoretical treatment of moral phenomena. Dr. Rosemarie Tong, another current ethics scholar, characterizes ethics as a "systematic, rational inquiry into the nature of and the relationship between the right and good, or the product of such an inquiry" (personal communication, October 1994).

Such inquiry is frequently pursued through two major approaches: meta-ethics and normative ethics.[1] Meta-ethics focus on the analysis of the meaning and nature of man's behaviors, while normative ethics focus on evaluating those aspects (i.e., identifying and assessing principles or criteria as a basis for judging what is moral, or what is good or bad). Referring to meta-ethics, Edel (1987) says they are ". . . Conceived as purely linguistic-logical analysis of moral discourse, a self-enclosed field quite apart from the "preaching" and "exhortation" of substantive or normative ethics" (p. 24). In contrast, normative ethics concentrate on norms, the generally accepted criteria used to evaluate the nature of behavior. They are described as "inquiry that attempts to answer the question of 'which general norm for the guidance and evaluation of conduct are worthy of moral acceptance and for what reason' " (Beauchamp & Childress, 1994, p. 4).

Today's ethics theories use either one or both of these two approaches to varying extents, thus creating a complex and broad base upon which current professional ethics are built. At the same time, ethics theories have tended to be reductionistic, typically positing one idea as key or central and then reducing everything else to that idea. Accordingly, sharp distinctions between, or separatist views of, different theories are cautioned against by some ethicists (e.g., Beauchamp & Childress, 1994). Indeed, a number of different theories have shaped current professional ethics, providing a rich texture for guiding professional practice.

ETHICS THEORIES AND SYSTEMS: PAST AND PRESENT

Contributions to today's approaches have come from major cultural centers over many centuries, primarily out of efforts to regulate human behavior and advance societies. Table 1, drawing on the content and organization of *A Companion to Ethics* (Singer, 1993), provides a sequence of historical development by noting civilizations that have influenced modern ethics thinking, beginning with the earliest contributions for which there is written record.

Current theory has evolved from ethical thought developed within these civilizations over a span of more than five thousand years, and

TABLE 1. Civilizations Influencing Modern Ethics Thinking

Ancient Ethics	Mesopotamia Egypt	4th millennium b.c.e.
Major Ethical Traditions	Indian Ethics	
	Buddhist Ethics	
	Classical Chinese Ethics	
	Jewish Ethics	
	Christian Ethics	
	Islamic Ethics	
Western Ethics	Ancient Greece	400-200 b.c.e.
	Medieval and Renaissance	11th-16th centuries
	Modern Western Morals and Ethics	17th century to present time

contributions from Western ethics systems of the past 2400 years have had particular influence on today's ethical theories. Brief descriptions of the three major systems constituting Western ethics (Ancient Greece, Medieval and Renaissance, and Modern Western Morals and Ethics) are presented next (a) to elucidate the modern understanding of structure in ethics, and (b) to provide a background for understanding current professional ethics.

Greek Influence

Early Greek influence, based considerably on the thinking of Socrates, Plato, and Aristotle, continues to pervade Western ethics theories. The essential focus of Greek ethics centered on two concepts of human behavior that have been translated as happiness and virtue (from the Greek *eudaimonia* and *arete*). As Rowe (1993) has stated, to the Greeks ". . . it was the fundamental questions–about the sort of life one should live . . . and about the criteria to be used in answering questions of that sort–which really mattered" (p. 130). Among translated writings from that period, one of signal influence is Aristotle's (1925/1987) *Nichomachian Ethics*, written in the third century b.c.e.[2] Aristotle emphasized the rational person and the virtuous life: "we become just by doing just acts" (from Ross, 1925/1954, p. 29). Identifying two forms of moral virtue, intellectual and moral excellence, he admonished, "It makes no small difference, then, whether we form habits of one kind or of another from our very youth; it makes a very great difference, or rather *all* the difference" (p. 29). The basic ethical guidance of Aristotle's writings is that man should pursue good moral or good ethical activity and that such activities will lead to a virtuous or noble life. While his writings attend in detail to the nature of ethical behavior, they do not do so with regard to the kind of undergirding principles constituting the essence of many current theories.

Medieval and Renaissance Influences

Medieval and Renaissance influences come from philosophical thought covering a 500-year period from about the 11th to the 16th centuries. Medieval ethics theories can be characterized as pre-scholastic, paving the way for the scholastic theories that emerged in the Renaissance. The high point of medieval thinking was between the mid 1300s and mid 1400s (Haldane, 1993), during which time the primary architects were two religious orders, the Dominicans and Franciscans. Indeed, early medieval thinking was influenced substantively by theology, with church leaders or the clergy serving as the moral philosophers of that period. They were concerned with normative questions (e.g., which virtues and behaviors were optimal). Morality in this period has been described as "neither systematic nor interested in what are now characterized as *meta-ethical* issues, that is, issues about the content and logical character of moral concepts" (Haldane, 1993, p. 139).

By the 11th and 12th centuries, however, scholasticism, a highly systematized approach to ethics, had emerged. Saint Thomas Aquinas (1224-1274) stands out as the greatest of medieval and scholastic philosophers, according to Haldane (1993), who credits him as perhaps the greatest of all philosophers born between Aristotle and Descartes. He points to Aquinas' genius as having been "in the capacity to see how Greek thought and Catholic doctrine might be synthesized into a Christian philosophy" (p. 141). Drawing on Aristotelian views, Aquinas developed a form of "consequentialist endaimonism," purporting that right action is conduct that either tends to promote or actually realizes human flourishing (p. 141). He insisted on the observance of nature's realities, believing that this approach to living would lead to God. His first principle regarding man's behavior was that "good is to be done and pursued and evil avoided" (p. 135). In his emphasis on conscience as necessary for distinguishing bad courses of action from good, he relates conscience to the practical or

right reason as set forth by the Greeks. Beyond his significant substantive contributions, Aquinas developed a form of inquiry that involved the explication of questions on major ethical issues supported
by arguments for and against them. Two significant Aquinas contributions are the *Summa Theologiae* and *Summa Contral Gentiles*.

Modern Western Ethical Thought

Modern ethics and moral philosophy, especially in the Western
world, have evolved considerably from Greek as well as medieval and
Renaissance teachings. In the composite, they are quite diverse, and
complex. Although most modern theories consider how to determine
whether behaviors and thoughts represent the highest or greatest good,
they do so in the context of strong challenge to earlier positions that either nature or God can function as the source of morality.

To facilitate an understanding of modern ethics thought, including
changes from earlier theories, a chronological perspective on its development is useful. Schneewind (1993) has suggested three stages for organizing modern ethical thought, beginning in the 17th century and
moving from (a) views of morality arising from an outside authority; to
(b) views defending humans as self-governing or autonomous; and finally to (c) current views more concerned with public morality than
with individual autonomy. Among major approaches to ethical inquiry
emerging in the 300 to 400 years since the end of the Renaissance in the
sixteenth century are those developed or expanded by several well-
known theorists, whose works appeared prior to the twentieth century,
including Kant, Bentham, and Mills. Following annotations of their
contributions to ethics theories are those of more contemporary thinkers.

Immanuel Kant's deontological ethics judge the rightness of an action
not only on external factors but on the action itself. In *Groundwork of the
Metaphysics of Morals*, Kant (1948) challenged the notion that "action
can only be right because it produces good" (Schneewind, 1993, p. 150).
He emphasized freedom as essential in any action and individual
autonomy as crucial to right actions: "The sole way in which we can be free
. . . is if our actions are determined by something within our nature. Before we can know what is good, we must determine what is right"
(Schneewind, 1993, p. 151). The central question for Kant is "what
ought I to do?" (O'Neill, 1993, p. 175). His writings focus on identifying "the maxims, or fundamental principles of action, that we ought to

adopt" (p. 176) and stress the compelling obligation or duty to act in accord with these maxims.[3]

Kant's overarching principle, which he identified as the Categorical Imperative or Universal Law, was that ethics must serve for all (i.e., they must be universal in nature and application). Moreover, the Categorical Imperative prescribes what individuals ought to do without reference to consequence. According to Kant, one should act with regard to only those maxims that would appropriately make universal law. Another Kantian principle emphasized respect for self and others. Arguing against indifference, Kant said: "failure to treat others or oneself as ends is once again seen as a failure of virtue or imperfect obligation" (cited in O'Neill, 1993, p. 179).

Jeremy Bentham (1748-1832), known as the architect of modern Utilitarianism, presented as his major contribution the view that ordinary people can get adequate guidance for action by consciously applying abstract moral principles. His work was complemented by that of John Stuart Mill (1806-1873), and, together, they are viewed as developing the "first detailed and systematic formulation" of Utilitarianism (Arras & Steinbock, 1995, p. 9). Their ethics relied on the principle of utility, or the "greatest happiness" principle, which stated that actions are right in proportion as they tend to promote happiness, and wrong as they tend to produce unhappiness. Referring to Mill's writings, O'Neill (1993) states, "Common sense, he said, morality which we all learn as children, represents the accumulated wisdom of mankind about the desirable and undesirable consequences of actions. Hence we can and must live by it . . ." (p. 152).

Utilitarians focus on the consequence of actions, choosing between actions on the basis of the outcome that produces the greater happiness; thus, theirs is known as a consequentialist theory or a teleological one (from the Greek *telos* meaning 'end'). Judging rightness of an action in terms of external goals, this theory is separated into three main subgroups: act, rule, and preference utilitarianism, with more frequent focus on act and rule utilitarianism. Act utilitarianism involves the consequences of specific acts, whereas rules utilitarianism relates to the consequences of general policies. As Arras and Steinbock (1995) explain, both of these approaches use rules to guide behavior; however, rules are "summaries of past experiences" for act utilitarianism, serving as rules of thumb to help in maximizing happiness (p. 12). In contrast, rule utilitarians seek and rely on those rules, even when the application of them does not necessarily maximize happiness in a particular situation.

Edel (1987) points out that the Utilitarian emphasis on "the greatest happiness for the greatest number played a vital role in the ascent of a democratic outlook because it was directed against the dominance of the few" (p. 31). Hegel (1770-1831), opposing Utilitarianism, took the view that morality was influenced by the context or the community in which one lives (Schneewind, 1993). In fact, between the time of the Utilitarian writings from the late 1700s to the 1880s and more modern ones emerging in the last half of the 20th century, a number of challenges arose regarding the basic nature and assumptions of ethical and moral thought and also their applications. Summarizing from Schneewind (1993), questions were raised by the relativists as to whether or not there is such a thing as moral knowledge, and by the logical positivists from their position that any ethics beliefs not complying with scientific tests "are not simply false–they are meaningless" (p. 155). Existentialists, such as Nietzsche and later Sartre, who purported that morality is based solely on the free-choice of each person, challenged any ethics system tied to universal law.

Although Utilitarian thinking continues to influence ethics and moral philosophy, Arras and Steinbock (1995) point out four objections to it: (1) the value or claim that happiness is the greatest good; (2) the requirement to calculate the probable consequence of every action (since, as these authors point out, such a task is impossible); (3) the responsibility assigned (i.e., that who is responsible is as, or more, important than what the outcome is); and (4) its inadequacy as a theory, given its conflict with some basic moral intuitions or beliefs.

Contemporary Theories

Meta-ethics. The meta-ethicists, who contributed greatly to the field of ethics from 1930 into the 1970s (Edel, 1987), returned to the study of moral principles. John Rawls, in his influential book *A Theory of Justice* (1971), emphasized principles of right action. Arguing that the right is prior to the good, he assumed a pro-Kantian view against Utilitarianism. Maintaining that a moral person must be guided by a sense of justice, he saw moral feelings as normal and necessary for the development of rules (Wilson, 1993). Although he advocated considering the welfare of the deprived or disadvantaged as well as that of the majority, he wrote that, since the issues are so complex, justice can only be achieved through some kind of contractual agreement on how the basic societal institutions are to be structured. Schneewind (1993) notes that Rawls tried to combine Hegelian notions regarding priority of the community with a reinterpretation of Kantian autonomy. Communitarians, opposing individualistic utilitarianism, purport instead the common good. Arras and Steinbock (1995) compare the two: "Where utilitarianism asks, 'Which policies will produce the greatest happiness, on balance, of all the individuals in society?' communitarianism asks, 'Which policies will promote the kind of community in which we want to live?'" (p. 27).

Ethics of care. More and more, since the 1970s ethics theories and writings have focused on social and political problems rather than on individual autonomy (Battin & Francis, 1988; Edel, 1987; Schneewind, 1993). Several recent developments in ethics thinking reflect this departure from liberal individualism, one of which is the emergence of the *ethics of care.* Indeed, some view today's ethics as being either (a) based theoretically on principles or (b) related to the ethics of care.

Beauchamp and Childress (1994) point to the emphasis in the ethics of care on traits valued in intimate personal relationships, among them sympathy, compassion, fidelity, discernment, and love. They explain that caring refers to "care for, emotional commitment to, and willingness to act on behalf of persons with whom one has a significant relationship" (p. 85), and they note that "the care ethic provides a needed corrective to two centuries of system-building in ethical theory and to the tendency to neglect themes such as sympathy, the moral emotions, and women's experiences" (p. 92). These authors also point out that, whereas traditional moral theory has focused on matters such as whether to lie or break confidentiality, the ethics of care stresses more "how actions are performed, which motives underlie them, and whether positive relationships are promoted or thwarted" (p. 86) than the actual decision made. Adson (1995) has described operative virtues imperative in ethical behaviors among healing professionals.

Feminist ethics. Congruent with the ethics of care has been the focus of recent moral thinking on concerns for underserved or less protected populations (e.g., minority groups). New approaches for understanding ethics have developed even for majority groups whose needs and issues had not been previously explored; for example, the development of ethics related to women, which received impetus from the feminist movement emerging in the 1960s. Since the sixties, with this impetus from the feminist movement, a number of theorists have contributed to the understanding of ethics regarding women's lives and experiences. Works such as the seminal thinking of Carol Gilligan (1982) raised awareness among ethicists and also among those interested in women's issues and female development about the possible, or actual, differences between how men approach moral issues and how women do. Subsequently, various philosophical approaches to the understanding of ethics as related to women have evolved; based on them, an array of feminist theories have developed.

Feminist writings give considerable attention to terminology and definitions; for example, the very definition of "feminist" is regarded carefully as well as variously among different approaches. Susan Wolf (1996), a contributor to feminism and bioethics, suggests that any definition of feminist include as many facets as possible, and she submits this understanding: ". . . feminist work takes gender and sex as centrally important analytic categories, seeks to understand their operation in the world, and strives to change the distribution and use of power to stop the oppression of women" (p. 8).

In understanding different views of women's ethics, it is essential to appreciate that feminine ethics (often equated with the ethics of care) differs from feminist ethics, the essence of which is described in Wolf's quote. Both theories have contemporary relevance since not all women consider themselves or their theories feminist. In fact, some women do not seek to examine or end the oppression of women, while some men contribute significantly to feminist ethics and would describe themselves as feminists. As this distinction implies, feminist ethics has developed beyond Gilligan's noble beginning, becoming a complex and diverse area of study. Because of this complexity and also the evolving nature of modern philosophy, it can seem difficult to identify essential themes and even more problematic to identify categories to guide the study of feminist ethics (Enns, 1992; Tong, 1996). One essential theme is presented by Jaggar (1991): "On the metaethical level, the goal of feminist ethics is to develop theoretical understandings of the nature of morality that treat women's moral experience respectfully but not uncritically" (p. 99). She identifies, as well, two assumptions common to all feminist ethics: (a) that the subordination of women is morally wrong, and (b) that the moral experience of women should be treated as respectfully as the moral experience of men (p. 97).

In an effort to identify recurring themes in feminist thinking, Enns (1992) suggests four basic approaches: liberal, cultural, radical, and socialist feminism. Although elucidating with respect to essential or recurring themes, her analysis reflects the challenging breadth of feminist thinking, a characteristic that parallels the development of any ethics system.

Applied ethics. Applied ethics[4] has come into its own in the last few decades, with an emphasis on ethics related to professions, business, communities, and other systems or venues including public policy. Singer (1986) wrote,

> To an observer of moral philosophy in the twentieth century, the most striking development of the past twenty years would not be any advance in our theoretical understanding of the subject, nor would it be the acceptance of any particular ideas about right and wrong. It would, rather, be the removal of an entire department of the subject: applied ethics. (p. 1)

The shift in emphasis to applied ethics was triggered by social and political developments, such as the Vietnam War, the civil rights movement, and student activism, which drew philosophers and ethicists into debate on the moral aspects of events like war, civil disobedience, and equality (Singer, 1986). The growing attention to professional ethics, one specific kind of applied ethics since the 1970s, is considered next.

DEVELOPMENT OF PROFESSIONAL ETHICS

The preceding historical overview notes the common threads as well as differences emerging during this development. It relates the contributions of various earlier systems to current Western ethics and moral thinking as they have developed in the last 300 to 400 years. This brief history underscores the centrality of each civilization's view of humanity and the world with respect to how each has determined moral and ethical thinking (i.e., to how each has viewed right and wrong). Whereas absolutists, for example, view behaviors generally seen as bad or negative (e.g., lying, stealing, killing) as never justifiable, relativists point to the meaning of a behavior, emphasizing the intention behind it. Generally, as noted above, ethics have been viewed by people as ways of behaving in accord with acceptable standards. As ethics thinking has developed, these ways of behaving and the standards that underlie them have become incorporated as basic principles into ethics theories.

Just as societies have produced their own ethical systems over the years, there has been in this century a developing interest among professions regarding ethics. Increased attention to applied ethics in the last several decades has contributed to the growing emphasis among the various professions in the Western world about ethics, which has led to the development of ethical principles or standards and ethical codes (although it is the case that some professions had begun such work early in the twentieth century). Professional ethics, then, is applied ethics developed to guide ethical behaviors or conduct within professions.

Most professions have now identified ethics principles and guidelines as important. Indeed, a profession's development and also its observance of an ethics code are seen currently as indicators of its having achieved a certain level of maturity. Not only are members of the profession guided by their code, and the next generation of professionals educated and trained by using the code to prepare for future professional activities, ethical codes also serve to inform the public on what they may expect regarding appropriate behavior from professionals. Health care ethics, for example, relies on fundamental principles to guide health care professionals with regard to what is right and what is wrong. Beauchamp and Childress (1994) have identified four clusters of such basic principles: respect for autonomy, nonmaleficence, beneficence, and justice. Edge and Groves (1994) identify seven basic principles of biomedical ethics: autonomy, veracity, beneficence, nonmaleficence, confidentiality, justice, and role fidelity.

Beyond observing their respective ethics codes, professionals across disciplines must also observe federal and state laws in carrying out their professional activities. Moreover, some argue that ethics guidelines should be observed by professionals in social as well as work contexts, a position reflecting the complexity of applying professional ethics.

ETHICS IN PSYCHOLOGY

In 1953, the American Psychological Association (APA) implemented psychology's first ethics code, and since then APA has established a record of ongoing review and revision to assure the currency and relevance of psychology's formally stated ethics principles. Indeed, some (e.g., Steininger et al., 1984) view APA as a pacemaker in its support of the development and revision of ethical guidelines for psychology. Revisions took place in 1977 and 1981 (APA, 1992), with an interim revision in 1989. The next revision, viewed as the first major revision since 1981 (Keith-Spiegel, 1994) took place in 1992. The most recent revision was accepted by the APA Council in 2002 and is generally viewed as expanding, enhancing, and sharpening the 1992 revision. Although the first couple of revisions were not major, each revision has had a somewhat different orientation and/or additional emphases; and, as might be expected, each has received mixed reactions. For example, the 1992 revision consisted of two parts (see Table 2). The first part included the Preamble and the six General Principles, which are aspirational in nature. The second part provided enforceable standards and covered eight major areas.

The 1992 revision met considerable, indeed varied, reaction, as reflected in a series of articles published in 1994 in the journal *Professional Psychology: Research & Practice*. The lead article, authored by Keith-Spiegel (1994) is entitled, "The 1992 Ethics Code: Boon or Bane?" setting the tone for the series. The summary article, written by Bersoff (1994), acknowledges the increased breadth of the new code and the attention given to important issues underattended in earlier codes. Also noted by Bersoff, however, are several criticisms related to lack of clarity, the use of qualifying language, and an appearance of protecting the profession rather than the public. In closing, Bersoff encourages the profession, in its next code revision, to stick more simply with

TABLE 2.The Principles and Standards of the 1992 and 2002 APA Ethics Code

	1992 Code	2002 Code
General Principles	A. Competence B. Integrity C. Professional and Scientific Responsibility D. Respect for People's Rights E. Concern for Others' Welfare F. Social Responsibility	A. Beneficence and Nonmaleficence B. Fidelity and Responsibility C. Integrity D. Justice E. Respect for People's Rights and Dignity
Standards	1. General Standards 2. Evaluation, Assessment, or Intervention 3. Advertising and Other Public Statements 4. Therapy 5. Discussing the Limits of Confidentiality 6. Teaching, Training Supervision, Research, and Publishing 7. Forensic Activities 8. Resolving Ethical Issues	1. Resolving Ethical Issues 2. Competence 3. Human Relations 4. Privacy and Confidentiality 5. Advertising and Other Public Statements 6. Record Keeping and Fees 7. Education and Training 8. Research and Publication 9. Assessment 10. Therapy

principles and to make absolutely clear its commitment to serve the public with integrity.

The 2002 revision continues to include the same basic components: an Introduction, a Preamble, five General Principles, and ten specific Ethical Standards (see Table 2). The Preamble and the General Principles remain aspirational in nature, and the Ethical Standards continue to present enforceable rules of conduct for psychologists. The 2002 APA code revision was developed to address some of the criticisms leveled against the 1992 revision. Indeed its development really started with acceptance of the 1992 code by APA's council of representatives at that time. The 2002 revision includes some additions to, and some deletions from the 1992 Code, examples of which are: social responsibility, sensitivity to the needs of students, and the acceptability of dual relationships. Each APA revision of the mode has been developed to serve the profession and the public, as noted above, and each has been used as well in the education and training of future professionals.

CONCLUSION

Current ethics focus on the meaning of ethical concepts and on how these concepts support moral judgment and moral behavior. They reflect a transition over the years from Aristotle's emphasis on the rational person and a virtuous life, with little attention to undergirding principles, to the development of more modern theories that, although they vary considerably in their emphases, rely considerably on basic principles and substantiating arguments for defining their essences. Each theory incorporates specific values and advances certain judgments essential in identifying and assessing moral behavior.

Modern theories continue to emphasize principles based on essential values that guide thinking about ethical issues and behaviors. Professional ethics, influenced considerably by both classical and modern theory, reflect these principles and values. They also respond to social and political developments, as demonstrated in the emergence of the ethics of care and feminist ethics in the past few decades with marked impact on professional ethics. Undoubtedly, modern theories will continue to change in response to emerging ethical and moral theories and also in response to social and political agendas, thus maintaining both currency and relevance.

NOTES

1. Some writers identify additional approaches; for example, Beauchamp and Childress (1994) identify normative and nonnormative ethics, dividing the latter into descriptive ethics, which involve what people report regarding their beliefs and action, and metaethics, which involve the analysis of ethics thinking and methods.

2. Although the ten books making up Aristotle's Nichomachian volume consider in some detail various issues relevant to his overall view of ethics and moral behavior, it is thought to be incomplete (see reference in Ross [1925/1954] regarding the likely editing by Aristotle's son, Nichomachus).

3. O'Neill (1993) describes Kant's ethics as difficult and systematic; he advises that, when studying Kant's work, three sets of influences be kept in mind: Kant's own writing (in the 1780s and 1790s); Kant's ethics, writings by his critics, which are largely negative; and Kantian ethics, which include the two sets just noted plus a broader array of ethical views that have emerged out of Kant's own ethics.

4. Not all ethics scholars support the term *applied ethics*. See Beauchamp and Childress (1994) for further discussion on their preference for the term *practical ethics*.

REFERENCES

Adson, M. A. (1995). An endangered ethic. The capacity for caring. *Mayo Clinic Proceedings, 70*, 495-500.

American Psychological Association. (1992). Ethical principles of psychologists and code of conduct. *American Psychologist, 47*, 1597-1611.

American Psychological Association. (2002). Ethical principles of psychologists and code of conduct. *American Psychologist, 57*(12), 1060-1073.

Aristotle. (1925/1987). *The nicomachean ethics*. New York: Oxford University Press.

Arras, J. D., & Steinbock, B. (1995). *Ethical issues in modern medicine*. Mountain View, CA: Mayfield Publishing Co.

Battin, M. P., & Francis, L. P. (1988). Foreward. In D. M. Rosenthal & F. Shehad (Eds.), *Applied ethics and ethical theory* (pp. vii-viii). Salt Lake City, UT: University of Utah Press.

Beauchamp, T., & Childress, J. F. (1994). *The principles of biomedical ethics* (4th ed.). New York: Oxford University Press.

Bersoff, D. N. (1994). Explicit ambiguity: The 1992 ethics code as an oxymoron. *Professional Psychology: Research & Practice, 25*(4), 382-387.

Edel, A. (1987). Ethics applied or conduct enlightened? In J. Howie (Ed.), *Ethical principles and practices* (pp. 24-48). Carbondale, IL: Southern Illinois University Pres

Edge, R. S., & Groves, J. R. (1994). *The ethics of health care: A guide for clinical practice*. Albany, NY: Delmar Publishers.

Enns, C. Z. (1992). Toward integrating feminist psychotherapy and feminist philosophy. *Professional Psychology: Research and Practice, 23*(6), 453-466.

Gilligan, C. (1982). *In a different voice*. Cambridge, MA: Harvard University Press.

Haldane, J. (1993). Medieval and Renaissance ethics. In P. Singer (Ed.), *A companion to ethics* (pp. 133-146). Cambridge, MA: Basil Blackwell Ltd.

Jaggar, A. M. (1991). Feminist ethics: Projects, problems, and prospects. In C. Card (Ed), *Feminist ethics* (pp. 78-104). Lawrence, KS: University of Kansas Press.

Kant, I. (1948). *Groundwork of the metaphysics of morals* (H. J. Paton, Trans.). London: Hutchinson (Original work published 1785).

Keith-Speigel, P. (1994). Teaching psychologists and the new APA ethics code: Do we fit in? *Professional Psychology: Research and Practice, 25*(4), 366-368.

Lewy, C. (1985). *Ethics.* Boston, MA: Martinus Nyhoff Publishers.

O'Neill, O. (1993). Kantian ethics. In P. Singer (Ed.), *A companion to ethics* (pp. 175-185). Cambridge, MA: Basil Blackwell Ltd.

Rawls, J. (1971). *A theory of justice.* Cambridge, MA: Harvard University Press.

Ross, D. (1925/1954). Introduction. In Aristotle's *The Nicomachean Ethics* (pp. v-xxiv). New York: Oxford University Press.

Rowe, C. (1993). Ethics in ancient Greece. In P. Singer (Ed.), *A companion to ethics* (pp. 121-132). Cambridge, MA: Basil Blackwell Ltd.

Schneewind, J. B. (1993). Modern moral philosophy. In P. Singer (Ed.), *A companion to ethics* (pp. 147-157). Cambridge, MA: Basil Blackwell Ltd.

Singer, P. (1986). *Applied ethics.* Oxford, England: Oxford University Press.

Singer, P. (1993). *A companion to ethics.* Cambridge, MA: Basil Blackwell Ltd.

Steininger, M., Jewell, J. D., & Garcia, L. T. (1984). *Ethical issues in psychology.* Homewood, IL: Dorsey Press.

Tong, R. (1996). Feminist approaches to bioethics. In S. M. Wolf (Ed.), *Feminism and bioethics: Beyond reproduction* (pp. 67-94). New York: Oxford University Press.

Webster's II. (1988). *Webster's II new riverside university dictionary.* Boston, MA: Houghton Mifflin Co.

Wilson, J. Q. (1993). *The moral sense.* New York: The Free Press.

Wolf, S. M. (1996). *Feminism and bioethics: Beyond reproduction.* New York: Oxford University Press.

Competence

Thomas F. Nagy

SUMMARY. Competence in mental health is explored in many roles, including that of researcher, author, teacher, supervisor, therapist, evaluator, consultant, forensic specialist, case manager, and administrator. It is viewed not only as a construct but also as an ongoing process within the individual. Five fundamental areas are examined: (1) Maintaining high standards of competence, (2) keeping within one's boundaries of competence and limitations of one's expertise, (3) maintaining competence in human diversity in practice and research, (4) engaging in continuing education in scientific and professional areas, and (5) protecting the welfare of others when standards are lacking. Guidance is also received from ethics codes, published standards of practice, federal and state laws, and institutional policies and regulations. *[Article copies available for a fee from The Haworth Document Delivery Service: 1-800-HAWORTH. E-mail address: <docdelivery@haworthpress.com> Website: <http://www.HaworthPress.com> © 2005 by The Haworth Press, Inc. All rights reserved.]*

KEYWORDS. Competence, standards, ethics, laws, guidelines, policies, professional roles

Address correspondence to: Thomas F. Nagy, PhD, 555 Middlefield Road, #212b, Palo Alto, CA 94301-2124.

[Haworth co-indexing entry note]: "Competence." Nagy, Thomas F. Co-published simultaneously in *Journal of Aggression, Maltreatment & Trauma* (The Haworth Maltreatment & Trauma Press, an imprint of The Haworth Press, Inc.) Vol. 11, No. 1/2, 2005, pp. 27-49; and: *Ethical and Legal Issues for Mental Health Professionals: A Comprehensive Handbook of Principles and Standards* (ed: Steven F. Bucky, Joanne E. Callan, and George Stricker) The Haworth Maltreatment & Trauma Press, an imprint of The Haworth Press, Inc., 2005, pp. 27-49. Single or multiple copies of this article are available for a fee from The Haworth Document Delivery Service [1-800-HAWORTH, 9:00 a.m. - 5:00 p.m. (EST). E-mail address: docdelivery@ haworthpress.com].

Digital Object Identifier: 10.1300/J146v11n01_03

INTRODUCTION

This article presents an analysis of the principle of competence in the mental health field, with accompanying examples and discussion. Professional competence is of critical importance, and constitutes the very bedrock of research, teaching, and clinical practice in the mental health field. In carrying out work, psychologists, psychiatrists, clinical social workers, and marriage and family therapists have a great potential for intervening in the lives of others in ways that can be either helpful or harmful. Without clear criteria for competence, there is potentially a risk of harm to individuals, families and groups, the research database, and, in a larger sense, the very society in which we live. Therefore, it is essential that professionals are mindful of the ethical requirements concerning competence in every aspect of their work, and it is incumbent upon them to continue upgrading their abilities over the course of their professional life as well.

Operating autonomously, usually with little or no consultation or direct scrutiny by their peers, therapists generally find themselves face-to-face in a small office, hospital room, or other setting with a distressed human being, couple, or family who could be greatly affected by their professional actions. The variability among these clients and patients is great, including children or the elderly, those of differing cultures and religious training, and those who are mentally retarded or cognitively impaired in other ways and therefore less able to assess the quality of the intervention that is offered. Many years of education, formal training, and supervision constitute the basis for the variety of roles that they engage in, but there still may be situations when practitioners feel a clinical and ethical challenge and will want to consult a code of ethics or practice guideline for advice.

The topics discussed in this article are based primarily upon the ethics codes of psychology, psychiatry, social work, and marriage and family therapy. They are, respectively, *The Ethical Principles of Psychologists and Code of Conduct* (American Psychological Association, 2002), the *Principles of Medical Ethics* (American Medical Association, 2001; American Psychiatric Association, 2001), the *Code of Ethics of the National Association of Social Workers* (National Association of Social Workers, 1996), and the *American Association of Marriage and Family Therapists Code of Ethics* (American Association of Marriage and Family Therapists, 1998). An appreciation of the substantial differences between the documents, both in form and content, can be acquired by consulting these codes (see Appendices, in this volume). Each code addresses the principle of competence in a somewhat different fashion; however, the psychology ethics code is by far the most lengthy and provides the most detailed operational definitions of competence in a variety of contexts. (For a detailed exposition of the Psychology ethics code, see Fisher, 2003, and Nagy, 2005.)

In considering the concept of competence in the broad diversity of roles played by mental health professionals, ideally each specialty area should be considered, including that of researcher, author, teacher, supervisor, therapist, evaluator, consultant, forensic specialist, case manager, and administrator, to name but a few. However, limited space prohibits addressing each of these roles in detail. By focusing the discussion upon three overarching roles, as discussed in the Psychology ethics code (that of researcher, teacher, and clinician), hopefully most other professional roles will be satisfactorily addressed as well, while exploring the implications of this important ethical principle.

In adhering to standards of competence, therapists should be keenly aware of both the "musts" and the "must nots" of their respective ethical codes. Although each code has a very different format and style, each requires mental health professionals to discharge their professional responsibilities within the limits of their professional competence without causing harm to individuals, groups, society, or the profession itself. In the field of psychology, as mentioned, the areas of work are specified as research, teaching, and clinical practice, and competence is defined by one's education, training, or experience. However, due to the unusual qualities brought by the patient or client, such as diagnosis, risk of harm to the patient or others, or legal complexities (e.g., child custody evaluation, mental competency to stand trial), there are situations that may challenge the competence of professionals. In these cases, even if they are able to provide only a minimal assistance, they must at least be vigilant to *avoid harming* others by their actions or their inaction. There are many cases in which the failure to act could result in substantial harm to individuals, such as ignoring consent forms for releasing confidential information to another or failing to notify Child Protective Services when a minor has been harmed by the patient.

Finally, by way of introducing this subject, it is important to note that competence does not only represent a construct that is ultimately achieved as a goal or an end point. It consists, in the main, of an ongoing process within the individual that, ideally, is in a constant state of flux and renewal. Indeed, mental health practitioners, researchers, and teachers create and recreate their competence daily, in many aspects of their professional work.

They maintain professional competence in a variety of ways, such as by participating in educational and growth-promoting activities (e.g., reading books and journals, participating in seminars, obtaining consultation or supervision, and seeking psychotherapy or other personally rehabilitative experiences on an as-needed basis).

GENERAL ETHICAL PRINCIPLES AND SPECIFIC RULES OF CONDUCT

The ethics codes for psychology, psychiatry, social work, and marriage and family therapy each have general principles stating the value or aspirational goals to be aimed at, as well as specific standards of conduct. The general principles or values inform professionals about the general ethical context and set the framework in which to carry out their work. The specific standards of conduct, on the other hand, provide direct guidance: the actual "musts" and "must-nots" for situations encountered in everyday practice. Both general principles and specific rules are important in conceptualizing and bringing into practice the elements of competent research, teaching, and practice of the mental health field.

The ethics code for psychologists establishes a useful framework by identifying five general concepts bearing on competence. The other professional disciplines (psychiatry, social work, and marriage and family therapy) address most of these same five areas, but some are covered in a more general or implicit fashion. They are as follows: (1) maintaining high standards of competence; (2) keeping within the boundaries of competence and limitations of one's expertise; (3) maintaining competence in human diversity in practice and research; (4) engaging in continuing education in scientific and professional areas; and (5) protecting the welfare of others when standards are lacking. As mentioned, these five goals are potentially applicable to each role played by professionals, either as researcher, teacher, or practitioner.

Maintaining High Standards of Competence

Clinicians should be aware of and meet the professional standards and requirements for the individuals and groups whom they serve. Formal ethical principles, published by professional associations are, of course, an excellent way of learning about these standards, but there are many other resources as well that are helpful in providing guidance. For example, many professional associations have guidelines or standards that help to educate their members about excellence in professional competence. They create special publications, such as the American Psychological Association's (1994) *Guidelines for Child Custody Evaluations in Divorce Proceedings*, the American Psychiatric Association's (2000) *Practice Guidelines: Treatment for Patients with Major Depressive Disorders*, the National Association for Social Work's (1989) *Standards for the Practice of Clinical Social Work*, and the American Association of Marriage and Family Therapist's (1994) *Guidelines for Nontraditional Techniques*. Although these publications usually do not require practitioner compliance with the same degree of rigor as does an ethics code or rule of conduct, they do provide helpful guidelines and advice and are easily accessible to members of the professional organization, and frequently to the public as well.

Frequently, professional associations, such as the International Society of Hypnosis and the Association for Applied Psychophysiology and Biofeedback, have their own codes of ethics and guidelines for clinicians and those doing research. In many cases, institutions such as universities and hospitals will provide therapists with concrete rules and aspirational guidelines that go beyond the principles outlined in ethics codes and are helpful in addressing specific aspects of research and clinical practice. These are generally available from the hospital or university's Institutional Review Board, an in-house committee that evaluates research proposals submitted for ethical compliance.

In addition, many other helpful documents are available to practitioners, as the product of collaboration of various boards, committees, task forces, and professional organizations. An example of the latter is the *Standards for Educational and Psychological Testing*, authored jointly by the American Educational Research Association, the American Psychological Association, and the National Council on Measurement in Education (1985). Also, special documents bearing on ethical practice are periodically created by such excellent and diverse professional associations as the National Academy of Sciences, the National Institutes of Health's Department of Health and Human Services, and the American Psychology-Law Society, to name a few. Mental health practitioners would do well to take advantage of the resources offered by these associations in supplementing their continuing education.

Competent research has always played an important role in the evolution of the science of human behavior. This ethical standard addresses the fundamental values that guide the planning and activities of those who carry out research, and is addressed by virtually every ethics code in the behavioral sciences. In addition to complying with ethical standards, investigators must also comply with the rulings of their respective Institutional Review Boards (formerly, human subjects protection committees) in carrying out research, as previously mentioned. They must also adhere to federal rules and regulations, as articulated by the National Institutes of Health's Office of Research Integrity if their research is federally funded, and the regulations of other relevant professional associations, such as the American Veterinarian Association, for research with animal subjects.

For the most part these regulatory standards are clear and straightforward: one knows which steps to take and what to avoid in order to be in compliance with a particular rule or guideline. Ethics codes also address some of these issues, such as the psychology ethics code's specific requirements for researchers about drawing up consent forms, deciding when to dispense with informed consent, offering incentives and providing for the safety of research participants, taking extra care when children are the focus of the study, and being aware of professional guidelines with animal research, to name a few (for a discussion of ethical considerations in research, see Meltzoff, in this volume). These standards have especially important implications for research involving the elderly, those who are very ill, those who are unable to provide consent (such as the mentally disabled or very young children), or those who are members of disadvantaged minority or ethnic groups.

Academicians, as represented by those teaching at the graduate, undergraduate, and secondary school levels, are responsible for instructing and supervising students as they progress through various developmental stages. They often constitute the very first exposure that students have to the science of human behavior. The National Standards for the Teaching of High School Psychology (American Psychological Association, 1999) is particularly helpful in providing guidance for secondary school teachers. As with the other subspecialty areas, it is important for teachers to participate in professional associations, remain current with the professional literature, and participate in formal continuing education activities on a regular basis in order to continuously update knowledge and expertise. By so doing, they maximize their ability to design courses, teach, mentor, and supervise with competence and objectivity. McGee (in this volume) and Callan and Bucky (in this volume) each discuss considerations in the education and training of mental health professionals.

Keeping Within the Boundaries of Competence and Limitations of Expertise

In recognizing their boundaries of competence, mental health practitioners and researchers regularly assess the requirements of a professional situation and determine whether or not they have sufficient skill to address it. Competence is generally measured by formal education, training, supervision and consultation, or other appropriate professional experiences. It is important to know whether or not one is venturing beyond one's boundaries of competence when exploring *terra incognita,* regardless of experience and seniority. For example, a clinician with twenty years of experience may have had virtually no experience diagnosing or treating a patient with dissociative identity disorder, as the epidemiology of this disorder is rather low. Before accepting such a patient into treatment, he/she should arrange to have professional resources available, such as an individual consultant or, perhaps, an experienced group of therapists that meets regularly and who are able to provide consultation on this difficult diagnostic category.

In recognizing the limitations of one's expertise, a therapist is keenly aware of what can reasonably be expected or accomplished with certain strategies, interventions, or techniques. Clinical interventions that lack an empirical or experiential basis provide the most obvious examples of failure to recognize the limitations of one's expertise. Several examples follow, involving specialized techniques such as hypnosis or biofeedback. Consider the therapist who has a good relationship with her patient, and has done good therapeutic work for a six-month period. Now her patient inquires about the use of hypnosis for management of migraine headaches. It would be unethical for this therapist, who may have read extensively about hypnosis but is lacking formal training, to attempt hypnosis on the strength of her patient's interest and her own self study. Alternatively, consider the patient who thinks that she may have a history of childhood sexual abuse and has never had therapy, and wishes to use hypnosis with this same therapist for her symptoms of panic disorder. Although she may have confidence in her therapist's ability and the technique itself, if hypnosis were improperly used she could be harmed by developing "memories" of childhood sexual abuse that may not be accurate (Edelman, 1978; Nagy, 1994; Nash, 1994). In short, although it may be true that others have confidence in the therapist's or consultant's abilities, it is the therapist's obligation alone to determine his or her own level of competence and when to refuse to intervene.

Another example would be the therapist who is competent to do biofeedback training for pain management, who also happens to believe that biofeedback not only relieves pain but also has therapeutic benefits for cancer. He may communicate this to his patient, directly or indirectly, and increase her hopes and expectancies where it is clearly not warranted. Biofeedback may indeed be a powerful intervention for patients with pain, but it may be misleading, fraudulent, and even abusive in some cases to promote it for purposes for which its efficacy has never been demonstrated. On the other hand, if preliminary research existed that showed a tendency for certain cancer patients to have more frequent remissions and a better quality of life as a result of biofeedback training, then such claims by a therapist could be supported, at least in a tentative fashion, with appropriate informed consent. The therapist should be cautious, however, that her own optimism does not result in false guarantees or assurances of recovery, lest the patient be dispirited and self-blaming for failing to achieve the promised results.

Another example of failing to recognize the limitations of one's expertise might be attempting to provide long-term psychotherapy over the telephone or via electronic mail or the Internet to people who have never been seen face-to-face and who have serious psychopathology, such as a personality disorder or bipolar affective disorder. Although the therapist may indeed be competent, he may be attempting to use his skill in a setting or a milieu for which its efficacy has never been established. Attempting to provide treatment for someone in an acute manic phase or an active alcoholic with borderline personality disorder exclusively over the telephone or over the Internet by means of electronic mail may or may not be possible; thus far the empirical evidence is lacking. Nevertheless, the patient begins such a process and enters an agreement with the therapist in good faith, paying for consultations, expecting to be helped by a mental health professional, and relying upon the therapist's assurances to engage in the process. It is possible, however, that little or no progress will occur using conventional interventions with individuals of these diagnostic categories, and that this "intervention" over the phone or online may essentially be the psychological equivalent of applying a "band-aid" to a broken leg and hoping for the best. Certainly, therapists should be aware of the benefits of new technology, and creative ways of offering their services to patients and clients. However, they should always assess these interventions cautiously, preserving a robust interest in the science of psychotherapy as well as the art, and take concrete measures to protect their patients from harm while using them.

Many therapists participate in some form of managed health care in rendering their professional services. Such a context may have limitations on the extent and type of treatment that will be reimbursed by the health care contract, resulting in truncated therapy and compromising what can reasonably be expected by the patient. By complying with the sharply reduced number of sessions allowed by the patient's contract, a therapist may in fact be attempting the impossible (Nagy, 1998). An example would be agreeing to treat an individual with a difficult diagnosis, such as anorexia nervosa, in six sessions, simply because that is all that the case manager and contract will initially allow. Certainly, treating therapists bear an obligation to petition for additional sessions when there is a compelling rationale. This is for the benefit of the patient, who may need additional therapy, as well as for the good of the clinician, as precedents exist for therapists to be sued for failure to seek additional sessions when the annual limit has been met (*Hughes v. Blue Cross of California*, 1988; *Wickline v. State of California*, 1986).

Keeping within the limits of one's expertise has particular implications for those performing psychological assessment. It is essential that those mental health providers using psychological tests do so in an appropriate manner, and be fully aware of the test's purpose and limitations. Using a Minnesota Multiphasic Personality Inventory as a means of assessing the patient's intelligence or using the Wechsler Adult Intelligence Scale as the sole basis for vocational counseling are examples of going beyond the inherent limitations of the instruments. Indeed behavioral scientists have many valid and powerful instruments of assessment at their disposal, but they must remember to remain within their own expertise and to be cognizant of the test's purpose for which norms exist. Further, when assessing those of a culture, race, or minority group for which the test has never been standardized, cautious interpretation and appropriate disclaimers must be used.

The ethical concept of competence has major implications for planning and carrying out research projects and the use of research assistants as well (for a discussion of ethical issues in research, see Meltzoff, in this volume). No matter how capable an individual may be in her own specialty area, she may be quite unsophisticated in a different area of study for a variety of reasons (e.g., type of population, the milieu, research design, etc.). According to the psychology ethics code, and implied to some extent by the other codes, investigators are obligated to carry out research on topics with which they already have at least a certain degree of familiarity, so as to minimize harm to research participants. If they are completely naive about a topic or a population, they are required to obtain some training or consult with others who are knowledgeable, so as to optimize the research protocol and minimize invasiveness or harm to others. The investigator who wishes to explore treatments for dyslexia with young children, but has never before worked with this population, should work with a co-investigator who is experienced with and knowledgeable about young children. In this way, not only will the planning and design of the research investigation likely be improved but also the risk to the children, if any, will be minimized. Likewise, the clinician who decides that he would like to investigate the impact of group therapy for chemically dependent patients and plans to videotape and observe sessions, but has never engaged in this type of research before, again would be wise to use a consultant or co-investigator familiar with these procedures and populations. By so doing, invasiveness would be minimized or alternate interventions could be developed that might be more palatable to the research participants without compromising the study.

At times, the lucrative incentives provided by business and industry may tempt researchers to exceed their limits of competence. Consider the investigator who is paid by a company that designs and sells computers to "prove" that a new piece of hardware is more efficient or user-friendly than one currently in use. It is possible that the researcher could generate such "evidence," but only by sacrificing robust methodology and creating a research design with a built-in bias in order to meet the company's needs. This might involve employing non-standardized instruments, non-objective techniques, or making unwarranted interpretations of the data in a way that would clearly not be supported by a well-designed study. Subsequently, when members of the public would be exposed to these results by means of product advertising, they would be unaware that these "research outcomes" derived from improper procedures, statistical techniques, or outright deception. Or, even more egregiously, consider the researcher who undertakes a project funded by an extremist organization to prove that a particular ethnic or cultural group is more prone to violence or criminal activity than another group. Again, such "outcomes" might be able to be fraudulently developed by means of using certain instruments, creating one's own non-validated instruments, or unwarranted extrapolations beyond the data. However, it would be clearly deceptive and unethical to do so, and the harm to individuals, society, and the knowledge base could be significant.

Professors and secondary school teachers are also responsible for providing instructional and training experiences that fall into their areas of expertise, again according to the psychology ethics code (for a discussion of ethical issues in teaching mental health professionals, see Callan & Bucky, in this volume). They should abide by guidelines and standards promulgated by various professional and regional associations and publications, as mentioned above. This involves teaching courses only when one has sufficient knowledge, in a manner that is as unbiased and objective as possible.

At the graduate level there may be more risks for overextending oneself, such as the instructor who teaches an introductory course in research with an animal laboratory to meet the demands of an institution with limited resources, but has inadequate training himself. Or consider the instructor who includes an experiential component with the course work, such as an ongoing, self-disclosing "therapy group," ostensibly for the purpose of teaching theories of group process. The professor who plays the role of didactic presenter on one day and group therapist on another places students in a confusing situation; they are simultaneously being asked to reveal private experiences in a quasi-therapy group while, at the same time, in the role of student, whose work is being formally evaluated and graded. There is little to suggest that competent teaching includes a classroom experience that requires inappropriate self-disclosure of the sort that would emerge in individual or group psychotherapy. On the contrary, this situation is potentially harmful to some students, and may exacerbate preexisting psychological conditions for others.

The temptation may be great, at times, for therapists and consultants to go beyond their level of competence, particularly when being paid by the hour to provide professional services of one sort or another. The inducement to exceed one's boundaries of competence may be particularly strong when a patient or organizational client has great faith in the professional's ability, based on a good personal relationship and general satisfaction with the services to date. However warranted this good faith may be, there could be problems later on if the professional attempts to provide further services for which he has little or no education or training. The risk to the consumer may increase as the psychopathology or complexity is greater or if legal factors are at work. An example would be the clinician who successfully provides individual psychotherapy to a depressed, high-level manager in a particular corporation, who then is persuaded by his patient to use his clinical skills in providing workshops to the other employees in the firm. He then offers seminars at the worksite reflecting his personal bias about good human relationships (e.g., authentic self-disclosure, honest communication, and confrontation with supervisors) without first being knowledgeable about how such behavior could affect ongoing working relationships and impact irrevocably upon the corporate system as a whole. He may be quite competent as an individual psychotherapist, but woefully inadequate as a corporate consultant, regardless of how a patient might esteem his clinical skills.

Caveats are particularly strong when there are obvious legal consequences to one's actions. A therapist should never presume competence in providing forensic services to a divorcing couple engaged in child custody litigation without some formal training and/or supervised experience. The assessment and testimony given by the therapist who undertakes this could have major, long-term implications for the lives of the parents and their children. Courts rely upon expert witnesses to provide competent testimony as a basis for legal and physical custody decisions, as well as visitation agreements. Incompetent assessment could result in a custody arrangement that would harm children and many other family members, and cause parents great financial sacrifices at a later time in attempting to reverse the court's ruling. Certainly it would be wise for all therapists to obtain at least minimal training in forensics, regardless of specialty area, in order to have a clear view of the risks inherent in this aspect of their work, how to develop skills for meeting them and when to refer.

Indeed there are many examples of going beyond the limitations of one's expertise, and alas, they are frequently not as transparent as the cases cited above. In reviewing the concept of competence one should consider all of the clinical and non-clinical roles played by professionals, whether as an individual or family therapist, an industrial-organizational consultant working with employees or managers, a child custody evaluator for a divorcing couple, or as a supervisor or mentor to aspiring trainees, to name a few. Finally, and most importantly, a certain degree of humility may be in order when judging one's own competence; as essential as it is to have confidence in one's abilities as a therapist, it is equally important to know when one's limits are being tested.

Maintaining Competence in Human Diversity in Practice and Research

Being aware of the range of human diversity is a requirement of most ethics codes, and acknowledges that (1) people differ greatly on a variety of criteria, and (2) various skills and training, commensurate with these differences, must be acquired by mental health professionals who interact with them. In reflecting upon the rich diversity within human beings, one considers the following variables: age, gender, race, sexual orientation, ethnicity, national origin, religion, disability, socioeconomic status, or any basis proscribed by law. Certainly it is important to be aware of one's own biases and how they may affect ones teaching, practice, or research. A systematic prejudice may exist against a member of a minority group, resulting in absence of objectivity, stereotyping, offensive humor, unfair treatment, hostility or some other unwarranted attitude or behavior, and ultimately flawed treatment or poorly designed research. Self-diagnosis of such a bias may be possible if one is aware of one's own dysphoric feelings, such as disgust, anxiety, anger, over-sensitivity, powerlessness, or other emotion when working with a particular individual or group. Unusual verbal or nonverbal behavior on the part of the therapist, such as poor eye contact, avoidance, sarcastic humor, physical gestures, aggressiveness, or other rejecting behaviors that seem to be out of character for the therapist may be indicators that a problem exists. If such telltale signs of bias do present themselves, they should herald a warning to the professional that steps must be taken to remedy the situation. These would include consulting a knowledgeable colleague, obtaining additional education or consultation in these areas, attending workshops, reading and studying, engaging in personal psychotherapy, and ultimately, referring the patient to another therapist, to name a few. Although health care professionals may feel well acquainted with each of the aspects of human variability, it may be useful to review them briefly as follows.

Age. Developmental issues manifest themselves continuously throughout the life of the individual, demanding a breadth of knowledge and array of skills commensurate with the person being served. The needs of the young child, at different ages, are unique, and differ from each other as they do from those of the adolescent or adult. Professionals who provide services, teach, or do research with these individuals must take these differences into account, and not presume competence unless education, training, supervision, or other appropriate experiences have provided the necessary skills.

It is also important to be aware of legal requirements as they may pertain to minors and the elderly. This has particular relevance to informed consent when counseling or conducting research with young children or adolescents, hospitalized mental patients, geriatric patients, or members of any disenfranchised group. Parents, legal guardians, or conservators must always be consulted and provide their consent before any clinical or research interventions are initiated.

Gender and sexual orientation. Gender may be considered a subculture unto itself, one into which an individual is born and on that has its own array of genetic predispositions, cognitions and perceptions, biases, and behavior patterns conditioned since childhood. A researcher who has a gender bias may unwittingly introduce distortions into any phase of a project, including formulations of hypotheses, data-collection, interpretation of data, and conclusions. Teachers who do not accept males and females equally may reflect their bias in unfair evaluations and grades, demeaning verbal and non-verbal behavior, inappropriate and damaging humor, or explicitly sexualized behavior, which clearly invites a dual role relationship or may be confusing or otherwise destructive to the student. Therapists and organizational consultants who have a gender bias may harm patients and clients, both by what they do and what they fail to do. Psychological assessment, psychotherapy, consulting with management, human relations work, and other direct services provide many opportunities for exposure to the opposite sex where the difference in social power is particularly significant. A professional with a bias could greatly impact the welfare of others, including, for example, invalid formal assessments and recommendations, consistent lack of progress or actual deterioration in psychotherapy, taking sides inappropriately in marital therapy, supporting a child custody arrangement which is damaging to the child, adversely influencing an employee's job, and making negative recommendations about hiring or firing which are not warranted by any objective criteria.

Professionals should also be accepting of the variety of sexual orientations, which make up humanity. Systematic bias or fear of homosexuals (or heterosexuals) can impair functioning in the same way that gender bias can, but frequently it manifests with greater intensity and consequences. Panicky feelings, avoidance, anger, or feelings of personal threat are frequently a part of homophobic reactions. If therapists are aware of their own prejudice against homosexuals or heterosexuals, they should decide to either limit their practice or professional contacts to those with whom they are comfortable, or obtain supervision, consultation, psychotherapy, or some other rehabilitative experience which will help them grow beyond this constricted way of responding. Certainly, in many cases, it will be impossible to avoid interacting with individuals who comprise the feared group, whether homosexual or heterosexual, such as in the classroom or work setting. Therefore, it is the wise individual indeed who welcomes such exposure as an opportunity to gain insight into his or her own negative reactions and is able then to initiate a growth process towards accepting those who differ in gender identity.

Race, ethnicity, national origin, and language. The United States has long had a tradition of welcoming immigrants from other lands, and indeed seems to constitute an amalgam of human diversity that is probably unparalleled in any other major country on earth. Such diversity poses a significant challenge to American psychotherapists and researchers to learn of the values, norms, social customs, idiosyncrasies, and other attributes of those from other cultures in order to properly study and serve them (cf. American Psychological Association, 1993; 2003). Prejudices based on race or national origin can severely impair one's ability to carry out work with first generation Americans, whether in academia, the consultation office, research, or any other setting. For example, the therapist working with a Japanese client should remember that avoidance of eye contact is not necessarily a clinical symptom, but is more likely a sign of respect for authority. Likewise, a Hispanic person's penchant for learning something of the therapist's personal life does not necessarily represent a narcissistic disregard for boundaries, but is a part of a strongly held cultural value that facilitates a good human relationship, without which therapy could not get underway.

Psychological assessment is greatly complicated when individuals from other cultures are being evaluated. Using language-based instruments that have not been standardized with populations of which the client or patient is a member may be inappropriate, yielding invalid profiles. Therefore, in performing assessments and generating reports one should be aware of the potential impact of using such instruments. A disclaimer should clearly indicate when the validity of an assessment is diminished due to inadequate norms. Culture-fair tests should be used whenever appropriate.

Many forms of bias or prejudice are less obvious, and do not necessarily result in a quantifiable or clearly observable result. Attitudes of negative bias and subtle rejection towards individuals in the classroom or workplace can essentially create a chronically hostile experience for the individual of a different race, culture, or ethnic group. It is the wise person who can identify his or her areas of weakness in accepting cultural diversity, and develop a strong commitment to increasing skills and broadening attitudes of acceptance.

Religion. Religious differences can also affect competence when there is a systematic prejudice on the part of the investigator, teacher, consultant, or therapist against individuals of a certain faith. This would manifest itself both in conceptual ways as well as in personal interactions, and could result in biased or poorly conducted research, substandard teaching or supervision, and incompetent consulting or psychotherapy. Whether the prejudice is against atheists, Mormons, Jews, Muslims, or representatives of any other religious faith makes little difference. The quality of the professional work will likely suffer and competence may be diminished unless this prejudice is addressed. If the professional cannot philosophically accept individuals of certain religious convictions, then he should be fastidious about referring such individuals to others.

When therapists and researchers serve or investigate members of the clergy, it is especially important to be familiar with the beliefs, values, habits, and other attributes that might affect their competence. Such special expertise can be obtained through consultation, formal study, or other didactic or experiential means.

Disability. In considering special skills needed to serve, teach, or investigate those with physical or mental impairments, one must be alert to the array of factors unique to each disability. The special needs of those with physical disabilities would include those who have sensory impairments (e.g., blind or hearing impaired), spinal cord or other severe injuries, chronic pain, chronic or degenerative diseases, fatal illnesses, or some other affliction that impairs their daily functioning. The array of mental disorders includes those who are mentally retarded, or those who have pervasive developmental disorders, autism, schizophrenia, dementias, or other brain disorders resulting from accidents or illnesses (e.g., stroke, heart attack, or any event resulting in brain anoxia and subsequent permanent damage).

Therapists, teachers, and researchers who are professionally involved with impaired or disabled individuals should first obtain the necessary education and training to increase their knowledge and skills. By so doing, they reduce the likelihood of harming students, clients or patients, or research participants by what they do or fail to do, and enhance the likelihood of successful outcomes.

Socioeconomic status. Special skills for working with those from a lower or higher socioeconomic status must be acquired by professionals before embarking upon a professional relationship with them. In practical terms, this might involve learning of any special needs or requirements of a student, patient, consultee, or research participant. For example, a therapist working with a homeless person must be adept at first helping the client meet his immediate needs, such as room and board, or getting a job, rather than beginning a course of long-term psychotherapy or dwelling upon the impact of early childhood experiences. Likewise, a battered woman living in a housing project will have special needs of protection and safe refuge, as well as concerns for the security of her children; she will be less interested in a therapy that fails to address these urgent issues, at least in some way. Furthermore, if a therapist is unaware of such exigencies and rigidly pursues a psychological intervention reflecting a particular orientation or theoretical framework without regard for the realities of the situation (e.g., immediate risks, danger to children, etc.), he runs the risk of jeopardizing the very safety of the patient or her dependents that he is attempting to help.

On the other hand, a very wealthy client seeking treatment may present certain problems that are also quite unique, creating dilemmas for therapists who commonly have little training or preparation for them. When money is no object, it may impact on the psychological service in subtle but profound ways. Consider the millionaire who is willing to pay the full fee and more for visits to a therapist, regardless of the productivity of the sessions; is he merely "buying a friend" instead of resolving his life problem or learning more adaptive behavior? Also, consider the wealthy client who may wish to fund his therapist's research in a new area, or donate a building to a university or hospital complex, in exchange for public recognition of his philanthropy. Indeed, there might be a strong inducement for the therapist to prolong treatment and continue working with this "lucrative" patient long after any therapeutic or consultative tasks have been completed. It is essential to monitor the therapist's conflicting motivations and interests when working with those who are very wealthy, in addition to being knowledgeable about their special needs and issues.

Researchers who study those of a lower or higher socioeconomic status likewise must appropriately educate themselves in order to successfully plan and carry out their study. The likelihood of valid results will be increased if the investigator takes into account dialects, dress, social behavior, and other factors which could impact upon the experimental design, research hypotheses, data gathering, interpersonal relationship with the investigator(s), or other aspects of the study. Failure to do so may not have such direct consequences for those involved as in the therapy setting, but it may have far greater implications in a larger sense by contributing to the knowledge base in a way that is biased or distorted.

Again, by way of summarizing, researchers, teachers, consultants, and therapists would each do well to seek education, training, or supervision as preparation for working with those of a significantly diverse socioeconomic status. Some factors to consider are how the socioeconomic status is reflected by interpersonal style or expression (formality vs. informality), ways of relating to authority figures (e.g., therapists, teachers, and others), language (usage of vernacular and slang), values, and goals.

Continuing Education and Professional Areas

It is essential for therapists, researchers, and teachers to remain well informed about their areas of expertise in the ever-expanding knowledge base. In fact, it is often a requirement of state licensing boards and professional associations that members engage in regular continuing education activities. This is readily accomplished by regularly perusing the scientific literature, seeking consultation or supervision as needed, maintaining membership in professional associations, and attending conventions, seminars, and workshops presented by one's county, state, or national professional association.

Many therapists choose to participate in peer consultation groups, a loose association of professionals meeting regularly to present cases and discuss clinical and scientific issues of mutual interest and benefit. Other examples of continuing education would include seeking individual or group consultation with senior clinicians to focus on a specific area or diagnosis (e.g., paranoid personality disorder, psychological aspects of chronic illness, etc.) or a particular psychological orientation or intervention (e.g., cognitive behavioral psychotherapy or dream interpretation).

In academia, there are many opportunities for expanding one's awareness of current literature. Those with academic appointments are generally engaged in research and publication throughout their career, in addition to their teaching responsibilities. Such research and writing generally requires a good awareness of the current psychological literature, at least in the area under study. Also, researchers and members of human subjects committees are regularly invited to attend continuing education seminars in many different parts of the country, sponsored by the National Institutes of Health's Office of Research Integrity. These workshops are of high quality, focusing upon research methodology, specific ethical issues involving the safety of research participants, and many other areas of interest. For those who teach at the secondary school level, there are also many opportunities for continuing education, as mandated by state and county Teachers' Associations.

Protecting Others' Welfare when Standards Are Lacking

Most ethics codes include the important mandate of avoiding harming others, founded conceptually over 2500 years ago upon the ancient Oath of Hippocrates, in its Latin form, *primum non nocere*– "above all, do no harm." But what are mental health professionals to do when specific standards are lacking? It may pose a risk to the mental health of some clients, and costly in other ways as well, to promote a clinical intervention or consultative strategy based on one's own idiosyncratic thinking or limited experience, absent research or other supporting experience. It may be true that much of what therapists do in the consulting room may be founded upon empirically validated techniques, or find some support in their experience and training; however, not every intervention can claim to be empirically validated. Indeed, there are some cases where researchers, therapists, teachers, and consultants specifically lack any guidance from the knowledge base, ethics codes, legal statutes, professional associations, institutions, or any other sources about how best carry out their work while safeguarding the welfare of patients and clients. In these situations, one's professional judgment must be relied upon to protect the safety and well-being of others.

Mental health professionals must always be alert to situations that may place others at risk of being harmed. The author has developed fourteen topical queries that may be used as guides in attempting to identify higher-risk situations of possible impaired competence (see Table 1). These questions are based, in part, on the author's earlier work (cf. Canter, Bennett, Jones, & Nagy, 1994). If any of these questions are answered in the direction of increasing the risk of exploitation or harm to another, then it is imperative that the individual take immediate steps to remedy the situation.

TABLE 1. Self-Questions for Minimizing the Risk of Harm when Using Innovative Techniques in the Absence of Standards or Guidelines

Topic	Query
Boundaries of competence	Are you practicing within your boundaries of competence, according to your formal training, supervision, or experience?
State and Federal laws and regulations, and institutional policies	Are you familiar with the current laws and regulations that pertain to your area of work that may provide guidance, though not actual answers to your questions (e.g., Health Insurance Accountability and Portability Act, Confidentiality rules and exceptions, IRB guidelines for human participants, or the appeal process in managed health care settings for extending therapy)?
Ethics codes and practice guidelines	Are you familiar with your professional association's Code of Ethics and any published guidelines or standards that may have a bearing on what you are about to undertake?
Innovative protocol, intervention, strategy, or approach	Are you about to engage in a new activity, research project, or intervention that has little or no referent in your training or professional experience (e.g., an inspired or intuitively novel therapeutic intervention)?
Uncertainty or apprehension about your work	Do you feel uncertain about how to proceed with respect to the impact of your work on others (e.g., research involving anxiety-evoking stimuli that you have never employed before?)
Confidence in data about client/patient and your intervention	Can you be sufficiently assured of a client or patient's diagnosis, history, or psychological makeup so as to proceed ahead with reasonable certainty that no adverse reactions will be triggered?
Risk of harm to another	Is there a possibility of harm to an individual, group, or organization, even though remote?
Impaired judgment or loss of objectivity	Is there a possibility that you may have impaired judgment or neutrality, or that you may be exploiting another as the result of a conflict of interest or an emerging dual role relationship (i.e., Are you sexually attracted? Are you considering offering psychotherapy to your student or supervisee?)
Prejudice, blind spots, and bias	Do you judge or have strong feelings about certain individuals with particular personal qualities so that your competence could be affected (e.g., gender, homosexuality, age, ethnicity, culture, religion, disability, socioeconomic status)?
Multiple role relationship	Are you altering your customary boundaries or limits by either engaging the individual in a secondary role (friend, co-author, or business associate) or attempting to increase or decrease your social distance (being artificially formal or inappropriately familiar)?
Exploiting the other for personal gain	Do you have something to gain by *using* the other for their knowledge or expertise, money, status, or some other attribute for your own personal or professional gain (e.g., "insider trading" on the stock market, free legal advice)?
Deceiving or manipulating the other	Are your statements accurate, or do they serve some secondary purpose for your own gain (i.e., are you attempting to prolong therapy for your own financial gain or influence others to behave in a certain way for your own benefit?)
Therapist avoidance or denial of reality	Are you systematically avoiding addressing certain topics or situations that you normally would confront (e.g., you never address the client's/patient's hostility or seductive behavior directed at you)?
Relinquishing your standard operating procedures	Do you find yourself changing your usual and customary practices in dealing with a particular individual or situation (e.g., you begin to spontaneously extend the length of your therapy sessions, or agree to meet a patient or research participant for dinner)?

As therapists, supervisors, researchers, and mentors in every sub-specialty, we should always remember that one way of taking action to protect the welfare of others includes consulting with those who are more knowledgeable and experienced. This would include seeking advice from formal resources, such as institutional review boards, state or county professional associations and ethics committees, one's national professional association, a state licensing board, or a university or hospital ethics center or office that accepts such inquiries. Advice can also be sought from other resources, both locally and nationally, such as senior practitioners (not necessarily friends) who are wise in matters of ethics and professional conduct, university professors or other ethicists who teach courses in ethics and professional conduct, and attorneys who specialize in mental health matters.

CONCLUSION

Maintaining professional competence in investigating and serving humankind is a process that lasts for the duration of the professional's life at work. This process reflects a dynamic interaction that involves formal training, continuing education, professional work, and personal life experiences. Although psychologists, psychiatrists, clinical social workers, and family and marriage therapists each have unique areas of specialty, each has essentially the same ethical mandate to remain within their boundaries of competence, and to avoid harming patients and clients in the course of their work.

In closing, it is important to note that individual practitioners who are not affiliated with any hospital or group, and who fail to participate in ongoing educational activities, may experience some professional isolation, resulting in a possible long-term decrement in competence as a consequence of the daily stresses of work. Participating in professional activities, consultation, and ongoing collegial interaction may be a good hedge against such isolation, and the risks to competence that it may bring. And finally, it must be remembered that competent practice presupposes good mental health in the practitioner and a lifestyle that sustains and promotes one's continued well-being. Indeed, this may be the most important ethical duty of each practitioner as it bears on competence: to care for and support the self first, and only then to offer resources to others.

REFERENCES

American Association of Marriage and Family Therapy. (1994). *Guidelines for non-traditional techniques.* Washington, DC: Author.

American Association of Marriage and Family Therapy. (2001). *AAMFT code of ethics.* Washington, DC: Author.

American Educational Research Association, American Psychological Association, & National Council on Measurement in Education. (1985). *Standards for educational and psychological testing.* Washington, DC: Author.

American Medical Association. (2001). *Principles of medical ethics, with annotations especially applicable to psychiatry.* Washington, DC: Author.

American Psychiatric Association. (2000). *Practice guidelines: Treatment for patients with major depressive disorders* (2nd ed.). Washington, DC: Author.

American Psychiatric Association. (2001). *The principles of medical ethics.* Washington, DC: Author.

American Psychological Association. (1993). Guidelines for providers of psychological services to ethnic, linguistic, and culturally diverse populations. *American Psychologist, 48*, 45-48.

American Psychological Association. (1994). Guidelines for child custody evaluations in divorce proceedings. *American Psychologist, 49*, 677-680.

American Psychological Association. (1999). *National standards for the teaching of high school psychology.* Washington, DC: Author.

American Psychological Association. (2002). Ethical principles of psychologists and code of conduct. *American Psychologist, 57*(12), 1060-1073.

American Psychological Association. (2003). Guidelines on multicultural education, training, research, practice, and organizational change for psychologists. *American Psychologist, 58*, 377-402.

Callan, J. E., & Bucky, S. F. (2005). Ethics in the teaching of mental health professionals. *Journal of Aggression, Maltreatment & Trauma, 11(3)*, 287-309.

Canter, M., Bennett, B., Jones, S., & Nagy, T. (1994). *Ethics for psychologists: A commentary on the APA Ethics Code.* Washington, DC: American Psychological Association.

Edelman, G. M. (1978). *The mindful brain.* Cambridge, MA: MIT Press.

Fisher, C. (2003). *Decoding the ethics code: A practical guide for psychologists.* Thousand Oaks, CA: Sage.

Hughes v. Blue Cross of California, 199 Cal. App. 3d 958 (Cal. App. 1988).

Meltzoff, J. (2005). Ethics in research. *Journal of Aggression, Maltreatment & Trauma, 11*(3), 311-336.

Nagy, T. (1994). Incest memories recalled in hypnosis–A case study. *The International Journal of Clinical and Experimental Hypnosis, 43*(2), 118-125.

Nagy, T. (1998). Managed health care, ethics, and behavioral medicine. In L. Barnill, & R. Small (Eds.), *Ethical and legal issues in the new mental health marketplace* (pp. 153-168). Washington, DC: American Psychological Association.

Nagy, T. (2005). Ethics in plain English: An illustrative casebook for psychologists. Washington, DC: American Psychological Association.

Nash, M. (1994). Memory distortion and sexual trauma: The problem of false negatives and false positives. *International Journal of Clinical and Experimental Hypnosis, 42*(4), 346-362.

National Association of Social Workers. (1989). *Standards for the practice of clinical social work.* Washington, DC: Author.

National Association of Social Workers. (1997). *Code of ethics of the National Association of Social Workers.* Washington, DC: Author.

Wickline v. State of California, 228 Cal. Rptr. 661 (Cal. Ct. App. 1986).

The Practice of Integrity
for Mental Health Professionals

David Mills

SUMMARY. The focus of this article revolves around accuracy and honesty in the mental health field. Integrity, both professional and personal, is the foundation of all mental health professionals' functioning. Honesty, fairness, and respect for others are necessary ingredients to professional behavior. Mental health professionals avoid misleading other individuals with regard to professional training and other areas of expertise. In professional roles, they clarify as early as feasible the nature of the expectations and activities in which they are engaged. *[Article copies available for a fee from The Haworth Document Delivery Service: 1-800-HAWORTH. E-mail address: <docdelivery@haworthpress.com> Website: <http://www.HaworthPress.com> © 2005 by The Haworth Press, Inc. All rights reserved.]*

KEYWORDS. Honesty, accuracy, federal trade commission, values, multiple relationships

Integrity is the centerpiece and arguably the most pervasive ethical (or moral) element in the *Ethical Principles of Psychologists and Code*

Address correspondence to: David Mills, PhD, P.O. Box 108, Little Deer Island, ME 04650.

[Haworth co-indexing entry note]: "The Practice of Integrity for Mental Health Professionals." Mills, David. Co-published simultaneously in *Journal of Aggression, Maltreatment & Trauma* (The Haworth Maltreatment & Trauma Press, an imprint of The Haworth Press, Inc.) Vol. 11, No. 1/2, 2005, pp. 51-62; and: *Ethical and Legal Issues for Mental Health Professionals: A Comprehensive Handbook of Principles and Standards* (ed: Steven F. Bucky, Joanne E. Callan, and George Stricker,) The Haworth Maltreatment & Trauma Press, an imprint of The Haworth Press, Inc., 2005, pp. 51-62. Single or multiple copies of this article are available for a fee from The Haworth Document Delivery Service [1-800-HAWORTH, 9:00 a.m. - 5:00 p.m. (EST). E-mail address: docdelivery@haworthpress.com].

Digital Object Identifier: 10.1300/J146v11n01_04

of Conduct (American Psychological Association [APA], 1992, 2002). Constructs associated with integrity include trust, fairness, respect for others, honesty, and the avoidance of doing harm or exploiting others.

Without integrity and its associated elements, it is difficult to conceive of the viability of an ethics code. Unless a patient is able to trust the honesty and the probity of the members of a profession and to accurately assume that these professionals will not be exploitive, the very profession itself will be suspect. While this article uses examples from the 1992 version of the psychology ethics code (APA, 1992), with references to its newest revision (APA, 2002), the subject of "integrity" is a critical part of other mental health codes. For example, integrity is cited in the Code of Ethics of the National Association of Social Workers (NASW; 1997) as one of that profession's six "core values." In the Code of Ethics for the American Association for Marriage and Family Therapy (AAMFT; 2001), "professional competence and integrity" represent one of the eight major ethical domains.

The evolution of psychology's codes reflects movement from general, exhortative tenets to more specific and precise statements and rules. With more than half a century of history, the Code has developed from general "be-honest-and-accurate-and-do-not-harm" elements to much more articulated listings of specific ingredients within such general constructs as honesty, accuracy, and the lack of harm. A good example of this kind of development is the evolution of the 1992 and 2002 Codes' inclusion of statements concerning sexual contact with patients (one form of dual relationship). Until the 1970s, such contact was implicitly assumed, per se, to be unethical but wasn't explicitly proscribed; however, explicit rules have developed over the past 20-25 years so that in the 1992 and 2002 Codes, such relationships are addressed in detail in several sections of the document (see, for example, Standards 1.17, 1.18, 1.19, 4.05, 4.06, 4.07, and 7.05 in the 1992 Code; 3.05, 6.05, 3.08, 10.05, 10.07, and 10.08 in 2002 Code). While these examples are probably the most articulated ones in the general movement within the Codes from the general to the specific, they are certainly not unique.

It is possible to break "integrity" into four sub-principles. The first of these would relate to a mental health professional's charge to describe accurately his or her qualifications and the professional services to be rendered. These descriptions must be presented in a way that is neither misleading nor deceptive. Secondly, the mental health professional is required to be aware of his or her own belief systems, values, and needs and their potential effect on his or her professional activities. The third sub-principle within integrity charges psychologists to clarify their roles as much as possible, and the fourth is a whole constellation of issues relating to improper and potentially harmful dual or multiple relation- ships. This article focuses on each of these four categories, discussing each generally and then providing specific examples that would relate to possible infractions of these standards.

ACCURATE DESCRIPTION OF QUALIFICATIONS/SERVICES

The standards associated with this topic, of course, revolve around the issue of honesty. A mental health professional is required to accu- rately represent his or her fee to potential clients (Standard 1.25 in 1992 version). In advertising, psychologists have the responsibility not only to avoid making false or deceptive statements themselves (Standard 3.03 in 1992 Code, Standard 5.01 in the 2002 Code), but also must make "reasonable efforts" to insure that others do not make false or deceptive statements about them. In general over the years, public statements (such as advertising) have progressed from requirements that the mental health professional present very little (but, of course, accurate) informa- tion, such as "name, rank and serial number" to allowing mental health professionals to publicly present almost anything about themselves and their practices as long as it is accurate and not false or misleading. While the details of the development of this "liberalization" of the Code is be- yond the scope of this article, it should be noted that these changes came as a result of both pressures from within the profession to allow psy- chologists to be more comprehensive in what they can say to potential patients; as well as from outside the profession from the consumer movement and from the Federal Trade Commission. Mental health pro- fessionals could be seen as being in restraint of trade by not allowing potential consumers enough information to make reasoned and reason- able decisions as to which mental health professionals to approach for needed services.

Apart from inaccuracy ("false or deceptive statements"), about the only proscription laid upon the psychologist is that testimonials from *current* patients or from "other persons who because of their particular circumstances are vulnerable to undue influence" are not solicited (Standard 3.05 in 1992 Code and Standard 5.05 in the 2002 Code).

A common violation of this honesty in advertising standard occurs when individuals who are performing clinical services but have degrees from other-than-clinical-programs identify themselves as having a degree in "clinical psychology." While there is no doubt that clinical training can occur in other than clinical training programs, a person must be scrupulous with regard to his or her credentials and must in no way present them in a way that could be misleading.

Case 1

A psychologist has moved to a new location and aggressively begins to advertise his services. He puts large paid advertisements in all the local newspapers that include his picture, a detailed description of his educational and work history, and a long listing of what he calls his "skills." The ad also states that he "slides" his fees on an as-needed basis and that he makes house calls.

The State Psychological Association's Ethics Committee receives multiple complaints that these ads are both over-reaching and unprofessional, and begins to investigate. The psychologist, in a detailed response to the Committee, satisfactorily substantiates the accuracy of his educational and work history. Not only does he note his graduate course work, but also he describes continuing education activities related to the "skill" areas outlined in the ad. He states that he does slide his fee for people who cannot afford his usual and customary fee, and, especially when in the early stages of working with agoraphobics, he does make house calls. When asked about the propriety of putting his picture in the ad, his response to the committee is, in essence, "Why not?"

The Ethics Committee, following a careful review of Section 3 of the code, finds *no* ethics violation by this psychologist. While some of the committee members have reservations about the propriety of certain elements of the ad, especially the picture, the ad is not seen as being inconsistent with ethical advertising.

AWARENESS OF BELIEF SYSTEMS, VALUES, AND NEEDS AND THEIR EFFECTS

This sub-section of the integrity portion of the code relates to two separate streams of activity. The first is associated with training issues and exhorts the psychologist not to practice outside of the areas in which he or she can demonstrate training. As an example, a psychologist who has not been trained to work with children should not do child work except in extraordinary circumstances in which there is no other option and then only under close supervision. Another common arena in which people tend to practice in apparent disregard to their training limitations in that of forensic psychology. Many psychologists with little or no training and experience in forensic psychology will hold themselves out as doing forensic work, and then not surprisingly do substandard work. At the same time, it is possible that any psychologist (irrespective of forensic training) can be "trapped" into court testimony when a legitimate subpoena relating to clinical activities has been received; even so, such a psychologist would be well-advised to seek close consultation with a colleague who is versed and experienced in the forensic arena.

The second relevant area to consider has to do with a psychologist's working with individuals whose very personal characteristics (or demographics) are seen by the psychologist as problematic or aversive. For example, for a psychologist who has very negative feelings toward gays or lesbians to attempt to do professional work with a gay or lesbian client could certainly lead to working at cross purposes with the client and lead to less than adequate services being rendered. A violation of this section could include making demeaning or otherwise derogatory statements to a client with regard to sexual orientation or some other significant characteristic. Psychologists are charged (Standard 1.09 in 1992 Code and Principle E in the 2002 Code) to respect the rights of others to have values, attitudes, and opinions differing from the psychologist's own. Not to show such respect could be seen as a violation of the Code.

Case II

A psychologist is working with a couple on their troubled marriage. Their relationship is one in which the husband is verbally abusive to and non-supportive of the wife's attempts to re-enter the world of work after their children have all grown and left the home. Prior to having children, the wife had a successful career as a credit manager for a local mortgage banking company, which is aggressively attempting to rehire her. The wife wants to resume her career but is being thwarted by her husband's aggressively expressed belief that, since he now earns enough to support the two of them (unlike her earlier period of work in which her income was necessary), she should stay at home and do, at most, volunteer work at the local Red Cross. While they are attempting to resolve this dilemma, their psychologist asks the wife to come in for an individual session during which he strongly advises her not to go back to work because "a good man is hard to find" and, since her income is not now needed, her taking a job could be seen as being self-indulgent. She angrily leaves both the individual session and the marital work, and brings charges against the psychologist with the State licensing board, which investigates the complaint.

The Board investigation substantiates the facts as described above. Additionally, the Board is told by the psychologist that this general issue is one to which he is especially sensitive since, when his own wife re-entered the working world, his own marriage fell apart. He states he was just attempting to keep this couple from experiencing the pain he himself had gone through.

The Board found the psychologist in violation of Standard 1.13 in the 1992 Code (Standard 2.06 in 2002 code) because it felt the psychologist's own personal problems in his marriage had attenuated his effectiveness with this couple. In addition, the Board found a violation of Standard 1.15 in the 1992 Code (located within Principle A in the 2002 Code) because he had attempted to use his professional influence inappropriately.

CLARIFYING ROLES AS MUCH AS POSSIBLE AND FUNCTIONING WITHIN THOSE ROLES

This section of this article also has two different sub-sections. The first as outlined in Standard 1.21 of the 1992 Code relates to a psychologist performing professional services for a person at the request of a third party. An example of such services is when a psychologist is requested to do a pre-employment evaluation of a job candidate by a potential employer. In such a situation, the potential employer would be the client, not the individual evaluated. Even so, the psychologist is charged to clearly and directly define the parameters of the evaluation with the person being evaluated before initiating the evaluation; for example, the psychologist should tell the person what his or her role is and what kind of data will be generated, as well as where and in what form those data will be reported (in this example, it would be reported to the company employing the psychologist). In this situation, the psychologist also needs to clarify for the person being evaluated what information, if any, can be reported or otherwise be made available to him or her. Not to clarify all these matters up-front could be seen as a violation of the code.

The second subsection in this "clarification" charge relates to the initial structuring of the therapeutic relationship and issues revolving around informed consent (Standards 4.01 and 4.02 in the 1992 Code and Standards 3.10 and 4.02(b) in the 2002 Code). It is not the intent of this article to outline all elements involved in initial structuring or informed consent (for a thorough discussion of these issues, see Golub, in this volume); however, there are critical issues that are essential to address. The psychologist must structure the relationship in a manner that is clearly understandable to the potential client, not using jargon or rhetoric that the client cannot reasonably be expected to understand. If the psychologist is to be supervised or may present this case to a case conference or in supervision, the client must be apprised of these facts and must agree to them. In addition and very importantly, issues revolving around confidentiality and exceptions to confidentiality must be spelled out in as much detail as is feasible (see Caudill & Kaplan, in this volume).

A number of potential ethical violations could occur by not adhering to these charges. For example, a psychologist who does an evaluation of an individual at the request of a third party but does not give the individual being evaluated adequate information about the particulars of this activity could be in violation of the Code. Another example might be a situation in which the client has not been informed of any limitations to confidentiality, but finds after the fact that the psychologist has an obligation to report information concerning such matters as child abuse or elder abuse. In these situations, the reporting itself is not a violation of the Code but not apprising the client *a priori* of the need to report such information would be.

Case III

A psychologist is asked by the state child protection agency to evaluate a man who is accused of sexually abusing his 6-year-old daughter. A contract between the psychologist and the agency is drawn up and the psychologist begins the evaluation. She clearly tells the father that her client is the agency and that it will pay all the bills for the evaluation. At the end of the evaluation with this man (who has a seventh grade education), he tells her "I don't want you to tell them (the agency) about any of this stuff between me and my little girl 'cause it's personal." The psychologist states that she has to tell the agency what she learned in the evaluation because, as she had told him earlier, the agency was her client. His response was "So what. Just cause they're your client don't mean you can tell them my personal stuff–that's just between me and you." The psychologist does send a comprehensive report to the State. While the father has not been abusive to his daughter, the psychologist's evaluation does raise serious questions about the quality of their relationship.

The father, through his court-appointed attorney, brings ethics charges against the psychologist for not clarifying issues around confidentiality. During the investigation by the APA Ethics Office, the psychologist admits to not explicitly discussing confidentiality with the father. The psychologist maintained that this issue should have been assumed by the father based on her informing him who her client was. Therefore, she did not believe further information was necessary.

The Ethics Committee disagreed and found that, especially with a person of such limited education, the psychologist had an obligation to explicitly clarify issues around confidentiality, and that not to do so was a violation of specific standards 1.21(a) and 5.01(a) in the 1992 Code (Correspond to standards 3.07 and 4.02 in the 2002 Code).

AVOIDING IMPROPER AND POTENTIALLY HARMFUL DUAL RELATIONSHIPS

Dual relationships (or multiple relationships) are probably the most potentially difficult and risky professional situations in which a psychologist can find himself or herself (see Clipson, in this volume). While the Code states that a psychologist should typically refrain from entering into a second relationship with a client, it does for example state that in many rural communities that have limited professional resources, it may not be feasible to avoid such multiple relationships. In such situations, the responsibility is on the psychologist to be sensitive to the potential harmful affects of such multiple relationships on those persons with whom they deal (Standard 1.17 in the 1992 Code; Standard 3.05 in the 2002 Code).

Except dual relationships that are of a sexual nature, and therefore *per se* unethical, a good rule of thumb is to be as open and frank about multiple relationships with patients or clients as possible. For those situations in which a dual relationship is unavoidable and when there is a great power differential between the psychologist and the client, it is strongly advised that a respected third party, agreeable to both individuals, be set up to mediate any possible difficulties or disputes that arise in the multiple relationship.

Psychologists are charged to ordinarily "refrain" from bartering with clients, but are allowed to do so only if the bartering is not clinically contraindicated and if the relationship is not exploitive (Standard 1.18 in the 1992 Code; Standard 6.05 in the 2002 Code). For a thorough discussion of bartering, see Gandolfo (in this volume).

Obviously, psychologists are not allowed to engage in exploitive relationships with individuals over whom they have control (e.g., research participants, employees, or students). Further, psychologists are not allowed to engage in sexual relationships with students or supervisees in situations for which they have evaluative or direct authority (Standard 1.19 in the 1992 Code and Standard 3.08 in the 2002 Code).

No area within the Code has attracted more attention than has the issue of sexual intimacies with current or former patients or clients. The Code is extremely clear with regard to sexual intimacies with *current* patients or clients (Standard 4.05 in the 1992 Code; Standard 10.05 in the 2002 version), stating that such behavior is always unethical. In addition, Standard 4.06 in the 1992 Code and 10.07 in the 2002 version state that psychologists will not accept as therapy patients or clients individuals with whom they have had earlier sexual contact. However, the issue of sexual contact with former therapy patients or clients is not so clear; earlier versions of the Ethics Code have not addressed this issue explicitly. Standard 4.07 in the 1992 Code and Standard 10.08 in the 2002 version deal with this matter in a way that strongly discourages sexual intimacies with former therapy patients or clients; however, if the sexual contact is initiated in the absence of any element of exploitation and only after two years post-termination, then it could be ethical if all parties are convinced that no element of exploitation is present. See Shavit (in this volume) for a thorough discussion of sexual contact between psychologists and patients.

It should also be noted that dual relationships typically include, as one of the relationships, a therapeutic one. The second (or other) possible relationship is not limited to being sexual; for example, a multiple relationship could include a therapeutic relationship concurrent with a business relationship. It should be noted again that non-sexual dual relationships in rural areas are very difficult to avoid. It takes a great deal of sensitivity and openness on the part of all parties to insure that there is no exploitation involved in these relationships.

The literature is rife with reporting of dual or multiple sexual relationships. This matter is certainly one of the most common and often-reported ethical violations. Again, the Code is very clear: sexual relationships with a current therapy patient or client are always unethical. They can never be justified on the basis of clinical or any other factors. All other dual relationships are discouraged, but under certain specified conditions and with judicious care and attention having been made are possible.

Case IV

A psychologist is seeing in therapy a client who almost matter-of-factly describes a sexual relationship she had had with her last therapist. Clearly, the client is not distraught over the relationship and seems upset only because the relationship has ended. The second psychologist suggests strongly that the client file ethics charges against the first psychologist, telling her quite appropriately that such relations are never ethical. The client refuses to file a complaint and refuses to allow the psychologist to release any information or to file a complaint herself. What options does the psychologist have?

This problem is not an uncommon one, and, in most jurisdictions, it is not an easy or comfortable one with which to deal. The second psychologist needs to know the laws in her state. In certain states, there is mandated reporting of therapist/client sexual contact (much like child sexual abuse reporting). In these states, the resolution is clear: the matter must be reported even in the absence of the client's permission. However, in states without mandated reporting, the second psychologist has an ethical dilemma. In this case, she has information of a serious ethical infraction, but does not have permission to do anything with that information. Accordingly, the client's explicit request not to break confidentiality must be honored. The issue can become a therapeutic one, as appropriate and provided if it does not sidetrack other critical therapeutic issues. Why the client engaged in the relationship and why she will not allow this information to be disclosed may be of dynamic (and, therefore, therapeutic) importance. At the very least, the second psychologist should tell the client that her earlier therapist was clearly breaching the Ethics Code and make information available to the client as to how and where one can file an ethics complaint.

Some psychologists in this bind have suggested meeting with the first psychologist to discuss the allegations without identifying their source. This "resolution" seems far from satisfactory and may end up breaching the client's confidentiality and possibly even putting the client in jeopardy. Accordingly, in the absence of mandated reporting or permission to breach confidentiality, there is no "good" resolution to this dilemma.

CONCLUSION

As described throughout this article, it is hard to visualize a situation in which professional integrity is not present in the context of overall ethical behavior. Integrity, both professional and personal, is certainly the foundation of all psychologists' professional functioning. Honesty, fairness, and respect for others are necessary ingredients to professional behavior. Psychologists avoid misleading other individuals with regard to professional training and areas of expertise. In professional roles, they clarify as early as feasible the nature of the expectations and activities in which they are engaged. Whenever possible, psychologists limit themselves to a single role with a professional client or patient. For the few situations in which such a single role is not feasible, sensitivity and open communication are necessary; however, under no circumstances is sexual contact with current patients or clients acceptable.

REFERENCES

American Association of Marriage and Family Therapy. (2001). *AAMFT code of ethics.* Washington, DC: Author.

American Psychological Association. (1992). Ethical principles of psychologists and code of conduct. *American Psychologist, 47,* 1597-1611.

American Psychological Association. (2002). Ethical principles of psychologists and code of conduct. *American Psychologist, 57*(12), 1060-1073.

Caudill, O. B., & Kaplan, A. (2005). Protecting privacy and confidentiality. *Journal of Aggression, Maltreatment & Trauma,* 11(1/2), 117-134.

Clipson, C. (2005). Misuse of psychologists' influence: Multiple relationships. *Journal of Aggression, Maltreatment & Trauma,* 11(1/2), 169-203.

Gandolfo, R. (2005). Bartering. *Journal of Aggression, Maltreatment & Trauma,* 11(1/2), 241-248.

Golub, M. (2005). Informed consent. *Journal of Aggression, Maltreatment & Trauma*, 11(1/2), 101-115.
National Association of Social Workers. (1997). *Code of ethics of the National Association of Social Workers*. Washington, DC: Author.
Shavit, N. (2005). Sexual contact between psychologists and patients. *Journal of Aggression, Maltreatment & Trauma*, 11(1/2), 205-239.

Professional and Scientific Responsibility: Integrity

Rodney L. Lowman

SUMMARY. This article addresses ethical issues associated with the concept of professional and scientific responsibility as related to Principle C, "Integrity" of the APA's 2002 Ethics Code. Differences between aspirational and enforceable ethical standards are noted and contextualized in APA's and other professional society's ethics codes. Three case examples are presented and discussed. *[Article copies available for a fee from The Haworth Document Delivery Service: 1-800-HAWORTH. E-mail address: <docdelivery@haworthpress.com> Website: <http://www.HaworthPress.com> © 2005 by The Haworth Press, Inc. All rights reserved.]*

KEYWORDS. Aspirational standards, Principle C, professional and scientific responsibility

> *Aspiration.* A strong desire for high achievement.
> (*American Heritage Dictionary*
> *of the English Language*, 1992, p. 110).

Address correspondence to: Rodney L. Lowman, PhD, Alliant International University, Office of the Provost, 10455 Pomerado Road, San Diego, CA 92131-1799 (E-mail: rlowman@alliant.edu).

[Haworth co-indexing entry note]: "Professional and Scientific Responsibility: Integrity." Lowman, Rodney L. Co-published simultaneously in *Journal of Aggression, Maltreatment & Trauma* (The Haworth Maltreatment & Trauma Press, an imprint of The Haworth Press, Inc.) Vol. 11, No. 1/2, 2005, pp. 63-70; and: *Ethical and Legal Issues for Mental Health Professionals: A Comprehensive Handbook of Principles and Standards* (ed: Steven F. Bucky, Joanne E. Callan, and George Stricker,) The Haworth Maltreatment & Trauma Press, an imprint of The Haworth Press, Inc., 2005, pp. 63-70. Single or multiple copies of this article are available for a fee from The Haworth Document Delivery Service [1-800-HAWORTH, 9:00 a.m. - 5:00 p.m. (EST). E-mail address: docdelivery@haworthpress.com].

Available online at http://www.haworthpress.com/web/JAMT
© 2005 by The Haworth Press, Inc. All rights reserved.
Digital Object Identifier: 10.1300/J146v11n01_05

Modern professional ethics straddles the canyon of attempting to set the highest possible (i.e., aspirational) standards and of trying to set reasonable, enforceable ethical values. The enforceable standards, if well developed, are ones that hopefully will not result in successful lawsuits against the promulgators or enforcers of ethics codes. This fundamental conflict is between the desire to hold professionals to the highest ideals or standards of practice and the fear of being successfully sued by perhaps less savory professionals or clients, who, in the rough-and-tumble real-world, can expertly be defended against (or become the aggressors against those who would be enforcers). In a highly litigious society, professional associations and state licensing boards, often the promulgators and enforcers of ethical standards, are understandably reluctant to push the envelope too far in the direction of rigorous enforcement of high standards.

By their nature, aspirational standards tend to be broad and general. They set the context for policy but they do not, in enforceable detail, define the policy in statutory form. An analogy might be between the Declaration of Independence and the Constitution of the United States. An even better analogy might be between the Constitution itself, still broad and policy making, and the statutory-enabling legislation that articulates in specific codified detail the laws that, in effect, implement the principle. The first document, and to some extent, the second one, are idealized manifestations inspiring action and belief. Statutory law, in contrast, is detailed and enforceable.

The role of aspirational standards in modern ethical practice and in the training of professional psychologists is largely undefined. With the 1992 major revision of the *Ethical Principles of Psychologists and Code of Conduct*[1] (American Psychological Association [APA], 1992), and continuing to the 2002 version of the Code (APA, 2002), the ethical principles and standards were split into two separate sections, one aspirational and one enforceable. The enforcement status of these principles is left somewhat ambiguous. For example, from the Principles, the Preamble and General Principles are *aspirational* goals to guide psychologists toward the "very highest ethical ideals" (APA, 2002, p. 3) of the profession of psychology. Although the Preamble and General Principles are not themselves enforceable rules of conduct, they still can be considered by psychologists in arriving at an ethical course of action but are not to be considered by ethics bodies either in interpreting whether the Ethical Standards have been violated or as a basis for imposing sanctions (APA, 2002, p. 3). The exact nature of the aspirational principles has to date not definitely been determined either in the professional literature or case law. Clearly, ethics bodies were not meant to enforce the aspirational Principles. Holding psychologists to a higher standard than usual and customary practice, a customary judicial standard for professionals, would also presumably be legally problematic.

Other professional associations' codes are also relevant. For example, the *Code of Ethics of the National Association of Social Workers* (National Association of Social Workers [NASW], 1999) also differentiates between Ethical Principles (broad statements that are overarching, such as values of service, social justice, and the dignity and worth of the person) and Ethical Standards that are much more specific and presumably enforceable. In contrast, the *Code of Ethics* of the American Association of Marriage and Family Therapists (AAMFT; 2001) does not make such a differentiation, instead identifying eight ethical areas that are presumably enforceable. However, this code also begins each of the statements with an overall statement that is orienting and somewhat aspirational in nature.

Currently, there is little empirical evidence to demonstrate whether or not having aspirational standards create the desired effect of improving the behavior of psychologists by setting high ideals. It remains to be determined empirically whether, because they are aspirational and not enforceable, such principles are largely ignored or taken less seriously. In many ways, aspirational standards are by their nature presumed to be more or less non-enforceable since they may hold out too high a standard for the typical practitioner. Mostly, psychologists are *required* by their ethical code to behave not necessarily at the highest level of performance but always at the minimally expected (i.e., usual and customary) level.

In the world of enforcement, law suits, and expert defenses, ethical standards perhaps necessarily focus on the goal of policing bad behavior more than they do on encouraging optimal behavior. Aspirational standards may therefore have minimal impact in contexts in which they are unenforceable. Although perhaps only those with strong super-egos, persons just beginning their professional careers, and those whose duties include ethical instruction are likely to take the aspirational standards very seriously, there is much to be learned from thinking about aspirational standards and, over time, in increasing the expected level of minimally acceptable performance.

With this background and context in mind, the purpose and apparent intent as well as the applications of aspirational Principle C of the APA's 2002 Ethics Code are addressed. It states:

Principle C: Integrity: Psychologists seek to promote accuracy, honesty, and truthfulness in the science, teaching, and practice of psychology. In these activities psychologists do not steal, cheat, or engage in fraud, subterfuge, or intentional misrepresentation of fact. Psychologists strive to keep their promises and to avoid unwise or unclear commitments. In situations in which deception may be ethically justifiable to maximize benefits and minimize harm, psychologists have a serious obligation to consider the need for, the possible consequences of, and their responsibility to correct any resulting mistrust or other harmful effects that arise from the use of techniques. (APA, 2002, p. 3)

ANALYSIS OF THE PRINCIPLE

This multi-faceted principle incorporates several ideas, all revolving around the concept of "integrity." The general theme in this Principle is psychologists' obligation to behave in a responsible, truthful, and accurate manner, both in their personal behavior (as it affects the practice of psychology), in their relationships to other professionals, and in their relationship to the profession itself.

This principle finds its way into several parts of the enforceable Ethical Standards. The requirement for "accuracy, honesty, and truthfulness" is codified in an enforceable way in several ethical standards, including 8.02 Informed Consent to Research, 9.03 Informed Consent in Assessments, and 10.01 Informed Consent to Therapy (defining the psychologist's responsibility for accuracy in research dealings with human participants, in assessment, and in therapy); 6.04 (c) Fees and Financial Arrangements and 6.06 Accuracy in Reports to Payors and Funding Sources (mandating accurate reporting and representation of fees); 7.03 Accuracy in Teaching (requiring accuracy in syllabi and in the presentation of psychological material in a classroom setting); and 8.07 Deception in Research (clarifying the circumstances and limitations for research that misleads participants), among others. Professional obligations to cooperate in issues involving honesty and integrity are covered by such standards as 8.14 (Sharing Research Data for Verification) and in a number of enforceable standards that prohibit sexual intimacies with psychotherapy clients (past and present) or the significant others or relatives of such clients (see Ethical Standards 10.05-10.08). Non-exploitative, non-fraudulent relationships among colleagues are governed by several standards, including 1.07 Improper Complaints, 3.08 Exploitative Relationships, 8.12 Publication Credit, and 8.15 Reviewers.

The general theme of all of these standards is that it is not enough to be competent in one's own work; the ethical psychologist is mandated to behave in certain ways in relationship to others and in the conduct of their work and, above all, must be honest, dependable, and reliable (also see Mills, this volume).

CASE VIGNETTES

Three short cases illustrate this Principle.

Principle C, Case 1

A counseling psychologist in independent practice received approximately two-thirds of his referrals from a large, market-dominant managed care firm. As the result of an aggressive campaign to wrest the contract away, another managed care company won the contract when it was up for renewal. Most of the existing providers were not to be included in the new company's provider list. In making referrals to the new managed care group, providers were authorized a few sessions of treatment to make the transition to the new set of providers. When the counseling psychologist met with his clients on their next visit after the announcement, he simply told the clients that they now had to seek their care through their new managed care group and gave them the telephone number to call to make the necessary arrangements. When the new providers sought information on the treatment and assessment rendered to date, the counseling psychologist refused to provide any information, stating he was not being paid to do so.

Principle C, Case 2

An Industrial-Organizational psychologist assessed job candidates for a client organization. She used a standard assessment battery but never completed job analyses for any of the positions for which the persons were being evaluated. Her contract provided payment only for her to give the tests and to report back to the client organization's management on the results. It did not pay for job analyses or to provide feedback to the person(s) assessed. An assessee who had been rejected for a position with the client firm contacted the psychologist and requested feedback on the results of the assessment. She refused, stating that her client was the organization, not the individuals assessed. Although the assessee never pursued the matter further, he remained convinced that he lost the job because of the results of his assessment.

Principle C, Case 3

A psychologist researcher and professor put out a call for participants in a research study. The plan was to gather information on a procedure that involved some physical discomfort. The researcher was under an imminent deadline for the submission of the results of his study to a granting agency. He had experienced difficulty in obtaining enough participants for the research. When the participant stated that she, on second thought, did not wish to participate in the study, instead of immediately honoring the request, the researcher met with her in a private room and spent a considerable period of time attempting to get her to change her mind. Finally, feeling threatened and intimidated, but wanting to end the conversation, she agreed to participate. She found the experiment aversive but stuck it out, angry with herself for not having been more assertive in saying no to participation.

Each of these cases identifies a breach in a psychologist's professional or scientific responsibilities that manifest less than optimal levels of professional integrity. The context in each case called for slightly different applications. The ethical issues associated with management mental health care (Case 1) are just now emerging (see, e.g., Haas & Cummings, 1994; Lowman & Resnick, 1994). The Industrial-Organizational context (Case 2) also raises its own unique ethical applications (see, e.g., Lowman, 1998). Research ethics (Case 3) have been more widely studied and reported (e.g., Stanley, 1996).

In each of these case examples, the psychologist could have done far more to be accurate, honest, and truthful in dealings with clients or those in the psychologist's care. The behavior of the psychologists in each of these cases was somewhat dishonest or inattentive to issues that should have been relayed. The focus in each case was more on the psychologist's needs or someone other than the client or person evaluated, resulting in inappropriate behavior that was ethically questionable. The occurrence of conflict is routine in many aspects of the practice of psychology; what is important is not its avoidance but rather how the psychologist handled or addressed that conflict. In these cases, the resolution of the conflict was entirely one sided and there appeared to have been little effort to minimize harm.

In all of these case examples, the psychologists behaved neither professionally nor in keeping with their responsibilities as psychologists. In each of these cases, the psychologist appeared to be more concerned with issues personally important to them as individuals than to the needs of their clients or the expected standard of professional behavior. In case 1, the psychologist failed to cooperate with colleagues when, regardless of the anger the psychologist might have felt toward the managed care situation, cooperation was clearly necessary. The psychologist was dishonest by omission in failing to provide information to the new treatment professionals.

In the second case, the psychologist did not necessarily have to provide the feedback requested in order to have behaved professionally. However, the terms of the engagement should have been made clear to the client organization and to the participants up front. When the psychologist encountered a situation in which the assessee requested feedback she had not expected to have been required to give, the issue(s) should have been worked through with the individual and the client organization, not simply summarily dismissed.

In the final case, the psychologist failed to behave responsibly by, in effect, fraudulently coercing an individual into a research role when a contrary decision about participation had been reached. Whatever their needs for research subjects and the like, psychologists must behave with scientific responsibility by following institutional research guidelines.

CONCLUSION

Although aspirational standards are not enforceable per se, their existence is intended to raise the level of the practice of psychology in all its many iterations and varieties. This article has identified aspects of aspirational and enforceable ethics codes. Limitations and values of aspirational codes are noted. The article also examined in detail one of the aspirational ethical principles, Principle C: Integrity, and provided illustrative case examples. Perhaps all of the cases could have been handled by the APA's enforceable Ethics Standards (APA, 1992), but the generic, aspirational principles remind us of the basis from which those more specific principles derive.

NOTE

1. *Ethical Principles of Psychologists and Code of Conduct* (APA, 2002). In this article this document will be referred to as Ethical Principles and Code.

REFERENCES

American Association of Marriage and Family Therapists. (2001). *AAMFT code of ethics*. Retrieved September 2, 2003 from, http://www.aamft.org/resources/LRMPlan/Ethics/ethicscode2001.asp

American Heritage Dictionary of the English Language (3rd ed.). (1992). Boston, MA: Houghton Mifflin.

American Psychological Association. (1992). Ethical principles of psychologists and code of conduct. *American Psychologist, 47*, 1597-1611.

American Psychological Association. (2002). *Ethical principles of psychologists and code of conduct*. Retrieved online September 2, 2003 from, http://www.apa.org/ethics

Haas, L., & Cummings, N. (1994). Managed outpatient mental health plans: Clinical, ethical, and practical guidelines for participation. In R. L. Lowman & R. J. Resnick (Eds.), *The mental health professional's guide to managed care* (pp. 137-149). Washington, DC: American Psychological Association.

Lowman, R. L. (Ed.) (1998). *The ethical practice of psychology in organizations*. Washington, DC: American Psychological Association.

Lowman, R. L., & Resnick, R. J. (Eds.). (1994). *The mental health professional's guide to managed care*. Washington, DC: American Psychological Association.

Mills, D. (2005). Integrity. *Journal of Aggression, Maltreatment & Trauma, 11*(1/2), 51-62.

National Association of Social Workers. (1999). *Code of ethics of the National Association of Social Workers*. Retrieved online September 2, 2003 from, http://www.naswdc.org/pubs/code/default.htm

Stanley, B. (1996). *Research ethics: A psychological approach*. Lincoln, NB: University of Nebraska Press.

Respect for People's Rights and Dignity

Rodney L. Lowman

SUMMARY. This article examines the nature and application of aspirational General Principle E (Respect for Peoples' Rights and Dignity) of the *Ethical Principles of Psychologists and Code of Conduct* (American Psychological Association [APA], 2002) and similar principles in other mental health professional ethics codes. Issues about aspirational versus enforceable standards are reviewed. Case examples and illustrations of the principle are provided. *[Article copies available for a fee from The Haworth Document Delivery Service: 1-800-HAWORTH. E-mail address: <docdelivery@ haworthpress.com> Website: <http://www.HaworthPress.com> © 2005 by The Haworth Press, Inc. All rights reserved.]*

KEYWORDS. APA ethics Principle E, peoples' rights and dignity

Aspirational Principle E of the *Ethical Principles of Psychologists and Code of Conduct* (American Psychological Association [APA], 2002) states:

Address correspondence to: Rodney L. Lowman, PhD, Office of the Provost, Alliant International University, 10455 Pomerado Road, San Diego, CA 92131-1799 (E-mail: rlowman@alliant.edu).

[Haworth co-indexing entry note]: "Respect for People's Rights and Dignity." Lowman, Rodney L. Co-published simultaneously in *Journal of Aggression, Maltreatment & Trauma* (The Haworth Maltreatment & Trauma Press, an imprint of The Haworth Press, Inc.) Vol. 11, No. 1/2, 2005, pp. 71-77; and: *Ethical and Legal Issues for Mental Health Professionals: A Comprehensive Handbook of Principles and Standards* (ed: Steven F. Bucky, Joanne E. Callan, and George Stricker,) The Haworth Maltreatment & Trauma Press, an imprint of The Haworth Press, Inc., 2005, pp. 71-77. Single or multiple copies of this article are available for a fee from The Haworth Document Delivery Service [1-800-HAWORTH, 9:00 a.m. - 5:00 p.m. (EST). E-mail address: docdelivery@haworthpress.com].

Available online at http://www.haworthpress.com/web/JAMT
© 2005 by The Haworth Press, Inc. All rights reserved.
Digital Object Identifier: 10.1300/J146v11n01_06

Principle E: *Respect for Peoples' Rights and Dignity*
Psychologists respect the dignity and worth of all people and the rights of individuals to privacy, confidentiality, and self-determination. Psychologists are aware that special safeguards may be necessary to protect the rights and welfare of persons or communities whose vulnerabilities impair autonomous decision making. Psychologists are aware of and respect cultural, individual, and role differences, including those based on age, gender, gender identity, race, ethnicity, culture, national origin, religion, sexual orientation, disability, language, and socioeconomic status and consider these factors when working with members of such groups. Psychologists try to eliminate the effect on their work of biases based on those factors when working with members of such groups. Psychologists try to eliminate the effect on their work of biases based on those factors, and they do not knowingly participate in or condone activities of others based upon such prejudices. (p. 4)

This issue has been a concern of the codes of ethics of most mental health oriented professions. For example, the *Code of Ethics of the National Association of Social Workers* (NASW; 1999) specifies, "Social Workers respect the inherent dignity and worth of the person" (p. 3). Additionally, the *Code of Ethics* of the American Association of Marriage and Family Therapists (AAMFT; 2001), which has little in the code that is "aspirational," does specify as a preamble to its Principle 1 (Responsibility to Clients): "Marriage and family therapists advance the welfare of families and individuals. They respect the rights of those persons seeking their assistance . . ." (p. 2).

ANALYSIS OF THE PRINCIPLE

APA's ethical principle will be taken as the major focus of this chapter; however, it would have been as easy to substitute the similar principle from a number of other ethics codes. In the case of the APA's principle, it is based on the concern by the Code's authors for the valuation of all humans and the minimization of discrimination on the basis of inappropriate factors (e.g., race, gender, etc.). The Principle encourages psychologists to become aware of differences among people and to value them. Much of the spirit of this code mirrors national and state anti-discrimination legislation (e.g., Age Discrimination Act of 1975; the Age Discrimination in Employment Act of 1967; the Civil Rights Act of 1991; Title VII of the Civil Rights Act of 1964; and the 5th and 14th amendments to the U.S. Constitution; see, e.g., Arvey & Faley, 1988). Protection from sexual orientation discrimination (see Bayer, 1987; Brown, 1996) is covered by statutes in some jurisdictions, primarily at the state and local level. Perhaps more controversial aspects are the issues of discrimination that concern language and socioeconomic status (e.g., Faunce, 1990), which, as ethical mandates and depending on the psychologist's obligation, may set the standards with which some psychologists might take issue or, at the least, feel the need for further definition and explanation.

Also potentially problematic from the perspective of defining aspirational principle is the assertion of psychologists' ethical obligations to respect the rights of individuals to privacy, confidentiality, self-determination, and autonomous decision-making (APA, 2002, p. 4). Similarly, the asserted rights to autonomy and self-determination, left undefined and without an operational definition (e.g., a statutory context or consensual agreement), may be controversial. Because the term "rights" is left undefined and generic, objections may be raised that there cannot be a right without a corresponding obligation to assure that right. If rights are merely asserted, independent of context, and left undefined, even a well-intentioned psychologist will have trouble knowing how to act in a manner consistent with those assertions. Since the asserted rights to confidentiality, self-determination, and autonomy are left rather general and global, these aspects of the Principle would become problematic were enforcement attempted from the aspirational Principle alone. As general principles, most psychologists would not disagree with the desirability of persons' privacy and confidentiality being protected, particularly as they relate to the practice of psychology. The constructs self-determination and autonomy, however, are more vague and, left undefined, do not clearly correspond to known statutes or legal obligations. Further elaboration of these constructs in the next revision of the code may be desirable. Similarly, the term discriminatory practices itself is left undefined. Because the aspirational principles are not directly enforceable, the danger is that psychologists may not take them seriously either in trying to understand and comply with them or, if they disagree with them, in trying to shape their future content.

The Principle thus illustrates the differences and the limitations of aspirational and enforceable codes. As broad statements of ideals, such principles can be of value. However, as specific, enforceable codes, such principles can fall short because of their lack of specificity and implied rather than stated obligations to behave (or not to behave) in a certain way. Note that several of the enforceable Ethical Standards (APA, 2002) are closely associated with this Principle. Ethical Standards 3.01 Unfair Discrimination; 3.02 Sexual Harassment; 3.03 Other Harassment; and 4.04 Minimizing Intrusions on Privacy, among others, all show a very close link with this more general principle. Privacy and confidentiality issues have their own section (Standard 4) in the enforceable section of the code. Generally, but not always, the Standards are more specific and more clearly point to measurable behavior.

CASE VIGNETTES

Three short case vignettes illustrating this Principle follow.

Principle E, Case 1

A psychologist employed in a mental health organization consisting largely of licensed professionals treated clients experiencing a broad range of mental health problems. He saw in intake a client complaining of depression and withdrawal. The client was then 49 years old and a fairly recent immigrant from an oppressive Latin American country. He spoke fluent Spanish and less-than-fluent English. The client was a prominent professional in his homeland but could not get the certifications or licensures he needed to practice his profession in this country. He was supported by public assistance and the charity of persons from his homeland. The psychologist, a white upper middle class male, diagnosed the depression and referred the client for a medication consult and suggested, in English, that short-term counseling might be helpful. The client followed through with the medication referral but not on the suggestion of short-term treatment.

Principle E, Case 2

A male heterosexual psychologist treated a male homosexual client for anxiety. He had never worked with homosexual clients prior to this client and was a little apprehensive about undertaking this treatment. However, he felt that he was tolerant and a good therapist and should get some experience with this population. The client disclosed that his lover had recently died from AIDS and that since the death, he had been sexually promiscuous and had engaged in unprotected sex. The therapist did not inquire about the patient's HIV status and did not attempt to address the sexual acting out. When the client developed a romantic attraction to him, despite his detailed knowledge of countertransference issues, the therapist felt that he could no longer be helpful to him and referred him to a gay psychologist colleague. The client reported to his new psychologist that he felt angry, hurt, and abandoned.

Principle E, Case 3

A psychologist-researcher, who was also an academic administrator, expressed clear preferences for certain types of research methodologies and actively opposed others. As the administrative head of his department and the supervisor of a dozen psychologists, he continued his long-standing pattern of ridiculing the approaches to the field taken by some of his colleague-subordinates while verbally and financially rewarding those whose research approach he valued. All of the professors to whom the negative comments and actions were directed were both competent and productive in their respective areas. He persistently disparaged the work of those that he wanted to leave, doing so behind their backs to other colleagues. He made fun of their approaches in public meetings. Although the psychologists complained privately to him that they felt discriminated against because of their methodologies and research interests, the administrator always reverted back to his prior behavior after a short interlude of changing his pattern of ridicule.

In the first case, the psychologist failed to account adequately for the recent immigrant's cultural context (see, e.g., Dana, 1996; LaFramboise, Foster, & Jones, 1996; Locust, 1995; Sue, 1996). Being a provider had been an important part of the client's life in his country of origin; this role was now absent and, at 49, the possibilities in his particular geographic area were realistically limited. The psychologist further failed to communicate the need for psychotherapy in terms the client could understand. The barriers to communication were not just linguistic; in the client's culture, psychotherapy may have been neither understood nor accepted. Taking the time to work through these issues would have enhanced the likelihood that the client would follow through with the recommendation.

In the second case vignette, there was a serious problem with the therapist's understanding and acceptance of his client's homosexuality (see, e.g., Brown, 1996). Had a female client experienced a romantic attachment to him, it is likely that he would have handled the transference appropriately. Referral might indeed have been appropriate if there was so little appreciation of the client's sexual orientation, but the manner of the referral was problematic. By summarily evicting the client from therapy, and by not processing the issues or accepting responsibility for his own reactions, the psychologist left the client feeling that there was something wrong with him and with his feelings.

The third case vignette illustrates a situation in which there was obvious bias in favor of certain approaches and subordinates and against others. Psychologist-administrators do not abdicate their responsibility to make judgements about the quality and character of their colleagues' work. Indeed, their professional duty is to assist their subordinates in being productive, if not in the particular institution at hand then in some other. What was problematic in this case is not that the administrator was evaluative, but the nature of his evaluations and the manner in which he chose to communicate them. The indirect expression of the administrator's evaluations, their persistence, and their apparently punitive nature support the notion of a pattern of discrimination and bias. What the psychologist may have rationalized as being witty jousts of a humorous nature were in fact statements that were neither reasoned nor appropriately directed. If the psychologist felt that the subordinates' research was inappropriate for this particular academic setting, then he should have dealt with those issues privately and in the context of a consensually agreed-upon determination of the department's research parameters. As it was, he inappropriately discriminated against certain competent and productive research methodologies while overly favoring others and failed to recognize his prejudices, which potentially could have had serious consequences on his subordinates' professional careers. Psychologists who become administrators do not cease to have an obligation to behave ethically or in a non-discriminatory manner. To the contrary, their behavior on assuming leadership roles becomes exemplary, in either the positive or negative sense.

CONCLUSION

The article examined aspirational Principle E of the APA ethics code concerning the professional's ethical obligations to respect peoples' rights and dignity. Similar principles appear in other examined ethical codes. The principle was illustrated with case examples. Perhaps all of the cases could have been handled equally well by the APA's enforceable Ethics Standards (APA, 2002), but the generic, aspirational principles remind us of the basis from which those more specific principles derive.

REFERENCES

Age Discrimination Act, 42 U.S.C. § 6101 (1975).

Age Discrimination in Employment Act (ADEA), 29 U.S.C. § 621, P.L. 90-202 (1967).

American Association of Marriage and Family Therapists. (2001). *AAMFT code of ethics*. Retrieved September 2, 2003 from, http://www.aamft.org/resources/LRMPlan/Ethics/ethicscode2001.asp

American Psychological Association. (2002). *Ethical principles of psychologists and code of conduct*. Retrieved September 2, 2003 from, http://www.apa.org/ethics

Arvey, R. D., & Faley, R. H. (1988). *Fairness in selecting employees*. Reading, MA: Addison Wesley.

Bayer, R. (1987). *Homosexuality and American psychiatry. The politics of diagnosis*. Princeton, NJ: Princeton University Press.

Brown, L. S. (1996). Ethical concerns with sexual minority patients. In R. P. Cabaj, & T. S. Stein (Eds.), *Textbook of homosexuality and mental health* (pp. 897-916). Washington, DC: American Psychiatric Press.

Civil Rights Act, 42 U.S.C. § 2000e, P.L. 88-352 (1964).

Civil Rights Act, 42 U.S.C. § 1981, P.L. 102-166 (1991).

Dana, R. H. (1996). Culturally competent assessment practice in the United States. *Journal of Personality Assessment, 66*, 472-487.

Faunce, P. S. (1990). Women in poverty: Ethical dimensions in therapy. In H. Lerman, & N. Porter (Eds.), *Feminist ethics in psychotherapy* (pp. 185-194). New York: Springer.

LaFromboise T. D., Foster, S., & James, A. (1996). Ethics in multicultural counseling. In P. B. Pedersen, J. G. Draguns, W. J. Lonner, & J. E. Trimble (Eds.), *Counseling across cultures* (4th ed., pp. 47-72). Thousand Oaks, CA: Sage Publications.

Locust, C. (1995). The impact of differing belief systems between Native Americans and their rehabilitation service providers. Special Double Issue: Spirituality, disability, and rehabilitation. *Rehabilitation Education, 9*, 205-215.

National Association of Social Workers. (1999). *Code of ethics of the National Association of Social Workers*. Retrieved online September 2, 2003 from http://www.socialworkers.org/pubs/code/code.asp

Sue, D.W. (1996). Ethical issues in multicultural counseling. In B. Herlihy, & G. Corey (Eds.), *ACA ethical standards casebook* (5th ed., pp. 193-204). Alexandria, VA: American Counseling Association.

The Concerned Mental Health Practitioner: Welfare of Others

Charles Clark

SUMMARY. A discussion is provided regarding a fundamental principle of psychology, a concern for other's welfare, as set out in the American Psychological Association's (2002) *Ethical Principles of Psychologists and Code of Conduct.* Although the principle concern for others' welfare is essentially aspirational in nature, this is an ethical principle that is at the core of the mental health professions' stated values, and that must be positively put into operation in a variety of professional contexts. Unlike so much else in professional ethics codes that involves injunctions of what not to do, or which attempts to limit the self-serving tendencies of professionals, this general principle is essentially positive, pointing to the need to approach others and to consider their welfare first. *[Article copies available for a fee from The Haworth Document Delivery Service: 1-800-HAWORTH. E-mail address: <docdelivery@haworthpress.com> Website: <http://www.HaworthPress.com> © 2005 by The Haworth Press, Inc. All rights reserved.]*

KEYWORDS. Welfare of the consumer, patient rights, dignity, social responsibility, avoiding harm, Hippocratic Oath

---

Address correspondence to: Charles Clark, PhD, 117 North First Street, Suite 103, Ann Arbor, MI 48104-4101.

[Haworth co-indexing entry note]: "The Concerned Mental Health Practitioner: Welfare of Others." Clark, Charles. Co-published simultaneously in *Journal of Aggression, Maltreatment & Trauma* (The Haworth Maltreatment & Trauma Press, an imprint of The Haworth Press, Inc.) Vol. 11, No. 1/2, 2005, pp. 79-87; and: *Ethical and Legal Issues for Mental Health Professionals: A Comprehensive Handbook of Principles and Standards* (ed: Steven F. Bucky, Joanne E. Callan, and George Stricker) The Haworth Maltreatment & Trauma Press, an imprint of The Haworth Press, Inc., 2005, pp. 79-87. Single or multiple copies of this article are available for a fee from The Haworth Document Delivery Service [1-800-HAWORTH, 9:00 a.m. - 5:00 p.m. (EST). E-mail address: docdelivery@haworthpress.com].

Digital Object Identifier: 10.1300/J146v11n01_07

It is a fundamental principle of psychology, as set out in the 2002 version of the American Psychological Association's (APA) *Ethical Principles of Psychologists and Code of Conduct*, that:

> Psychologists strive to benefit those with whom they work and take care to do no harm. In their professional actions, psychologists seek to safeguard the welfare and rights of those with whom they interact professionally and other affected persons, and the welfare of animal subjects of research. When conflicts occur among psychologists' obligations or concerns, they attempt to resolve these conflicts in a responsible fashion that avoids or minimizes harm. Because psychologists' scientific and professional judgments and actions may affect the lives of others, they are alert to and guard against personal, financial, social, organizational, or political factors that might lead to misuse of their influence. Psychologists strive to be aware of the possible effect of their own physical and mental health on their ability to help those with whom they work. (APA, 2002, General Principle A)

The 1992 version of the APA's *Ethical Principles of Psychologists and Code of Conduct* states that:

> Psychologists seek to contribute to the welfare of those with whom they interact professionally. In their professional actions, psychologists weigh the welfare and rights of their patients or clients, students, supervisees, human research participants, and other affected persons, and the welfare of animal subjects of research. When conflicts occur among psychologists' obligations or concerns, they attempt to resolve these conflicts and to perform their roles in a responsible fashion that avoids or minimizes harm. Psychologists are sensitive to real and ascribed differences in power between themselves and others, and they do not exploit or mislead other people during or after professional relationships. (APA, 1992, General Principle E)

These statements of principle articulate an essential difference between psychology as one of the behavioral sciences and one of the human service professions, and other scientific and professional pursuits that are not necessarily predicated on a contribution to the welfare of others. This value is not one confined to the APA Ethics Code. As Keith-Spiegel and Koocher (1985) have indicated, the promotion of the welfare of consumers served by a profession is a theme repeated in most statements of professional ethics. The *Code of Ethics of the National Association of Social Workers,* for instance, states in its Preamble that a "historic and defining feature of social work is the profession's focus on individual well-being in a social context and the well-being of society" (National Association of Social Workers [NASW], 1999). The first principle of the American Association for Marriage and Family Therapy's (AAMFT) *Code of Ethics* similarly provides that "Marriage and family therapists advance the welfare of family and individuals . . ." (AAMFT, 1998, Principle 1).

At first blush, a concern for others' welfare appears to be an obvious and self-evident ethical principle for mental health practitioners and one that requires little explication, no matter how difficult it may be to put into action. A closer look reveals that its meaning is elusive and its application inevitably ambiguous. Its referents may be clear enough: the others about whose welfare clinicians must be concerned would include any person affected by clinical assessment or intervention, teaching, supervision, and research, and even the animal subjects of research. The nature of their welfare that is to be protected is harder to specify, however, as is the nature or expression of concern that psychologists, marriage and family therapists, social workers, or other clinicians must have. As Kendler (1993) pointed out with reference to one profession, "American psychology from its earliest days has been concerned with promoting human welfare. But the meaning of the term has remained as vague as it is today . . ." (p. 1050). Nor is this ambiguity confined to this one ethical issue. Indeed, Kendler's analysis of ethical conflicts within psychology indicates that there are no psychological rules by which valid ethical principles in general can be identified, and thus no psychologically valid way of directing or determining the correct resolution of ethical conflicts.

One question that arises regarding the notion of concern for the welfare of others is how this concern is delimited and differentiated from other concerns. Is it co-extensive, for instance, with social responsibility, social justice, or respect for the rights, dignity, and worth of the person? Those issues, never clearly differentiated from concern for the welfare of others, are raised in the ethics documents of mental health professions. The case can be made that not only are these ethical issues separate from this concern, but that they are secondary to it. As Clark (1993) argued, social responsibility may be seen to have two unequal components, one a primary concern about humans as individuals, and the other a derivative concern for social change and betterment; social responsibility may be understood ultimately as responsibility owed to individual human beings.

This general principle of concern for others' welfare, universal to the mental health professions however it is articulated, indicates that while practitioners may engage in their discipline as a livelihood or as a source of personal satisfaction and gratification, professional work that is separated from others' welfare is incomplete. Mental health practice has an essential moral component. In its attention to others, behavioral science is in this sense at least a social science. Its contacts and involvement with others, such as research subjects, students, and therapy clients, means that to divorce mental health practice from any obligation to contribute to others' welfare is to risk harming others, or at least to act in disregard of their welfare.

Human contact is frequent or inevitable in a number of other sciences or professions as well, but the individuals with whom psychologists, social workers, marriage and family therapists, counselors, and other clinicians interact are, by the intimate nature of their transactions, in a uniquely vulnerable position. Without the requirement of a positive intent from mental health professionals to help these individuals in some way, they may well be harmed. Consider the case of a psychologist who operates a call-in radio program with the express purpose of providing drive-time entertainment. She calculates that while she is unlikely to do any individual much good, given the fleeting nature of the contact she has with them, neither is she likely to do anyone any harm. In another case, a therapist who works in an affluent community has long since realized that there are few constraints operating to limit the frequency of his sessions with clients or the length of their treatment. With no explicit theoretical rationale, he develops a policy of seeing all clients three times a week, with the expectation that they will see him for at least two years.

In both of these situations, in the absence of any obvious harm to the individuals the professionals have rationalized that no harm is done. But the decisions to practice a profession in these ways were not explicitly oriented to a positive attention to the welfare of the individuals affected by their work. In these hypothetical situations, the practice instead seems to be primarily, and essentially, an economic enterprise conducted for the professional's personal benefit. In this amoral climate, in which an analysis of the ways a service might be detrimental to individuals was not performed, the potential damage would not have been anticipated, and would in fact have been disregarded. The welfare of the individuals affected by these professionals has not been safeguarded, and has actually been put at risk.

It is often the case that there are multiple and even competing demands on clinicians regarding the welfare of others; therefore, successful attention to the welfare issue generally implies a deliberate consideration of who is likely to be affected by psychological activities and services, and in what manner. Attention needs to be turned not only to the many possible individuals or groups that could be affected, but also to the interaction effects. For example, helping one individual to achieve goals may affect the interests of someone else, perhaps adversely, from that person's point of view. This dynamic of undesirable if not unanticipated consequences is seen in many situations involving treatment, as in the vignettes presented in Table 1.

It is a basic prescription of the Hippocratic Oath, a progenitor of other professional codes of ethics, to do no harm: ". . . I will prescribe regimen for the good of my patients according to my ability and my judgment and never do harm to anyone . . ." (Glanze, Anderson, & Anderson, 1992, p. 379). The 1992 APA ethics code appreciates that this avoidance of harm is not simple to achieve. In part this is due to the fact that harm is relative, or a matter of whose ox is gored. That is, a good result for one individual in treatment or in research may have what another person might recognize as an entirely negative effect. Even in respect to the person who enjoys a good consequence, there are often enough un-

TABLE 1. Vignettes Demonstrating Undesirable Consequences of Treatment

---

Vignette 1

A psychologist who has been assessing and treating a client presenting complaints of chronic pain following a seemingly minor accident determines that a substantial amount of the client's subjective complaint is a function of secondary gain. The psychologist receives a subpoena from the client's attorney, who is pressing a personal injury claim on the client's behalf. The psychologist knows that a full disclosure of her findings is unlikely to be seen, at least by the client, as beneficial.

Vignette 2

A therapist suspects that the basis for a client's lifelong misery and poor adjustment is childhood sexual abuse. Although the client initially reports no memories of sexual abuse, the clinician undertakes the recovery of the dissociated material he feels underlies the client's problems. Using hypnosis and other techniques, the client indeed comes to report memories of being sexually abused by her father and mother at a young age. The client wishes to confront her aged parents, and then to file a lawsuit against them to obtain money that will cover the expenses of her ongoing therapy.

pleasant concomitants. An appreciation of the ramifying and various effects of change in the social systems in which individuals live will lead to the conclusion that in many cases no good can be done without some possible adverse effect on the recipient of the benefit, or on others affected by the recipient or more generally by the actions of the mental health professional. The ethical dilemma in situations such as the vignettes in Table 1 does not stem from the failure to avoid all harm, which may be inevitable. The problem, if there is one, arises instead in respect to a failure to weigh, in the term of the general principle of concern for the welfare of others, the possible effects of intervention or other action on a variety of individuals who are likely to be affected.

If neither the risks nor the benefits of empirical findings or clinical assessment can be predicted in advance, it is nonetheless important that the professional report results accurately. Responsible practice requires objectivity and the honest reporting of findings, observations, and conclusions, even if one or another individual or group interested in the issue and affected by the clinician would not view those results as contributing to their benefit, and might even view them as harmful. Mental health practitioners cannot be entirely effects-oriented, and their integrity cannot be compromised by a desire to maximize good outcomes, at least to someone, or to minimize pain to everyone. In some instances, it simply may not be possible to avoid or even anticipate harm altogether, either harm as any reasonable person would view it, or harm as seen through the eyes of one of the persons affected. Moreover, to fail to take action may itself do harm to the welfare of others (e.g., failure to report empirical findings, or failure to advise a court of law regarding the psychological status of an individual plaintiff or defendant who has been the subject of assessment or treatment).

Of course, the welfare of others is not possible to identify with certainty in every instance, whether or not those affected themselves can state where their interests lie. It might be obvious enough that it would be to a child's benefit, for instance, to grow up in a loving and supportive family. But when the family structure has broken down, it may not be as clear that the child would benefit from the continued joint custody of the now-divorced parents, as opposed to the sole custody of only one of the parents. It might be obvious enough that it is to the benefit of an individual who is severely depressed to prevent a suicide and to preserve life. But, as in some debilitating or terminal illnesses, when life itself has become dependent on respirators and feeding tubes, when nearly all physical control and independent function has been lost, and when the individual requests aid in dying, it is not clear that the preservation of life does benefit the individual. In such cases, while society in the form of the law or religious and other institutions may hold that there is benefit to continued life and to society itself in upholding the sanctity of life by never acquiescing to a patient's request for assisted suicide, it may not be apparent to many thoughtful and ethically sensitive persons whose interests must be served to protect the welfare of others.

Inherently, therefore, an attempt to support the welfare of others involves conflict between competing obligations and concerns. While attention to others' welfare is made difficult by problems of identifying those affected by psychologists' actions, in weighing competing or conflicting demands and in identifying essential benefits and detriments accruing to particular individuals, it is the professional's position vis-a-vis the individuals he or she affects that most threatens harm to them.

The problems of potential exploitation may originate in a perfectly appropriate attitude of professional caring, as in the following example, but may come about because of a neglect of the effects of the relationship itself on both parties. A psychologist had been treating a young woman from a chaotic family background who rapidly developed an obsessive attachment to the therapist. As weeks went by, the woman sent cards, letters, and small gifts, and made increasingly frequent telephone calls to the therapist. She permitted the psychologist to read her diary, which included romantic and rescue fantasies centering on the psychologist. In sessions, the client sat close to the psychologist, and repeatedly attempted to make physical contact. The psychologist soon acquiesced to her attempts, and a pattern of rapidly escalating physical and sexual contact began.

The positions psychologists, social workers, counselors, and other therapists occupy in relation to research subjects, students, supervisees, clients, or others can best be conceptualized for the purpose of this discussion as ones involving differential power. The power of the professional may be real, as when a psychologist as teacher assigns grades or a social worker as supervisor controls the conditions of employment and promotion. The clinician's power may only be apparent, however, when ascribed to that professional by someone affected by the clinician. In many instances the attribution of power, either real or imagined, is an intrinsic part of psychological and mental health activities. Arguably, the ascription of power to a professional as therapist, that is the power to understand the client, the power to discern the causes and dynamics of a client's distress, and the power to employ effective techniques to produce relief or improvement, is at the heart of effective therapeutic intervention. Power differences between clinicians and those with whom they interact are neither good nor bad in and of themselves; to some extent they are inevitable.

Some differences in power, however, are unnecessarily enhanced or are even created by professionals who, consciously or not, seek primary benefit for themselves, not for those with whom they interact. Because of the great potential for harm that arises in relation to differences in power, mental health clinicians must acknowledge an obligation to limit and control, to the extent feasible and compatible with professional effectiveness, both real and apparent power differentials. To fail to do so is to mislead the person, and to open the door to an exploitation of the power difference that exists.

CONCLUSION

A concern for others' welfare cannot be accomplished passively, or by simply avoiding disrespect of individual differences and rights. Although the principle concern for others' welfare is essentially aspirational, this is an ethical principle that is at the core of the mental health professions' stated values, and that must be positively put into operation in a variety of professional contexts. Over and above operational derivatives of this principle, however, such as the need to refrain from all sexual contact with clients, the general principle must inform, in a proactive and positive manner, psychologists' professional activity in all arenas. Unlike so much else in professional ethics codes that involves injunctions of what not to do, or which attempts to limit the self-serving tendencies of professionals, this general principle is essentially positive, pointing to the need to approach others and to consider their welfare first.

REFERENCES

American Association for Marriage and Family Therapy. (1998). *AAMFT code of ethics*. Washington, DC: Author.

American Psychological Association. (1992). *Ethical principles of psychologists and code of conduct*. Washington, DC: Author.

American Psychological Association. (2002). *Ethical principles of psychologists and code of conduct*. Washington, DC: Author.

Clark, C. R. (1993). Social responsibility ethic: Doing right, doing good, doing well. *Ethics & Behavior, 3,* 303-327.

Glanze, W. D., Anderson, K. N., & Anderson, L. E. (1992). *The Mosby medical encyclopedia* (Rev. ed.). New York: Plume.

Keith-Spiegel, P., & Koocher, G. P. (1985). *Ethics in psychology: Professional standards and cases.* New York: Random House.

Kendler, H. H. (1993). Psychology and the ethics of social policy. *American Psychologists, 48,* 1046-1053.

National Association of Social Workers. (1999). *Code of Ethics of the National Association of Social Workers.* Washington, DC: Author.

Social Responsibility
and the Mental Health Professions

Erica H. Wise

SUMMARY. While mental health professionals tend to primarily focus on their professional responsibilities toward the specific members of the public whom they serve, many are also concerned about positively impacting the broader society or culture in which they live and work. This notion of social responsibility is addressed in the ethics codes of both psychologists and social workers. This article reviews how this notion is addressed for these two mental health professions and also examines the changes that have occurred for psychologists between the 1992 and 2002 ethics codes. Finally, some general issues regarding the role of mental health professionals in changing society are considered. *[Article copies available for a fee from The Haworth Document Delivery Service: 1-800-HAWORTH. E-mail address: <docdelivery@haworthpress.com> Website: <http://www.HaworthPress.com> © 2005 by The Haworth Press, Inc. All rights reserved.]*

KEYWORDS. Ethics, social responsibility, mental health, psychology, social work

---

Address correspondence to Erica H. Wise, PhD, Department of Psychology, CB# 3270, University of North Carolina at Chapel Hill, Chapel Hill, NC 27599-3270.

[Haworth co-indexing entry note]: "Social Responsibility and the Mental Health Professions." Wise, Erica H. Co-published simultaneously in *Journal of Aggression, Maltreatment & Trauma* (The Haworth Maltreatment & Trauma Press, an imprint of The Haworth Press, Inc.) Vol. 11, No. 1/2, 2005, pp. 89-99; and: *Ethical and Legal Issues for Mental Health Professionals: A Comprehensive Handbook of Principles and Standards* (ed: Steven F. Bucky, Joanne E. Callan, and George Stricker) The Haworth Maltreatment & Trauma Press, an imprint of The Haworth Press, Inc., 2005, pp. 89-99. Single or multiple copies of this article are available for a fee from The Haworth Document Delivery Service [1-800-HAWORTH, 9:00 a.m. - 5:00 p.m. (EST). E-mail address: docdelivery@haworthpress.com].

Digital Object Identifier: 10.1300/J146v11n01_08

This article will focus on how psychologists and social workers address the issue of their responsibility to positively impact the broader society or culture in which they live and work. More specifically, it will focus on how the notion of social responsibility is differentially addressed in the 1992 and 2002 American Psychological Association (APA) ethics codes for psychologists and the Code of Ethics of the National Association of Social Workers (1996). Generally, the issue of social responsibility is framed as a responsibility to address the underlying causes of human suffering through social action and by directly having an impact on social policy. Mental health professionals tend to focus on their ethical and legal duties towards the members of the public whom they serve. Even when mental health services are provided to a group or an organization, the emphasis remains on responsibility towards clearly defined individuals within that group or organization. While the ethics codes for social workers and psychologists share a primary focus on ethical duties towards clients, they do also each address the issue of broadly defined social responsibility. The ethics codes of these mental health professions both reflect and shape the attitudes of practitioners towards this important issue. In addition to reviewing how these issues are considered in the ethics codes of these two groups of mental health professionals, differences for psychologists between the APA's 1992 and 2002 ethics codes will also be considered.

SOCIAL WORKERS AND SOCIAL RESPONSIBILITY

The preamble of the Code of Ethics of the National Association of Social Workers (1999 revision) states, "Fundamental to social work is attention to the environmental forces that create, contribute to, and address problems in living" (p. 1) and later that "Social workers also seek to promote the responsiveness of organizations, communities, and other social institutions to individuals' needs and social problems" (p. 1). In outlining broad ethical principles or core values, the code of ethics for social workers states a core value of "Social Justice." This ethical principle and core value is quoted below in its entirety:

> Social workers challenge social injustice. Social workers pursue
> social change, particularly with and on behalf of vulnerable and
> oppressed individuals and groups of people. Social workers' so-
> cial change efforts are focused primarily on issues of poverty, un-

employment, discrimination, and other forms of social injustice. These activities seek to promote sensitivity to and knowledge about oppression and cultural and ethnic diversity. Social workers strive to ensure access to needed information, services, and resources; equality of opportunity; and meaningful participation in decision making for all people. (p. 4)

Under the Ethical Standards section of the social work ethics code, Standard (6) is devoted to social responsibility. It is entitled "Social Workers' Ethical Responsibilities to the Broader Society" and consists of four sections. This standard is broadly aspirational and sets a high standard for social workers to directly impact the world around them in order to improve the lives of individuals. Section 6.01 Social Welfare states that:

Social workers should promote the general welfare of society, from local to global levels, and the development of people, their communities, and their environments. Social workers should advocate for living conditions conducive to the fulfillment of basic human needs and should promote social, economic, political, and cultural values and institutions that are compatible with the realization of social justice.

Section 6.02 Public Participation specifically enjoins social workers to involve others in shaping public policy and states, "Social workers should facilitate informed participation by the public in shaping social policies and institutions." Section 6.03 Public Emergencies represents a shift in emphasis and states, "Social workers should provide appropriate professional services in public emergencies to the greatest extent possible." Section 6.04 Social and Political Action is remarkably sweeping in its requirement that social workers act to change society for the better. This important and far-reaching section is quoted below in its entirety:

6.04 (a) Social workers should engage in social and political action that seeks to ensure that all people have equal access to the resources, employment, services, and opportunities they require to meet their basic human needs and to develop fully. Social workers should be aware of the impact of the political arena on practice and should advocate for changes in policy and legislation to improve social conditions in order to meet basic human needs and promote social justice.

6.04 (b) Social workers should act to expand choice and opportunity for all people, with special regard for vulnerable, disadvantaged, oppressed, and exploited people and groups.

6.04 (c) Social workers should promote conditions that encourage respect for cultural and social diversity within the United States and globally. Social workers should promote policies and practices that demonstrate respect for difference, support the expansion of cultural knowledge and resources, advocate for programs and institutions that demonstrate cultural competence, and promote policies that safeguard the rights of and confirm equity and social justice for all people.

6.04 (d) Social workers should act to prevent and eliminate domination of, exploitation of, and discrimination against any person, group, or class on the basis of race ethnicity, national origin, color, sex, sexual orientation, age, marital status, political belief, religion, or mental or physical disability.

It is readily apparent that the social work code of ethics sets an extremely high standard for social workers to have a positive impact on the world around them. There are some clear and interesting contrasts with how this issue is dealt with in the ethics code for psychologists.

PSYCHOLOGISTS AND SOCIAL RESPONSIBILITY

As with the social work code of ethics, most of the *Ethical Principles of Psychologists and Code of Conduct* (APA, 1992, 2002) are primarily focused on the specific and general responsibilities psychologists have towards those with whom they work. This section will include an examination of how these codes differentially address the issue of social responsibility.

1992 code. In the 1992 ethics code, the seven sentences in Principle F (Social Responsibility) represent a dramatic shift from the primary focus described above. This aspirational principle speaks to the notion of social action and social relevance. It is a charge to all psychologists to strive toward changing the world in a positive manner. This charge is broadly directed to both psychological scientists and practitioners. Beyond the expectation that psychologists comply with the law, Principle F introduces the controversial notion that psychologists should take a pro-active stance in the development and promulgation of more humane law and social policy. Finally, psychologists are asked to participate in pro bono activities. This overview of the 1992 ethics code for psychologists will continue with an examination of each of the general concepts embedded in this principle in terms of its meaning and implications. The first three sentences address the issue of making our knowledge and services generally available to the public in the interest of enhancing welfare and mitigating the causes of human suffering:

> Psychologists are aware of their professional and scientific responsibilities to the community and the society in which they work and live. They apply and make public their knowledge of psychology in order to contribute to human welfare. Psychologists are concerned about and work to mitigate the causes of human suffering. (APA, 1992, Principle F)

The first sentence is stated as a moral imperative that is fleshed out in the subsequent sentences. The second sentence moves from the notion of awareness of social responsibility to call for the application and dissemination of knowledge to enhance human welfare. The third sentence broadens the concept of social responsibility to include the prevention of human suffering. The following vignettes provide examples of how psychologists might use their knowledge of research and treatment interventions to improve human welfare:

1. Dr. A. serves on the board of the local Planned Parenthood Association. In that capacity she has helped to develop improved counseling techniques for aiding in the decision-making process of women who have an unwanted or unplanned pregnancy.
2. Dr. B. is an academic psychologist with a specialization in the area of adult development and aging. He attends monthly meetings and serves on the Advisory Board of a local hospital, which offers a day treatment program for the elderly.

The fourth sentence addresses itself to scientists and echoes the issues outlined above by stating: "When undertaking research, they strive to advance human welfare and the science of psychology." The following vignette provides an example of socially relevant research:

3. Dr. C. does research examining the impact of homelessness on children's academic performance and peer relationships.

The fifth sentence, "Psychologists try to avoid misuse of their work," seems to stand out from the rest of the principle; it does serve to focus the attention of the psychologist on the importance of striving to avoid negative consequences arising from our professional and scientific activities. The following vignette illustrates a psychologist taking affirmative action to avoid misuse of his research findings:

4. Dr. D. communicates his concerns about possible misuse of research data to a corporation that he learns has been using his data to exclude older workers from a training program. His research has demonstrated age-related decrements in learning novel material under highly specific laboratory conditions.

The sixth sentence is the most radical and controversial of Principle F: "Psychologists comply with the law and encourage the development of law and social policy that serve the interests of their patients and clients and the public." This aspect of Principle F enjoins psychologists to go beyond compliance with current laws in order to take an active role in public policy development. The following vignettes provide examples of how psychologists might become involved in social advocacy and public policy development:

5. Dr. E. consults, at no charge, with the Mental Health Commission of her state on issues related to services for individuals suffering from chronic and persistent mental illness. This is her area of expertise.
6. Dr. F. is a member of a multidisciplinary study group whose task is to coordinate state services for at-risk children and families. This group makes recommendations to the state legislature.

Finally, in the seventh sentence, the issue of pro bono work is addressed: "They are encouraged to contribute a portion of their professional time for little or no personal advantage." The following vignettes provide examples of pro bono activities:

7. Dr. G. routinely participates in volunteer training at a local rape crisis center.
8. Dr. H. routinely donates two to three hours per week of his private practice time to see clients for a reduced fee.
9. Dr. I. offers Parent Effectiveness classes on the first Tuesday of each month at her daughter's elementary school. The workshops are free of charge and are sponsored by the PTA.

Taken as a whole, Principle F is a broad and complex aspirational principle.

2002 code. In the 2002 ethics code, the General Principles section has been significantly revised with each principle having been reformulated and retitled. The most striking change regarding the topic under consideration is that there is no longer a principle entitled "social responsibility." While the new General Principle B, "Fidelity and Responsibility," does incorporate several of the issues addressed in the 1992 General Principle F, much of the sweeping and provocative language has been removed. There are now only two sentences in the new General Principle B that relate even tangentially to social responsibility as we have defined it. The second sentence informs psychologists that, "They are aware of their professional and scientific responsibilities to society and to the specific communities in which they work," and the final sentence is the reminder that, "Psychologists strive to contribute a portion of their professional time for little or no compensation or personal advantage." Conspicuously absent in the 2002 code is the sweeping call for psychologists to contribute to human welfare and to mitigate the causes of human suffering through their research and by impacting law and social policy.

Several other sections of the 1992 and 2002 *Ethical Principles of Psychologists and Code of Conduct* also address the issue of social responsibility. The Preamble to the 1992 code states that psychologists' " . . . goal is to broaden knowledge of behavior and, where appropriate, to apply it pragmatically to improve the condition of both the individual and society." The first sentence of the Preamble to the 2002 Code states, "Psychologists are committed to increasing scientific and professional knowledge of behavior and people's understanding of themselves and others and to the use of such knowledge to improve the condition of individuals, organizations, and society." The third sentence is, "They strive to help the public in developing informed judgments and choices concerning human behavior." In the 1992 code, Ethical Standards 1.15 and 1.16 refer respectively to the need to take steps to ensure that our influence and our work are not misused. Ethical Standard 3.04 informs psychologists that statements made in media presentations need to be " . . . based on appropriate psychological literature and practice." Interestingly, although the sections on research responsibilities (6.07 and 6.10) address responsibilities towards research participants, they do not echo the aspirational call found in Principle F to conduct research relevant to the advancement of human welfare. This silence on the need for social relevance in research in the enforceable portion of the code may reflect a reluctance to interfere with the scientist's academic freedom and freedom of inquiry. On a more pragmatic level it may also reflect the difficulty in developing a universally agreed upon distinction between pure versus applied research. In the 2002 ethics code, Ethical Standard 5.04 is similar to the 1992 Ethical Standard in that it informs psychologists, "When psychologists provide public advice or comment via print, internet, or other electronic transmission, they take precautions to ensure that statements (1) are based on their professional knowledge, training or experience in accord with appropriate psychological literature and practice . . ."

In a survey of members of the APA (Good, Simon, & Coursey, 1981), 96% of those who responded indicated that they participated in at least one public interest activity. In particular, 67% reported engaging in pro bono activities, 35% reported conducting research or writing that was directed towards the understanding or solution of social problems, and 20% reported that they actively engaged in community or social action. As the authors pointed out, there was an interesting trend that emerged in that psychologists were most likely to offer pro bono services and least likely to engage in direct social action. Writing or conducting research on social issues fell in between. This may reflect the ambivalent attitude that many psychologists hold toward the undertaking of direct social action. It would be of interest to replicate this survey of psychologists to determine our current level of involvement in the range of public interest activities. Based on the earlier discussion of the social work code of ethics, it would be reasonable to hypothesize that social workers participate more actively than do psychologists in direct political or social action.

As indicated above, several important concepts are embedded in the 1992 Principle F. Most psychologists would agree that the knowledge gained from psychological research can have direct relevance to many important social issues and concerns. For example, in the past decade, articles have reviewed research related to abortion (Adler, David, Major, Roth, Russo, & Wyatt, 1992), cultural and historical perspectives on grief (Stroeb, Gergen, Gergen, & Stroebe, 1992), and homelessness (Jones, Levine, & Rosenberg, 1991), to name just a few. More recently, a social paradigm was presented that outlined how psychologists might directly impact laws and social policy related to persons with disabilities (Gill, Kewman, & Brannon, 2003). These authors also point out that the APA has also taken a strong stand on encouraging cultural competence and opposing discrimination. The issues become more complex when controversial positions are taken. For example, the pro-choice versus right to life debate is a particularly controversial moral/religious topic. Rather than taking a definitive moral position, the APA has taken a public health perspective and has provided a review of the psychological factors associated with abortion. In contrast, the Council of Representatives of the APA takes the position that homelessness is harmful and contributes to mental illness (APA Council of Representatives, 1991). A cursory review of the Letters section of the *APA Monitor* attests to the controversial nature of the social issues on which the APA as an organization and psychologists in particular have taken a stance. Most psychologists would agree that while moral convictions are a personal matter, relevant psychological research can meaningfully inform public health debate.

Interest in the notion of preventing mental health problems dates back at least three decades (e.g., Caplan, 1964). More recently, psychologists have proposed highly sophisticated models for studying and implementing prevention-oriented public health initiatives in the mental health field (Coie et al., 1993). Although a comprehensive review of this area is outside the scope of this article, it is important to note that psychologists may differ on how they would propose to effectuate social change. Albee (1982) has suggested that psychologists need to advocate actively for social change at a political level. His stance on this issue is strikingly similar to the position endorsed by the social workers in their code of ethics. Humphreys and Rappaport (1993) argue persuasively that, for example, current research on the issue of substance abuse may be inadvertently maintaining a political status quo. They go on to assert that psychologists need to be involved in actively challenging harmful social and political policies. In contrast, Fox (1993) has argued that promoting psychological issues through the legal system may actually serve to maintain existing social inequities. These authors call our attention to the fact that interventions in social policy and law may be more complex than they appear. Although we as psychologists may agree with the concept of social activism, these activities must be approached thoughtfully and in an informed manner.

In summary, the ethics codes for social workers and psychologists are similar in that both tend to primarily focus on ethical responsibilities towards clearly identifiable individuals or groups. While they do both address the issue of the responsibility that mental health professionals have to change the broader culture, they do this in very different ways.

The social workers ethics code incorporates remarkably sweeping language in enjoining social workers to effectuate positive social change. This concept is included in the preamble and the core value statements and in the ethical standards portions of their code. In contrast, for psychologists, even in the 1992 APA ethics code, there is a clear distinction between the sweeping social responsibilities outlined in the aspirational portion of the code and the more limited references to this issue in the enforceable portions of the code. This difference is more marked when comparing the social work ethics code with the 2002 ethics code for psychologists in that the aspirational portion of the new psychology code no longer enjoins psychologists to take action to directly influence public policy and law. It is likely that these contrasting approaches to the issue of social responsibility reflect some deeply held assumptions as well as essential historical and philosophical differences between these two mental health professions.

REFERENCES

Adler, N. E., David, H. P., Major, B. N., Roth, S. H., Russo, N. F., & Wyatt, G. E. (1992). Psychological factors in abortion: A review. *American Psychologist, 47,* 1194-1204.

Albee, G. W. (1982). Preventing psychopathology and promoting human potential. *American Psychologist, 37,* 1043-1050.

American Association of Marriage and Family Therapy. (1998). *AAMFT code of ethics.* Washington, DC: Author.

American Psychological Association. (1992). Ethical principles of psychologists and code of conduct. *American Psychologist, 47,* 1597-1611.

American Psychological Association. (2002). Ethical principles of psychologists and code of conduct. *American Psychologist, 57*(12), 1060-1073.

American Psychological Association Council of Representatives. (1991). Resolution on homelessness. *American Psychologist, 46,* 1108.

Caplan, G. (1964). *Principles of preventive psychiatry.* New York: Basic Books.

Coie, J. D., Watt, N. F., West, S. G., Hawkins, J. D., Asamow, J. R., Markman, H. J. et al. (1993). The science of prevention: A conceptual framework and some directions for a national research program. *American Psychologist, 48,* 1013-1022.

Fox, D. A. (1993). Psychological jurisprudence and radical social change. *American Psychologist, 48,* 234-241.

Gill, C. J., Kewman, D. G., & Brannon, R. W. (2003). Transforming psychological practice and society: Policies that reflect the new paradigm. *American Psychologist, 58,* 305-312.

Good, P., Simon, G. C., & Coursey, R. D. (1981). Public interest activities of APA members. *American Psychologist, 36,* 963-971.

Humphreys, K., & Rappaport, J. (1993). From the community mental health movement to the war on drugs: A study in the definition of social problems. *American Psychologist, 48,* 892-901.

Jones, J. M., Levine, I. S., & Rosenberg, A. A. (1991). Homelessness research, services and social policy. *American Psychologist, 46,* 1109-1111.

National Association of Social Workers. (1996). *Code of ethics of the National Association of Social Workers.* Washington, DC: Author.

Stroebe, M., Gergen, M. M., Gergen, K. J., & Stroebe, W. (1992). Broken hearts or broken bonds: Love and death in historical perspective. *American Psychologist, 47,* 1205-1212.

CONFIDENTIALITY PRIVILEGE, CONSENT, AND PROTECTION

Informed Consent

Muriel Golub

SUMMARY. This article focuses on informed consent and the components to be reviewed with clients in the first session or as early as possible thereafter. Recent changes that give patients greater autonomy in the treatment process are also presented. The process of obtaining informed consent or informed refusal places a new responsibility on the practitioner. Informed consent as it pertains to clinical practice, supervision and training, and psychological research is also discussed. *[Article copies available for a fee from The Haworth Document Delivery Service: 1-800-HAWORTH. E-mail address: <docdelivery@haworthpress.com> Website: <http://www.HaworthPress.com> © 2005 by The Haworth Press, Inc. All rights reserved.]*

Address correspondence to: Muriel Golub, PhD, 3610 South Bristol Street, #105, Santa Ana, CA 92704.

[Haworth co-indexing entry note]: "Informed Consent." Golub, Muriel. Co-published simultaneously in *Journal of Aggression, Maltreatment & Trauma* (The Haworth Maltreatment & Trauma Press, an imprint of The Haworth Press, Inc.) Vol. 11, No. 1/2, 2005, pp. 101-115; and: *Ethical and Legal Issues for Mental Health Professionals: A Comprehensive Handbook of Principles and Standards* (ed: Steven F. Bucky, Joanne E. Callan, and George Stricker) The Haworth Maltreatment & Trauma Press, an imprint of The Haworth Press, Inc., 2005, pp. 101-115. Single or multiple copies of this article are available for a fee from The Haworth Document Delivery Service [1-800-HAWORTH, 9:00 a.m. - 5:00 p.m. (EST). E-mail address: docdelivery@haworthpress.com].

Digital Object Identifier: 10.1300/J146v11n01_09

KEYWORDS. Informed consent, self determination, autonomy, competence, values, patient exploitation, voluntariness

The doctrine of informed consent requires a health practitioner (physical and/or mental) to make a reasonable disclosure to his patient regarding the goals, procedures, risks, and often costs of a proposed course of treatment. The American Psychological Association's (2002) code of ethics and standards of behavior directs the psychologist to protect the welfare of the consumer, accept responsibility for the consequences of his own actions, and practice within the boundaries of his competence and training. Informed consent involves educating a patient who is mentally competent and who has a good knowledge of what will be likely to occur in treatment about the requirements, limitations, possible "side effects," and desired and/or likely outcomes of the treatment. This patient must then enter into treatment with the particular provider in a freely voluntary manner, without coercion, duress, or deceit, and with the assurance that any decisions made will not alter the patient's access to quality clinical care. In short, there are four components necessary to informed consent: patient competency; disclosure of relevant information; patient understanding of that material; and voluntariness of the consent without undue influence by the practitioner or others.

The concept and the doctrine of the right of the patient to provide informed consent has an established history, with a special landmark occurring in 1914. At that time, a New York Judge who later became a Supreme Court Justice, Benjamin Cardozo, wrote that, "Every human being of adult years and social mind has a right to determine what shall be done with his own body; and a surgeon who performs an operation without his patient's consent commits an assault for which he is liable in damages" (*Schloendorf v. Society of New York Hospital*, 1914, p. 93). Judge Cardozo went on to indicate that this was true except in cases of an emergency in which it was necessary for treatment to commence while the patient was unconscious. Informed consent is particularly rooted in the concept that patients have the right to determine whether or not to undertake the course of treatment, rather than have this dictated to them or imposed upon them by the physician or by any other members of the patient's environment. In earlier centuries, health professionals had traditionally functioned in a paternalistic system, in which it was believed that their superior knowledge made it necessary for patients to defer to the practitioner's judgement; the mere presence of the patient was taken as an assumption of their consent to treatment.

In 1960, this principle of self-determination was reaffirmed, and further guidelines were established. The question of what information was needed in order for a person to make such judgments was addressed by the court in the state of Kansas. It was established that, "The duty . . . to disclose . . . is limited to those disclosures which a reasonable . . . practitioner would make under the same or similar circumstances . . ." (*Natanson v. Kline*, 1960, p. 1106). There have been a number of case decisions in the years that followed, each reaffirming and amplifying this concept of self-determination by the patient, with the requirement that the practitioner be the provider of relevant information, providing the "education" that is needed by the patient in order to adequately weigh the facts and come to an informed decision.

The reliance on community (of physician) standards was rejected in 1972, when it was determined that, "Respect for the patient's right of self-determination on particular therapy demands a standard set by law for physicians rather than one which physicians may or may not impose upon themselves" (*Canterbury v. Spence*, 1972, pp. 783-784). The questions asked or not asked by patients cannot determine the information that is provided for them. There are numerous situations in which the patient does not even have sufficient information to know what questions are germane and would elicit the information that is needed. It is now clearly stated in case law that the practitioner must provide adequate and relevant information whether or not the patient inquires about it. This is considered an active "affirmative duty" on the part of the practitioner.

Lest patients be put in a position in which they become frightened or overwhelmed by the information presented to them regarding the proposed plan and procedures of treatment, the courts have also required that the practitioner has a similar active "affirmative duty" to disclose what the results would be from declining to undergo the proposed treatment procedures or tests (*Truman v. Thomas*, 1980, p. 312). It is also necessary to respect the patient's explicit demand to not be given this information. (It is important for the protection of the practitioner that any of the above choices and actions be documented in writing.)

The most grievous violation of this doctrine of informed consent took place during the Nazi regime, when tens and perhaps even hundreds of thousands of prisoners of the Nazi regime were unwillingly and forcibly used as subjects for Nazi "medical experimentation and research." This resulted in the Nuremberg Code (1949) and the Declaration of Helsinki (World Medical Association, 1964/1975). Although these concentrated primarily on the rights of subjects of research, nevertheless each of these influenced the development of the emphasis on the rights of patients of (physical health and/or mental health) clinical treatment practitioners, particularly in the area of the right to self-determination.

The history of the development of the medical (and later, the psychological as a subset of the medical) profession has had as a primary goal the practitioner's obligation to not only "do no harm" (non-maleficence), but also to work actively in the direction of the benefit of the patient. This has traditionally reinforced the notion that patients do not have the wisdom, or specialized knowledge, to practice self-determination by making informed judgments in the course of the treatment of their health. However, both law and ethics now dictate that the patient has the right to refuse treatment (or various parts of treatment) that the practitioner has determined in his/her own mind to be likely to be beneficial to the patient. The process of obtaining informed consent before treatment or research is a derivative of the right to self-determination.

The process of obtaining informed consent or informed refusal places a new responsibility on the practitioner. First, it is necessary to make sure that patients both know and understand their diagnosis, presented in non-technical terms so that the language of the presentation is clearly understandable at the developmental, verbal, intellectual skills, and reading level of each patient. It is necessary that, if the languages of the practitioner and the patient are different, or in the situation in which the patient is hearing-impaired, attempts be made to enlist the help of a third party as needed, so as to assure that the facts, ideas, and concepts being presented to the patient are in fact understandable by the patient. Both the risks and the benefits of treatment need to be explained to the patient, along with the risks and benefits of not receiving treatment. If there are alternative forms of treatment, these, too, need to be presented to the patient, along with direct and/or indirect types of side effects that the patient can anticipate may occur in each situation.

According to Wenning (1993), it is especially important to go through the process of informed consent prior to initiating long-term psychotherapy. He points out that potential benefits include, symptom relief, personality change, improved interpersonal functioning, heightened self-esteem, an improved ability to take responsibility for problems, and a greater sense of options. However, he also points out that there are a number of possible adverse treatment reactions, such as the possibility of the patient receiving this type of treatment becoming increasingly dependent upon the therapist, in which case there is the possibility that the patient's capacity for autonomous functioning may become undermined and lessened. In other situations, it is possible that there may be a deterioration of personality functioning, a feeling of shame about needing psychotherapy, devaluation by others (both by individuals and social agencies/institutions), as well as unwanted changes or damages in relationships outside the therapy setting. It is, of course, also possible that the treatment will lead to no changes either in the presenting symptoms or in the life circumstances of the patient.

In addition to providing all of the information already discussed, it is incumbent upon the practitioner to ascertain that patients are mentally competent, understanding what is being said, realizing that this information applies to them at the present time, and being able to appreciate the potential consequences of their decisions. According to Stromberg et al. (1988), "The general rule is that a patient is presumed to have decision making capacity unless a specific determination to the contrary is made" (pp. 607-608). It is important to note here that a minor is not considered able to give informed consent; in this situation, as well as in situations in which it is believed that the patient is not competent to give informed consent, then this process must involve the legal guardian(s) of the patient. This does not, however, relieve the practitioner of the responsibility of explaining to the patient, as fully as the patient can understand, what is going to happen, and why.

One way in which guidelines as to the nature and quantity of information that is necessary can be established is to consider what any "reasonable person" would want to know and to take into account in their decision making process. The concept of informed consent was articulated in 1972 by the California Supreme Court, when the following parameters were defined:

> We employ several postulates. The first is that patients are generally persons unlearned in the medical sciences and therefore, except in rare cases, courts may safely assume the knowledge of patient and physician are not in parity. The second is that a person of adult years and in sound mind has the right, in the exercise of control over his own body, to determine whether or not to submit to lawful medical treatment. The third is that the patient's consent to treatment, to be effective, must be an informed consent. And the fourth is that the patient, being unlearned in medical sciences, has an abject dependence upon and trust in his physician for the infor-

mation upon which he relies during the decisional process, thus raising an obligation in the physician that transcends arm-length transactions. From the foregoing axiomatic ingredients emerges a necessity, and a resultant requirement, for divulgence by the physician to his patient of all information relevant to a meaningful decisional process. (*Cobbs v. Grant*, 1972, p. 513)

INFORMED CONSENT IN CLINICAL PRACTICE

One component in the realm of informed consent has to do with the practitioner's making clear to the patient the type and extent of the practitioner's education, experience, and training in a specific area. In psychology, as in its medical counterparts, no psychologist has education, training, and experience in all of the possible psychological situations that may be encountered. This is especially true in such areas as working with culturally diverse populations, or with such subgroups of society as women, children, gays and lesbians, the elderly, the chronically ill, and the physically, educationally, and emotionally disabled or handicapped. Working with such diverse populations when not adequately trained and/or supervised to do so is unethical behavior, and may be additionally regarded by the Psychology Licensing Boards of various states as being illegal.

A further area of consideration in this regard has to do with whether or not the psychologist has indicated to the patient what the psychologist's own value system is about, especially since the psychologist must be certain that he/she is not imposing his/her own values on the patient. This seems self-evident in areas such as sexuality, religion, culture, and emphasis on education and/or the work ethic. It is sometimes less clear, as in such areas as whether or not to encourage a patient to rebel against a repressive environment, or to accept and adapt to it. In addition, there are often subtle and sometimes not-so-subtle repercussions on the social relationships of the patient as a result of the intervention of the practitioner.

One area in which there is fairly often an unexpected side effect of psychological treatment is in the area of marital and/or significant relationships. It is very important that patients in marital or other significant relationships understand that there may be a change in the nature, duration, and sometimes even the permanence of that relationship. This is particularly true in the area of separation or divorce coming as a result of a change brought about by the psychological treatment of one or both parties to the relationship. Patients need to weigh in advance whether this is a risk they wish to take; it is not within the purview of the practitioner to make this decision.

While the data regarding the ethical and legal requirements to provide informed consent are sufficient reason to warrant the process of informed consent, there is another important reason to implement this process in psychotherapy. First, a number of studies have indicated the likelihood that the use of informed consent procedures makes patients less anxious, more likely to follow the treatment plan, be more alert to unexpected negative results of the treatment, and help them to recover more quickly. In addition, it is the job of the psychologist to aid in the establishment of a therapeutic sanctuary, a place of safety and trust within which the work of psychotherapy can be done by the patient. The foundation for this sanctuary is laid in the first few sessions. A comprehensive process of informed consent leads to the development of the therapeutic alliance, aiding in the patient's acquisition of knowledge of the structure and process of psychotherapy as well as an awareness of the possible risks to be encountered.

Each patient comes into the therapy setting with a set of expectations. Since many patients have had limited exposure to psychological treatment, these expectations may have developed from varied sources, including popular television shows or hearsay from neighbors or friends. The patient often holds the expectation that the psychologist has some "magical" power, and can/will do something that will "magically" change the course of the patient's life. Regardless of the source of the development of these expectations, they are generally not grounded in a realistic picture of what psychotherapy is about and what one can expect. However, if the practitioner fails to perform some expected result, there is often a sense of injury on the part of the patient. From the very beginning of therapy, the patient needs help in establishing what is reasonable to expect, from the therapist, from the process, and from patients themselves.

It is the therapist's responsibility to advise the patient about the process itself (what it is like, what to expect, what not to expect), as well as to advise about the specific positive and negative consequences that may come about through participation in psychotherapy. As discussed earlier in this chapter, it is the clinician's responsibility, for example, to advise the patient that: he may get worse before he gets better; there is a possibility of regression; it is likely that he will not get better right away; and he may have to deal with the fears and anxieties that are engendered by the process itself, in addition to the original issues that brought him to the therapeutic situation. Patients need to know that they have the right to make choices regarding the form of treatment, and that the use of that right, with its accompanying increase in patient participation in the treatment process, will lead to increased feelings of joint effort which are an important part of the therapeutic alliance itself.

As indicated earlier in this article, another area to be discussed deals with other alternatives that might exist within the community, including the alternative of non-treatment. A review must be made of the benefits and consequences of those alternatives. These alternatives might include self-help groups within the community, low cost or sliding scale community agencies, other modalities of psychotherapy (e.g., group, marital, family), facilities that work primarily with the special group(s) of which the patient may be a member (e.g., women, children, American Indian, Hispanic, etc.), inpatient versus outpatient treatment when appropriate, and a myriad of other possible alternatives that exist within various communities, alternatives of which each practitioner should be aware. Some but not necessarily all other alternatives include individual self-help books and programs, educational training for personal effectiveness, crisis intervention systems and hot-lines, as well as legal, medical, and religious intervention.

It is very important, in these days of managed care and often very limited insurance coverage, that the patient understand what these financial limits are, and how they will impact on both the treatment itself and on their choice of a particular form(s) of treatment. It is especially important within the mental health field for patients to fully understand that they will likely become financially responsible for the costs incurred by the treatment choices they make. In addition, some plan or prospective measure needs to be put into effect to evaluate the patient's response to treatment, whether that plan includes standardized assessment techniques, behavioral observations by both the patient and the practitioner, or other techniques and criteria.

Patient participation in the decision-making regarding the process leads to a reduction in the belief that the therapist is magical or all-powerful, or that the process of psychotherapy is something that is done "to" the patient "by" the psychologist. Regarding the therapist, the patient needs and has the right to know the boundaries of the therapist's competence, as well as the therapist's training and professional orientation. The patient also needs and is entitled to know the therapist's professional strengths and weaknesses.

Also to be discussed is the question of the limits of confidentiality that can expected to exist within the therapeutic sanctuary. Included should be issues of danger to self and others, the mandated requirements for child abuse or elder abuse reporting, loss of confidentiality by court subpoena, as well as the waiver of confidentiality in any case in which the patient, as plaintiff, presents his mental/emotional status as an issue.

The limits of the therapeutic relationship need to be clarified, particularly that dual relationships of any nature are not an option, and that sexual contact between a therapist and a patient is neither permitted nor useful, but rather is counterproductive to the therapy process, damaging to the patient, and both unethical and illegal.

In the development of a sanctuary where some stability and some consistency is required, the patient needs to know about the therapist's availability, both long and short range. What hours and days of the week is the therapist available? How many appointments per week are feasible? Does the therapist have some flexibility in scheduling, as may be appropriate in the patient's changing situation? What kind of vacation coverage is usual? What happens in emergencies? What is the psychologist's policy regarding telephone contacts? What provisions are made for other coverage if the therapist is not available in an emergency? What happens when suddenly in the course of therapy things feel as though they are falling apart, and the patient feels that only with contact with the therapist can he somehow put himself/herself back together again?

The patient also needs to understand the role of assessment in psychology. Why is it used? When is it used? How is it used? What will happen to the results? Will they be used in the development of a treatment plan? Will the results be somehow integrated into future sessions? Will there be formal feedback? Who will see the results? And certainly, what is the cost, not only in money, but also in time, energy, and upset? What will the evaluation process engender, and what can the patient expect as a result of it?

The patient has the right before beginning psychological treatment to know what the questions are that he should be asking, and to know as much as possible about what realistically can be expected. Giving the patient these parameters provides a foundation for stability and constancy, both of which are fundamental parts of the trust and safety that are essential if successful psychological treatment is to occur.

The patient also needs to know that he has the freedom to terminate treatment at any time if he feels that he is not able to establish a suitable relationship with the practitioner, and also has the right to ask for consultation and supervision if he feels that he is in an untenable bind with the therapist that cannot be resolved on their own. The patient should further be aware of the role of collegial consultation, discussing with the practitioner such parameters as when consultation will involve protecting the identity of the patient and when (with the use of a signed release) the consultation will involve sharing the identity of the patient. The patient also needs to know the purpose of consultation: that it helps the therapist maintain objectivity; that it deepens the understanding of the dynamics of the therapist-patient relationship; and that it helps the therapist to locate and heal blind spots in his own vision as he looks at the therapeutic process.

Somewhere in those first few sessions as the process of therapy becomes more apparent, and the patient becomes more informed and more able to make suitable consent, he needs to know that this relationship may not be an ongoing one with permanence to the point at which the patient feels healed, given certain circumstances. The patient needs the protection of knowing what will happen if the treatment process needs to be interrupted. One example of this might be if the practitioner feels that he has gone as far as he can go with this particular person, and that treatment by another person, another modality, or another approach might be advisable.

The replacement of individual psychotherapy with group psychotherapy, which may or may not be conducted by the same therapist, is another major change. The patient needs to know in advance that, as changes seem advisable, the therapist will not unilaterally "toss" the patient out to some other person or modality, but that these are choices that will be made with mutual discussion. It is also important for him to know with confidence that while these are options that the therapist must keep in mind, the choices will be a mutual one. Additionally, the patient needs to know that should the patient or the therapist move away, provisions will be made to relocate the patient into a suitable relationship in order to continue the work.

Psychotherapy may be a useful and powerful means of helping a patient make changes that will lead to a life that feels more satisfying, more productive, and more comfortable. This process is made possible by the development of trust and safety, and a feeling of confidence in the therapist and in the process itself. Informed consent helps construct the foundation of trust and safety, and represents one very positive example of combining ethical and legal integrity with basic good therapeutic practice.

INFORMED CONSENT IN PSYCHOLOGICAL RESEARCH

The background and the development of the doctrine of informed consent as required in medical and psychological research has its development in a manner very similar to that explained at the beginning of this chapter. At the Nuremberg war trials of 23 Nazi physicians who were indicted for crimes against humanity, the following judicial summary was adopted, and has served as a basis for the consent requirements that researchers must follow. This judicial summary states:

> The voluntary consent of the human subject is absolutely essential. This means that the person involved should have legal capacity to give consent; should be so situated as to be able to exercise free power of choice, without the intervention of any element of force, fraud, deceit, duress, overreaching, or other ulterior form of constraint or coercion; and should have sufficient knowledge and comprehension of the elements of the subject matter involved as to enable him to make an understanding and enlightened decision. The latter element requires that before the acceptance of an affirmative decision by the experimental subject there should be made known to him the nature, duration, and purpose of the experiment; the method and means by which it is to be conducted; all inconveniences and hazards reasonably to be expected; and the effects upon his health or person which may possibly come from his participation in the experiment. The duty and responsibility for ascertaining the quality of the consent rests upon each individual who initiates, directs, or engages in the experiment. It is a personal duty and responsibility which may not be designated to another with impunity. (Keith-Spiegel & Koocher, 1995, pp. 389-390, originally published in the *Journal of the American Medical Association*, 1946)

The current factors under focus revolve around ensuring that research participation is, in fact, entered into in a voluntary, informed, and knowledgeable way. Several major problems are encountered here, in addition to the general problems dealing with the obtaining of truly informed consent for treatment.

One special area of difficulty is in the area of voluntariness. Is consent truly "voluntary" if a large amount of money or some other powerful incentives are offered in exchange for participation? In addition, we need to look at factors such as social pressure, social prestige, and an appeal to the potential participant's sense of altruism.

While ostensibly voluntary, there are often subtle implications that to not participate would be a sign of weakness, immaturity, or any of a number of other negative characteristics. One area in which this is particularly a problem is when the researcher is also the college professor who is attempting to use students as research subjects. Here there is an inherent risk that refusing may subject the student to the displeasure of the professor, thereby in some way affecting the grades, evaluations, or future recommendations that might be given by that particular professor regarding the student(s) who refused to participate. Another condition under which the concept of "voluntariness" may be violated is when an employer requires that an employee fill out research questionnaires, etc., either as a condition of remaining employed or as one condition of potentially gaining employment.

As is also the case in other forms of psychological (or medical) participation, the research subject must retain the right to withdraw at any time; this right should be made explicit during the informed consent phase of the introduction of the research study. This is also the case with children who are subjects, although they may not be able to verbalize fully their desire to withdraw from the experimental situation. Here, it is the responsibility of the researcher to monitor the behavioral cues of the child subjects, and when appropriate to inquire of the child subject whether or not they wish to withdraw from the task. Many of the same risks apply to research as apply to participation in other areas of psychological practice, and the researcher has the responsibility to disclose them to potential subjects before participation is begun. These certainly include not only the obvious ones such as loss of privacy or confidentiality, loss of self-esteem, stress, and discomfort, but also those not quite so obvious as potential feelings of shame, embarrassment, and negative feelings about having been deceived. This list is not meant to be all-inclusive, but rather is included to direct the researcher's thinking along these lines.

One important area that must be considered in terms of informed consent for research is in the area of deception of research subjects, where it is believed that such deception is absolutely necessary in order to attain accurate research findings. Not only does the researcher have the responsibility to make the fullest disclosure possible, but additionally has the responsibility to monitor and remediate areas of discomfort or upset that the research subject has experienced and/or developed as a result of the research participation, and certainly as a result of the deception (if deception is involved in the research design).

INFORMED CONSENT IN SUPERVISION AND TRAINING

This article would not be complete without at least some mention of the importance of informed consent in the areas of supervision and training. It is, of course, both legally and ethically required that those who work under the supervision of a license issued to another must state this (preferably in writing) to all those with whom they interact on a professional basis. This is true not only in the case of clinical practice, but also in the case of research and any other form of professional participation.

One area that has been sorely neglected insofar as informed consent is concerned has to do with the explicitness of the standards and expectations that are held by both the supervisor and the supervisee about the other. Supervisees need to know, in advance, how they will be evaluated, what information the supervisor will use in that evaluation, and what criteria are to be met. They have a right to know, too, what information that they reveal to the supervisor will be kept confidential.

Unfortunately, it is still not unusual for the same person to serve as a supervisor and as a (quasi-official or even official) therapist as well. While combining these two roles may seem to be useful and convenient, there develops and remains a distinct blurring of the boundaries between the rights and obligations of the supervisor-supervisee relationship and that of the patient-therapist relationship.

The supervisee is entitled to know the qualifications, education, training, and experience that is held by the supervisor, just as the supervisor must have the same information about the supervisee. Since the supervisor cannot supervise in an area in which he/she is not themselves qualified, it is very much in the interest of all concerned (and especially in the interest of the patient) that this be common and respected knowledge between supervisor and supervisees.

The supervisor is expected to carefully inform the supervisee of the goals and objectives that the supervisee is expected to reach, or at least work toward. It is also expected that the supervisor help the supervisee understand due process as it relates to all concerned, as well as helping the supervisee understand what they can do to protect all concerned from physical and/or emotional harm. It is also important that the supervisor help the supervisee learn about and use wisely all resources (including the supervisor, but extending into the community) that are available.

Finally, a supervisor has the responsibility to be careful not to impose upon the supervisee his/her own theoretical biases, as well as refraining from allowing the supervisee to develop total dependence upon the supervisor. The supervisor has to walk the fine line of allowing the supervisee to make their own mistakes, while simultaneously taking wise steps to ensure the well-being of the patient.

Persons interested in a more complete discussion of this area, developed to assist supervisors in accomplishing their task in the most efficient and most professional manner possible, are referred to Austin, Moline, and Williams (1990; pp. 230-237).

REFERENCES

American Psychological Association. (2002). Ethical principles of psychologists and code of conduct. *American Psychologist, 57*(12), 1060-1073.

American Psychological Association, Committee for the Protection of Human Participants in Research. (1982). *Ethical principles in the conduct of research with human participants*. Washington, DC: American Psychological Association

Austin, K. A., Moline, M. E., & Williams, G. T. (1990). *Confronting malpractice: Legal and ethical dilemmas in psychotherapy*. Thousand Oaks, CA: Sage Publications, Inc.

Canterbury v. Spence, 464 F.2d 772 (D.C. Cir. 1972).

Cobbs v. Grant, 502 P.2d 1 (Cal 1972).

Keith-Spiegel, P., & Koocher, G. P. (1985). *Ethics in psychology: Professional standards and cases*. New York: Random House.

Natanson v. Kline, 350 P.2d 1093 (1960).

Nuremberg Code. (1949). In *Trials of war criminals before the Nuremberg Military Tribunals under Control Council Law No. 10* (Vol. 2, pp. 181-182). Washington, DC: U.S. Government Printing Office.

Schloendorf v. Society of New York Hospital, 105 N.E. 92 (N.Y.1914).

Stromberg, C. D., Haggarty, D. J., Leibenluft, R. F., McMillian, M. H., Mishkin, B., Rubin, B., & Trilling, H. R. (1988). *The psychologist's legal handbook*. Washington, DC: The Council for the National Register of Health Service Providers in Psychology.

Truman v. Thomas, 611 P.2d 902 (Cal. 1980).

Wenning, K. (1993). Long-term psychotherapy and informed consent. *Hospital & Community Psychiatry, 44*(4), 364-367.

World Medical Association. (1964/1975). *Declaration Of Helsinki: Ethical principles for medical research involving human subjects.* Adopted by the 18th World Medical Association General Assembly Helsinki, Finland, June 1964; amended by the 29th World Medical Association General Assembly, Tokyo, Japan, October 1975. Retrieved October 19, 2003 from, http://www.wma.net/e/policy/pdf/17c.pdf

Protecting Privacy and Confidentiality

O. Brandt Caudill
Alan I. Kaplan

SUMMARY. This article discusses the confidentiality of communications between therapist and patient and the scope of, and exceptions to, the privilege preventing such communications from being disclosed. Ethical principles, statutes, and case law will be explored. *[Article copies available for a fee from The Haworth Document Delivery Service: 1-800-HAWORTH. E-mail address: <docdelivery@haworthpress.com> Website: <http://www.HaworthPress.com> © 2005 by The Haworth Press, Inc. All rights reserved.]*

KEYWORDS. Confidentiality, privilege, waiver, exceptions, litigation

There can be little doubt that confidentiality is an essential prerequisite to effective psychotherapy. Patients frequently assume that the confidentiality of their communications with the psychologist is absolute. However, in the last two decades there have been numerous exceptions carved out to confidentiality, of which both psychologists and patients

---

Address correspondence to: Alan I. Kaplan, JD, Law Offices of Alan I. Kaplan, 1925 Century Park East, Suite 500, Los Angeles, CA 90067-2706 (E-mail: Aikaplan1@aol.com).

[Haworth co-indexing entry note]: "Protecting Privacy and Confidentiality." Caudill, O. Brandt, and Alan I. Kaplan. Co-published simultaneously in *Journal of Aggression, Maltreatment & Trauma* (The Haworth Maltreatment & Trauma Press, an imprint of The Haworth Press, Inc.) Vol. 11, No. 1/2, 2005, pp. 117-134; and: *Ethical and Legal Issues for Mental Health Professionals: A Comprehensive Handbook of Principles and Standards* (ed: Steven F. Bucky, Joanne E. Callan, and George Stricker) The Haworth Maltreatment & Trauma Press, an imprint of The Haworth Press, Inc., 2005, pp. 117-134. Single or multiple copies of this article are available for a fee from The Haworth Document Delivery Service [1-800-HAWORTH, 9:00 a.m. - 5:00 p.m. (EST). E-mail address: docdelivery@haworthpress.com].

Digital Object Identifier: 10.1300/J146v11n01_10

need to be cognizant. The situation is complicated by the interaction be-tween confidentiality and issues of the psychotherapist-patient privi-lege.[1] Generally, confidentiality requires information to be kept private, with certain exceptions that will mandate or allow disclosure. The issue of privilege relates to whether the communications can be disclosed in court.

While the confidentiality of psychologist's communication is often assumed, the reality is that confidentiality must have a basis in statute or case law to be upheld. It has only been in the last fifty years that legisla-tures have provided statutes specifically codifying confidentiality and exceptions to confidentiality. The professional associations for psycho-therapists (most notably the American Psychological Association [APA]) have been in the forefront of defining the scope of confidentiality and the duties a psychologist has to preserve confidentiality. Some states, such as California, have enacted broad statutes governing the confiden-tiality of information from patients.[2]

CONFIDENTIALITY BY CASE LAW

A number of state courts have articulated and protected the confiden-tiality rights of patients, most notably the 1970 California Supreme Court decision in *In re Joseph E. Lifschutz*.[3] There was no comparable decision by the United States Supreme Court until 1996 when the Court decided *Jaffee v. Redmond*.[4] This case arose from the killing of a man by police officer Redmond. A wrongful death action was commenced, and a lower court ordered the defense to provide to the plaintiff (the es-tate of the dead man) the records of a licensed clinical social worker named Karen Beyer, who had approximately 50 counseling sessions with Officer Redmond after the shooting. The Supreme Court noted that all 50 states had enacted some form of psychotherapist-patient privi-lege, but that the federal courts were not uniform in applying such privi-lege at the federal level. In upholding the existence of the privilege and the importance of confidentiality, the court stated in pertinent part:

> In contrast to the significant public and private interest supporting recognition of the privilege, the likely evidentiary benefit that would result from the denial of the privilege is modest. If the privi-lege were rejected, confidential conversations between psycho-

therapists and their patients would surely be chilled. Particularly when it is obvious that the circumstances that give rise to the need for treatment will probably result in litigation. Without a privilege, much of the desirable evidence to which litigants such as petitioners seek access–for example, admissions against interest by a party, is unlikely to come into being. This unspoken "evidence" will therefore serve no greater truth-seeking function than if it had been spoken in privilege. That is appropriate for the federal courts to recognize a psychotherapist privilege under Rule 501 as confirmed by the fact that all 50 states and the District of Columbia have enacted into law some form of psychotherapist privilege . . .[5]

In arriving at its decision, the Supreme Court made specific note of the 1992 APA Ethical Principles[6] and the requirement of the psychologist to disclose the relevant limits on confidentiality to the patient.[7]

SELECTED STATUTES MANDATING CONFIDENTIALITY

California Civil Code Sections 56 through 56.37 (the Confidentiality of Medical Information Act) were enacted originally in 1979 (and later amended) to regulate the field of health care records disclosure. Section 56.10 prohibits the release of health care records without patient authorization. However, in certain instances a practitioner *must* disclose patient information if compelled to do so (subject to the patient's constitutional privacy rights) (see Table 1). In addition, a health care provider also *may* disclose patient information in certain situations (see Table 1). In Section 56.11, the Code provides specific requirements permitting a patient to validly authorize the release of their health care records if the authorization contains certain statutorily mandated language, and provided that the patient understands the scope of the authorization that the patient is signing.

The Code also provides that a patient whose records have been used or disclosed in violation of the Code and who has sustained economic loss or personal injury as a result, may recover compensatory and punitive damages not to exceed $3,000, attorney's fees up to $1,000, and the costs of litigation.[8] Finally, any violation of the Code that results in economic loss or personal injury to a patient is punishable as a misdemeanor,[9] and any practitioner who willfully discloses confidential information is subject to a license revocation proceeding before the Board of Psychology.[10]

TABLE 1. Circumstances in Which Patient Information Must or May Be Disclosed

---

Patient information *must* be disclosed in the following instances:

   (a) by a court;

   (b) by a board, commission, or administrative agency for the purpose of adjudication;

   (c) by a board, commission, or administrative body which is conducting an investigation and has issued a subpoena of its own;

   (d) by an arbitrator or arbitration panel which has lawfully issued a subpoena;

   (e) by a search warrant lawfully issued to a government law enforcement agency;

   (f) when otherwise specifically required by law.

Patient information *may* be disclosed in the following circumstances:

   (a) to other health care providers to facilitate treatment of the patient;

   (b) to an insurance plan to facilitate payment for health care services or, in some circumstances, to a government agency that funds health care;

   (c) to persons or entities providing billing services to the practitioner;

   (d) to peer review boards;

   (e) to malpractice insurance companies;

   (f) to any licensing authority such as the Board of Psychology conducting a general investigation (providing that identifying information is removed from the records);

   (g) to the county coroner in the course of an investigation by the coroner's office;

   (h) to public agencies, clinical investigators, health care research organizations and accredited public or private nonprofit educational or health care institutions for bona fide research purposes;

   (i) when retained by the patient's employer, a practitioner may disclose information relevant to the patient's ability to work;

   (j) to an insurance carrier who hires a practitioner;

   (k) to a group practice pre-paid health care service plan by providers who contract with the plan. The information may also be transferred among providers that contract with the plan, for the purpose of administering the plan;

   (l) to insurance plans under certain circumstances;

   (m) to probate court investigators in the course of a guardianship or conservatorship proceeding in order to help to determine whether the patient is in need of a conservatorship;

   (n) to tissue banks processing the tissue of a decedent;

   (o) when disclosure is otherwise authorized by law.

In 1955, the United States Court of Appeals for the District of Columbia Circuit, in the case of *Taylor v. United States*,[11] commented on the importance of confidentiality as follows:

> In regard to mental patients, the policy behind such a statute is particularly clear and strong. Many physical ailments may be treated with some degree of effectiveness by a doctor, whom the patient did

not trust, but a psychiatrist must have his patient's confidence or he cannot help him. The psychiatric patient confides more utterly than anyone else in the world. He exposes to the therapist not only what his words directly express; he lays bare his entire self, his dreams, his fantasies, his sins, and his shame. Most patients who undergo psychotherapy know that this is what will be expected of them, and that they cannot get help except on that condition. It would be too much expected of them to do so if they knew that all they say–and that all the psychologist learns from what they say–may be revealed to the whole world from a witness stand.'[12]

In recent years, the issue of confidentiality has led to numerous battles over the extent to which psychologists and other mental health professionals may disclose information in family court matters involving custody and visitation. There has been a proliferation of both lawsuits and licensing board actions around the country dealing with alleged breaches of confidentiality in a forensic setting. This will be discussed in more detail below, but is an additional area of which psychologists must be cognizant.

Finally, the United States Congress has enacted the Health Insurance Portability and Accountability Act (HIPAA),[13] a comprehensive and incredibly detailed statutory scheme that addresses the confidentiality of patient's records. It is beyond the scope of this article to address the sweep of HIPAA; however, psychologists should beware that if their state does not have a sufficiently restrictive scheme for protecting confidentiality, HIPAA may come into play. For states that have a pre-existing comprehensive scheme dealing with the confidentiality of medical information, such as California, HIPAA may have significantly less impact. Because the various states have different statutory schemes governing confidentiality, the first area to be examined will be the confidentiality provisions of national organizations for psychologists and other therapists.

THE APA'S ETHICAL PRINCIPLES REGARDING CONFIDENTIALITY

The APA's Ethical Principles have addressed confidentiality in numerous respects, including addressing the duty to maintain confidentiality with specific ethical principles and trying to delineate the psychologist's obligations to maintain confidentiality. The most recent revisions of the APA ethics code[14] became effective January 1, 2003. These principles deal with confidentiality under section 4 and include the following provisions:

Under Principle 4.01, psychologists have "a primary obligation" to take reasonable precautions to protect confidentiality, including an obligation to recognize that the limits of confidentiality may be regulated by law, institutional rules, or professional or scientific relationships. Under Ethical Principle 4.02, psychologists are required to discuss with persons, including patients and organizations with which they have a scientific or professional relationship, the relevant limits of confidentiality and the "foreseeable uses" of the information generated through their psychologist activities. This is also required to be reflected in a written informed consent under Ethical Principle 3.10. This principle dictates that the discussion of confidentiality should occur at the inception of the relationship, unless this is not feasible or is contraindicated, and other points as warranted by new circumstances.

Ethical Principle 4.02(c) also imposes on psychologists the duty to explain to patients the risks to their privacy and confidentiality of electronic transmission of the information. In short, psychologists who are using anything from cell phones and faxes to the Internet must be conscience of and disclose limitations on confidentiality from using technology.

Ethical Principle 4.03 requires that written permission must be obtained to record the voices or images of individuals to whom services are provided. In addition a failure to obtain such permission in advance could subject a psychologist to civil suit or criminal prosecution if the recording violated federal or state statutes.[15]

Ethical Principle 4.04 deals with the sensitive issue of how to minimize intrusions on confidentiality. Subsection (a) stipulates that the psychologist include in their written and oral reports and consultations only information that is germane to the purpose for which the communication is made. This is obviously a subjective standard and may lead to some confusion in the future. Further, the question of who determines what is germane is open to dispute.

Subsection (b) of section 4.04 provides that the psychologist only discuss confidential information for appropriate scientific or professional purposes, and only with individuals who are concerned with those matters. Thus, if a psychologist were to disclose to a colleague information about a patient because it was amusing or bizarre, even if the patient was not identified, it would arguably be a violation of this Ethical Principle.

Ethical Principle 4.05 allows disclosures as authorized with the appropriate consent of the client or patient. In addition, under subsection (b), a psychologist may disclose confidential information without the consent of the patient as mandated or permitted by law for purposes such as (1) to provide needed professional services; (2) to obtain appropriate professional consultations; (3) to protect the patient or others, including the psychologist, from harm; or (4) to obtain payment.

Ethical Principle 4.06 governs the common practice of obtaining consultations with colleagues and provides that psychologists do not disclose information that could lead to the identification of a patient or research participant, unless the psychologist has obtained prior consent from the patient. This principle also stipulates that they only need to disclose information to the extent necessary.

Ethical Principle 4.07 governs the use of confidential information in writing, lectures, and public media. This principle provides that psychologists do not disclose in their writing, lectures, or public media confidential or personally identifiable information concerning patients, students, research participants, or other recipients of their services unless they take reasonable steps to disguise the person or organization, obtain consent in writing to do so, or there is a legal authorization for doing so.[16]

Similar provisions can be found in the ethical principles of the American Association for Marriage and Family Therapists, the California Association of Marriage and Family Therapists, the National Association of Social Workers, and the American Psychiatric Association.[17]

EXCEPTIONS AND LIMITATIONS TO CONFIDENTIALITY

In the last ten to twenty years, numerous exceptions have been carved out to the general principle of confidentiality, and the extent to which these principles apply varies from state to state. There are many exceptions to the confidentiality rules, all of which deal with specialized circumstances and which, viewed, as a whole, should not be read as swallowing up the general confidentialities principles in any sense!

Danger to self or others. If a patient represents an immediate danger to themselves or to others, they can be involuntarily hospitalized,[18] in which event confidential information about the patient can be revealed to law enforcement authorities and to hospital personnel pursuant to the

1967 Lanterman Petris Short Act[19] ("LPS" Act). When the Supreme Court decided *Jaffee,* it left open the question of whether a dangerous patient exception or duty to warn, like *Tarasoff v. Regents of the University of California,*[20] would be recognized. The Federal circuit courts have disagreed to some extent on the existence of such a duty. The Tenth Circuit Court of Appeal in *United States v. Glass*[21] held that a therapist was allowed to disclose a serious threat if the disclosure was the only means of averting harm. The Sixth Circuit Court of Appeal in *United States v. Hayes*[22] recognized that a therapist may have a duty to warn the prospective target of a patient's threats but found that the psychotherapist-patient privilege still precluded the therapist from testifying about the threats in a later prosecution.

Commission of a crime. A patient who seeks treatment to aid them or anyone else in the commission of a crime does not have a right of confidentiality with respect to communications relevant to the commission of the crime.

Court appointment. When a court appoints a practitioner to evaluate a patient and orders the practitioner to submit an evaluative report, the patient has no right of confidentiality because the court has already ordered the practitioner to report on the patient's condition.

Sanity proceedings. Where a patient is involved in a criminal proceeding and their sanity is at issue, they may be evaluated by one or more practitioners for the purpose of reporting to the court. In such situations, the patient's mental state is directly at issue, and the practitioner is required by the court to report their findings.

Competency proceedings. When a patient is involved in a proceeding to determine their competence (e.g., a guardianship or conservatorship proceeding), the practitioner may be called upon to perform an evaluation to determine the patient's competence. Again, such an evaluation is primarily for the benefit of the court and is usually court-ordered, as a result of which there is no right of confidentiality.

Public records. Occasionally a patient requires a practitioner to file a report with a public agency on behalf of the patient. In such events, the information is only confidential to the extent that the public agency's records are held confidential.

Child abuse. Where the patient is a child and the practitioner reasonably suspects child abuse, they must report the facts constituting the suspected child abuse to the Department of Children Services. Additionally, reporting is mandated where the patient is an adult, but the perpetrator is still living with minors.[23] Among the most common exceptions to confidentiality are state statutes requiring psychologists and other mental health professionals to report instances of suspected child sexual abuse. California's statute is typical and requires a mandated reporter who has knowledge of or observes a child in his or her professional capacity, or whom he or she knows or reasonably suspects has been the victim of child abuse to report verbally and in writing.[24]

While reference will be made to the child abuse reporting laws in the State of California as an example, a comprehensive listing of the state's statutes governing child abuse reporting can be found in the book, *Mandating Reporting Of Suspected Child Abuse, Ethics, Law, & Policy* by Seth C. Kalichman (1995). Generally, a reasonable suspicion is defined to mean that it is objectively reasonable for a person to entertain a suspicion based upon facts that could cause a reasonable person in a like position, and drawing when appropriate on his or her training or experience, to suspect child abuse or neglect.[25]

Sexual abuse is defined to mean sexual assault or sexual exploitation, including statutory rape, rape in concert, incest, sodomy, and any sexual contact between the genitals or anal opening of one person and the mouth or tongue of another. Any intentional touching of the genitals, or intimate parts with the clothing covering them, of a child for purposes of sexual arousal or gratification, etc., is also sexual abuse.[26] In addition, physical abuse includes "unlawful corporal punishment or injury," which means a situation where a person deliberately inflicts on a child cruel or inhumane corporal punishment, or an injury that results in a traumatic condition. This definition does not include all forms of corporal punishment and does not include the necessary use of reasonable force by peace officers or public school officials trying to quell a disturbance.[27] The term child abuse is defined to mean a physical injury that is inflicted by other than accidental means on a child by another person.[28]

Neglect is defined to mean the negligent treatment or maltreatment of a child by a person who is responsible for the child's welfare, under circumstances that indicate harm or threatened harm to the child. Severe neglect means the neglectful failure of a person having the care or custody of the child to protect the child from severe malnutrition, or medically diagnosed non-organic failure to thrive. General neglect means the failure to provide adequate food, clothing, shelter, medical care, or supervision where no physical injury has occurred.[29]

While almost every state requires reporting of child sexual abuse and child physical abuse, some states allow discretionary or mandatory reporting of emotional abuse inflicted on a child. In California, this is a permissive report. New Mexico, Texas, Wyoming, Nevada, Massachusetts, Kansas, and Maine include emotional abuse as a mandated reporting category. Other statutes are more vague or use ambiguous language; for example, Maryland's definition requires an injury inflicted by inhumane treatment or as a result of a malicious act.[30]

In *Searcy v. Auerbach*,[31] a California psychologist was sued. Michael Searcy had taken his daughter, Stacy, from her home in Texas to his home in California. He then asked Dr. Auerbach to evaluate her. Dr. Auerbach gave Mr. Searcy a written opinion stating his belief that Stacy had been sexually abused while in her mother's custody. Mr. Searcy contacted the police and a child welfare agency in Houston and gave them Dr. Auerbach's written opinion. The Texas officials then called California child protective service officials, who subsequently spoke with Dr. Auerbach. He repeated to them the statements made in his written opinion. However, Dr. Auerbach made no effort to contact authorities about his evaluation of Stacy.

Sandra Searcy discovered the written opinion and sued for libel and slander. Dr. Auerbach claimed immunity under California's Child Abuse Reporting Law. The 9th Circuit Court of Appeal, however, found that Dr. Auerbach was not entitled to immunity because: (a) he did not make a report as required, and actually violated the statute by failing to make the report required under section 11166, and (b) he disclosed his opinion to Mr. Searcy, who is not a person authorized to receive it under Penal Code section 11167.5 (which limits the individuals who can receive the report, generally to law enforcement individuals or people charged with investigating such reports). Dr. Auerbach tried to argue that giving his report to Michael Searcy could be considered an intermittent step toward reporting the abuse to Texas or California agencies. The 9th Circuit rejected this argument and held that the report could only be made to a state agency. The court decision also implies that Dr. Auerbach would not have had immunity for a direct report to Texas, because his only immunity was for reporting to California agencies.

With modern communications, including the Internet, psychologists need to be aware that information received about child abuse that occurred in a state outside their own can only be reported to an agency and state in which they are licensed. That agency can then notify sister-state agencies even where a report is authorized under the particular statute in question. If the psychologist distributes the report to individuals that are not specified in the statutory scheme, he or she may be successfully sued and may be outside the scope of any immunity. Of course, a false report of child abuse would be almost per se libel and slanderous.

Elder abuse. A patient over the age of 65, who the practitioner believes is the victim of physical or emotional abuse, may also trigger a reporting requirement.[32] California and a number of other states have enacted mandatory elder abuse statutes that are modeled after the child abuse reporting laws. If a psychologist practices in a state where such a statute is in effect, then he or she may have mandated reporting duties analogous to those in child abuse reporting. The elder abuse laws are somewhat broader in scope and address financial abuses of elders, as well as physical and sexual abuse of elders. In addition to California, Florida has a comprehensive scheme to protect elders, entitled The Adult Protective Service Act.[33]

Deeds and wills. If a patient dies and a communication is important to help decide an issue concerning a deed of conveyance, will, or other writing executed by the patient, the practitioner may disclose confidential information for that purpose.[34]

Suit against practitioner. A patient who files a suit against a practitioner for breach of duty, or a patient who is a party to litigation filed by a practitioner against the patient, voids any right of confidentiality with respect to communications relevant to the resolution of that litigation.

Heirs. If a communication between a deceased patient and a practitioner is important to an issue between parties claiming through the deceased patient, disclosure may be compelled.[35]

Patient litigant exception. If the patient has filed a lawsuit putting in issue their emotional state, and if a court orders that disclosure of mental health records is warranted, there is no right of confidentiality at that point.[36]

Waiver. If a patient signs a proper written waiver, there is no right to confidentiality.

Dependent abuse. Persons between the ages 18-64 who are mentally or physically dependent on another person and who are the subject of abuse may present to a practitioner. If a practitioner suspects that these facts have merit, they must report the abuse to the appropriate agency.[37]

COMMON BREACHES OF CONFIDENTIALITY

In the author's experiences, it is somewhat rare to have a suit over breach of confidentiality outside the forensic setting (discussed below) without other issues being present, such as alleged dual roles or sexual relationships with patients. A rapidly growing area of both civil suits and complaints to licensing boards, for different categories for mental health professionals, concerns statements that are made by a treating therapist in a court setting. These can be collectively referred to as forensic breaches of confidentiality. While there is no immediate method of tracking how many such cases are being filed in the various state and federal courts, it is clear that the number of such cases is on the rise.

The general issue these cases present, and the divergent results nationwide, are demonstrated by reviewing three cases that were decided at approximately the same time: *Werner v. Kliewer*,[38] *Cutter v. Brownbridge*,[39] and *Dolin v. Von Zweck*.[40]

In *Cutter v. Brownbridge*, a licensed clinical social worker was a psychotherapist for a man for approximately six years. The social worker agreed to maintain all communications and diagnoses in confidence. While the man and his wife were involved in a bitter divorce, the social worker, voluntarily and not as a result of a subpoena or any other legal requirement, wrote a declaration disclosing the man's diagnosis as well as damaging personal details. This was attached by the man's wife for suspension of his visitation rights and was filed in court. The man sued the therapist, claiming invasion of privacy and breach of confidentiality. The social worker tried to have the case thrown out on the general California litigation privilege, which immunizes parties and witnesses in litigation from being sued. However, the California Court of Appeal held that the state statutory immunity was subordinate to the right of privacy (Article I, Section 1 of the California Constitution), and therefore, the social worker could be sued.

By contrast, in *Werner v. Kliewer*, Mrs. Werner was also embroiled in a custody battle and was having suicidal feelings, which led her to voluntarily admit herself to a hospital. While there, she saw Dr. Kliewer, a psychiatrist. Before the hospitalization, Mrs. Werner did not have any difficulty with daily tasks, such as preparing her children for getting ready for school, and the children found her present behavior to be frightening. She left the hospital against medical advice after a few days. At the request of Mrs. Werner's husband, Dr. Kliewer wrote a letter to the judge hearing the custody matter expressing his concern that she might be a risk to herself, and should be evaluated further. Dr. Kliewer disclosed the behavior that her children found frightening, and disclosed her suicidal threats. The letter was shared with the judge, the parties' attorneys, and court officials. Mrs. Werner sued Dr. Kliewer, claiming breach of confidentiality, but the Kansas Supreme Court upheld the dismissal of all claims, including invasion of privacy against the psychiatrist. The Kansas Supreme Court held that the state's legitimate concern for the best interest of Mrs. Werner's children outweighed any other concerns, including invasions of her privacy.

In *Dolin v. Von Zweck*, a Massachusetts Appellate Court dealt with an analogous situation also arising from a custody battle. Dr. Von Zweck had treated Mrs. Dolin and the Dolin children, but had never met Mr. Dolin. Dr. Von Zweck wrote a letter for use by a maternal aunt who was seeking custody of the children. The letter contained statements that could have been construed as defamatory to Mr. Dolin, whom Dr. Von Zweck had never met. Mr. Dolin had a psychiatric expert testify, who criticized Dr. Von Zweck's behavior. The Appellate Court held that Dr. Von Zweck was immune from suit, because of the Massachusetts litigation privilege. Thus, whether a psychologist may be liable for forensic breach of confidentiality may well hinge on the position taken by his or her state's supreme court on the competing interest litigation privilege versus privacy.

An anomalous case is *Cheatham v. Rogers*,[41] where a Texas appellate court allowed a father in a custody battle to obtain psychotherapy records of the personal therapy of the therapist who served as court appointed counselor for the children. Thus, the number of cases dealing with this area has proliferated. Certain general principles can be derived and should be followed by psychologists who wish to avoid potential liability.

Avoiding liability. First, a psychologist who has treated more than one individual needs the consent of all participants in the therapy to be able to disclose any information to anyone. A partial consent is ineffective in most instances to justify any type of disclosure. Second, both courts and licensing boards have reacted negatively to psychologists or other psychotherapists interjecting themselves into litigation where their involvement was not requested by the court. A mental health professional should proceed with extreme caution where he or she is requested to provide any type of statement in court. The first inquiry should be whether everyone whose consent is necessary has given appropriate consent, and whether the consent is in writing. Additionally, psychologists must be cautious about commenting on the mental state of people that they have not treated or assessed since such statements would be speculative and would violate the *Specialty Guidelines for Forensic Psychologists*.[42] Stewart Greenberg and Daniel Shuman[43] provide an excellent discussion of the differences in roles. In addition, if a psychologist is going to express any opinion regarding visitation or custody, he or she should recognize that the current trend is to view such statements as inappropriate unless he or she has been formally appointed as a child custody evaluator. Any statements that are made in a custody proceeding should comply with the APA's *Guidelines for Child Custody Evaluation in Divorce Proceedings*.[44]

TECHNICAL BREACHES OF CONFIDENTIALITY

In recent years, therapists have made use of voicemail, cell phones, and the Internet for communications with patients. However, it is imperative that therapists be conscious of the ways in which these technologies can be used to breach confidentiality. Generally, a psychologist who is dealing with someone over the Internet runs a number of risks, one of which is that they are opening their computer systems to potential attack by viruses. In addition, one of us (O.B.C.) has seen a circumstance where a communication from a therapist to a personal friend was inadvertently copied to a patient who was in the therapist's e-mail address book, which created difficulties. Because of the ease with which e-mail can be sent, the risk of communications being sent to unintended recipients is as much of a potential problem as hacking the therapist's computer system is.

Voicemail presents its own set of problems, because a person who can guess or learn the therapists' voicemail code would be given information by the system itself, which would allow access to patient communication. One of us (O.B.C.) has seen some circumstances where individuals were able to obtain the therapist's access code and accessed voicemail messages, then presented the information contained in the voicemail messages as if it was information learned directly from the therapist. A key problem here is the use of predictable voicemail codes. As with home alarm codes, the more predictable the code, the easier it is for a third party to anticipate and use it to the therapist's detriment. Finally, cell phones are widely used, but also well known to be capable of being intercepted advertently or inadvertently, and therapists should use caution in having confidential communications over cell phones.

A recent case from Massachusetts underscores how different the application of the psychotherapist-patient privilege can be from state to state. For example, the Massachusetts Supreme Court in *Commonwealth v. Olivera*[45] concluded that the psychotherapist-patient privilege is not self-executing and that there must be an affirmative assertion of it by a patient or a psychotherapist to prevent privileged therapy records from being disclosed. The court concluded that the requirement that the privilege be asserted affirmatively was not a mere technicality, because the judge attempting to make a privilege determination from the records themselves would often have no information as to the professional status of the individuals whose communications with the patient were reflected in the record. Under Massachusetts law, a person who is a staff psychologist, but who did not meet licensure or educational requirements as a psychotherapist under their privilege law, was someone whose sessions with the patient would not be privileged.[46] Similarly, a psychologist who had a doctoral degree in education, but no degree in psychology, did not constitute a psychotherapist for the purpose of the Massachusetts privilege.[47]

The *Olivera* case arose in the context of a criminal defendant contesting his conviction for sexually molesting his girlfriend's two daughters. California, on the other hand, has taken the position that a criminal defendant does not have a right to access the psychotherapy records of a complaining witness/victim except under extraordinary circumstances.

An example of the types of cases that have been brought regarding the psychotherapist-patient privilege is the Connecticut case of *Cabrera v. Cabrera*,[48] where a father contended that the statutory psychotherapist-patient privilege did not apply to marital counseling sessions because the term "marital counseling" was not used in the privilege statute. Although there was no statutory or case law in point, the appellate court of Connecticut concluded that marital counseling was covered by the privilege unless the privilege was waived. In this case, the father claimed that his wife, by calling a psychiatrist to the stand who testified about her psychological condition, waived her psychotherapist-patient privilege that arose with a psychologist who had conducted both marital counseling sessions and individual psychotherapy sessions. The court noted that under Connecticut law, to result in a waiver of the privilege there must be two components: (a) A party must have put his or her own mental health in issue; and (b) the court must find it is more important to the interests of justice that the communications be disclosed and that the relationship between the person and the psychologist be protected.

Yet another contrast is found in *O'Neill v. O'Neill*,[49] where a Florida Appellate Court concluded that a mother's psychotherapist-patient privilege could be invaded after she was admitted to a psychiatric ward of the local hospital following making suicidal threats and saying she would harm her children. Florida courts have apparently recognized an exception to the psychotherapist-patient privilege, where a "calamitous event" such as a parent's attempted suicide occurs during a pending custody dispute. The courts have found that the mental health of the parent is then sufficiently at issue to invade the privilege. The court in the *O'Neill* case felt that the mother's hospitalization and her threats to the children warranted invading her privilege. There is no indication that this decision would be followed in other jurisdictions, but it is illustrative of how the cases vary from jurisdiction to jurisdiction.

CONCLUSION

A patient's expectation of privacy in communications with a therapist is now protected at both the federal and state levels. Psychologists must be aware of what local state law provides regarding the scope of confidentiality and the exceptions to the psychotherapist patient privilege, to avoid being subjected to civil suits and/or administrative action by licensing boards for improper disclosures.

NOTES

To locate references located in this article, please use the online database Lexis-Nexis. After you are in the database, choose the *Legal Research* option. For Cases: Go to *Get a Case* and type in party name or use citation. For State-based codes: Go to desired state and enter type of code.

1. See in this volume Alan I. Kaplan, *Therapist-Patient Privilege: Who Owns the Privilege*, 11(1/2) *Journal of Aggression, Maltreatment & Trauma*, 135-143 (2005).

2. Confidentiality of Medical Information Act (Cal. Civ. Code § 56 et seq.).

3. *In Re Lifschutz*, Supreme Court of California, 2 Cal. 3d 415, 85 Cal.Rptr. 829, 467 P.2d 557 (1970).

4. 518 U.S. 1, 116 S.Ct. 1923 [135 L.Ed.2d 337] (1996).

5. *Jaffee v. Redmond* supra at 518 U.S. 1 at p.12-13.

6. American Psychological Association, *Ethical Principles of Psychologists and Code of Conduct* (Author, 1992).

7. *Supra* at Footnote 20.

8. Cal. Civ. Code § 56.35.

9. Cal. Civ. Code § 56.36.

10. Cal. Bus. & Prof. Code § 4992.3 (m).

11. 222 F.2d 398, 401 (1955).

12. 222 F.2d 398, 401 (1955).

13. Pub.L. No.101-191, 110 Stat.1936 (1996).

14. American Psychological Association, *Ethical Principles of Psychologists and Code of Conduct* (Author, 2002).

15. For example, under Cal. Penal Code § 631 and 632 the recording of a conversation without a person's consent may be grounds for criminal prosecution and a statutory penalty.

16. There have been occasional cases where mental health professionals have been sued for failing to adequately disguise patients in such writings or public statements [e.g., *Doe v. Doe,* 93 Misc. 2d 201, 400 N.Y.S.2d 668 (1977)].

17. See appendices to this volume for the reprints of the most recent versions of the ethics codes of the APA, the American Association for Marriage and Family Therapists, the National Association of Social Workers, and the American Psychiatric Association.

18. For a thorough discussion of the duty to protect, see also in this volume Simone Simone & Solomon M. Fulero, *Tarasoff and the Duty to Protect,* 11(1/2) *Journal of Aggression, Maltreatment & Trauma,* 145-168 (2005).

19. Cal. Welf. & Inst. § ?5000 *et. seq.* (1969).

20. *Tarasoff v. Regents of the University of California,* 17 Cal.3d 425, 551 P.2d 334, 131 Cal.Rptr. 14 (1976).

21. 133 F.3D 1356 (10th Cir. 1998).

22. 227 F.3d 578 (6th Cir. 2000).

23. Cal. Penal Code § 11166, *et. seq.*

24. Cal. Penal Code § 11164, *et seq.*

25. Cal. Penal Code § 11166(a)(1).

26. Cal. Penal Code § 11165.1.

27. Cal. Penal Code § 11165.4.

28. Cal. Penal Code § 11165.6.

29. Cal. Penal Code § 11165.2.

30. In most states, the failure to make a mandated child abuse report is grounds for civil suit and criminal prosecution. There have been a surprising number of criminal cases around the country brought against therapists and others for failing to make mandated child abuse reports. For example, *Henry v. Everhard,* 309 Ark. 336, S.W.2d 467 (1992); *Rosecrans v. Kinson,* 154 Mich. App. 381, 397 N.W.2d 317 (1986); *People v. Caviani,* 10 Cal.App. 4th Supp. 20 (1992); *State v. Hurd,* 135 Wisc.2d 266, 400 N.W.2d 42 (1986).

31. 980 F.2 609 (9th Cir. 1992).

32. Cal. Welf. & Inst. Code § 15630-15631.

33. Either Florida or California statutes can be looked to for model or typical reporting provisions.

34. Cal. Evid. Code § 1021, 1022.

35. Cal. Evid. Code § 1019.

36. Cal. Evid. Code § 1016.

37. Cal. Penal Code § 15630.

38. *Werner v. Kliewer,* 289 Kan. 285, 710 P.2d 1250 (1985).

39. *Cutter v. Brownbridge,* 183 Cal. App.3d 836, 228 Cal. Rptr. 545 (1st Dist.1986).

40. *Dolin v. Von Zweck,* 19 Mass. Ct. 1032, 447 N.E.2d 200 (1985).

41. 824 S.W.2d 321 (Tex.App.-Taylor 1992).

42. Committee on Ethical Guidelines for Forensic Psychologists, *Specialty Guidelines for Forensic Psychologists,* 15(5) Law & Human Behavior 655-665 (1991).

43. Stewart A. Greenberg & Daniel W. Shuman, *Irreconcilable Conflicts Between Therapeutic and Forensic Roles,* 28(1) Professional Psychology: Research and Practice 50-57 (1997).

44. American Psychological Association, *Guidelines for Child Custody Evaluation in Divorce Proceedings,* 49(7) American Psychologist 677-680 (1994).

45. *Commonwealth v. Olivera,* 438 Mass. 325 (2002).

46. *Commonwealth v. Mandeville,* 396 Mass. 393 (1982).

47. *Commonwealth v. Rosenberg* 410 Mass. 347 (1991).

48. *Cabrera v. Cabrera,* 23 Conn. App.330, 580 A2d 1227 (1990).

49. *O'Neill v. O'Neill* 823 So.2d 837 (Fla. App. 2002).

Therapist-Patient Privilege:
Who Owns the Privilege?

Alan I. Kaplan

SUMMARY. The psychotherapist-patient privilege prevents the disclosure of confidential communications between psychotherapists and their patients in a variety of judicial proceedings. It applies to any confidential communications between those persons defined by statute as able to form a confidential psychotherapist-patient relationship. The privilege is held by the patient and the psychotherapist. If the patient is incompetent or a minor, another authorized person may exercise the privilege on the patient's behalf. Exceptions to the privilege exist where it has been waived, or where competing principles of justice outweigh the privilege. *[Article copies available for a fee from The Haworth Document Delivery Service: 1-800-HAWORTH. E-mail address: <docdelivery@haworthpress.com> Website: <http://www.HaworthPress.com> © 2005 by The Haworth Press, Inc. All rights reserved.]*

KEYWORDS. Privilege, therapist-patient, testimony, evidence, confidentiality

Address correspondence to: Alan I. Kaplan, JD, Law Offices of Alan Kaplan, 1925 Century Park East, Suite 500, Los Angeles, CA 90067-2706 (E-mail: Aikaplan@aol.com).

[Haworth co-indexing entry note]: "Therapist-Patient Privilege: Who Owns the Privilege?" Kaplan, Alan I. Co-published simultaneously in *Journal of Aggression, Maltreatment & Trauma* (The Haworth Maltreatment & Trauma Press, an imprint of The Haworth Press, Inc.) Vol. 11, No. 1/2, 2005, pp. 135-143; and: *Ethical and Legal Issues for Mental Health Professionals: A Comprehensive Handbook of Principles and Standards* (ed: Steven F. Bucky, Joanne E. Callan, and George Stricker) The Haworth Maltreatment & Trauma Press, an imprint of The Haworth Press, Inc., 2005, pp. 135-143. Single or multiple copies of this article are available for a fee from The Haworth Document Delivery Service [1-800-HAWORTH, 9:00 a.m. - 5:00 p.m. (EST). E-mail address: docdelivery@haworthpress.com].

Available online at http://www.haworthpress.com/web/JAMT
© 2005 by The Haworth Press, Inc. All rights reserved.
Digital Object Identifier: 10.1300/J146v11n01_11

INTRODUCTION

California courts and the California Legislature have long recognized that confidentiality is an indispensable element of effective psychotherapy and psychological research. Accordingly, the Legislature has enacted a variety of statutes over the years designed to shield confidential disclosures between patients and psychotherapists from being revealed in judicial proceedings. Unlike other confidentiality rules and the constitutional right of privacy,[1] the psychotherapist-patient privilege applies only to the attempted disclosure of confidential communications in judicial or administrative proceedings. This includes trials, depositions, and subpoenas for the examination of records. The current psychotherapist-patient privilege statute in California provides that, unless the privilege has been waived, or an exception to the privilege applies:

> The patient, whether or not a party, has a privilege to refuse to disclose, and to prevent another from disclosing, a confidential communication between patient and psychotherapist if the privilege is claimed by: (a) the holder of the privilege; (b) a person who is authorized to claim the privilege by the holder of the privilege; or (c) the person who was the psychotherapist at the time of the confidential communication, but such person may not claim the privilege if there is no holder of the privilege in existence or if he is otherwise instructed by a person authorized to permit disclosure.[2]

This article will discuss the various factors that determine whether or not the psychotherapist-patient privilege applies at all, and if it does apply, whether an exception nevertheless requires the disclosure of confidential information.

Definition of "Psychotherapist"

In order for the privilege to apply, the communication must be confidential and it must be divulged to the "psychotherapist." In general, the definition of "psychotherapist" is rather broad in most states. For example, in California[3] it includes the following persons:

1. a psychiatrist;
2. a person who the patient reasonably believes to be a psychiatrist (whether or not such person is in fact licensed to practice medicine);

3. a licensed psychologist;
4. a licensed clinical social worker;
5. a credentialed school psychologist;
6. a licensed marriage, family and child counselor;
7. a registered psychological assistant;
8. a registered marriage, family and child counselor intern;
9. a registered associate clinical social worker;
10. registered interns working for authorized nonprofit community counseling organizations;[4]
11. psychological interns working within a clinical program at an accredited or approved college or university;
12. marriage, family and child counseling interns;
13. a registered nurse who possesses a Masters Degree in psychiatric mental health nursing;
14. a governmental agency or a person contracting with a governmental agency;[5]
15. an agency that receives funding from community United Funds, or a run-away house or a crisis resolution center;[6]
16. a licensed educational psychologist.[7]

The definition of "psychotherapist" has been broadened tremendously over the years but still includes, in general, only those persons specifically authorized by law to perform psychotherapy, or persons who the patient reasonably believes are psychiatrists. Additionally, persons rendering mental health treatment or counseling services to consenting minors are also included within the general definition of psychotherapist.

Definition of "Holder of the Privilege"

The primary holder of the privilege is the patient, if the patient is a legally competent adult. A patient is defined as:

A person who consults a psychotherapist or submits to an examination by a psychotherapist for the purpose of securing a diagnosis or preventive, palliative, or curative treatment of his mental or emotional condition or who submits to an examination of his mental or emotional condition for the purpose of scientific research on mental or emotional problems.[8]

If the patient is not legally competent, privilege holders can include the patient's legal guardian or conservator, a deceased patient's personal representative (executor-administrator), and a minor patient's attorney or social worker in a dependency proceeding under Welfare and Institutions Code Section 300. Of course, the therapist is also a holder of the privilege and has a duty to assert the privilege on behalf of the patient.[9]

Many questions regarding who holds the privilege arise in dependency proceedings, in which children are often deemed holders of the privilege and can exercise it through their counsel. However, the social worker may also be deemed a holder, and even over the objection of the patient and their attorney, the therapist can be compelled to give the court and social worker circumscribed information to accomplish the information gathering goal of the therapy (to provide the court with information to ensure that the minor patient receives necessary services) but the details of the therapy should remain confidential.[10] While a parent is normally the holder of a young child's privilege, a parent who allegedly abuses the child cannot use the privilege to prevent disclosure of the abuse.[11]

The issue also commonly arises in custody disputes, where parents can disagree about who has the authority to exercise the privilege. In such cases, and particularly where the therapist suspects abuse by one or both parents, disclosure of confidential patient information should be refused until the Court issues an order delineating who is entitled to receive this information. The therapist should advise both parents (and the Court) in writing if they believe that disclosure of information about the therapy will harm the minor patient.

Subject to the foregoing and other special rules that apply to various categories of minors and incompetents, the patient is the most important holder of the privilege, and in general, other than the therapist, only those who have the legal authority to exercise the patient's privilege where the patient is legally incompetent can be considered holders of the privilege.

Confidentiality of the Communication

A communication is not protected by the privilege unless it is transmitted in the course of a treatment relationship and transmitted in confidence, which means that, so far as the patient is aware, no one will learn of the communication other than those who are present to further the interests of the patient in the consultation or those to whom disclosure is reasonably necessary for the transmission of the information or the accomplishment of the purpose for which the psychotherapist is consulted.[12] Accordingly, the privilege is not destroyed if the patient makes a disclosure in the context of a group treatment session, since the presence of the other group members is for the benefit of all the others, including the witness/patient, and is designed to facilitate the patient's treatment.[13]

Sometimes, a patient will have ulterior motives in submitting to psychotherapy. For example, in *People v. Cabral*,[14] a prisoner initiated contact with a psychologist who ran a sex offender treatment program. The prisoner was under the belief that submitting to the program would reduce his possible prison sentence. The prisoner contended (and the court accepted his contention) that the prisoner also sought treatment from the psychologist. The prisoner wrote a letter to the psychologist admitting to the molestation. The court ordered that the letter was admissible because the *primary* purpose of the consultation was to reduce the prisoner's sentence. Accordingly, even though a patient may seek psychotherapy in part for valid clinical reasons, the psychotherapist-patient privilege does not apply unless the *predominant* reason for seeking treatment was to obtain needed help, rather than for other motives irrelevant to treatment.

Providing that the privilege applies, it prevents even the disclosure of a therapist's patients' names, even where law enforcement authorities are conducting a search for such patients to determine if they were sexually molested by the therapist.[15]

EXCEPTIONS TO THE PRIVILEGE[16]

There are a number of circumstances in which psychotherapist-patient communications must be disclosed in court proceedings even where the "holder" of the privilege (i.e., the patient) objects:

1. *Patient/litigant exception.* Where the patient brings a legal proceeding alleging that they have suffered psychological injury due to a defendant's conduct.[17] In such cases, the courts have articulated a balancing test between the defendant's right to a fair trial and a patient's right to confidentiality, and have determined that a patient who raises the issue of their own mental competence creates the necessity for disclosure of such confidential information as is necessary to permit the court to fairly adjudicate the patient's claim.[18] Additionally, a criminal defendant who raises the question of their own sanity will be held to have waived their psychotherapist-patient privilege, thereby permitting

disclosure of communications made in the course of treatment or hospitalization.[19]

2. *Competency proceedings.* In a proceeding held to determine the competence of a patient, such as a guardianship proceeding, a conservatorship proceeding, or a commitment proceeding.[20]

3. *Commission of a crime.* If the services of a psychotherapist are sought or obtained to enable a patient to commit or plan to commit a crime or tort, or to escape detection or apprehension after the commission of a crime or tort, there is no psychotherapist-patient privilege.[21]

4. *Heirs of deceased patient.* There is no privilege as to a communication between parties "all of whom claim through a deceased patient regardless of whether the claims are by testate or intestate succession or by *inter vivos* transaction."[22]

5. *Breach of duty.* In cases involving a breach of duty by the psychologist arising out of their relationship with the patient, there is no psychotherapist-patient privilege as to any communications between the psychologist and the patient.[23]

6. *Deceased patient–will.* In a communication from a deceased patient concerning their intent in executing a will or other dispositive instrument, there is no psychotherapist-patient privilege.[24]

7. *Public reports.* Where a psychologist is required by law to report information to a public employee or for inclusion in the public record, there is no psychotherapist-patient privilege as to that information.[25]

8. *Dangerous patient.* Where a psychotherapist has reasonable cause to believe that the patient is dangerous to himself or to the person or property of another, and that disclosure is necessary in order to prevent the threatened danger, there is no psychotherapist-patient privilege.[26]

9. *Tarasoff.* Where a patient expresses a credible threat of injury to an identifiable victim, the therapist not only has the right but the obligation to warn the intended victim.[27, 28]

10. *Court-appointed psychotherapist.* Where a psychotherapist is appointed by a judge or by the Board of Prison Terms to examine a patient, there is no applicable psychotherapist-patient privilege.[29]

11. *Child abuse reporting.* Where a psychotherapist is required to report child abuse, the psychotherapist-patient privilege does not apply to prevent such a report.[30] Interestingly, although the privilege does not prevent a child abuse report, it can preclude the psychotherapist from testifying to the court regarding the same information that they set forth in the report.[31]

12. *Elder abuse*. A psychotherapist who suspects that their elderly patient is being abused in the home or in another setting has a right and duty to report such abuse to the applicable authorities.[32]

13. *Coroner's inquiries*. Where a coroner is investigating the cause of a patient's death, they have the right to obtain the patient's psychological treatment records for the purpose of said investigation, notwithstanding any potential psychotherapist-patient privilege.[33] Such information may not be further disclosed to other persons or agencies after receipt by the coroner, and must be sealed after the investigation has ended.[34]

14. *Waiver*. Where a patient voluntarily discloses a material part of a confidential psychotherapist-patient communication, they may well be deemed to have waived the privilege, thus requiring full disclosure in any judicial proceeding.

APPLICATION OF THE PRIVILEGE

As a practical matter, the application of the privilege is fairly straight-forward and does not (or should not), as a matter of course, require great sophistication or legal acumen by the psychotherapist. If the patient claims that the psychotherapist-patient privilege applies, and objects to the disclosure of confidential patient information, or declines to sign a written waiver allowing such disclosure, the psychotherapist is required by law to claim the privilege on behalf of the patient and should not disclose the requested information unless a court has reviewed the privilege claim and has specifically ordered such disclosure. In this way, the psychologist can avoid making complicated legal determinations as to whether one exception or another to the privilege may apply. This is not, and should not, be a burden for psychologists, as the issue should be addressed directly to the legal system.

In most circumstances, if the patient has waived the privilege, and if they have an important right that depends on such a waiver, their attorney will advise them to sign a written release for the requested information, which would then absolve the psychologist of any liability for release of records or of testimony. In the instances where the patient does not consent to the release of the requested information, the attorneys involved in the judicial or administrative proceeding have ready access to the courts to obtain a ruling as to whether or not the material should be released. It is therefore critically important that psychologists who are in possession of privileged information have the courage to endure attempts at intimidation by non-patients or counsel involved in judicial or administrative proceedings, and to clarify that such matters are not within the purview of psychologists but should be determined by the courts.

Additionally, under Article 1, Section 1 of the California Constitution, each patient has a constitutional right of privacy and other confidentiality rights separate and apart from the psychotherapist-patient privilege. Accordingly, even if a psychologist decides that one of the psychotherapist-patient privilege exceptions applies, they could still incur serious liability to the patient if they disclose confidential information without either the patient's consent or a specific order of court.[35] Accordingly, a psychotherapist who zealously guards the patient's privacy, even at the expense of receiving some intimidating threats from members of the legal community, will nevertheless be pursuing the safest course and that most conducive to a healthy psychotherapeutic relationship.

NOTES

1. Cal. Const. art. 1, § 1.
2. Cal. Evid. Code § 1014 (a)-(c).
3. Cal. Evid. Code § 1010.
4. Cal. Bus. & Prof. Code § 2909(d).
5. Cal. Fam. Code § 6924(a)(1)(A & B).
6. Cal. Fam. Code § 6924(a)(1)(C & D).
7. Cal. Fam. Code § 6924(a)(2)(C) and Cal. Bus. & Prof. Code § 4986, *etseq.*
8. Cal. Evid. Code § 1011.
9. Cal. Evid. Code § 1013(a) & (b).
10. *In re Kristine W.*, 94 Cal.App.4th 521, 528 (2001).
11. *In re Mark L.*, 94 Cal.App.4th 573 (2001).
12. Cal. Evid. Code § 1012.
13. *Farrell v. Superior Court*, 203 Cal.App.3d 521, 527, 250 Cal.Rptr. 25 (1988).
14. *People v. Cabral*, 12 Cal.App.4th 820, 15 Cal.Rptr.2d 866 (1993).
15. *Scull v. Superior Court*, 206 Cal.App.3d 784, 254 Cal.Rptr. 24 (1988).
16. See also in this volume O. Brandt Caudill and Alan I. Kaplan, *Protecting Privacy and Confidentiality*, *11(1/2) J. Aggression, Maltreatment & Trauma*, 117-134 (2005).
17. Cal. Evid. Code § 1016.
18. *In re Lifschutz*, 2 Cal.3d 415, 424-425, 85 Cal.Rptr. 829 (1970).
19. *People v. Mickle*, 54 Cal.3d 140, 190, 284 Cal.Rptr. 11 (1991).
20. Cal. Evid. Code §§ 1004, 1025.
21. Cal. Evid. Code § 1018.
22. Cal. Evid. Code §§ 1000, 1019.
23. Cal. Evid. Code § 1020.

24. Cal. Evid. Code §§ 1021, 1022.

25. Cal. Evid. Code § 1026.

26. Cal. Evid. Code § 1024; *Menendez v. Superior Court* (1992) 3 Cal.4th 435, 11 Cal.Rptr.2d 92 (holding that the psychotherapist-patient privilege still applies if the patient's only threat is directed to the psychotherapist rather than to some outside third party).

27. *Tarasoff v. Regents of the University of California*, 17 Cal.3d 425, 131 Cal.Rptr. 14 (1976). See also, Cal. Welf. & Inst. Code § 5328(r).

28. For a discussion of *Tarasoff* in this volume, see Simone Simone and Solomon M. Fulero, *Tarasoff and the Duty to Protect, 11(1/2) J. Aggression, Maltreatment & Trauma,* 145-168 (2005).

29. Cal. Evid. Code § 1017(a) & (b).

30. Cal. Penal Code § 11171(b).

31. *People v. Stritzinger*, 34 Cal.3d 505, 194 Cal.Rptr. 431 (1983).

32. Cal. Welf. & Inst. Code § 15630 *et.seq.*

33. Cal. Gov't Code § 27491.8.

34. Cal. Gov't Code §§ 27491.8(b) & (d).

35. See Chapter 23, supra.

Tarasoff and the Duty to Protect

Simone Simone
Solomon M. Fulero

SUMMARY. The *Tarasoff I* and *Tarasoff II* cases were decided by the California Supreme Court in 1974 and 1976, respectively. These cases involved the murder of a young woman by her ex-boyfriend, who had been a patient at a University counseling center. The parents of the young woman sued, alleging negligence. *Tarasoff I* set forth a "duty to warn" on the part of psychotherapists. Upon rehearing in *Tarasoff II*, the decision was upheld but modified. The court ruled that when a therapist determines, or should have determined, that a patient presents a serious danger of violence to another, the therapist has a "duty to protect" that other person. In this article, we address subsequent cases that have arisen under the "duty to protect" doctrine, and analyze some of the legal issues that these cases have raised. *[Article copies available for a fee from The Haworth Document Delivery Service: 1-800-HAWORTH. E-mail address: <docdelivery@haworthpress.com> Website: <http://www.HaworthPress.com> © 2005 by The Haworth Press, Inc. All rights reserved.]*

KEYWORDS. Tarasoff, duty to protect, law, ethics

Address correspondence to: Solomon M. Fulero, PhD, JD, Department of Psychology, Sinclair College, Dayton, OH 45402 (E-mail: sol.fulero@sinclair.edu).

[Haworth co-indexing entry note]: "Tarasoff and the Duty to Protect." Simone, Simone, and Solomon M. Fulero. Co-published simultaneously in *Journal of Aggression, Maltreatment & Trauma* (The Haworth Maltreatment & Trauma Press, an imprint of The Haworth Press, Inc.) Vol. 11, No. 1/2, 2005, pp. 145-168; and: *Ethical and Legal Issues for Mental Health Professionals: A Comprehensive Handbook of Principles and Standards* (ed: Steven F. Bucky, Joanne E. Callan, and George Stricker) The Haworth Maltreatment & Trauma Press, an imprint of The Haworth Press, Inc., 2005, pp. 145-168. Single or multiple copies of this article are available for a fee from The Haworth Document Delivery Service [1-800-HAWORTH, 9:00 a.m. - 5:00 p.m. (EST). E-mail address: docdelivery@haworthpress.com].

Digital Object Identifier: 10.1300/J146v11n01_12

TARASOFF DOCTRINE

"Protective privilege ends where the public peril begins," concluded Judge Tobriner in the famous *Tarasoff v. Regents of the University of California* (*Tarasoff I*; 1974, at 566; cited in Fulero, 1988) decision rendered by the California Supreme Court. The Court's decision compelled psychotherapists in California to warn potential victims of psychotherapy patients who represented a threat of imminent danger to them. The *Tarasoff* decision had its genesis at the precise moment a young man fell in love with a young woman, an obsessive love that ultimately culminated in the death of Tatiana Tarasoff and left a legacy of liability for mental health professionals.

Medical and mental health professionals have traditionally viewed confidentiality as the *sine qua non* of efficacious treatment (Denkowski & Denkowski, 1982). For this reason, concerned professional organizations raised objections to the Tarasoff ruling, arguing that the duty to warn would jeopardize the sanctity of confidentiality within the therapeutic relationship. In response, the California Supreme Court agreed to rehear and ultimately to vacate its original decision. Instead, the 1976 decision in *Tarasoff v. Regents of the University of California* (*Tarasoff II*) imposed upon psychotherapists in California a legal duty to protect third parties from harmful acts perpetrated by their patients, even if the protective intervention requires a breach of the patient's confidentiality. Having moved from a specific "duty to warn" to a more general "duty to protect," the revised or amended decision increased the options available to clinicians, but also increased the ambiguity inherent in the situation by providing only vague suggestions as to how to discharge the newly imposed legal duty (Mills, Sullivan, & Eth, 1987).

Post-*Tarasoff* cases have employed the same key concepts and legal principles that guided the *Tarasoff* decision. However, courts in different jurisdictions have interpreted these components differently, and they have either expanded, restricted, or rejected the original *Tarasoff* doctrine. This has resulted in vastly diverse rulings that vary from jurisdiction to jurisdiction. The permutation of the *Tarasoff* legal requirements has created a wake of confusion for mental health professionals in an already abstruse and difficult situation (Kamenar, 1984). Mental health professionals must determine how to satisfy both their legal duty to protect as well as their concomitant ethical obligation to maintain the confidentiality of their patients' disclosures. The conflict created by these inextricably interwoven but often conflicting concepts sometimes results in a clinical dilemma for which mental health professionals find little guidance in existing ethical codes.

THE LEGACY OF LIABILITY

The actual implications of the *Tarasoff* decision are easily misunderstood, since law journals, mental health literature, and judicial opinions commonly misrepresent the decision. This leaves many mental health professionals somewhat confused about their responsibilities regarding their patients who threaten violence (Southard & Gross, 1982). Much of the literature that reviews *Tarasoff* provides only a condensed version of the background of the case (Gehring, 1982; Gurevitz, 1977). Thus, many mental health professionals have been exposed to only superficial knowledge of the events that led to the *Tarasoff* decision, that is, the actual seminal case law that first required psychotherapists to protect third parties. The actual *Tarasoff* facts have been presented in varying degree of detail by commentators such as Crocker (1985), Gehring (1982), Goodman (1985), Gurevitz (1977), Kermani and Drob (1987), Knapp and VandeCreek (1982), Lamb, Clark, Drumheller, Frizell, and Surrey (1989), Matflerd (1992), Mills (1984), Mills et al. (1987), Oldham (1978), Quinn (1984), Roth and Meisel (1977), Runck (1984), Schwartz (1985), Slovenko (1988), Sonkin (1986), Southard and Gross (1982), and VandeCreek and Knapp (1989), among others. A review of the facts will illustrate how psychotherapists' decisions, even those decisions made with good intentions but with an incomplete understanding of relevant legal requirements, can have far reaching repercussions.

Material facts. Prosenjit Poddar, a 25-year-old student from Bengal, India, entered graduate school in September 1967 at the University of California at Berkeley to earn a Master's Degree in Naval Engineering (Quinn, 1984; Slovenko, 1988; VandeCreek & Knapp, 1989). He had been born into the Harijan caste, the social stratum allotted to so called "untouchables," a position that lies virtually outside acceptable society. Poddar's social position would have prevented him from having an opportunity for advanced education and a professional career in India (Slovenko, 1988; Vandercreek & Knapp, 1989). His own countrymen referred to Poddar as *gabhir jaler mach*, literally translated as a "deep water fish," because he revealed so little of himself (Slovenko, 1988).

Poddar lived in the International House, which also hosted folk-dancing classes during the fall semester of 1968. He enrolled in the dance class and met a young American student, Tatiana Tarasoff, an immature 19-year-old student from a disturbed home. The couple exchanged a casual New Year's Eve kiss, which led Poddar to believe that Tatiana's passion for him matched his for her. When Tatiana told Poddar she did not want an intimate relationship with him and was involved with other men, Poddar plunged into a severe depression. During his period of depression, he cried, spoke disjointedly, and neglected his appearance, his health, and his studies. The young couple continued to meet occasionally. In his obsession with Tatiana, Poddar surreptitiously taped parts of their conversations during these meetings. Afterwards he would spend hours dissecting the recorded conversations with his roommate in order to determine Tatiana's feelings for him (Mills, 1984; Mills et al., 1987; Schwartz, 1985; VandeCreek & Knapp, 1989).

Tatiana went to Brazil on vacation in the spring of 1969 (Goodman, 1985), and Poddar's emotional condition began to improve (Schwartz, 1985). A friend persuaded him to seek treatment from the student health services at Cowell Memorial Hospital, an affiliate of the University of California at Berkeley (Southard & Gross, 1982; VandeCreek & Knapp, 1989). On June 5, 1969, Poddar was seen at the student health service by Dr. Gold, a psychiatrist on the hospital's inpatient staff (Goodman, 1985; Mills et al., 1987; Quinn, 1984; VandeCreek & Knapp, 1989). Dr. Gold diagnosed Poddar with paranoid schizophrenia (Goodman, 1985). Uncharacteristically, Dr. Gold told Poddar in the initial evaluation that he appeared quite disturbed. The psychiatrist prescribed a neuroleptic and arranged for Poddar to receive weekly psychotherapy with Dr. Lawrence Moore, a 34-year-old clinical psychologist on the outpatient staff (Mills, 1984; Mills et al., 1987; Oldham, 1978; Slovenko, 1988). Shortly before Dr. Moore began Poddar's psychotherapy, the psychologist had been traumatized by the attempted suicide of his wife and her attempted murder of their child (Slovenko, 1988).

Although Poddar distrusted the psychologist and feared that Dr. Moore would betray him, they continued to meet weekly for a total of eight sessions (Slovenko, 1988). In the course of psychotherapy, Dr. Moore determined that Poddar had a pathological attraction to a young woman who had rejected him (Quinn, 1984) and that Poddar fantasized about harming her (Kermani & Drob, 1987; Mills, 1984; Slovenko, 1988). On August 18, 1969, Dr. Moore determined from Poddar's remarks in therapy that Poddar planned to kill the young woman when she returned from vacation (Mills et al., 1987; Oldham, 1978; Schwartz, 1985). Although Poddar did not specifically name Tatiana Tarasoff as his intended victim, Dr. Moore had obtained sufficient information to be aware of her identity (Crocker, 1985; Kermani & Drob, 1987). Poddar's friend had informed Dr. Moore that Poddar intended to buy a gun (Mills, 1984; Mills et al., 1987; Slovenko, 1988). Poddar also confessed to Dr. Moore his intention to buy a weapon (Quinn, 1984), and subsequently purchased a pellet gun (Slovenko, 1988). Dr. Moore could not dissuade Poddar from his threat to kill Tatiana (Southard & Gross, 1982), and when Dr. Moore confronted Poddar about the gun, Poddar refused to relinquish it (Slovenko, 1988).

Dr. Moore considered Poddar a danger to Tatiana (Crocker, 1985), and on August 20th sought consultation with Dr. Gold, the initial evaluating psychiatrist, and with Dr. Yandells, the assistant director of the department of psychiatry. Dr. Yandells substituted for Dr. Harvey Powelson, Moore's supervisor and director of the department of psychiatry, who was away on vacation at the time (Quinn, 1984). The three professionals concurred that Poddar should be committed involuntarily for evaluation (Goodman, 1985; Kermani & Drob, 1987; Mills, 1984; Mills et al., 1987; Quinn, 1984; Schwartz, 1985; VandeCreek & Knapp, 1989).

Dr. Moore contacted the campus police both by phone and by letter to recommend that Poddar be committed for a 72-hour emergency psychiatric evaluation pursuant to the existing commitment law (Kermani & Drob, 1987; Knapp & VandeCreek, 1982; Oldham, 1978; Quinn, 1984; Southard & Gross, 1982; VandeCreek & Knapp, 1989). Only two months previously, California had enacted the Lanterman-Petris-Short Act (1969), which designated the city police as agents authorized to pick up individuals who needed psychiatric evaluation (VandeCreek & Knapp, 1989). Neither the campus police nor the mental health professionals had a clear understanding of how to implement involuntary commitment under the new law. In addition, only two hospitals in Berkeley were legally authorized to hold involuntary psychiatric patients; the university hospital had no such legal authorization (Mills et al., 1987; Schwartz, 1985). Dr. Moore followed up his telephone request with a letter to the campus police:

> At times he appears to be quite rational, at other times he appears quite psychotic . . . [C]urrently the appropriate diagnosis for this is paranoid schizophrenic reaction, acute and severe. He is at this point a danger to the welfare of other people and himself. That is, he has been threatening to kill an unnamed girl who he feels has betrayed him and has violated his honor. He has told a friend of his

. . . that he intends to go to San Francisco to buy a gun and that he plans to kill the girl. He has been somewhat more cryptic with me, but he has alluded strongly to the compulsion to "get even with" and "hurt" the girl. (Slovenko, 1988, p. 148)

The university police questioned Poddar in the presence of Tatiana's brother, Alex, who was also Poddar's friend and roommate (Slovenko, 1988). They released Poddar when he denied any intent to kill Tatiana, who was still in Brazil, and promised to stay away from her (Kermani & Drob, 1987; Knapp & VandeCreek, 1982; Quinn, 1984). Poddar never returned for further treatment with Dr. Moore (Knapp & VandeCreek, 1989; Mills, 1984; Mills et al., 1987; Quinn, 1984).

Dr. Powelson, Director of the department of psychiatry, became outraged when he returned from vacation and learned that Poddar had been questioned by the campus police (Slovenko, 1988). He immediately ordered the campus police to return Dr. Moore's letter. Dr. Powelson further ordered Dr. Moore to destroy all of his clinical notes that pertained to Poddar and demanded that Moore take no further action to commit Poddar (Kermani & Drob, 1987; Oldham, 1978; Quinn, 1984; VandeCreek & Knapp, 1989). When Dr. Moore's professional judgment was overruled by his superior (Schroeder, 1979), no further measures were taken to deter Poddar from his intention to kill Tatiana, and no efforts were made to warn Tatiana or her family of her potential danger (Knapp & VandeCreek, 1989; Quinn, 1984). Tatiana returned to Berkeley in the fall and once again rebuffed Poddar's advances. In the meantime, Poddar had left the International House and had moved within a few blocks of Tatiana's home; he had also invited Alex to live with him (Goodman, 1985; Gurevitz, 1977; Quinn, 1984; VandeCreek & Knapp, 1989). Two months after the campus police had exacted Poddar's promise not to harm Tatiana, he went to her home with his gun and demanded to see her (Mills, 1984; Quinn, 1984). Tatiana refused to see Poddar, and he grew increasingly more insistent. When Tatiana screamed, Poddar shot her with his pellet gun, and she ran from the house with Poddar in pursuit. He caught her and stabbed her repeatedly with a kitchen knife. After he stabbed Tatiana to death, Poddar returned to her home and phoned the police (VandeCreek & Knapp, 1989).

Although prosecuted for first-degree murder (Mills, 1984), Poddar was convicted of second-degree murder by the jury (Mills et al., 1987). Poddar attempted to have the original murder charge reduced to manslaughter on the grounds that his paranoid schizophrenia rendered him incapable of reasonable, meaningful consideration of the nature of his act prior to the murder. However, the jury agreed with the court-appointed psychiatrist that Poddar was schizoid rather than schizophrenic (Schwartz, 1985), and he was convicted of second-degree murder (Mills et al., 1987; VandeCreek & Knapp, 1989). Subsequently, the Court of Appeals reduced the verdict to voluntary manslaughter (*People v. Poddar*, 1972; Schwartz, 1985) and confined Poddar to the Vacaville Medical Facility (Slovenko, 1988). The California Supreme Court eventually reversed his conviction in February 1974 because the judge had failed to give adequate instruction to the jury in regard to "diminished capacity" (*People v. Poddar*, 1974; Mills et al., 1987; Slovenko, 1988; VandeCreek & Knapp, 1989). Poddar was released, and it was agreed not to retry him, on the condition that he immediately return to India. Dr. Moore was dismissed from the clinic after Tatiana was killed. Poddar returned to India and eventually married a lawyer, leaving behind a legacy of liability to mental health professionals (Goodman, 1985; Mills et al., 1987; Slovenko, 1988).

The Tarasoff duty. While the state pursued the criminal case against Poddar, Tatiana's parents filed a wrongful death civil suit against the University regents, the psychotherapists, and the campus police (Goodman, 1985; VandeCreek & Knapp, 1989). The suit alleged that (a) the defendants failed to detain a dangerous patient, (b) Dr. Moore failed to comply with his duty to warn others about his dangerous patient, (c) Dr. Powelson abandoned a dangerous patient by failing to hospitalize Poddar, and (d) all the defendants breached their duty to safeguard their patient and the public (Kermani & Drob, 1987; Southard & Gross, 1982). However, at the time Tatiana's parents filed suit, no specific case had established a legal duty for psychotherapists to warn or to protect potential victims of their patients. The issue was therefore dismissed by the trial court but became the crux of the appeal to the California Supreme Court (Mills, 1984). The civil suit was considered twice by the California Supreme Court. Eventually, both sides agreed to an out-of-court settlement, with the amount of the settlement undisclosed and sealed by court order (Schwartz, 1985), although it was rumored to be $50,000 (Slovenko, 1988). No actual liability was found against any of the defendants since the participants agreed to the out-of-court settlement (Southard & Gross, 1982). The two court decisions became known as *Tarasoff I* and *Tarasoff II*.

Tarasoff I. Tarasoff I came about as a result of the initial civil suit filed by Tatiana Tarasoff's family (Mills et al., 1987). After more than 13 months of deliberation (Gurevitz, 1977), the California Supreme Court established a duty to warn in California (*Tarasoff v. Regents of the University of California*, 118 Cal. Rptr. 129, 529 P.2d 533, [1974]; cited in Fulero, 1988). Prior to *Tarasoff I*, no court had recognized a legal duty to warn the potential victim of a patient (Cohn, 1983).

The *Tarasoff I* decision appears to have its basis in two distinct lines of previous cases: (a) cases in which physicians were required to breach confidentiality to report contagious diseases to public health authorities, and (b) cases in which mental institutions were held liable for harm perpetrated by patients who were negligently released or who escaped (Fulero, 1988). In particular, the *Tarasoff I* decision applied a precedent in which a physician was found liable for failure to notify a patient's wife that her husband was infected with tuberculosis (Appelbaum & Appelbaum, 1990; VandeCreek & Knapp, 1989). The *Tarasoff I* court decided that a cause for action for "failure to warn" existed against the campus police and against both therapists (Southard & Gross, 1982), and the case was reinstated.

Tarasoff I engendered controversy among professionals and disciplines from the day of its inception. Justice Tobriner, who wrote the California Supreme Court majority decision, determined that the complaint was essentially based on two grounds: (1) the defendants' failure to warn Tatiana of her impending damage, and (2) the defendants' failure to confine Poddar pursuant to the Lanterman-Petris-Short Act (Kermani & Drob, 1987). Despite Dr. Moore's efforts to detain Poddar, the court described him as having carelessly disregarded Tatiana's life and safety (Gurevitz, 1977). In the opinion of Meyers (1987), Dr. Moore "behaved with exemplary rectitude" (p. 191), but Dr. Powelson exhibited outrageous behavior when he subverted his subordinate's treatment plan, falsified records by arranging to have the campus police destroy Dr. Moore's letter, and when he ordered Dr. Moore to falsify medical records by obliterating all references to Poddar's threats. On the other hand, Southard and Gross (1982) condemn Dr. Moore's interventions as rash because Tatiana was in Brazil and already out of harm's way at the time Poddar made his threats. Apparently, Southard and Gross believe that dangerousness exists only in discrete increments; they failed to consider that patients can continue to represent a danger to others, despite the patient's protestations to the contrary.

In view of the facts of the case and issues involved, the imposition of a specific court-mandated duty to warn caused an uproar within the professional community (Quinn, 1984). The American Psychiatric Association, the Northern California Psychiatric Society, and several other organizations united to file an *amicus curiae* brief to challenge the court's decision. Their brief challenged the decision on several points, but most stridently protested the fact that therapists cannot reliably predict their patients' violent acts, and that warning would constitute a breach of confidentiality (Everstine et al., 1980; Kermani & Drob, 1987; Mills, 1984; Quinn, 1984; Schwartz, 1985). Even though the professional organizations maintained that breach of confidentiality jeopardizes the trust necessary for effective psychotherapy (Everstine et al., 1980) and would both deter people from seeking therapy and inhibit their disclosures, the court regarded their fears as too speculative (Slovenko, 1988) and thus rejected both major arguments (Everstine et al., 1980; Kermani & Drob, 1987). The *Tarasoff I* court held that "public policy favoring protection of the confidential character of patient-psychotherapist relationships must yield in instances in which disclosure is essential to avert danger to others; the protective privilege ends where the public peril begins" (*Tarasoff I*, at 566; cited in Fulero, 1988, p. 184).

Tarasoff II. In response to the *amicus curiae* brief, the California Supreme Court agreed to rehear the case and rendered the second *Tarasoff* decision in 1976 (Southard & Gross, 1982). The *Tarasoff II* decision vacated the *Tarasoff I* decision, which lost any further binding legal authority (Slovenko, 1988; VandeCreek & Knapp, 1989).

The second decision exempted the campus police but found the therapists potentially liable (Southard & Gross, 1982). The court reaffirmed its earlier decision but redefined the newly established duty as a duty to *protect* potential victims (Fulero, 1988).

> When a therapist determines or pursuant to the standards of his profession should determine, that his patient presents a serious danger of violence to another, he incurs an obligation to use reasonable care to protect the intended victim against such danger. The discharge of this duty may require the therapist to take one or more of various steps depending upon the nature of the case. Thus it may call for him to warn the intended victim or others likely to apprise the intended victim of danger, to notify the police, or take whatever steps are reasonably necessary under the circumstances. (*Tarasoff II*, cited in Quinn, 1984, p. 322)

With its re-statement, the court moved away from the specificity of an unequivocal duty to "warn" toward a broader, more general duty to "protect" (Zeiss, 1995). However, the new holding represented something of a Pyrrhic victory for mental health professionals. Even though the re-decision afforded psychotherapists more flexibility to choose the most appropriate intervention (Beck, 1990a; Weinstock & Weinstock, 1989), it also increased the ambiguity already inherent in this type of situation with its vague and limited suggestions as to how to discharge the duty (Mills et al., 1987). The court's holding failed to specify the class of persons who would be required to issue a warning, what steps were reasonable to discharge the duty to protect, and how reasonably to know when a patient is sufficiently dangerous (Mills, 1984).

So, the casual kiss exchanged by a young couple eventually culminated in a legal duty imposed upon mental health professionals to protect potential victims of their patients. In addition to having established a legal duty to protect third parties, *Tarasoff* also served as the precedent for cases with similar themes. However, different courts have reached vastly different conclusions with regard to the relevant legal principles and key concepts involved. Before examining the subsequent cases, which further complicate and obscure the duty to protect, it is necessary to explore the relevant legal principles and key concepts on which the cases pivoted.

KEY CONCEPTS IN TARASOFF-TYPE SITUATIONS

The *Tarasoff* decision hinged upon certain key concepts and legal principles. The potential for liability underscores the need for mental health professionals to be familiar with these special issues, which include: (a) fiduciary relationship, (b) prediction of dangerousness, (c) foreseeability, (d) identifiable victim, (e) reasonable care, and (f) duty to protect. In order to determine how and when mental health professionals must legally and ethically exercise their duty to protect third parties, they must understand the conceptual framework of the case and how the relevant concepts and principles function within the domain of duty to protect.

Fiduciary relationship. Under traditional common law, no person had any legal duty to protect a third person (George, 1985; Oldham, 1978). The prototypical example is that one can stand at the edge of a pond and watch someone drown without liability for failure to jump in the water and save the person from death. Eventually the courts did create a duty for persons engaged in "public callings" to protect those persons with whom they had a *special relationship*, e.g., employers to employees, public carriers to passengers, innkeepers to guests, and bar owners to inebriated patrons (Beigler, 1984; George, 1985; Greenberg, 1984; VandeCreek & Knapp, 1989). This provided a basis for including situations in which a "special relationship" is said to exist (VandeCreek & Knapp, 1989). Thus, a "fiduciary relationship" is the special relationship recognized by the law as one of trust and confidence between two parties, e.g., the relationship between doctor and patient, within which the patient can communicate without fear of disclosure (Crocker, 1985).

Tarasoff broke new legal ground by holding the psychologist responsible even though he had no existing relationship with the victim or her family. Until the *Tarasoff* ruling, duty existed only when the defendant had a special relationship to both the victim and the patient (Eberlein, 1980). The California Supreme Court cited *Restatement of the Law Second, Torts* (American Law Institute, 1965; cited in Miller, Doren, VanRybroek, & Maier, 1988; also cited in Fulero, 1988, 1992) and determined that the therapist-patient relationship satisfied the essence of the common-law dictum that liability can be imposed only if the defendant has some special relationship to the dangerous person or to the potential victim (Kermani & Drob, 1987). The court determined that, as individuals engaged in a public calling, psychotherapists must assume some responsibility for the safety of both the patient and any third parties threatened by that patient (Crocker, 1985; George, 1985; Lamb et al., 1989; Southard & Gross, 1982). Thus the existence of the fiduciary relationship allows an extension of the therapist/patient relationship to include any third party known to be threatened by the patient. Specifically, the *Tarasoff* court decided that the police who detained and then released Poddar had no duty to warn Tatiana because they had no "special relationship" with either Poddar or Tatiana (Oldham, 1978). On the other hand, the court deemed that Dr. Moore did have a special relationship with Poddar, which created an obligation for Dr. Moore to protect Tatiana (Beigler, 1984; VandeCreek & Knapp, 1989). In other words, therapists have a special relationship with potential victims of their patients sufficient to impose liability for harm that comes to them under certain conditions.

Prediction of dangerousness. The *Tarasoff* court ruled that confidentiality must yield when the therapist has determined, or should have determined, that a patient presents a serious danger to another person (Cohn, 1983; Fulero, 1988). The legal status of dangerousness invokes the need for special protective measures designed to protect others from harm at the hands of the dangerous person (Pollack, Gross, & Weinberger, 1982).

The concept of "danger" does not describe actual harm but merely signals that the potential for or the possibility of harm exists (Simon, 1990). The task of mental health professionals requires evaluating individuals to determine if they have the potential to cause harm to others (Pollack et al., 1982). Dangerousness does not exist as an inherent quality in an individual; it results from a number of factors (Slovenko, 1988), many of which are transient situational variables (Searight & Pound, 1994). Dangerousness lies on a continuum of infinite degrees of risk and may be activated in any given context by psychological and/or social factors (Monahan, 1981; Sonkin, 1986). Legal requirements force on-the-spot clinical evaluations of the patient's potential for harm into a dichotomy of dangerous versus non-dangerous (Kaufman, 1991). However, Meyer, Landis, and Hays (1988) argue that individuals should be ranked according to their perceived potential for harm because dangerousness fluctuates over time and in response to multiple variables (Kaufman, 1991).

Mental health professionals actually inherited the duty to predict dangerousness nearly a century ago, albeit in another context. When it became apparent in the late 1800s that the penal system could not successfully reform all criminals, emphasis shifted from rehabilitation to protection of society. Clinicians who were first asked to explain criminal behavior were now asked to predict it as well. This new requirement was predicated on legal needs rather than on empirical evidence. Thus clinicians inherited and assumed an unjustified reputation for having the ability to predict future dangerous behavior (Pollock, 1990). The legal community, the courts, legislators, and society in general all appear to believe that mental health professionals, on the basis of their training and experience, have the special technical knowledge necessary to assess dangerousness and have charged them with that responsibility (Cocozza & Steadman, 1978). Thus the *Tarasoff* decision rests upon an existing assumption that mental health professionals have the expertise and unique skills to predict the dangerous behavior of their patients (Dix, 1983).

Unfortunately, the judicial system has ignored a large body of psychological research that demonstrates the high level of inaccuracy of mental health professionals in predictions of dangerousness (Beigler, 1984; Ewing, 1991; Monahan, 1981). In 1974, the American Psychiatric Association established a task force that determined that psychiatrists had not reliably demonstrated any ability to predict future violence and thus had not manifested psychiatric expertise in that area. Ironically, these findings were made public just prior to the *Tarasoff I* ruling

(Carlson, Friedman, & Riggert, 1987). Data indicate that attempts to predict future dangerousness have an accuracy outcome of less than 50% (Miller et al., 1988). Mental health professionals make about two erroneous predictions for every correct prediction of violence by their patients (Oppenheimer & Swanson, 1990). Other writers have elaborated on the inaccuracy of predictions of dangerousness, as demonstrated by subsequent acts of violence (Beck, 1987a; Cocozza & Steadman, 1978; Knapp, VandeCreek, & Shapiro, 1990; Oppenheimer & Swanson, 1990; Stromberg, Schneider, & Joondeph, 1993). Still, their relative inability to predict notwithstanding, mental health professionals still have standards of care to assess dangerousness. However, the *Tarasoff II* court emphasized that it required non-negligent behavior rather than a perfect performance from mental health professionals (Kaufman, 1991).

Foreseeability. The *Tarasoff* court ruled that the peril must be foreseeable and the victim identifiable (Southard & Gross, 1982); thus foreseeability determines duty to protect (Slovenko, 1988). In the wake of *Tarasoff*, Mills (1984) performed an analysis of subsequent cases and determined that most of the cases rested on the issue of foreseeability. Within this domain, the psychotherapist must determine if the threat is serious and if the potential harm is both imminent and serious (Slovenko, 1988). Foreseeability of danger in the form of violence has three accepted criteria: (a) a history of violence, (b) threats in regard to a specific person, and (c) an apparent motive (Beck, 1987b; Beck, 1990b; Matflerd, 1992). Danger can be categorized as *clearly foreseeable* if the patient meets two of the three conditions, as *questionably foreseeable* if the patient meets only one criterion, and as *unforeseeable* if none of the criteria are met (Beck, 1987b).

Identifiable victim. The psychotherapist has no requirement to interrogate a patient or to conduct a special investigation to determine the victim's identity (Lamb et al., 1989), but is required to exercise "a moment's reflection" which may inadvertently reveal the victim's identity (Fulero, 1988). Once the therapist determines, or should have determined, a foreseeable victim of danger, the therapist is liable for exercising reasonable care to protect that potential victim.

Standards of reasonable care. Although the *Tarasoff I* ruling exempted the campus police from potential liability, it provided a standard of "reasonable care" against which the obligations of psychologists and psychiatrists would be measured in similar cases (Gross & Robinson, 1987). *Tarasoff II* (1976) set forth the principle that when a therapist determines, or pursuant to the standards of his profession should determine, that his patient presents a serious danger of violence to another, he incurs a serious obligation to use reasonable care to protect the intended victim from such danger. This principle has since become a national standard for psychiatric practice (Beck, 1987a). Even though the undefined, nebulous term "reasonable care" has not been operationalized, it exists to establish liability rather than to provide a definitive guideline.

A legal obligation exists when a psychotherapist knows, or should have known, the patient poses a serious threat to another person. If the psychotherapist fails to take appropriate steps to avert the foreseeable danger, and that patient subsequently harms someone, liability may be found (Southard & Gross, 1982). Malpractice, or professional negligence, can result in liability if a psychotherapist, by negligent acts of commission *or* omission, fails to meet the minimal standards of care in exercising a court-recognized duty and his or her negligence results in injury to another person (Crocker, 1985; Eberlein, 1980; Kamenar, 1984; VandeCreek, Knapp, & Herzog, 1987).

To determine the existence of professional negligence, the law asks the following questions: (1) Was a duty of care owed? (2) If so, what was the duty? (3) Was the duty of care breached? (4) Did damages result? and (5) Were the damages "proximately caused" by the professional's act or omission? Duty of care is a legal term used to denote a special relationship inferred by the law between two or more parties, based on a specific fact pattern. Duties of care arise and lapse as people move through their daily lives. For example, the driver of a car owes a duty of care to passengers and to certain other road users. The operator of a supermarket owes a duty of care to shoppers. Once a special relationship and the resulting duty of care has been established, the court must then determine: "But for the actions of the defendant, would the plaintiff have been injured?" and "Was this type of injury foreseeable?" Once duty of care questions have been answered, questions of reasonableness must then be resolved.

The use of reasonable care in the therapy relationship means, "what a professional with comparable training and experience in the same community would have done when faced with a similar situation" (Mills et al., 1987, p. 72). If injury to a victim occurs, the adequacy of the therapist's conduct is measured against the traditional negligence standard of reasonable care under the circumstances (Crocker, 1985). Judicial inquiry considers the foreseeability of harm to the victim and measures the psychotherapist's judgment and conduct against the reasonable degree of skill, knowledge, and care ordinarily exercised by other members of the same professional speciality (Fulero, 1988; Mills et al., 1987; Slovenko, 1988).

The legal determination of the accepted standard of care rests on the test of reasonableness (VandeCreek et al., 1987). When a recognized conventional therapeutic practice already exists, the standard of care for that practice suffices (Mills, 1984). However, certain situations have no reliable, clinically-validated paradigms (e.g., the prediction of violent behavior); thus no standard convention exists, and the interventions vary among psychotherapists (Mills, 1984; Simon, 1990). A standard of care can be established by consulting several appropriate and expert mental health professionals from the particular community in which the case arises (Erickson, 1993).

SUBSEQUENT CASES

As of 1990, over 70 published legal cases have involved mental health professionals and facilities named as defendants in suits regarding breach of the duty to protect (Beck, 1990a). The *Tarasoff* decisions have tipped the scales in favor of the protection of society rather than toward the preservation of absolute confidentiality (Cohn, 1983). Since the original *Tarasoff* holdings in California, courts across the land have not consistently interpreted, applied, or accepted a universal definition of when and how the duty to protect arises and when it has been discharged (Greenberg, 1984; Kermani & Drob, 1987; Knapp et al., 1990; Searight & Pound, 1994). States in which *Tarasoff*-type cases have come to trial have responded by either expanding, restricting, or rejecting the *Tarasoff* doctrine, both by court rulings and by statute.

Duty varies by court rulings. Gradually the *Tarasoff* duty to protect has gained prominence in the legal and psychiatric communities (Goodman, 1985) and provoked a trend toward acceptance as a public policy (Mills et al., 1987). The second major decision that imposed a duty to warn was rendered in New Jersey in 1979 with the case of *McIntosh v. Milano* (Fulero, 1988; Kamenar, 1984). Like the *Tarasoff* case, it too involved a dangerous outpatient. Lee Morgenstein, a drug user, admitted to his therapist, Dr. Milano, that he was having fantasies about his neighbor, Kimberly McIntosh, and was engaged in stalking her. In therapy, Morgenstein also made threats against Kimberly and her boyfriends. Dr. Milano talked to the boy's parents several times but never warned Kimberly or her parents. Morgenstein subsequently induced

Kimberly to go with him to a local park where he shot her in the back and killed her (Beck, 1987b; Gehring, 1982; Kamenar, Kermani & Drob, 1987; Shapiro, 1983; VandeCreek & Knapp, 1989). In the *McIntosh* case, the duty to protect by warning the victim overrode the duty to maintain the patient's confidentiality (Greenberg, 1984).

As its acceptance grew, the *Tarasoff* doctrine spread across the country. Some jurisdictions interpreted the scope of *Tarasoff* in much broader terms (Beigler, 1984; Dickens, 1988; Kermani & Drob, 1987; Miller, 1986) and increased the frontiers of liability for psychotherapists (Meyers, 1984). Other jurisdictions restricted the duty and thus the potential for liability.

Using *Tarasoff* as a precedent, the court in *Bellah v. Greenson* (1977; see Goodman, 1985; Meyers, 1984; Mills, 1984; Southard & Gross, 1982) accepted the *Tarasoff* premise in 1977, but narrowed the duty by exempting California psychiatrists from liability for failure to warn others of their patients' suicidal tendencies and from liability for property damage when a young female patient committed suicide while in therapy. On the other hand, in the case of *Peck v. Counseling Service of Addison County* (1985), the Vermont Supreme Court extended the *Tarasoff* duty to encompass *all* mental health professionals and extended their liability to include property damage, under certain circumstances (Fulero, 1988; Stone, 1986). John Peck, a 31-year-old alcoholic outpatient with temporal lobe epilepsy, threatened to burn down his father's barn. However, when he promised his counselor that he would not carry out his threat, his counselor did not alert her supervisor or the patient's father of the threats (Beck, 1987b; Fulero, 1988; Matflerd, 1992). The therapist, who held an M.A. in educational psychology, was held to the same professional standard established for the court by the expert testimony of a psychiatrist.

Cases that have broadened the *Tarasoff* doctrine do not reflect the statistical reality of mental health professionals' lack of reliable predictions (Kaufman, 1991). In *Mavroudis v. Superior Court for County of San Mateo* (1980; Kermani & Drob, 1987), the court ruled in 1980 that for the *Tarasoff* duty to exist, the danger posed by the patient must be imminent, and the victim readily-identifiable (Fulero, 1988; Meyer et al., 1988; Southard & Gross, 1982). Upon his release from an institution, a psychiatric inpatient beat his parents, who had not been warned that he posed a danger to them (Southard & Gross, 1982). The court ruled that disclosures about the patient are not required if the patient does not pose an imminent threat to an identifiable victim (Kermani &

Drob, 1987). The court also found no need to interrogate or conduct a special investigation to determine the victim's identity.

John Patterson was released from the state hospital into the custody of his mother. Two months later, during a scuffle with her, he accidentally shot and killed his mother. Patterson's psychiatrist was found negligent for not having read an emergency room notation from two years prior to the shooting during which time Patterson was said to have paced the floor and threatened his mother for money (Beck, 1987b; Kermani & Drob, 1987; VandeCreek & Knapp, 1989). The Patterson case, called *Davis v. Lhim* (1983; see Fulero, 1988), resulted in a decision that accepted the basic *Tarasoff* duty to protect as applied to a readily identifiable victim but extended liability to include the actions of a patient who had no history of violence and did not appear to represent an *imminent* threat to his victim at the time of his release.

Some decisions have extended the domain of *Tarasoff* to include a duty to protect unidentifiable victims of patients who have not even communicated a threat of violence. The case of *Jablonski by Pahls v. United States* (1983) illustrates the beginning of a trend toward a stricter standard of liability for psychotherapists. Jablonski killed his common-law wife, Melinda Kimball, while in outpatient treatment at the VA. Jablonski had refused to reveal the location of his previous psychiatric treatment and to release his medical records. The psychiatrists advised Jablonski to commit himself voluntarily and advised Melinda to leave him during his evaluation (Appelbaum, 1984; Beck, 1987b; Kamenar, 1984; Slovenko, 1988; Sonkin, 1986). However, a federal court found that an affirmative duty to warn had existed and upheld liability even though the patient had not verbalized threats against anyone, let alone against a specific individual (Fulero, 1988; George, 1985; Kamenar, 1984; Slovenko, 1988).

Another case that extended *Tarasoff* came about when Ulysses "Butch" Cribbs, Jr., a VA outpatient, bought a gun at Sears, and three weeks later opened fire at a Thanksgiving show for children in an Omaha nightclub. Cribbs had not made threats against anyone, nor did he display signs of dangerousness during therapy (see Goldman & Jacob, 1991; Kermani & Drob, 1987; Slovenko, 1988). A Nebraska court, in *Lipari v. Sears, Roebuck & Company* (1980; see Beck, 1987b; Mills, 1984) ruled that the *Tarasoff* doctrine would be applied even when a specific victim was not known and the potential threat was to an unknown class of people. In neither case had the patient voiced any threats to their psychotherapists.

One of the most provocative expansion rulings occurred in *Hedlund v. Orange County* (1983) in which a California court held that the duty to pro-

tect extended to a child through the mother (Fulero, 1988). Two psychotherapists were found negligent for failure to warn LaNita Wilson of threats
their patient made against her. When the patient shot LaNita, her minor
son, Darryl, was seated next to her and witnessed the traumatic incident
(George, 1985; Slovenko, 1988; Sonkin, 1986; VandeCreek & Knapp,
1989). The psychotherapists were held liable for emotional injury to a
fourth party who acquired third-party status, and the concomitant right to
protection, as an extension of his mother's third-party right to protection.

On the other hand, in *Thompson v. County of Alameda* (1980), another California court ruled that the *Tarasoff* decision did not apply to
nonspecific threats made against nonspecified persons (Gross & Robinson, 1987; Kamenar, 1984; Mills, 1984). James F., a juvenile molester,
killed a neighborhood child within 24 hours of his release into the custody of his mother, even after having clearly stated his intention to kill
his next molestation victim (Beck, 1987b; George, 1985; Kermani &
Drob, 1987; Meyers, 1987; Slovenko, 1988; Southard & Gross, 1982).
Ironically, the *Thompson* decision that the victim must be identifiable
and the danger must be foreseeable had been rendered by the California
Supreme Court only three days before that same court rendered the almost opposite *Lipari* decision. In a similar vein, other suits have also restricted the *Tarasoff* doctrine that limits psychotherapist liability for
harm caused by their patients (Kaufman, 1991).

In *Brady v. Hopper* (1983), a Colorado court interpreted the duty as
applicable only when the therapist has privileged information of a serious threat directed at a specific, identifiable person (Fulero, 1988;
Kermani & Drob, 1987). Dr. John J. Hopper, a Colorado psychiatrist,
treated John W. Hinckley, Jr., the would-be assassin of President Rea-
gan. Hinckley had made no specific threats of violence, had no history
of violence, and exhibited no warning signs of dangerousness (Goodman, 1985; Kermani & Drob, 1987). The *Brady* court refused to extend
the *Tarasoff* doctrine in this case (Kermani & Drob, 1987; Slovenko,
1988; VandeCreek & Knapp, 1989) and limited the duty to protect as
applicable only to specific threats made against specific victims.

Since *Tarasoff*, most courts have found that a duty to protect third
parties exists as a matter of law; however, Beck (1987b) has found no
clear fact pattern or legal theory that distinguishes cases well enough to
predict the outcome of court decisions to impose *Tarasoff* liability from
those that did not impose liability. The duty to protect remains subject to
judicial interpretation on a case-by-case basis. Thus, the variability of

the existing court decisions obfuscates rather than clarifies matters for mental health professionals (Lane & Spruill, 1980, p. 204).

Statutory approaches. The *Tarasoff* case itself applied only in California. Both "duty to protect" laws and confidentiality requirements are imposed by the individual states and not by federal legislation or federal trial law. Thus, specific laws vary from state to state, and the relative balance between confidentiality and duty to protect also varies from jurisdiction to jurisdiction (Zeiss, 1995; Fulero, 1988, 1992). In many states, as subsequent cases have defined the legal duty of mental health professionals toward the potential victims of their patients, there have been statutes enacted to specify the parameters of the duty, and methods to discharge it.

Duty to protect statutes have been passed in California, Colorado, Illinois, Indiana, Kentucky, Louisiana, Maryland, Massachusetts, Minnesota, Montana, New Hampshire, New Jersey, Ohio, and Utah, thus far. They permit discharge of the duty by warning the intended victim or by notifying the police. Seven of these states consider the duty discharged when the mental health professional seeks involuntary commitment for the threatening patient. Kentucky and Ohio mental health professionals can satisfy their duty to protect by notifying the police if the threat is not to an identifiable person. In addition to warning the intended victim or notifying the police, Colorado also allows the duty to be discharged through "other appropriate action." On the other hand, mental health professionals in Minnesota can contact law enforcement authorities only if they were unable to contact the potential victim (Knapp et al., 1990, p. 294).

Florida, New York, and Tennessee have enacted statutes that grant immunity to therapists from breach-of-confidentiality suits based on having warned an identifiable victim of a patient's threats. Whereas these statutes permit psychologists to warn intended victims, they do not *require* protective actions by therapists (Stromberg et al., 1993). Illinois also has a privileged communication act, which allows mental health professionals to breach confidentiality without incurring liability (Gray & Harding, 1988). On the other hand, Maryland and Texas have statutes that do not allow mental health professionals to breach confidentiality to warn potential victims, even when their lives are at risk (Gray & Harding, 1988; Knapp & VandeCreek, 1982).

CONCLUSION

In summary, states and legal jurisdictions have exhibited significant variability in their response to Tarasoff. This has resulted in a plethora of interpretations of the *Tarasoff* doctrine, which has confused many mental health professionals about legal issues relevant to their duty to protect third parties as well as about the confidentiality issues of their patients. In the practice of psychotherapy, most mental health professionals will encounter at least one patient who represents a danger to others. *Tarasoff* legislation and litigation will continue to affect clinical practice for many years to come (Pietrofesa, Pietrofesa, & Pietrofesa, 1990), but no one universal law clearly articulates the duty to protect. The variability of the parameters of the duty to protect and the permutations of the legal requirements for discharging that duty underscores the need for mental health professionals to have an awareness of the legal onus peculiar to their own geographic location. Without adequate knowledge of their specific legal requirements, either by case law or statute, mental health professionals will not be able to satisfy either their legal or their ethical obligations.

REFERENCES

Appelbaum, P. S. (1984). The expansion of liability for patients' violent acts. *Hospital and Community Psychiatry, 35*(1), 13-14.

Appelbaum, K., & Appelbaum, P. S. (1990). The HIV antibody-positive patient. In J. C. Beck (Ed.), *Confidentiality versus the duty to protect: Foreseeable harm in the practice of psychiatry* (pp. 121-140). Washington, DC: American Psychiatric Press, Inc.

Beck, J. C. (1987a). The potentially violent patient: Legal duties, clinical practice, and risk management. *Psychiatric Annals, 17*(10), 695-699.

Beck, J. C. (1987b). The psychotherapist's duty to protect third parties from harm. *Mental & Physical Disability Law Reporter, II*(2), 141-148.

Beck, J. C. (1990a). The basic issues. In J. C. Beck (Ed.), *Confidentiality versus the duty to protect: Foreseeable harm in the practice of psychiatry* (pp. 1-8). Washington, DC: American Psychiatric Press, Inc.

Beck, J. C. (1990b). Current status of the duty to protect. In J. C. Beck (Ed.), *Confidentiality versus the duty to protect: Foreseeable harm in the practice of psychiatry* (pp. 9-21). Washington, DC: American Psychiatric Press, Inc.

Beigler, J. S. (1984). Tarasoff v. confidentiality. *Behavioral Sciences and the Law, 2*(3), 273-289.

Bellah v. Greenson, 81 Cal.App.3d 614, 141 Cal.Rptr. 92 (1977).

Brady v. Hopper, 570 F.Supp. 1333 (D.Colo. 1983).

Carlson, R. J., Friedman, L. C., & Riggert, S. C. (1987). The duty to warn/protect: Issues in clinical practice. *Bulletin of the American Academy of Psychiatry and the Law, 15*(2), 179-186.

Cocozza, J. J., & Steadman, H. J. (1978). Prediction in psychiatry–An example of misplaced confidence in experts. *Social Problems, 25*(3), 265-276.

Cohn, J. B. (1983). Harm to third parties in psychotherapy. *American Journal of Forensic Psychology, 1*(2), 15-18.
Crocker, E. M. (1985). Judicial expansion of the Tarasoff doctrine. Doctors' dilemma. *The Journal of Psychiatry and Law, 13*(1-2), 83-99.
Davis v. Lhim, 335 N.W.2d 481 (Mich.Ct.App. 1983).
Denkowski, K. M., & Denkowski, G. C. (1982). Client-counselor confidentiality an update of rationale, legal status, and implications. *The Personnel and Guidance Journal, 60*(6), 371-375.
Dickens, B. M. (1988). Legal limits of AIDS confidentiality. *Journal of the American Medical Association, 259*(23), 3449-3451.
Dix, G. E. (1983). A legal perspective on dangerousness: Current status. *Psychiatric Annals, 13*(3), 243, 247, 251, 255, 256.
Eberlein, L. (1980). Legal duty and confidentiality of psychologists–Tarasoff and Haines. *Canadian Psychology, 21*(2), 49-58.
Erickson, S. H. (1993). Ethics and confidentiality in AIDS counseling: A professional dilemma. *Journal of Mental Health Counseling, 15*(2), 118-131.
Everstine, L., Everstine, D. S., Heymann, G. M., True, R. H., Frey, D. H., Johnson, H. G., et al. (1980). Privacy and confidentiality in psychotherapy. *American Psychologist, 9*, 828-840.
Ewing, C. P. (1991). Preventive detention and execution. The constitutionality of punishing future crimes. *Law and Human Behavior, 15*(2), 139-163.
Fulero, S. M. (1988). Tarasoff–10 years later. *Professional Psychology: Research and Practice, 19*(2), 184-190.
Fulero, S. M. (1992). Recent developments in the duty to protect. *Psychotherapy in Private Practice, 10*(1-2), 33-43.
Gehring, D. D. (1982). The counselor's "duty to warn." *The Personnel and Guidance Journal, 6-1*(4), 208-210.
George, J. C. (1985). Hedlund paranoia. *Journal of Clinical Psychology, 41*(2), 291-294.
Goldman, D. L., & Jacob, T. (1991). Anatomy of a second generation Tarasoff case. *Canadian Journal of Psychiatry, 36*(1), 35-38.
Goodman, T. A. (1985). From Tarasoff to Hopper: The evolution of the therapist's duty to protect third parties. *Behavioral Sciences and the Law, 3*(2), 195-225.
Gray, L. A., & Harding, A. K. (1988). Confidentiality limits with clients who have the AIDS virus. *Journal of Counseling, and Development, 66*(5), 219-223.
Greenberg, L. T. (1984). The evolution of *Tarasoff*. Recent developments in the psychiatrist's duties to warn potential victims, protect the public, and predict dangerousness. *The Journal of Psychiatry and Law, 12*(3), 315-348.
Gross, D. R., & Robinson, S. E. (1987). Ethics, violence, and counseling: Hear no evil, see no evil, speak no evil? *Journal of Counseling and Development, 65*(7), 340-344.
Gurevitz, H. (1977). Tarasoff. Protective privilege versus public peril. *American Journal of Psychiatry, 134*(3), 289-292.
Hedlund v. Orange County, 669 P.2d 41 (Cal. 1983).
Jablonski by Pahls v. United States, 712 F.2d 391 (9th Cir. 1983).
Kamenar, P. D. (1984). Psychiatrists' duty to warn of a dangerous patient. A survey of the law. *Behavioral Sciences and the Law, 2*(3), 348-350.

Kaufman, M. (1991). Post-Tarasoff legal developments and the mental health literature. *Bulletin of the Menninger Clinic, 55*(3), 308-322.

Kermani, E. J., & Drob S. L. (1987). Tarasoff decision. A decade later dilemma still faces psychotherapists. *American Journal of Psychotherapy, 41*(2), 271-285.

Knapp, S., & VandeCreek, L. (1982). Tarasoff, Five years later. *Professional Psychology, 13*(4), 511-516.

Knapp, S., VandeCreek, L., & Shapiro, D. (1990). Statutory remedies to the duty to protect: A reconsideration. *Psychotherapy, 27*(2), 291-296.

Lamb, D. H., Clark, C., Drumheller, P., Frizzell, K., & Surrey, L. (1989). Applying *Tarasoff* to AIDS-related psychotherapy issues. *Professional Psychology: Research and Practice, 20*(l), 37-43.

Lane, P. J., & Spruill, J. (1980). To tell or not to tell: The psychotherapist's dilemma. *Psychotherapy: Theory, Research, and Practice, 17*(2), 202-209.

Lanterman-Petris-Short Act, Cal. Welf. & Inst. § ?5000 *et. seq.* (1969).

Lipari v. Sears, Roebuck & Co., 479 F.Supp. 185 (D.Neb. 1980).

Matflerd, C. (1992). The aftermath of *Tarasoff.* A review of the duty to protect or warn. *Carrier Foundation Medical Education Letter, 174,* 1-5.

Mavroudis v. Superior Court of San Mateo County, 102 Cal. App. 3d 594 (1980).

McIntosh v. Milano, 168 N.J. Supr. 466, 403 A.2d 500 (N.J. Supr.Ct. 1979).

Meyer, R. G., Landis, E. R., & Hays, J. R. (1988). *Law for the psychotherapist.* New York: W. W. Norton & Company.

Meyers, C. J. (1984). The legal perils of psychotherapeutic practice (Part II): Coping with *Hedlund and Jablonski. The Journal of Psychiatry and Law, 12*(l), 39-47.

Meyers, C. J. (1987). Hard cases: The "duty to warn" as a felt necessity of our time. *The Journal of Psychiatry and Law, 12*(l), 39-47.

Miller, R. D. (1986). *Currie v. United States: Tarasoff* comes South. *Mental and Physical Disability Law Reporter, 10*(6), 577, 605.

Miller, R. D., Doren, D. M., VanRybroek, G., & Maier, G. J. (1988). Emerging problems for staff associated with the release of potentially dangerous forensic patients. *Bulletin of the American Academy of Psychiatry and the Law, 16*(4), 309-320.

Mills, M. J. (1984). The so-called duty to warn: The psychotherapeutic duty to protect third parties from patients' violent acts. *Behavioral Sciences and the Law, 2*(3), 237-257.

Mills, M. J., Sullivan, G., & Eth, S. (1987). Protecting third parties: A decade after Tarasoff. *American Journal of Psychiatry, 144*(l), 68-74.

Monahan, J. (1981). *The clinical prediction of violence.* Beverly Hills, CA: Sage.

Oldham, J. T. (1978). Liability of therapists to non-patients. *Journal of Clinical Child Psychology, 7*(3), 187-188.

Oppenheimer, K., & Swanson, G. (1990). Duty to warn: When should confidentiality be breached? *The Journal of Family Practice, 30*(2), 179-184.

Peck v. Counseling Service of Addison County, 499 A.2d 422 (Vt. 1985).

People v. Poddar, 103 Cal.Rptr. 84 (1972).

People v. Poddar, 518 P.2d 342 (Cal. 1974).

Pietrofesa, J. J., Pietrofesa, C. J., & Pietrofesa, J. D. (1990). The mental health counselor and "duty to warn." *Journal of Mental Health Counseling, 12*(2), 129-137.

Pollock, N. L. (1990). Accounting for predictions of dangerousness. *International Journal of Law and Psychiatry, 13*(3), 207-215.

Pollack, S., Gross, B. H., & Weinberger, L. E. (1982). The concept of dangerousness for legal purposes. In B. H. Gross, & L. E. Weinberger (Eds.), *New directions for mental health services: The mental health professional and the legal system, 16*. San Francisco: Jossey-Bass.

Quinn, K. M. (1984). The impact of Tarasoff on clinical practice. *Behavioral Sciences and the Law, 2*(3), 319-329.

Roth, L. H., & Meisel, A. (1977). Dangerousness, confidentiality, and the duty to warn. *American Journal of Psychiatry, 134*(5), 508-511.

Runck, B. (1984). Survey shows therapists misunderstand Tarasoff rule. *Hospital and Community Psychiatry, 35*(5), 429-430.

Schroeder, L. O. (1979). Legal liability–A professional concern. *Clinical Social Work Journal, 7*(3), 194-199.

Schwartz, D. W. (1985). The obligation to assess dangerousness. *New York State Journal of Medicine, 85*(2), 67-68.

Searight, H. R., & Pound, P. (1994). The HIV-positive psychiatric patient and the duty to protect: Ethical and legal issues. *International Journal of Psychiatry in Medicine, 24*(3), 259-270.

Simon, R. I. (1990). The duty to protect in private practice. In J. D. Beck (Ed.), *Confidentiality versus the duty to protect: Foreseeable harm in the practice of psychiatry* (pp. 23-41). Washington, DC: American Psychiatric Press, Inc.

Slovenko, R. (1988). Commentary: The therapist's duty to warn or protect third persons. *The Journal of Psychiatry and Law, 16*(1), 139-209.

Sonkin, D. J. (1986). Clairvoyance vs. common sense: Therapist's duty to warn and protect. *Victims and Violence, 1*(1), 7-22.

Southard, M. J., & Gross, B. H. (1982). Making clinical decisions after Tarasoff. *New Directions for Mental Health Services, 16*, 93-101.

Stone, A. A. (1986). Vermont adopts Tarasoff: A real barn-burner. *American Journal of Psychiatry, 143*(3), 352-355.

Stromberg, C., Schneider, J., & Joondeph, B. (1993). Dealing with potentially dangerous patients. *The Psychologist's Legal Update, 2*, 1-12.

Tarasoff v. Regents of the University of California, 13 Cal. 3d 117, 529 P.2d 533, 118 Cal. Rptr. 129 (1974). (Tarasoff I).

Tarasoff v. Regents of the University of California, 17 Cal. 3d 425, 551 P.2d 334, 131 Cal Rptr. 14 (1976). (Tarasoff II).

Thompson v. County of Alameda, 167 Cal.Rptr. 70 (1980).

VandeCreek, L., & Knapp, S. (1989). *Tarasoff and beyond: Legal and clinical considerations in the treatment of life-endangering patients*. Sarasota, FL: Professional Resource Press.

VandeCreek, L., Knapp, S., & Herzog, C. (1987). Malpractice risks in the treatment of dangerous patients. *Psychotherapy, 24*(2), 145-153.

Weinstock, M. D., & Weinstock, D. (1989). Clinical flexibility and confidentiality. Effects of reporting laws. *Psychiatric Quarterly, 60*(3), 195-214.

Zeiss, R. A. (1995). Ethical and legal responsibilities with sero-positive HIV clients. *The Behavior Therapist, 18*(10), 197-199.

GENERAL ETHICAL STANDARDS
IN PRACTICE

Misuse of Psychologist Influence:
Multiple Relationships

Clark R. Clipson

SUMMARY. In no other area of professional ethics must psychologists rely on their own judgment than in the area of multiple relationships. Yet ironically, because of the wide variety of types and possible outcomes in dual relationships and boundary crossings, psychologists are given less guidance in this area of ethical decision-making than in any other. As a result, psychologists' emotional conflicts and personal needs are more likely to interfere with their judgment in this area. This article will review important dynamics of multiple relationships and boundary violations,

Address correspondence to: Clark R. Clipson, PhD, 3921 Goldfinch Street, San Diego, CA 92103 (E-mail: clarkclipson@hotmail.com).

[Haworth co-indexing entry note]: "Misuse of Psychologist Influence: Multiple Relationships." Clipson, Clark R. Co-published simultaneously in *Journal of Aggression, Maltreatment & Trauma* (The Haworth Maltreatment & Trauma Press, an imprint of The Haworth Press, Inc.) Vol. 11, No. 1/2, 2005, pp. 169-203; and: *Ethical and Legal Issues for Mental Health Professionals: A Comprehensive Handbook of Principles and Standards* (ed: Steven F. Bucky, Joanne E. Callan, and George Stricker) The Haworth Maltreatment & Trauma Press, an imprint of The Haworth Press, Inc., 2005, pp. 169-203. Single or multiple copies of this article are available for a fee from The Haworth Document Delivery Service [1-800-HAWORTH, 9:00 a.m. - 5:00 p.m. (EST). E-mail address: docdelivery@haworthpress.com].

Digital Object Identifier: 10.1300/J146v11n01_13

while also providing a model for assisting psychologists in avoiding exploitive or harmful dual relationships. *[Article copies available for a fee from The Haworth Document Delivery Service: 1-800-HAWORTH. E-mail address: <docdelivery@haworthpress.com> Website: <http://www.HaworthPress.com>* © 2005 by The Haworth Press, Inc. All rights reserved.]*

KEYWORDS. Ethics, multiple relationships, dual relationships, professional boundaries

Multiple, or dual, relationships occur any time a psychologist interacts professionally with another person in more than one capacity (Bennett, Bryant, VandenBos, & Greenwood, 1990). Such relationships may involve mixing a professional role (e.g., therapist, evaluator, supervisor, teacher, researcher) with a non-professional role (e.g., friend, lover, business partner, relative), or juxtaposing two professional roles (i.e., therapist and supervisor, therapist and student). These roles may occur concurrently or sequentially. Sometimes a dual relationship may exist in a more subtle fashion when a psychologist steps outside the boundaries of the professional role.

Multiple relationships are not prohibited in the current version of the American Psychological Association's (APA) *Ethical Principles of Psychologists and Code of Conduct* (2002), hereafter referred to as the Ethics Code. Indeed, many types of multiple relationships cannot be avoided and some may even be sought out. Not all are inherently harmful, and some are extremely beneficial to both participants. Even so, all multiple relationships provide fertile ground for problems to arise, and most psychologists believe that multiple relationships must either be approached with caution or avoided altogether (Kitchener, 1988).

Because not all dual relationships are harmful, because of the wide diversity in types of dual relationships, and because of the limited research base in this area, psychologists are given little guidance in how to navigate blurred boundaries or multiple roles in the ethics literature. Legal and regulatory guidelines are vaguely written or non-existent, and psychologists complain that the Ethics Code does not adequately address these issues (Pope & Vetter, 1992). As a result, professionals must rely on their own judgement more in this area of their professional conduct than in any other. Under such circumstances, psychologists are prone to commit errors in judgement more often in this area than in areas where there are more explicit guidelines available. Indeed, violations in the area of dual relationships, including sexual intimacies with clients, make up the majority of disciplinary actions by state licensing boards, the most frequent type of complaint to ethics committees, and result in the largest financial losses in malpractice suits (Pope & Vasquez, 1991). As a result, there is little wonder that the profession, as well as the public, is starting to sit up and take notice.

MULTIPLE RELATIONSHIPS IN THE APA'S CODE OF ETHICS

Historically, interest in dual relationships began with those involving sexual relations between psychologists and their clients, students, and supervisees. As the APA's Ethics Code has developed over the years, there has been increasing attention devoted to the explicit prohibition against these types of sexual dual relationships (see Ethics Code Sections 3.05, 10.05, 10.06, 10.07, and 10.08). More recently, there has been increased attention focused on non-sexual multiple relationships, both in the Ethics Code and in the literature. Dual relationships involving sexual behavior will not be discussed in this chapter as they are addressed in depth elsewhere (see Shavit, this volume), as is a discussion of bartering (see Gandolfo, this volume).

The primary reference to multiple relationships in the Ethics Code is found in Section 3.05(a):

> A multiple relationship occurs when a psychologist is in a professional role with a person and (1) at the same time is in another role with the same person, (2) at the same time is in a relationship with a person closely associated with or related to the person with whom the psychologist has the professional relationship, or (3) promises to enter into another relationship in the future with the person or a person closely associated with or related to the person. A psychologist refrains from entering into a multiple relationship if the multiple relationship could reasonably be expected to impair the psychologist's objectivity, competence, or effectiveness in performing his or her functions as a psychologist, or otherwise risks exploitation or harm to the person with whom the professional relationship exists. Multiple relationships that would not reasonably be expected to cause impairment or risk exploitation or harm are not unethical.

This passage echoes themes found elsewhere in the Ethics Code, including the injunction that psychologists "take reasonable steps to avoid harming" others (Section 3.04) and that they "do not exploit persons over whom they have supervisory, evaluative or other authority" (Section 3.08).

From this excerpt it is clear that dual or multiple relationships are not prohibited. Indeed, there is acknowledgement that avoiding such relationships is both impossible, and perhaps even undesirable in some instances. For example, a colleague working with a Native American population felt he would not be accepted as a potential therapist to this community were he not to deliberately engage in multiple relationships by participating in community events such as pow-wows and round-ups (R. Morton, personal communication, November 14, 1993). Other writers addressing ethical issues related to rural or other ethnic populations similarly discuss the frequent inevitability or need for the psychologist to participate in a dual relationship (Barnett & Yutrzenka, 1993; Haas & Malouf, 1989).

With not all non-sexual multiple relationships being prohibited, the Ethics Code goes on to warn against psychologists forming relationships that appear "likely" or "reasonably might" lead to problems. It is at this point that errors in the individual psychologist's judgement can impair their evaluation of the likelihood or reasonableness that entering into a new role with another person could lead to problems. These errors in judgement are most likely to arise out of the psychologist's own unexamined needs or countertransference reactions to the other person (Tansey & Burke, 1989).

The Ethics Code identifies four potential risks of psychologists forming multiple non-sexual dual relationships. These include impaired objectivity, interference with the psychologist's professional performance, harm to the other party, and exploitation of the other party. With the first two risks, a psychologist's effectiveness is compromised. It is difficult to confront a client if the therapist is hoping to form a friendship after the conclusion of therapy. An evaluator's conclusions may be influenced if there is a possibility that the person being assessed will become their client. When a psychologist is not free to say what needs to be said in the best interest of the client, supervisee, or student, everyone loses. The psychologist loses a sense of integrity and the opportunity to offer potentially important information to the other person, while the other person is left with a diluted experience.

With the latter two risks, the other person's well-being is compromised. When a psychology graduate student is not passed to candidacy because of something their professor/therapist learned about them in therapy, a professional career is unfairly jeopardized. When a therapist asks a client for a favor, the client's sense of trust is damaged: whose needs are being met in this relationship? The harm to those damaged by exploitive dual relationships can include difficulties with trust, feelings of loss and anger, guilt, depression or anxiety, diminished self-esteem, emptiness, isolation, and even disturbances of identity (Peterson, 1992; Pope & Bouhoutsos, 1986).

The 1992 Ethics Code introduced a new element, in that not only is entering into a harmful dual relationship prohibited, but also even *promising* such a relationship in the future is advised against. The promise itself is understood as being sufficient in some cases to compromise a psychologist's effectiveness or to endanger the well-being of another. Focusing on the attainment of the new relationship may result in the sacrifice of the original goals shared by the participants (Canter, Bennett, Jones, & Nagy, 1994). For example, both therapist and client may compromise their honesty if they believed a social relationship would ensue after termination.

Canter et al. (1994) point out that the rule against promising a future relationship does not prevent the psychologist from explaining the rule to another person. However, they caution the psychologist not to mislead the other person into believing that having a different kind of relationship is a shared goal. They also warn the psychologist of the possibility of the other person misunderstanding the psychologist's intentions, as it may be easy to see the psychologist's explanation as a veiled message that a future relationship is indeed a possibility.

In Section 3.06 of the 2002 version of the APA Ethics Code, we see that, "Psychologists refrain from taking on a professional role when personal, scientific, professional, legal, financial, or other interests or relationships could reasonably be expected to (1) impair their objectivity, competence, or effectiveness in performing their functions as psychologists or (2) expose the person or organization with whom the professional relationship exists to harm or exploitation." As the first part of this section advises against entering into another type of relationship if a professional relationship existed first, this section asserts that a professional relationship may be inappropriate if any other type of relationship was pre-existent. It is the professional (especially a therapeutic) relationship that is understood to be of primary importance, as it carries the greatest risk of harm or exploitation. However, the authors of the Ethics Code recognize that it may not always be possible or necessary to avoid entering into such a dual relationship. Again, such a decision is left to the judgement of the psychologist, with all the inherent risks and responsibilities.

The Ethics Code by itself will probably never contain sufficient guidance to professionals struggling with the complexities of multiple relationships. As Keith-Spiegel and Koocher (1985) write: "It is probably impossible to create clear guidelines for psychologists with regard to dual-role relationships not involving sexual intimacy, since each situation presents unique features that must be considered" (p. 267). Psychologists must rely on expositions of the Code, on Ethics Committee decisions regarding specific cases, and ultimately, on consultation with colleagues in order to successfully navigate the perilous and often uncharted seas of dual relationships. The remainder of this article will consequently look beyond the limits of the Ethics Code for help in this journey.

RESEARCH ON DUAL RELATIONSHIPS

Surprisingly little research has been conducted in the area of nonsexual dual relationships. This is especially baffling considering the relative wealth of data available on sexual dual relationships (Pope & Bouhoutsos, 1986) and the number of complaints against psychologists in this area (Ethics Committee of the APA, 1988). However, there are several reasons why so few studies may have been undertaken. First, as stated above, nonsexual dual relationships, unlike their sexual counterparts, are not inherently problematic; consequently they do not compel such scrutiny. Secondly, dual relationships are extremely complex and situational, making it difficult to apply a general rule across individual cases. Finally, there are inadequate definitions when it comes to addressing types of dual relationships.

In what may be the earliest study on nonsexual dual relationships, Tallman (1981) noted that about one-third of a sample of 38 psychotherapist respondents had formed social relationships with some of their clients. Of particular interest was the fact that although the sample was equally divided along gender lines, it was only male therapists who developed social relationships with their clients. Another third of the sample, in this case mostly women, stated that they had attended a special event in their client's lives, such as a wedding or Bar Mitzvah. While the first group of psychologists developed friendships with their clients, the second group stated that attendance at these special events was an isolated event designed to support their clients rather than provide an avenue for socializing. The final third of Tallman's sample could not justify social contacts with clients outside the office under any circumstances.

Pope, Tabachnick, and Keith-Spiegel (1987) surveyed the ethical beliefs and practices of 1,000 clinical psychologists, and included several items regarding nonsexual dual relationships among their questions. It is interesting to note how many of the psychologists who participated admitted to certain practices, at least on occasion. For example, 12% of their sample stated that they had become friends with a former client. Approximately 3% said they had provided therapy to a friend. Almost 8% reported they had invited clients to an office open house. Another 9% stated they had provided therapy to someone who was also a student or supervisee. Almost 3% had provided therapy to someone employed by them. Over 24% reported that they had attended a client's special event, such as a wedding. For all these situations, the vast majority of respondents stated that they had never participated in these practices, while another sizable contingent said that they had occurred "rarely."

A later study by Borys and Pope (1989) involving over 4,000 psychiatrists, psychologists, and social workers found a similar pattern of practices among all three professions as related to dual relationships. While usually far less than 10% of their sample admitted engaging in a dual relationship with their clients with any regularity, significant numbers of the respondents stated that they had disclosed details of personal stresses (38%), gone out to eat with a client after a session (21%), provided therapy to a current student or supervisee (10%), and bought goods or services from a client (21%), with at least "a few clients." Such a trend points to a phenomenon typical of dual relationships: while few psychologists engage in these practices with any regularity, almost all of us are at risk to become involved in a harmful or exploitive dual relationship at any given time. However, some of us may be more at risk than others.

In a further analysis of their data, Borys and Pope (1989) found a significant gender difference suggesting that male therapists tend to engage in nonsexual dual relationships more than do female therapists, and that these relationships involve female clients far more often than male clients. This pattern has been found consistently in studies addressing sexualized dual relationships, where a higher status male (e.g., therapist, professor, supervisor, administrator) is much more likely to engage in a sexual relationship with a lower status female (e.g., client, student, supervisee, or employee) (Holroyd & Brodsky, 1977; Pope & Bouhoutsos, 1986; Pope & Vasquez, 1991) than is any other possible gender combination (high status female to low status male, female to female, male to male). The fact that this pattern also occurs in nonsexual dual relationships raises some interesting questions, the most important of which is: Does a nonsexual dual relationship tend to lead to a sexual one? There is ample reason to believe that it can.

As with familial incest, sexual involvement between therapist and client may be the culmination of a more general breakdown in roles and relationship boundaries that begin on a nonsexual level. This link was predicted by the systems perspective, which views disparate roles and behaviors within a relational system as interrelated. Changes in one arena are expected to affect those in other realms of behavior. The results of the current study suggest that the role boundaries and norms in the therapeutic relationship, just as those in the family, serve a protective function that serves to prevent exploitation (Pope & Vasquez, 1991).

PARAMETERS OF A DUAL RELATIONSHIP

Numerous models for ethical decision-making have been generated in recent years (Haas & Malouf, 1989; Handelsman, 1991; Rest, 1983; Woody, 1990). Recognizing the relative lack of guidance provided by the Ethics Code in the area of dual relationships, several writers called for increased structure in making decisions in this area (Borys & Pope, 1989; Keith-Spiegel & Koocher, 1985; Pope & Vasquez, 1991). In an attempt to provide a framework for decision-making in this area, various psychologists have attempted to define the parameters of a dual relationship.

Roll and Millen (1981) were the first to address non-sexual dual relationship issues, but limited their remarks to psychologists responding to requests for psychotherapy from acquaintances. Their suggestions include: (1) avoid doing so if possible, (2) be aware of possible transference, (3) obtain consultation while making a decision, (4) maintain boundaries, (5) be aware of one's own values, (6) be prepared to lose the friendship, (7) be vigilant regarding confidentiality, (8) recognize when treatment should be terminated, and (9) insure that one's own needs are met to avoid abusing the client.

Kitchener (1988) offered three guidelines to assist in determining if a dual relationship has a high probability of being harmful or not. The first guideline states that as the *incompatibility of expectations* increases between roles, so will the potential for harm. Second, as the *obligations* associated with different roles diverge, the potential for loss of objectivity and divided loyalties increases. Finally, as the *power and prestige* differential between the professional's and the consumer's roles increase, so does the potential for exploitation. Kitchener sums up her position in the following manner:

> . . . when the conflict of interests is great, the power differential large, and the role expectations incompatible, the potential for harm is so great that the relationships should be considered *a priori* unethical. At the other extreme, when the conflict of interests is small or non-existent, the power differential small, and the role expectations compatible, there is little danger of harm. (Kitchener, 1988, p. 220)

Gottlieb's (1993) decision-making model is built upon Kitchener's, and also identifies three dimensions of a dual relationship. The first is that of *power*, defined as the amount of influence the psychologist may have in relation to another person. The second dimension is that of *duration of the relationship*, recognizing that power increases over time. The third is *clarity of termination*, referring to the likelihood of further contact between the two parties. Gottlieb then suggests that a psychologist follow five steps in employing his model.

Step 1. Assess the current (primary) relationship according to the three dimensions. If the level of power is high, the duration of the relationship prolonged, and termination unclear, then a further relationship is probably best avoided.

Step 2. If the conditions outlined in the first step are not met, the contemplated (secondary) relationship should also be assessed according to the three dimensions. If the same conditions delineated above apply, then a dual relationship should be avoided.

Step 3. Examine the two relationships for role incompatibility using Kitchener's (1988) model, noting expectations, divergence of obligations, and increase in power differential. As incompatibility increases, a dual relationship should be avoided.

Step 4. If the psychologist believes it may be acceptable to proceed, consultation should be initiated with a colleague. Decisions should be made conservatively and with the best interest of the other party in mind.

Step 5. After consulting with a colleague, discuss a decision to proceed with the other person. If the other person is competent and chooses to engage in the secondary relationship, then the psychologist may proceed.

These models, while helpful in delineating a step-by-step approach to decision-making in the area of dual relationships, are limited in certain respects. First, while they both address the crucial dimension of power, they neglect the equally important dimension of intimacy. Duration of relationship may be related to the potential for intimacy, but these two parameters are not necessarily correlated. In addition, the needs and intentions of the two people involved are inadequately addressed.

Any professional relationship can be understood as involving the three dimensions of power, intimacy, and need fulfillment. *Power* may be defined as the degree of control one has in a relationship, such as may be represented by the capacity to evaluate, influence, or judge. Power exists on a continuum from domination to submission, with the people involved either involved in a power struggle or playing out some complementary balance of power. A therapist has power over a client, because the client has come for help. A teacher or supervisor has power because they are to grade or evaluate. In a professional relationship, the power aspect of the relationship is formalized through the granting of a license, with the assumption that the professional will use their power for the benefit of a client, student, supervisee, or research subject.

In non-professional relationships, such as friendships, family relations, or business acquaintances, the power relationships are not usually so well defined and may be more flexible. In business relationships, there is often no assumption made that the person who holds the power will use that power for the benefit of the other person. The power differential and expectation in a professional relationship most closely resembles the relationship between parent and child, where society expects the parent to use their greater experience and control to the benefit of their children. This is not to suggest a complete parallel in this regard, for there are many important differences. For example, professional relationships involve the element of choice.

Intimacy is defined as the degree to which one person allows the other person to get to know them. It generally refers to the conscious choice to tell or show someone else something about ourselves, but can also involve unintentional revelations about ourselves. Intimacy exists on a continuum from complete self-disclosure to a guarded secretiveness. In a professional relationship, the person who occupies the more powerful position generally shares the least about themselves. Clients, students, supervisees, and research subjects usually know little about the lives of their therapists, teachers, supervisors, or investigators. Of course the converse is also generally true, in that the person in the less powerful position generally engages in the most self-disclosure. With greater intimacy comes greater vulnerability. In non-professional relationships, the level of intimacy may be either more mutual or more equally restricted. Family relations and friendships usually involve greater mutuality of self-disclosure, while acquaintances and business relations usually employ an implicit restriction on self-disclosure. Indeed, the relative lack of self-disclosure on the part of the more powerful member of the professional relationship makes the exceptional occasions one decides to use self-disclosure as a therapeutic or educational technique very influential.

Need fulfillment refers to the question of whose needs a relationship is designed to meet. A relationship can be mutually fulfilling, fulfilling in a complementary way, or it can meet only one person's needs. Most professional relationships are designed to be fulfilling in a complementary manner, in which the needs of the less powerful, more vulnerable member are accorded greater concern than those of the more powerful, less vulnerable member. This does not mean that the psychologist/therapist/teacher's needs are not important or not being met. It means that the psychologist suspends their shared needs (to be liked, to be understood, to seek help, etc.) in favor of complimentary and agreed-upon needs, such as to be paid, to occupy a role of status, and to develop greater skill and competency. Non-professional relationships are marked by a tendency to be mutually fulfilling (meeting shared needs), while any exploitive relationship fulfills the needs of one member of the relationship at the expense of the other person.

Acknowledging that there is always the risk of harm in any dual relationship, with these three parameters of power, intimacy, and need fulfillment in mind, dual relationships can be assessed in terms of their level of risk. Table 1 illustrates risk levels in terms of these three parameters. At a mild level of risk, the dual relationships tend to share a common power differential (such as that between teacher and supervisor), a low degree of self-disclosure on the part of the psychologist, and the fulfillment of complementary needs specific to the roles each member of the relationship plays. At a more moderate level of risk, the dual relationships share a dissimilar power differential (such as that between friend and therapist), a higher degree of self-disclosure on the part of the psychologist, and the fulfillment of mutual needs within the relationship. At a severe level of risk, the relationship's power differential remains dissimilar, self-disclosure tends to be high on the part of the psychologist, and the focus of the relationship becomes the gratification of the psychologist's needs.

DUAL RELATIONSHIPS INVOLVING PSYCHOTHERAPY

Probably no area of dual relationships has received more attention than that of becoming friends with former psychotherapy clients (Keith-Spiegel & Koocher, 1985; Pope & Vasquez, 1991; Rest, 1983; Tallman, 1981). There are a number of reasons for this interest. Foremost is the natural wish to develop a friendship with a client that the psychologist likes or with whom significant interests are shared. Our profession occupies a rather unique position in this regard. If an attorney, physician, teacher, or member of the clergy develops a friendship with a client, patient, student, or parishioner over time, there is not the inherent degree of risk involved as between psychotherapists and their clients. This risk is manifest in four primary ways. First, if a therapist anticipates forming a friendship with a client, the therapist may refrain from confrontation in an effort to avoid conflict or a threat to the desired friendship. Second, the therapist may develop a blind spot to a client's problem area, seeing the client as more effective than they may actually be. This could result in either idealizing the desired client/friend, or in prematurely ending the therapy so that the friendship might begin. Third, the client may limit self-disclosure in order to lower the risk of being rejected. Fi-

TABLE 1. Factors in the assessment of risk of harm in dual relationships.

Level of risk	Parameters
Mild	Power differential–high Psychologist's level of intimacy–low Need fulfillment–complementary
Moderate	Power differential–low Psychologist's level of intimacy–high Need fulfillment–mutual
Severe	Power differential–high Psychologist's level of intimacy–varies Need fulfillment–exploitive

nally, the loss of the anticipated friendship could be harmful to the client should the relationship not work out. Such a painful resolution to the therapeutic alliance could dilute whatever benefit the client had derived from therapy as well as become yet another problem with which the client needs to cope. In addition, becoming friends with a client may preclude their ever returning for treatment.

In Pope et al.'s (1987) study of psychologists' beliefs and behavior about ethical issues, 58% of the respondents stated that they had become friends with at least one former psychotherapy client. Approximately 79% stated that they believed it was ethical for a psychologist to form a friendship with a former client, at least under some circumstances. Despite the inherent risks outlined above, clearly this is an issue with which most psychologists wrestle.

If a psychologist is considering the pursuit of a friendship with a current or former client, there are several questions upon which he/she should reflect. What does this wish to be friends represent? Is there something about the transference relationship (e.g., a pull to rescue the client, or protect them from having to deal with the pain of separation) that fuels this wish? Is there a void or problem area in the therapist's life that this desired friendship might fill or resolve? Is the therapist attempting to avoid dealing with the pain of losing the client in his/her life? Considering the nature of the therapeutic relationship, what are the chances that the friendship could ever be truly mutual? How would the therapist feel about explaining the decision to become friends with a client to one's spouse or colleagues? How would the therapist handle the ongoing need to protect the client's confidentiality; for instance, in reply to a question of how the two became friends?

Once the therapist has thought through these questions, if he/she still feels that pursuing a friendship with a client is acceptable, consultation with a colleague is advisable to ensure that the psychologist is not deceiving themselves or overlooking any important information. The next step would be to discuss this issue with the client, taking some time to consider the feelings that arise in both parties as this wish is considered consciously. If the decision to pursue a friendship holds up after this kind of rigorous and honest self-examination, then it may be appropriate.

While most psychologists probably avoid taking on friends as clients, the Pope et al. (1987) study indicates that more than 47% of the respondents do not believe that seeing friends as clients is necessarily unethical in all situations. However, the psychologist who is approached by a friend (or family member) to provide therapy should carefully consider any possible motivation for doing so. In most communities, there are other mental health professionals to whom a referral can be made, and any potential problems of a dual relationship avoided (Canter et al., 1994).

Seeing a friend in therapy can be tempting and gratifying to one's grandiosity, especially if the friend makes a plea to the psychologist's familiarity with the situation ("You know me already; I'd have too much to explain to anyone else"), to the psychologist's expertise ("You're the best in town to treat my problem"), or to the psychologist's vulnerability ("If I can't see you I won't go to anyone else for help"). However, few other situations so vividly highlight the importance of having a professional detachment with a client. What if the therapist learns something disturbing about their friend? Will the therapist confront the client/friend if it may mean risking the friendship? How can the therapist reasonably hope to maintain a lack of investment in the outcome of the therapeutic work? How will the therapist deal with their friend's judgement about the quality of their work together? Finally, how will the boundary between the therapeutic alliance and the friendship be established?

A related and far more common dilemma for the psychologist occurs when he/she is approached by a friend or acquaintance and asked for advice (Keith-Spiegel & Koocher, 1985). While it is again tempting for the therapist to use their expertise and knowledge of a given situation to provide assistance, this situation is fraught with difficulty. Because of the relative power accorded to the psychologist because of their training and advanced degree, his/her advice, however casually given, is often accorded significant importance. The friend may act on advice given when the psychologist had insufficient information, or when the psychologist was more interested in sounding like an expert than in considering the best interest of the friend. The friendship can be threatened if the psychologist's advice results in an undesired outcome to the friend. The psychologist may be blamed and held responsible. In situations such as this, the psychologist can of course provide emotional support and information. If a situation is at all serious, however, the friend is best referred to another professional for assistance and the potential risk to both parties avoided altogether.

Psychologists often gain new clients through acquaintances, colleagues, or clients who respect their work. When considering whether to take on a new referral, the nature of the relationship between the referral source, the potential client, and the therapist should be carefully considered. If the referral is from an acquaintance, what is the likelihood that the psychologist will meet the new client socially? How would boundaries be maintained if the therapist were to run into the new client because of membership in a common social group (church, school, etc.)? How would the therapist be influenced by what the potential client may say about therapy to their mutual friend?

Situations in which current therapy clients make a referral can be complex. What is the client's motivation behind the referral? Does the client hope to gain a new importance to the therapist by making referrals? Does the client have a particular investment in the outcome of the referred person's therapy? Is competition or "sibling rivalry" between the two clients likely to jeopardize both people's therapeutic work? Can the therapist ensure that he/she will not unintentionally disclose confidential information to one of the clients? Each of these questions must be given careful consideration so that the best interests of both the current and potential clients can be preserved. This is especially the case when the two clients are husband-wife or parent-child.

The Ethics Code (APA, 2002) does not prohibit psychologists from accepting gifts or favors from clients. Apart from the clinical issues involved (the client's motives), the ethical issue is primarily one of determining the effect accepting a gift or favor may have on the therapeutic relationship. Caution should be used as complaints of exploitation may be made if the client's motives were manipulative or if the client is later disappointed with therapy.

The value of the gift is an important dimension to consider, especially in relation to the client's socioeconomic status. However, psychologists should never accept gifts that exceed minimal value, no matter what the client's financial situation. The APA Ethics Committee once reprimanded a psychologist for accepting a Porsche automobile from a client, even when the psychologist pointed out that his client was so wealthy that the expense was negligible (Keith-Spiegel & Koocher, 1985). Regardless of the client's financial position, an expensive or highly valued gift is likely to unduly influence the therapist and should be avoided and examined in therapy.

Another issue to consider is the temporal context under which the gift is given. In general, it may be far more appropriate to accept small or handmade gifts given around holidays or termination than those offered at a seemingly random time. Haas and Malouf (1989) warn in particular of gifts that are accompanied by the statement, "I just saw this and it reminded me of you." Gifts given at times other than those mentioned above are more likely to have clinical significance, and are again best refused and the motivations behind them examined.

Gifts and favors should of course never be directly solicited from clients. The client will inevitably become aware of the bind that such a request puts them in, with the resulting detrimental effect of all boundary violations. These types of situations will be discussed further below.

There are some instances where therapeutic goals are more likely to be achieved outside the therapist's office. These situations might include treatment of various phobias (e.g., flying, driving, being out in public), eating disorders, stress reduction, and crisis intervention. Whenever these interventions are contemplated, careful consideration is required to ensure that professional boundaries are maintained and conflicts of interest are avoided. Whenever the psychologist considers the use of an "in-situ" intervention, he/she should consider three things (Keith-Spiegel & Koocher, 1985). First, the psychologist should question his/her own motivation and need for utilizing this technique. Is it really necessary to achieve adequate results? Is there any research data to support the intervention? Does this intervention satisfy the therapist's need to spend more time with the client or break up the monotony of the office routine? Second, the therapist should develop a specific treatment plan justifying the intervention as the most effective way of achieving the desired outcome. If the issue is a client's sexual inhibition, does the therapist really need to accompany the client to an X-rated movie, or could the client view such a video by themselves in the privacy of their own home? Finally, the therapist should take steps to ensure that the client understands the proposed intervention, is adequately prepared for it, and provides freely given consent for it.

In addition, interventions carried out apart from the therapist's office can raise unexpected complications. For example, who should pay for the airline tickets and the therapist's time should the therapist and client decide to take a short flight together to practice in real life the skills learned in systematic desensitization? How will the therapist manage their own anxiety as a passenger in a car driven by a client recovering from a driving phobia? As much as possible, these issues need to be thought out before they are undertaken, perhaps in consultation with a colleague experienced in such techniques.

It is a seemingly universal experience among therapists that they run into their clients outside the office. In small or isolated communities the reality of bumping into clients or the inevitability of multiple roles is a daily fact of life. However, even in large urban settings, psychologists must be prepared to deal with these same issues.

Barnett and Yutrzenka (1993) delineate the conditions that often serve to make the avoidance of dual relationships unavoidable in rural settings. First, the sparse population: when there are a limited number of people within a given area, these people are more likely to see each other on a regular basis. Second, the towns in a rural setting tend to be small and isolated from one another. Third, rural areas often have very limited health care choices generally, and even more limited mental health services from which to choose. Fourth, rural settings offer relatively limited personal privacy compared to urban settings. Finally, there is greater overlap of personal and professional relationships in a rural setting where choices are limited: if there is only one psychologist in town, that is the one the fourth grade teacher is likely to see, even if the psychologist's child is in her class.

Psychologists in rural settings often have to make an extra effort to ensure that acquaintances do not run into each other in the waiting room. They routinely must deal with the question of how to act towards a client they meet in the supermarket, park, or restaurant. In many cases, this type of role confusion is so engrained in the community that clients and professionals alike have no difficulty adjusting to the situation. With more disturbed clients, however, embarrassing situations can result.

When a psychologist is presented with a situation where he/she is asked to see a client with whom they are likely to share multiple relationships, the psychologist should determine if there is any alternative available. Only if there is not should the psychologist proceed to establish a professional relationship. It is when charges of exploitation, prejudice, or harm are made in a situation where the "small world hazard" was known in advance and alternatives were available but not utilized that psychologists are held responsible by investigating ethics committees (Keith-Spiegel & Koocher, 1985).

In those situations, rural or urban, where a psychologist accidentally runs into a client, the therapist should leave it up to the client to decide whether to acknowledge him/her. If anyone is with the client, it would be natural for them to ask the client how they know anyone who speaks to them, and the client should be given the choice of whether to disclose the fact that they are in therapy. If the client says hello, the therapist should also acknowledge the client, keeping the interaction limited to whatever is appropriate to the situation. The extra-therapeutic encounter should be discussed during the next therapy session.

PSYCHOLOGICAL EVALUATIONS

Performing psychological evaluations (psychological testing) for friends or their family members raises many of the same issues as those for therapy. Psychologists may be enticed to perform such services because of appeals to their expertise, or because the request seems so harmless. For example, a psychologist who specializes in psycho-educational assessment may be asked by a friend to evaluate her child for school readiness or a learning problem. Because of the "non-emotional" nature of the evaluation, the psychologist may be tempted to acquiesce. However, there can of course be many emotional factors involved in academic performance. The psychologist may overlook significant information in order to preserve the friendship, and deprive the child of an adequate evaluation and treatment plan. Or the psychologist could over-react to information learned about his/her friend through the child, which could either threaten the relationship or result in the evaluator taking inappropriate action. The friendship could also become endangered if the friend is unhappy with the conclusions reached by the evaluator (Binder & Thompson, 1995).

The Ethics Code (APA, 2002) does not prohibit psychologists from performing psychological evaluations with current clients, or from seeing as clients those who were previously evaluated by the psychologist. Certain work settings (such as in forensics) will preclude such a dual relationship, recognizing the potential bias such a relationship may produce. Standard 7.03 of the 1992 Ethics Code addressed this issue directly in a forensic setting, noting that a dual relationship in court-related matters can compromise "professional judgement and objectivity."

When a psychologist considers evaluating a current client, several questions need to be considered. What is the psychologist's motivation for taking on another role with the client? Does the psychologist have the necessary qualifications to conduct the evaluation, or would another professional be more suitable? How might the relative formality of the testing situation affect the therapeutic alliance? How might the psychologist and/or the client handle any "bad news" that results from the evaluation? Would the psychologist's need to preserve the therapeutic relationship affect his/her interpretation of the test data or the way the data was interpreted to the client? Would the client's need to preserve the therapeutic relationship affect their participation and level of self-disclosure? There may indeed be times where careful examination of these questions leads the psychologist to conclude that it would not be harmful to the therapeutic relationship to proceed with conducting the evaluation. There may even be instances where utilizing a previous professional relationship may be the only way to obtain a valid evaluation, such as in the case of a disturbed child who has difficulty forming attachments. But there may be other situations where referral to a qualified colleague may be preferred in order to avoid the risk of jeopardizing the therapy or to ensure that the client does not feel exploited.

In situations where a person previously evaluated by a psychologist approaches that professional about becoming a client, many of the same questions apply. There may be many situations where it is appropriate to accept this person as a client. However, this would not be appropriate in any forensic situation, nor should the psychologist ever consider a person they are currently evaluating as a potential client. Such a consideration could again serve to obfuscate the psychologist's judgement and the necessary detachment needed for an accurate evaluation.

ACADEMIC SETTINGS

While is it typical for therapists and their clients to make special arrangements to limit social contact with one another outside of the office, this is not the case for psychology professors and their students. Indeed, there are often special events (e.g., departmental socials, faculty-student retreats) that are designed to encourage such interactions and relax formal role distinctions. Indeed, many graduate and undergraduate students have benefited from becoming friends and colleagues with their professors. These types of mentoring relationships prove valuable in forming a professional identity and may open doors career-wise.

However, professors have a great deal of power over their students, which if used to the student's detriment can ruin a career. While a client can "fire" a therapist, a student may feel that they are unable to escape the influence of a faculty member who may hold a grudge against them or who may attempt to use personal information to keep the student from graduating or advancing to candidacy. Students often feel powerless in dealing with professors they perceive as exploitive, as university grievance committees are usually composed of other faculty members who may be in sympathy with their colleagues. Professional ethics committees rarely become involved with student complaints unless they are extreme, preferring in most cases to have the complaints resolved at the level of the university (Keith-Spiegel & Koocher, 1985).

Blevins-Knabe (1992) outlines several issues that relate to dual relationships between professors and their students. Students often implicitly trust their professors with sensitive personal information, as they might a therapist. They trust their professors will not use this information to exploit them. This can be a special risk in situations where the professor is grading the student on non-objective criteria, or where the faculty member is part of a committee making decisions about the student's academic standing. When a professor learns information about a student that he/she believes may compromise that student's competence as a professional, the professor has an obligation to use this information responsibly. This might include directly speaking with the student about whatever concerns the professor might have, or raising the concern with the student and his/her advisor.

Faculty members are also required to be objective and fair in providing evaluations of students [see Section 7.06 of the Ethics Code]. Instances in which professors have responded to criticism from students by giving them poor evaluations have been noted by the APA Ethics Committee (Keith-Spiegel & Koocher, 1985). Additionally, faculty members are encouraged not to allow personal biases to influence their evaluations or grading of students.

An all too common situation that arises out of students socializing with professors are charges of favoritism from other students. When a student and a faculty member are perceived as friends by other students, this can compromise the role of the professor (Blevins-Knabe, 1992). Other students may feel that it is "who you know, not what you know" that is most important in academic success. The professor may feel exploited by the student who seeks to use the friendship to gain access to information about tests or to receive special consideration on grading. The student may feel exploited if the professor asks for special requests or issues a social invitation.

Several authors (Blevins-Knabe, 1992; Keith-Spiegel & Koocher, 1985) suggest that it is best for faculty members to restrict their social contact with students to casual or university-related events until the student graduates. They also note that while there may be many ways in which on-going friendships with a professor may benefit a student, there is always the risk that the relationship may become problematic, leaving the student without an important reference. These writers suggest that a letter of recommendation could be placed in the student's file before a social relationship is formed as one way to protect the student.

Some professors design their classes to include "affective" or "experiential" material. It is not uncommon, for example, that a teacher of a group therapy class requires the students to serve as group members, sharing their own conflicts and feelings, to allow other students to practice their therapy skills. Other classes may require students to practice regression techniques (e.g., bodywork, hyperventilation, etc.) with one another in order to gain competence. These classes have a certain appeal to students, and many professors feel that it is the only way to teach certain skills short of bringing clients to class. When complaints are filed with ethics committees about such classes, the dual roles of student/client and professor/therapist are usually at the root of the problem. The most common complaints allege unfair evaluations based on the professor's subjective experience of the student's participation rather than on more objective criteria such as test performance, or poor evaluations based on personal information the student revealed during the class. Keith-Spiegel and Koocher (1985) suggest five recommendations for programs to follow when experiential courses are offered:

1. Inform students at the outset about course requirements and the justification for the requirements.
2. Assist any student who elects not to take a class that contains experiential content in finding an alternative class or in devising a substitute experience.
3. Use a professor who is not a core faculty member to teach such classes to limit the possibility of personal information influencing the student's progress through the program.
4. Whenever possible, develop objective grading criteria that does not utilize knowledge of student's problems or their willingness to share them as part of the criteria. If this is not possible, offer the course for "credit" only.
5. Make some attempt to screen students for the class. Offer any student who appears likely to be harmed by an experiential class an alternative class or experience.

The relationship between supervisor and supervisee raises many of the same issues relative to dual relationships, as do those between professors and students. Indeed, it is not uncommon for a student to have a professor also serves as a supervisor. Such a dual relationship in itself is not unethical (Canter et al., 1994). However, it is important for both parties to be aware that a poor grade received in the classroom could negatively impact the supervisory relationship, especially if the student feels that the grade was not based on objective criteria.

Section 3.08 of the 2002 Ethics Code specifically mentions supervisees as a group with whom psychologists should avoid potentially harmful or exploitive dual relationships. Social relations may compromise a supervisor's objectivity in providing feedback or evaluations. Interns and supervisors may conspire to avoid issues or topics that might threaten the social relationship (Slimp & Burian, 1994).

Supervisors should be alert to signs that they are starting to engage in a dual relationship with their interns. They should note tendencies to treat their supervisees differently based not on their training needs, but on personal regard or attraction. Supervisors may also find themselves disclosing personal information designed to have their interns like or understand them, rather than in the interest of the student's growth. Finally, supervisors should guard against placing their students in the middle of political battles that are typical of most institutions (Horn, 1995).

Despite some of the similarities between supervision and psychotherapy, Slimp and Burian (1994) cite a number of writers who argue against supervisors doing therapy with their interns. The Board of Psychology in California expressly prohibits supervisors from hiring interns who were former psychotherapy clients (California Department of Consumer Affairs, 1995). Supervisors are required to evaluate their interns, and evaluations are antithetical to the therapeutic process. Evaluations should be based on the student's performance as a clinician, not on their personal conflicts (Slimp & Burian, 1994). Supervision should serve only to identify areas of personal conflict that are impacting the intern's professional performance. For resolution of these conflicts, the student should either be referred for psychotherapy or seek out treatment on their own.

FORENSIC SETTINGS

As suggested above, the issue of multiple relationships between psychologists and their clients takes on even greater importance in a forensic setting than in a clinical one. In court, every effort must be made to ensure that the testimony of the psychologist designated as an expert is untainted by bias resulting from a previous or multiple relationships. In the rare instances where a multiple relationship is unavoidable, the nature of these relationships must be clarified to all parties involved in the case.

Section 7.03 of the Ethics Code (APA, 1992) addressed the issue of multiple relationships in a forensic setting:

> In most circumstances, psychologists avoid performing multiple and potentially conflicting roles in forensic matters. When psychologists may be called on to serve in more than one role in a legal proceeding–for example, as a consultant or expert for one party or for the court and as a fact witness–they clarify role expectations and the extent of confidentiality in advance to the extent feasible, and thereafter as changes occur, in order to avoid compromising their professional judgement and objectivity and in order to avoid misleading others regarding their role.

This standard is echoed in the *Specialty Guidelines for Forensic Psychologists* (Committee on Ethical Guidelines for Forensic Psychologists, 1991), and states the goal of psychologists avoiding multiple relationships whenever possible in a forensic setting. Although there may be exceptions to this rule, most forensic experts believe strongly that such exceptions are fraught with the risk of harm to the clients involved (Canter et al., 1994).

The most common situation that comes up involving multiple relationships in a forensic situation is that of a psychologist being asked by the court to testify about a client. Section 7.05 of the Ethics Code (APA, 1992) stated that having a prior professional relationship with a client does not preclude a psychologist from testifying as a fact witness, but also admonishes professionals to consider ways in which the previous relationship may affect their opinions and judgement, and to disclose any potential conflict to the relevant parties.

Psychologists may find themselves forced to testify regarding their clients against their will, or they may see it as in their client's best interests to testify on their behalf. In either event, the therapist must be aware of any tendency to act as an advocate for their client, as this is not a legitimate role for the psychologist to play. In court, the psychologist's purpose is to supply the court with facts, and to also express any limitations regarding those facts (Canter et al., 1994).

In the vast majority of cases where a psychologist is requested by the court to conduct a psychological evaluation on a current or former therapy client, the Ethics Code (APA, 2002) makes it clear that the psychologist should not do so. In the role of therapist, the client's welfare is most important, while in the role of forensic evaluator, objectivity and accuracy in presenting data is paramount, resulting in the extreme likelihood of these two roles coming into conflict. If the assessment were not to prove favorable to the client, the therapeutic relationship could be irreparably damaged. In the rare cases where the therapist agrees to also serve as an evaluator, the possibility of bias should be acknowledged in all reports, depositions, and testimony, along with any limitations that might be relevant to the rendered opinions (Canter et al., 1994).

BOUNDARY VIOLATIONS

While most discussions of multiple relationships focus on the more moderate violations discussed above (or the most extreme violation of therapist sexual abuse), it is important to also attend to the wide variety of lesser and more complex boundary crossings that may or may not result in a boundary violation (Gutheil & Gabbard, 1993). In any professional relationship, there is a thin line between the roles that both parties explicitly agree to and the various other roles that either party can so easily be enticed to enter. As Kilman (1994) puts it:

> For the most part, the problem for psychologists is not the recognition and avoidance of clear dual relationships, the problem lies in the more subtle blurring of roles. Most dual relationship problems it turns out, begin with "good intentions" to be "helpful" and from these innocuous beginnings therapist and patient can start down the slippery slope which leads to the impairment of the therapist's judgement, loss of unself-interested objectivity and to the compromise of patient safety/trust essential to any therapeutic work. (p. 2)

It would be a mistake to assume, however, that all boundary crossings are inevitably bad. It could be argued that boundary crossings occur with great regularity in any therapeutic relationship, and are noted and used to the client's benefit by the sensitive therapist who carefully monitors and interprets these crossings as part of transference and countertransference reactions. Under these conditions, one could argue that such boundary crossings are necessary in order for the therapeutic alliance to be maintained, much as the tightrope walker must begin to lose his balance before the central nervous system can compensate and allow a return to balance.

Several writers (Pope & Vasquez, 1991; Slimp & Burian, 1994) point out that a review of the therapist sexual abuse literature often notes that lesser boundary violations tend to precede the actual sexual acting out within the therapeutic relationship. Other writers caution that because of this "after-the-fact finding" in cases of therapist sexual abuse, the legal system (and plaintiff's attorneys in particular) automatically apply this reasoning to all cases in which a client complains of being harmed by a boundary violation on the part of the therapist. Thus any boundary crossing is perceived as wrong and inevitably harmful (Gutheil & Gabbard, 1993). It is important to recognize that what constitutes a boundary crossing or violation is somewhat relative, depending upon which theoretical orientation is adopted and on the context of the behavior. For example, touching a client may be frowned upon in psychodynamic psychotherapy, but is considered essential when conducting a sensory-perceptual examination as part of a neuropsychological evaluation.

Whenever psychologists discuss the issue of boundaries, it is assumed that everyone understands and agrees on what constitutes a professional boundary. Like most, this is probably not a good assumption. Gutheil and Gabbard (1993) delineate nine dimensions of the professional boundary to facilitate psychologists' reflection on their own behavior.

Role

While difficult to define, the professional role is essentially what the therapist, supervisor, or professor is supposed to do. The psychologist may step outside their role when they put their needs first, or they may be lured outside their role by client demands. One way of conceptualizing which demands the psychologist is supposed to gratify is by distinguishing libidinal demands (those which are related to the client's need to be loved) from growth demands (those which may be related to the client's need for flexibility and sensitivity on the part of the therapist).

Time

Professional relationships are bounded by time (i.e., the length of the therapy session, class, or supervisor session). For many clients, the time limits on their sessions provide structure and a container that they find reassuring, as they know they will only have to experience the pain of remembering and reliving for a set time. The time of day in which a session takes place can also be part of a boundary, as sessions which occur outside of usual working hours are more at risk of being viewed by the client and others as taking away from the psychologist's personal time and giving that time to the client. Giving clients extra time through the use of telephone calls may also represent a boundary violation unless they are allowed only under certain explicit conditions.

Place

Professional relationships typically occur within an office, a hospital, or a classroom. While there may be legitimate reasons to see clients or students elsewhere (e.g., in their homes, in court, in jail), making an exception to the customary standard should be well thought out with regard to the psychologist's motivations and the possible impact on the professional relationship.

Money

The financial dimension of the professional relationship defines it as a business relationship, placing it squarely in the world of work, not love. Passively allowing a client to run up a large debt or letting the billing lapse is quite different than making a decision to see a client for free or a low fee and discussing this decision with the client. When the psychologist neglects the financial aspect of a professional relationship, he/she betrays his/her own conflict in this area, leading inevitably to feelings of anger. The psychologist is then in the uncomfortable position of either denying his/her legitimate needs or asserting needs that have accumulated excessive emotional energy.

Gifts and Services

As discussed above, small or handmade gifts given during a holiday or at the end of a professional relationship may be received by the psychologist without constituting an ethical violation. When the psychologist allows excessive giving on part of the client, or worse comes to expect it, then a boundary violation occurs.

Clothing

The manner in which a professional dresses represents a social boundary. Excessively revealing or outright seductive clothing could lead to harmful effects for the client. Allowing or encouraging a client to wear inappropriate clothing would also constitute a boundary violation.

Language

How the psychologist and their clients, students, or interns address one another is another important dimension of boundary. Using first names may in some instances create a false sense of intimacy or may be infantilizing to a client. The tone used between both parties is also relevant, as anger and seductiveness are most often conveyed in terms of the tone used in speech. Choice of words and the use of profanity need to be carefully considered in relation to the client, student or intern with whom the psychologist is dealing. What may be a way of joining with one person may be offensive to another.

Self-Disclosure

Self-disclosure is a powerful tool in the therapist's arsenal, as it may strengthen the therapeutic alliance, reduce feelings of isolation and self-criticism, and foster a more realistic perception of the therapist and of the client's own self. However, few other aspects of the professional boundary are so subject to misuse. Careful self-examination is needed to ensure that self-disclosure is not done to gratify the therapist's unfulfilled needs in their private lives. Disclosure of many facts in the therapist's life may be a burden to a client, where exploration of the client's fantasies about the therapist may prove more beneficial.

Physical Contact

Psychologists hold many different views regarding the use of touch with their clients. The most conservative limit their physical contact to a handshake, while more liberal therapists believe it is appropriate to hug clients or provide comfort by touching their backs or extremities. There may be occasions where it seems inhumane to refuse to touch a client, such as in cases involving HIV+ or acutely grief-stricken clients. Like all other boundaries, however, careful thought should go into all decisions to have physical contact with a client. Pope, Sonne, and Holroyd (1993) provide useful questions for psychologists to consider in relation to their own decisions about touching clients.

Reflecting upon the above nine dimensions of professional boundaries will hopefully make it easier for psychologists to monitor their own behavior, and prevent boundary crossings from becoming boundary violations.

In an interesting exploration of boundary violations across several professions, Peterson (1992) notes that boundary violations can be distinguished from a boundary crossing, as all violations share in common four characteristics. Focusing on the therapist-client relationship, she notes that while in a professional relationship the therapist suspends their needs to meet the needs of the client, when a boundary violation occurs a *role-reversal* occurs, wherein the therapist's needs become primary. In a professional relationship, the therapist and client mutually agree on the goals they are working towards, but a boundary violation occurs when the therapist has a *secret agenda* of which the client is unaware. In a professional relationship, the therapist uses their status and expertise for the benefit of the client, but in a boundary violation the therapist *misuses their position of power and trust*. Finally, in a professional relationship the client should feel free to make choices without risking a loss of integrity or the loss of the therapeutic alliance. When a boundary violation occurs, however, the client is placed in a *lose-lose situation* where either one outcome or the other is inevitable.

An example should make these characteristics clear. Suppose a dependent, somewhat histrionic client starts to cry at the end of session, and the therapist allows her to remain in the office for several minutes beyond the end of her scheduled session. The therapist, failing to attend to his feelings of sexual attraction and his wish to rescue and protect this client, suggests that she move her appointment to later in the day when he has no one scheduled after her, in case she needs some extra time.

In the example above, the therapist has put his needs above those of the client, who needs to learn to tolerate some limits. The therapist also has a secret agenda of which the client is unaware. He is indulging his sexual attraction to her, while she believes that he must really care for her if he is willing to spend extra time with her. The therapist is misusing his position of power and trust, acting as though he is merely conducting a psychotherapy session when he is actually giving in to his sexual fantasies. Finally, the client is in a lose-lose position, as she loses a sense of integrity if she continues to indulge the therapist's wishes, and she risks losing the therapeutic relationship she values if she states that she does not want to be seen at the end of the day for longer than usual.

It is important to note that the client could "lose" in another way if and when the therapist recognizes what he is doing and attempts to reestablish appropriate therapeutic boundaries. By telling the client she must leave the session after the usual time, she may feel a sense of rejection or abandonment once she is no longer "special" enough to warrant extra time. These feelings may also occur if the therapist becomes more aloof in response to the recognition of his own sexual attraction to the client. The issue of how to resolve problematic multiple relationships will be addressed later in this article.

As this example demonstrates, exploitation of those with less power than the psychologist can be subtle. Therapists may burden clients with requests they may feel unable to deny and that go beyond their responsibilities. Similarly, supervisors can ask favors of their interns that can make the intern feel they have no choice in the matter, or that they risk a poor evaluation should they refuse. The same could apply to professors and students. In these situations, the client, intern, or student is unable to make a truly autonomous decision. It is like when the insensitive parent presents their child with an untenable choice: do what I say (which they know the child does not want or need to do) or risk the loss of parental love (or risk emotional or physical abuse).

PREVENTING PROBLEMATIC MULTIPLE RELATIONSHIPS

Conservative writers in the field of dual or multiple relationships take a position that seems simplistic and unrealistic. While acknowledging that dual relationships per se are not unethical, they view such relationships as so fraught with the potential for exploitation they recommend that if a dual relationship can be avoided, it would be unwise not to do so.

However, even Section 3.05 of the Ethics Code (APA, 2002) recognizes that dual relationships are unavoidable. They may be expected in rural areas or small towns, and among certain ethnic, religious, professional, or university communities. When a psychologist has no choice but to enter into a dual relationship, then his/her foremost priority must be to avoid causing harm. Whatever efforts to avoid harm are taken should be carefully documented, and should always include efforts to clarify one's role with all parties, informing the other parties of any possible negative consequences, and following well-established treatment or research protocols (Keith-Spiegel & Koocher, 1985).

The literature identifies several steps that can be taken to avoid entering into exploitive or harmful multiple relationships. Pope and Borys (1989) focus on the training of psychologists. They recommend that students be exposed to the research literature on dual relationships, especially those involving therapist sexual abuse. Dual relationships should be explored in all areas of training as they arise, and institutions are encouraged to make explicit policy statements regarding dual relationships, especially between professors and students. Perhaps most important, training programs are encouraged to provide safe and supportive environments in which students and supervisors can discuss anxiety-laden issues that may lead to unethical dual relationships. Sexual feelings, aggressive impulses, and financial conflicts are examples of some of the issues that interns need to be able to bring up with their supervisors. Continuing education in these areas is also important for therapists who are already practicing.

Becoming more educated about dual relationships is a necessary but not sufficient way of preventing problematic dual relationships. In addition, psychologists must remain sensitive to both the pull from their clients as well as their own needs that would lead them into a potentially harmful dual relationship. Experienced psychologists will become aware of certain clients who may be more likely to initiate a dual relationship, such as those with personality disorders. Seasoned practitioners should also remain sensitive to their own areas of conflict and need, especially as life events bring stress and loss. By staying in touch with oneself, the psychologist can be sure to be the first one to know if a dual relationship is negatively affecting treatment. This is far better than finding out through a client, or worse, an attorney.

There are certain warning signs that psychologists can be aware of that may lead them to question whether they are approaching a professional boundary, or whether that boundary has already been breached. These may include strong feelings toward a client, either positive or negative, as well as relaxation of the structured boundaries of time and place. Other warning signs may include excessive or unwarranted self-disclosure, gratification of a client's libidinal impulses, or touching a client. Psychologists may wish to use the Exploitation Index developed by Epstein and Simon (1990) as a structured self-assessment instrument. To assist in identifying early warning indicators of boundary violations, this instrument poses questions to the therapist related to eroticism, exhibitionism, dependency, power-seeking, greediness, and enabling.

In thinking through possible dual relationship situations, it is useful to consider whether the anticipated dual relationship will keep the client from making autonomous decisions. It may be equally important to consider the impact on the professional's life. Many dual relationships may be experienced by the psychologist as inhibiting them in either their personal or professional roles, apart from the impact on the client's life. Many psychologists find it helpful to consider worst-case scenarios when contemplating a course of action related to dual relationships.

The importance of consultation in evaluating dual relationships cannot be overstated (Canter et al., 1994; Pope & Vasquez, 1991). Especially in an area of ethical decision-making that is so emotionally charged, the relatively objective perspective of a colleague detached from the situation can bring to light aspects of the decision that were avoided or denied by the individual. Indeed, avoidance of seeking out consultation in situations about which a psychologist feels particularly anxious should perhaps be viewed as a warning sign. Consultation can be useful in understanding the dynamics of a boundary violation or dual relationship, in finding an effective way to resolve a problem, and in creating the least possible harm. Any consultation meetings regarding a dual relationship should be documented in the event that a complaint is later filed by a client.

Once a problematic dual relationship or boundary violation and possible ways of resolving it have been identified, the psychologist should take action. Waiting for the client to take the initiative is likely to breed further injury and anger if the client feels harmed by the relationship. This will only create more problems for the client, and increase the likelihood that a complaint will be filed with an ethics committee.

RESOLVING PROBLEMATIC MULTIPLE RELATIONSHIPS

Section 3.05(b) of the Ethics Code is explicit in its demand that psychologists attempt to resolve harmful multiple relationships:

> If a psychologist finds that, due to unforeseen factors, a potentially harmful multiple relationship has arisen, the psychologist takes reasonable steps to resolve it with due regard for the best interests of the affected person and maximal compliance with the Ethics Code.

Psychologists may initially go into denial when confronted with the reality of having entered an uncomfortable dual relationship or having committed a boundary violation. They want the problem to go away, or hope the client will not notice. If they recognize the violation as being harmful to the client, the professional is likely to also experience a sense of shame and impaired self-worth. After all, most psychologists are highly motivated to help others, and the thought that they may have caused harm is disturbing to all but the most psychopathic therapists. Associated with these other feelings is the sense of terror: the fear of what must be faced about oneself, the possibility of facing investigation by an ethics committee or licensing board, and having to face the client.

Once the psychologist accepts that a boundary violation or harmful dual relationship has been committed, he/she must make the uncomfortable choice between self-protection and self-examination. While in a self-protective stance, the psychologist engages in rationalization in an attempt to justify their actions, and/or minimizes the impact of their actions on the client. But if the psychologist is courageous enough to choose the path of self-examination, there are four difficult, but potentially rewarding, questions to answer (Peterson, 1992). First, how did this happen? Second, what is going on for me that led to this result? What need was served by my entering into this multiple relationship? Third, why this particular client? And finally, how did I give myself permission to commit this ethical violation? How did I lose empathy for the client? And what was the faulty logic that I engaged in to justify my actions? Other decisions may follow or aid in this line of self-examination, such as seeking out consultation or entering treatment.

Making a decision to acknowledge a boundary violation to a client is admittedly risky, because it could be viewed legally as an admission of guilt. The threat of being sued or investigated makes many psychologists fearful of discussing the violation and attempting to restore balance in the relationship. However, in avoiding this challenge the psychologist compromises their integrity and the restoration of trust will be impossible.

In order to face their client and admit their mistake, a psychologist must let go of perfectionistic beliefs about their professionalism. They must also relinquish control over the outcome, and be willing for the client to be seen by another professional if the conflict cannot be resolved. They must also trust that they are choosing the right path, and know that they have the opportunity to alleviate their own shame as well as the client's sense of injury. Beginning a frank discussion with the client with the words "I have allowed treatment to take a turn that is no longer serving your best interests" is the first step towards reaching a resolution and restoring a client's sense of integrity and reality.

During this unusual type of meeting with a client, the psychologist must be open to hearing the client's experience of the boundary violation without becoming defensive and justifying his/her actions. Using empathy-building skills, the psychologist needs to effectively respond to any pain he/she might have caused. Feelings of remorse and sorrow expressed by the therapist will result in a sense of acceptance and validation for the client. If mutual acceptance is possible, it will lead to a renewed and perhaps stronger therapeutic alliance. If such mutual acceptance is not possible, it is in the client's best interest to be referred to another practitioner so that he/she can resolve these issues and get on with the business of dealing with their own lives.

The psychologist's efforts to resolve a boundary violation or harmful dual relationship can have a powerful impact on their clients. When the psychologist tells the client what happened from his/her side of the relationship, the client gains a sense of clarity. When the psychologist explores the truth about themselves and takes responsibility for his/her actions, the client gains a sense of safety. When the psychologist acknowledges the wrong that he/she has done, the client gains a sense of control. When the psychologist faces their shame and accepts the consequences of their actions, the client gains a sense of validation. Putting aside the therapist's own needs and returning to their proper professional role can be extremely confirming for a client.

CONCLUSION

This article has emphasized the central reliance that psychologists must have on their own judgement in dealing with multiple relationships. Because of the wide variety of types and possible outcomes in dual relationships and boundary crossings, psychologists are given less guidance in this area of ethical decision-making than in any other. As a result, psychologists' emotional conflicts and personal needs are more likely to interfere with their judgement in this area. Education about dual relationships is an important first step, but psychologists must find support from their colleagues to undergo continued rigorous self-examination if they are to avoid violating professional boundaries and causing harm through multiple relationships. Consultation remains the best safeguard against possible harm to our clients.

REFERENCES

American Psychological Association. (1992). *Ethical principles of psychologists and code of conduct.* Washington, DC: Author.
American Psychological Association. (2002). *Ethical principles of psychologists and code of conduct.* Washington, DC: Author.

Barnett, J. E., & Yutrzenka, B. A. (1993). Nonsexual dual relationships in professional practice, with special applications to rural and military communities. *The Independent Practitioner*, 243-248.

Bennett, B. E., Bryant, B. K., VandenBos, G. R., & Greenwood, A. (1990). *Professional liability and risk management*. Washington, DC: American Psychological Association.

Binder, L. M., & Thompson, L. L. (1995). The ethics code and neuropsychological assessment practices. *Archives of Clinical Neuropsychology, 10*, 27-46.

Blevins-Knabe, B. (1992). The ethics of dual relationships in higher education. *Ethics and Behavior, 2*, 151-163.

Borys, D. S., & Pope, K. S. (1989). Dual relationships between therapist and client: A national study of psychologists, psychiatrists and social workers. *Professional Psychology: Research and Practice, 20*, 283-293.

California Department of Consumer Affairs. (1995). *Laws and regulations relating to the practice of psychology*. Sacramento, CA: California Office of State Publishing.

Canter, M. B., Bennett, B. E., Jones, S. E., & Nagy, T. F. (1994). *Ethics for psychologists: A commentary on the APA Ethics Code*. Washington, DC: American Psychological Association.

Committee on Ethical Guidelines for Forensic Psychologists. (1991). Specialty guidelines for forensic psychologists. *Law and Human Behavior, 15*, 655-665.

Epstein, R. S., & Simon, R. I. (1990). The exploitation index: An early warning indicator of boundary violations in psychotherapy. *Bulletin of the Menniger Clinic, 54*, 450-465.

Ethics Committee of the American Psychological Association. (1988). Trends in ethics cases, common pitfalls, and published resources. *American Psychologist, 43*, 564-572.

Gandolfo, R. (2005). Bartering. *Journal of Aggression, Maltreatment & Trauma, 11*(1/2), 241-248.

Gottlieb, M. C. (1993). Avoiding exploitive dual relationships: A decision-making model. *Psychotherapy, 30*, 41-48.

Gutheil, T. G., & Gabbard, G. O. (1993). The concept of boundaries in clinical practice: Theoretical and risk-management dimensions. *American Journal of Psychiatry, 150*, 188-196.

Haas, L. J., & Malouf, J. L. (1989). *Keeping up the good work: A practitioner's guide to mental health ethics*. Sarasota, FL: Professional Resource Exchange, Inc.

Handelsman, M. M. (1991, August). An ounce of prevention: Practice ethical reasoning. In D. J. Lutz (Chair), *Full-time academicians in part-time practice: ethical and legal concerns*. Symposium conducted at the annual meeting of the American Psychological Association, San Francisco, CA.

Holroyd, J. C., & Brodsky, A. M. (1977). Psychologist's attitudes and practices regarding erotic and nonerotic physical contact with patients. *American Psychologist, 32*, 843-849.

Horn, D. (1995). Boundary issues in supervision. *The California Psychologist, 12*, 30.

Keith-Spiegel, P., & Koocher, G. P. (1985). *Ethics in psychology: Professional standards and cases*. New York: Random House.

Kilman, B. (1994). Examining multiple role relationships. *San Diego Psychologist Newsletter, 3*, 1-3.

Kitchener, K. S. (1988). Dual role relationships: What makes them so problematic? *Journal of Counseling and Development, 67*, 217-221.

Peterson, M. R. (1992). *At personal risk: Boundary violations in professional-client relationships*. New York: W.W. Norton and Company.

Pope, K. S., & Bouhoutsos, J. C. (1986). *Sexual intimacy between therapists and patients*. New York: Praeger Press.

Pope, K. S., Sonne, J. L., & Holroyd, J. (1993). *Sexual feelings in psychotherapy: Explorations for therapists and therapists-in-training*. Washington, DC: American Psychological Association.

Pope, K. S., Tabachnick, B. G., & Kieth-Spiegel, P. (1987). Ethics of practice: The beliefs and behaviors of psychologists as therapists. *American Psychologist, 42*, 993-1006.

Pope, K. S., & Vasquez, M. J. T. (1991). *Ethics in psychotherapy and counseling: A practical guide for psychologists*. San Francisco: Jossey-Bass Publishers.

Pope, K. S., & Vetter, V. A. (1992). Ethical dilemmas encountered by members of the American Psychological Association. *American Psychologist, 47*, 397-411.

Rest, J. (1983). Morality. In P. H. Mussen (Series Ed.) & J. Flavell & E. Markman (Vol. Eds.), *Handbook of child psychology: Vol. 3, Cognitive development* (4th ed., pp. 556-629). New York: Wiley.

Roll, S., & Millen, L. (1981). A guide to violating an injunction in psychotherapy: On seeing acquaintances as patients. *Psychotherapy: Theory, Research and Practice, 18*, 179-187.

Shavit, N. (2005). Sexual contact between psychologists and patients. *Journal of Aggression, Maltreatment & Trauma, 11*(1/2), 205-239.

Slimp, A. O., & Burian, B. K. (1994). Multiple role relationships during internship: Consequences and recommendations. *Professional Psychology: Research and Practice, 25*, 39-45.

Tallman, G. (1981). *Therapist-client social relationships*. Unpublished manuscript, California State University, Northridge.

Tansey, M. J., & Burke, W. F. (1989). *Understanding countertransference: From projective identification to empathy*. Hillsdale, N.J.: The Analytic Press.

Woody, J. D. (1990). Resolving ethical concerns in clinical practice: Toward a pragmatic model. *Journal of Marital and Family Therapy, 16*, 133-150.

Sexual Contact
Between Psychologists
and Patients

Natalie Shavit

SUMMARY. This article discusses sexualized dual relationships between psychologists and patients, including both sexual contacts while treatment is in progress and after its termination. The reported prevalences of sexual contact between psychologists and patients and between psychologists and former patients are discussed as well as practitioners attitudes towards these two types of relationships. The profiles of both psychologists and patients likely to be involved are outlined as are the clinical and professional consequences of these behaviours. Finally, the APA Ethics Code (2002) is examined to determine whether its inclusions in these areas are adequate and to shed more light on clinicians' continued roles and responsibilities even after treatments have concluded. *[Article copies available for a fee from The Haworth Document Delivery Service: 1-800-HAWORTH. E-mail address: <docdelivery@haworthpress.com> Website: <http://www.HaworthPress.com> © 2005 by The Haworth Press, Inc. All rights reserved.]*

Address correspondence to: Natalie Shavit, LLB, PsyD (E-mail: NRS614@yahoo.com).

[Haworth co-indexing entry note]: "Sexual Contact Between Psychologists and Patients." Shavit, Natalie. Co-published simultaneously in *Journal of Aggression, Maltreatment & Trauma* (The Haworth Maltreatment & Trauma Press, an imprint of The Haworth Press, Inc.) Vol. 11, No. 1/2, 2005, pp. 205-239; and: *Ethical and Legal Issues for Mental Health Professionals: A Comprehensive Handbook of Principles and Standards* (ed: Steven F. Bucky, Joanne E. Callan, and George Stricker) The Haworth Maltreatment & Trauma Press, an imprint of The Haworth Press, Inc., 2005, pp. 205-239. Single or multiple copies of this article are available for a fee from The Haworth Document Delivery Service [1-800-HAWORTH, 9:00 a.m. - 5:00 p.m. (EST). E-mail address: docdelivery@haworthpress.com].

Digital Object Identifier: 10.1300/J146v11n01_14

KEYWORDS. Sexual contact, psychologists, patients, termination, ethics, clinical consequences

Even before the fourth century B.C. emergence of the Hippocratic Oath, healers were told not to become sexually intimate with patients (Brodsky, 1989). Surprisingly, it was relatively recently that the American Psychological Association (APA) explicitly prohibited psychologists from being sexually intimate with their patients. Up until 1979, complaints pertaining to therapist sexual misconduct were virtually nonexistent; indeed, the APA Ethics Committee dealt with only four such complaints from 1970-1974. In dramatic contrast, since the inclusion of the ban on this behavior, sexual misconduct cases became steadily more numerous, and are now reported as being the second largest category of complaints, with only child custody complaints being more frequent (Hunsaker, 1998).

Since psychologists have been faced with the possibility of civil and criminal law suits, complaints to ethics and licensing boards, and large financial and professional liability for sexual contact with their patients, research on the prevalence and harm of such relationships has been forthcoming. State-run organizations and self-help groups have sprung up in several places around the country and on the internet to provide support, information, and assistance to victims of therapist sexual misconduct (Haspel, Jorgenson, Wincze, & Parsons, 1997). Examples of these include the Walk-In Counseling Center in Minneapolis, the Boston Association to Stop Therapist Abuse, Therapist Exploitation Link Line, and AdvocateWeb. Such resources increase the public's awareness about therapist-patient sex and its consequences; further, they rally state legislatures, professional associations, and licensing boards to work on prevention, punishment, and compensation where it is warranted (Haspel et al., 1997).

The most current *Ethical Principles of Psychologists and Code of Conduct* (APA, 2002) outright forbids engaging in sexual intimacies with current patients and with former patients within, at the very least, two years after therapy is terminated (Standards 10.05, 10.08). Similarly, section 1.2 of the American Association of Marriage and Family Therapy's (AAMFT) *Code of Ethics* (1998) prohibits sexual intimacies with current clients and for two years following termination of services, while section 1.09(c) of the 1999 *Code of Ethics of the National Association of Social Workers* (NASW) states that social workers should not "under any circumstances" engage in sexual activities with current clients and only under "extraordinary circumstances" with former clients. Several basic values underscore these prohibitions. According to the ethical principle of abstinence, clinicians are to refrain from serving their own gratification beyond professional satisfaction and financial remuneration when treating patients (Smith & Fitzpatrick, 1995). Thus, the only appropriate return for services is the professional fee paid by the patient to the therapist. The principle of neutrality, derived from psychoanalytic theory, maintains that the patient's welfare and needs are of primary concern in the treatment relationship, so the therapist must not impose personal opinions that do not further therapy progression (Smith & Fitzpatrick, 1995). A further relevant principle is that clinicians must strive to further a patient's independence and autonomy (Smith & Fitzpatrick, 1995). This principle translates into not fostering over-dependence or keeping the treatment going indefinitely, maintaining the patient's self-determination. Western concepts of human dignity are the foundation of all these ethical guidelines (Simon, 1998).

The definition of sexual involvement intended by the APA Code (1992) includes a range of behavior from sexual intercourse to kissing and even verbal sexual invitations (Canter, Bennett, Jones, & Nagy, 1994). A commentary on the 1992 APA Code (Canter et al., 1994) explained that the term "sexual intimacies" encompasses a broader range of behavior than sexual intercourse, and can include "kissing, any erotic or romantic hugging, touching, or other physical contact" (p. 96). It can also cover actions like masturbation or verbal sexual invitations that do not involve touch.

REPORTED PREVALENCE
OF THERAPIST-PATIENT SEXUAL CONTACT

Data from studies investigating the prevalence of therapist-patient sexual involvement have been obtained via national, anonymous direct and indirect surveys of both therapists and patients (Pope & Vetter, 1992). The initial nationwide survey to look at sexual involvement between therapist and patient was done by Holroyd and Brodsky in 1977 with a sample consisting of 500 male and 500 female licensed psychologists. They found that 7.7% of their 700 respondents admitted to having had erotic contact with patients. Nearly 11% of the men acknowledged erotic contact with their patients, and 5.5% admitted having sexual intercourse. For female psychologists, 1.9% admitted erotic contact and 0.6% admitted sexual intercourse. Furthermore, it was almost always a male therapist engaging in erotic contact with a female patient; 80% of those who acknowledged sexual contact with a patient had done so with more than one person; and 70% of the male and 88% of the female psychologists regarded such behavior as never being to the patient's benefit. No differences between those who did and did not engage in non-erotic contact were found by theoretical orientation (Holroyd & Brodsky, 1977).

Comparable results were obtained by Pope, Levenson, and Schover (1979), with approximately 12% of male therapists and 3% of female therapists in the sample of 481 members of Division 29 (Psychotherapy) admitting to sexual involvement with at least one patient. Only 2% believed, however, that such relationships could be of benefit. Of note is that 43% of respondents who had sexual contact with clients or students in this study endorsed that such involvement was clearly not beneficial to either party. These beliefs were not found to be linked to gender.

In 1988, Pope conducted a review of all the therapist sexual misconduct studies published in the US between 1983 and 1987, and obtained a prevalence rate of 8.3% for males and 1.7% for females acknowledging such behavior. In 1991, Stake and Oliver surveyed 320 licensed psychologists in Missouri via anonymous questionnaires to examine particular behaviors rather than directly asking about actual sexual involvement per se. They arrived at an incident rate between 2.2% and 7.3%, depending on the definition of sexual misconduct.

Pope, Tabachnick, and Keith-Speigel (1987) conducted a comprehensive survey about psychologists' beliefs and behaviors in practice. On items related to therapist-patient sexual involvement, their research found that only 1.9% of the 456 respondents acknowledged engaging in sexual contact with a patient, and only 2.6% acknowledged engaging in erotic activity with a patient. These figures were lower than those obtained by Holroyd and Brodsky (1977). By way of explanation, the authors theorized that perhaps due to the added press that therapist sexual misconduct had received, there may have been an actual decrease in the violations of this nature taking place in the field.

Borys and Pope (1989) studied dual relationships among 4,800 mental health professionals. Of their 2,133 respondents, only 0.2% of the women and 0.9% of the men admitted to having been sexually intimate with an ongoing patient. These data were also lower than those previously reported for women (2.5-3.1%) and for men (7.1-12.1%) in earlier research (Gartrell, Herman, Olarte, Feldstein, & Localio, 1987;

Holroyd & Brodsky, 1977; Pope, Kieth-Spiegel, & Tabachnick, 1986). Similar to Pope, Tabachnick, and Keith-Speigel's (1987) conclusion, Borys and Pope proposed the possibility that the decline may represent an actual drop in such behavior; alternatively, they also proposed that it may be that the added publicity that this topic had received decreased the willingness to admit to sexual misconduct, especially since it has been recognized in several states as a felony, and/or that the wording of their survey instrument led to misinterpretation. "It is possible that participants may have interpreted 'engaging in sexual activity with an ongoing client' as referring to sexual intimacies with someone who was still a patient at the time of this survey rather than sexual intimacies with any patient-past or present-before termination of therapy" (p. 289).

Gender differences. Gender differences in the acknowledgment of sexual contact with patients have been variable in the research. The reported rates for male psychologists have typically been between 5-12%, whereas female rates have ranged from 1-3% (Bouhoutsos, Holroyd, Lerman, Forer, & Greenberg, 1983; Gartrell et al., 1987; Holroyd & Brodsky, 1977; Pope et al., 1986). However, in Akamatsu's (1988) and Pope et al.'s (1987) findings, both genders' incidence rates were in the 2-3% range. Based on the report of the Ethics Committee (APA, 1999), 72% of the sexual dual-relationship allegations involved male psychologists with adult female patients. In that year, "there were three cases in the female-female, one case in the female-male, and no cases in the male-male categories of complaints" (Ethics Committee of the APA, 1999, p. 706). Based on the sample of clinicians insured by the American Professional Agency, there has been a rise in the number of claims against female therapists accused of sexual misconduct, from both female and male patients, and there have been instances where the female psychologists have had their patients' babies (E. Marine, personal communication, September 24, 1999). When female clinicians have admitted to sexual involvement with a patient, they tend to report being in love, and the patient is more likely to also be female (Rigby-Weinberg, 1986, cited in Collins, 1999, p. 57). In a study by Benowitz (1994) on the experiences of female patients sexually exploited by female versus male psychotherapists, of the 15 female-female dyads where therapist-patient sexual involvement had occurred, 20% of the clinicians identified as heterosexual, 20% as bisexual, and only 40% as lesbian. The remaining 20% did not indicate their sexual preference. For 20% of the therapists in the study, it was their first sexual encounter with another woman. The author stated that the data supported the idea that "therapists who are not comfortable with their feelings of same-sex attraction may be at higher risk for acting inappropriately with their clients" (p. 72). In addition, since 33% of the therapists were married to men at the time of the sexual involvement, a heterosexual orientation or marriage to a man "are not clear predictors that female therapists will refrain from sexual contact with female clients" (p. 72).

Differences have been apparent in the belief about the therapeutic benefit of sexual contact with patients between male and female psychologists (Holroyd & Brodsky, 1977), with females thinking it less beneficial and being more likely to report that their patients experienced negative consequences from sexual contact with a prior therapist (Holroyd & Bouhoutsos, 1985). Collins' (1999) study found no significant difference in attitudes of male and female psychologists about the ethicality of sexual contact with current patients, although the female therapists perceived the impact of such contact to be more harmful. Female therapists have been more in favor of compulsory reporting of therapist-patient sexual contact (Gartrell et al., 1987). Stake and Oliver's (1991) research confirmed that women clinicians showed a higher sensitivity to sexual misconduct issues but found no significant gender differences with respect to reported overt sexual contact with patients. While no exact data were provided, a lower rate of sexual misconduct was obtained regarding the male therapists compared to prior research, but similar incidence was reported by female therapists. The researchers also offered that the drop in the male prevalence rate may have been the result of the increased negative press that sexual involvement had received recently both in the professional and the legal arenas.

ATTITUDES REGARDING THERAPIST-PATIENT SEXUAL CONTACT

To examine attitudes regarding psychiatrist-patient sexual contact, Herman, Gartrell, Olarte, Feldstein, and Localio (1987) conducted a national sample of 1,423 practicing psychiatrists. Ninety-eight percent described it as "always inappropriate" and "usually harmful." Nonetheless, a surprising result was that 4.5% of the respondents believed that if the therapist fell in love with the patient, the sexual contact could be appropriate. Those clinicians who admitted to having had sexual contact with at least one patient ($n = 84$ respondents) were more prone to entertaining exceptions to the rules, with 10% countenancing sexual relations with patients and 19% of them believing it could be of benefit to the treatment. One

55-year-old divorced psychiatrist who acknowledged having sex with three female patients wrote that his last encounter was "a loving relation to a healthy human being I'd come to know" and that it "in no way had the usual sordid tinge" (Herman et al., 1987, p. 167). Almost 10% of the offender group as compared with only 1% of the non-offender group thought that it could sometimes be a valid treatment intervention. The researchers note that those who felt regret about their sexual intimacy with a patient focused more on the negative results on themselves rather than on those for the patient. Regarding policy recommendations, the offenders were more likely to oppose the idea of imposing sanctions in response to therapist-patient sexual relations than the non-offenders (34% versus 13%).

Conte, Plutchik, Picard, and Karasu (1989) surveyed 101 psychotherapists on a variety of ethical issues. Only 80% believed that sexual intimacy between therapist and patient was grounds for malpractice, with the remainder considering it just unethical. They found no significant differences among the three professions represented (psychologists, psychiatrists, and social workers) nor were any significant gender differences obtained.

The attitudes and behaviors of 366 male members of the American Counseling Association were researched by Thoreson, Shaughnessy, Heppner, and Cook (1993). Sexual contact with patients, defined as sexual intercourse or direct genital stimulation, was reported by 1.7% of the respondents; 94.6% rated this as professional misconduct. They found that attitude was the most reliable correlate of engaging in sexual contact with a current patient. In a subsequent national study of female members of American Counseling Association, Thoreson, Shaughnessy, and Frazier (1995) examined both attitudes and behaviors about sexual contact in a variety of professional relationships ($N = 377$). They found a prevalence rate of 0.7% for female counselors who acknowledged sexual contact with a patient during the treatment. However, in these same counselors' prior experience as either students, patients, or supervisees, 5.2% reported sexual contact during the course of that prior professional relationship. These disparate rates were explained in terms of the level of power held in the relationship, with sexual contact more common when these women are in the lower power role (e.g., as students, patients, or supervisees) as opposed to when they are in the higher power role (e.g., as counselors). Between 85% and 95% believed such contact to be harmful and to constitute misconduct.

PATIENTS AT RISK

Therapist-patient sexual contact often starts with a vulnerable patient and an emotionally unfulfilled therapist (Steres, 1992). Studies that

have looked at patient characteristics have shown that the female victims are typically 12 to 16 years younger than their male therapists
(Bouhoutsos et al., 1983; D'Addarrio, 1977). These patients have been
profiled as lonely, depressed, and having poor self-esteem, with a history of incest or other abusive relationships, leaving them vulnerable to
further exploitation (Coleman & Schaefer, 1986). Pope and Bouhoutsos
(1986) presented three groups of patients, differing in terms of their
level of risk in becoming sexually intimate with their therapists. The
low risk group includes relatively high-functioning, neurotically organized patients with no history of psychiatric hospitalization and
who have had stable relationships in their lives. The moderate risk
group have had troubled relationships, are more dependent, and are
likely to be personality disordered. The high risk group are the more
borderline organized patients, with histories of psychiatric hospitalizations, attempted suicides, and substance abuse issues. They are
also more likely to be survivors of rape and/or incest, thereby placing
them at a higher susceptibility to repeated victimization. This correlate has been refuted by Wohlberg, McGraith, and Thomas (1997),
who stated that although "it feels as if there is a disproportionate
number of survivors of childhood sexual abuse, the percentages are
consistent with the prevalence within the population at large" (p. 4).
In Pope and Vetter's (1992) study, only 32% of patients who had had
sexual relations with their therapists had been sexually abused as
children.

CLINICAL CONSEQUENCES
OF THERAPIST-PATIENT SEXUAL CONTACT

The therapy relationship is not an egalitarian one. Patients come to
therapy in a vulnerable state, seeking support and assistance from a more
knowledgeable professional (Herman et al., 1987). "[T]he therapist comes into the relationship with all the power and authority of the expert
who has something to sell . . . what is being sold is a promise that the relationship will help the patient improve his or her personal life" (Brodsky,
1986, p. 156). The clinician gathers as much data on the patient as possible, including their most private thoughts and experiences, but the patient
learns very little in the way of personal details about the therapist. Central
to the trust necessary for the benefits of the therapy process is the clini-

cian's promise not to misuse the power position for personal gratification (Herman et al., 1987). Sexual involvement uses and manipulates this unequal distribution of power (Smith & Fitzpatrick, 1995). Moreover, owing to the nature of the alliance, a patient may believe that any sexual advance made upon him/her by the therapist is part of what is necessary and/or beneficial to the treatment (Pope, 1988). Brodsky (1986) stated that sexual intimacy with patients always implies exploitation and hence distress or damage.

An analogy is often drawn between therapist-patient sexual involvement and incest because, like parents, therapists can abuse the greater power they have in the dyad and can manipulate patients' vulnerability, trust, and dependence on them for safety and help (see, e.g., Freud, 1958; Searles, 1959; Seto, 1995). Masters and Johnson (1976) have also compared therapist-patient sexual involvement to rape or incest, creating "therapeutic orphans" who are not in a position to provide a meaningful consent. Finkelhor (1984) likened sexual intimacy between therapist and patient to adult-child sex or child sexual abuse since "in the context of a therapeutic relationship, a patient is not really free to say yes or no. Even if the patient liked it, a moral wrong would have been committed" (p. 18). The incidence rates of incest and therapist-patient sex are similar (Kardener, 1974). Both a parent and a therapist are to place the child/patient's well-being as paramount. Both allow a close, dependent relationship for a specific goal, that of ultimate independence and autonomy. A successful therapy, like successful child rearing, will enable a child or patient to freely pursue his/her own life. Consequently, to engage in sexual contact with a patient or a child is to violate a critical boundary and a societal taboo. Both types of the taboo involve fantasies and wishes based on oedipal phenomena (Pope, 1990b). Abusers are often unable or unwilling to think through the consequences of their actions on their victim, instead focusing on their own gratification and feelings of affection (Pope, 1990b). Both kinds of abusers are frequently respected, prominent, and law abiding citizens on every other front (Pope, 1990b). Herman et al. (1987) felt that this comparison captures both the reality and the mechanisms in process in the therapeutic encounter.

Bouhoutsos et al.'s (1983) work showed that 90% of clinicians reported that patients who had been sexually involved with a previous therapist had suffered as a result of that involvement. The harm included inability to trust, reluctance to obtain further professional help, serious depressions, hospitalizations, and suicide. Coleman and Schaefer (1986) also listed depression and other affective disorders, adjustment disorders, and substance abuse as adverse effects of therapist-patient sexual contact. Pope (1988) believed that the fact that 10% from Bouhoutsos et al.'s study (1983) did not report harm is probably due to the delayed onset of the destructive effects. Following on this view, Holroyd and Bouhoutsos (1985) later discovered that many of those clinicians who perceived no adverse effects were in fact those who engaged in such therapist-patient sexual intimacy and so were biased in their reporting. Similarly, Herman et al. (1987) found that those clinicians who had had sexual contact with their own patients were more likely to believe such contact to be of benefit.

Feldman-Summers and Jones (1984) examined the symptoms of women who reported having been sexually involved with their therapists. Their study included 14 heterosexual Caucasian women who responded to advertisements announcing that people who had had sexual contact with their therapist or doctor were needed for research. This group was matched to another group of 10 women who had not engaged in sexual contact with their therapists. The researchers found that the women who had been sexually involved with their therapists reported increased rage, mistrust, and more psychosomatic and psychological symptoms. Severity of the detriment done by the sexual contact was shown to be related to the severity of the patients' symptoms before the treatment, prior sexual abuse, and the marital status of the therapist. The authors concluded that "if the client is suffering already from substantial psychological problems or if the therapist is married, the sexual contact will likely be even more harmful to the client" (p. 1060).

A 1992 survey by Pope and Vetter showed that half of their sample of 647 clinical and counseling psychologists had treated at least one patient who had been sexually intimate with a previous clinician. A total of 958 patients were identified in their study. Of these, 90% were rated to have been harmed by this contact, and 87% of all the patients were women.

The Walk-In Counseling Center in Minneapolis, Minnesota, based on its work with both victims and perpetrators of therapist-patient sex, reported that the most recurrent theme of those patients who experienced a therapist's sexual misconduct is loss of trust. The sexual involvement impacted their attitudes towards therapists at large as well as professional and legal structures, licensing boards, and the schools responsible for producing these clinicians (Pope & Bouhoutsos, 1986). Pope (1988) described what he termed 'therapist-patient sex syndrome.' Its symptoms include ambivalence, guilt, isolation, cognitive impairment, feelings of emptiness, identity and boundary dysfunction, difficulty with trust, sexual confusion, over-controlled hostility, mood lability, and/or an increased risk of suicide. He suggested that there exists a comparable effect between victims of child abuse, rape, and spousal abuse and those patients who have been sexually involved with their therapists, one that resembles traits of borderline personality disorder, histrionic personality disorder, and posttraumatic stress disorder. Schoener and Gonsiorek (1990) rejected this syndrome based on the variability of patient-victim characteristics seen in their Minneapolis clinic.

In a dissertation by D'Addario (1977), sexual contact with therapists was determined to be "detrimental, if not devastating" by the four female patients in the study. Not only were their presenting problems not treated in the therapy, but they were exacerbated by feelings of rage, loneliness, and abandonment. Nonetheless, they exhibited an unexpected degree of rationalization, denial, and understanding of the therapists' issues, all of which included sexual dysfunction.

In 1976, Taylor and Wagner reviewed the 34 cases of therapist-patient sexual involvement cited in the professional literature to date and rated them according to positive, negative, or mixed outcome. They found that 16 cases were determined to be negative, and 7 cases were determined to be positive. It is difficult to generalize from the results owing to the variability in reporting criteria. The empirical findings, based on both patient self-reports and the reports of their subsequent therapists, demonstrate that serious harm is a far more likely consequence of therapist-patient sexual involvement on the patients (Pope & Bouhoutsos, 1986).

In 1984, Vinson (cited in Pope & Bouhoutsos, 1986, p. 62) compared the symptoms of male and female patients who had been sexually intimate with their therapists and found that men did not perceive negative impact on their lives to the extent that women did. Likewise, the men who responded to Feldman-Summers and Jones' (1984) announcements seeking out men who had had sexual contact with their therapists stated that their experience was positive. This is similar to the perceptions of male sexual abuse survivors (J. Slavin, personal communication, February 6, 2000). Overall, the male patients reported nine times fewer symptoms than the females, who identified depression, hopelessness, alienation, and emotional numbness as the most troubling effects.

The research has not accounted for the gender differences in the impact of therapist-patient sexual abuse on the patients. When women do become abused in this way, they may feel more free to seek out psychological assistance and to express psychological symptoms, and more able to accept themselves as having been victims of sexual misconduct. Given current gender stereotypes, and in particular the male ethic of self-reliance (Finkelhor, 1984), men may have greater difficulty perceiving themselves as victims of a sexual offense or seeing themselves in the role of victim at all. The discrepancies between the genders' symptomatology may also be a function of the underreporting of male negative effects from sexual misconduct, the underreporting of incidence of sexual involvement with male patients, and/or a much lower actual incidence of males being victims of therapist sexual misconduct.

PROFESSIONAL CONSEQUENCES OF THERAPIST-PATIENT SEXUAL CONTACT

Therapist-patient sexual activity is negligence per se, a dereliction of the greatly ambiguous and greatly controversial standard of care (Simon, 1998), which may be defined as the care that prudent and reasonable therapists give to their patients (Grosso, 1998). When psychologists have been found guilty of sexual misconduct, they have had to face sanctions, license revocations and suspensions, and expulsion from professional organizations, and have been ordered to obtain therapy in the hopes of rehabilitation.

Legal sanctions. A review of the pertinent court cases by Austin, Moline, and Williams (1990, cited in Corey, Corey, & Callahan, 1995, p. 154) revealed that there was no successful defense available to therapists who had had sex with their patients. The courts viewed the behavior as an abuse of transference, whereby the power differential between the two parties vitiates patient consent (e.g., *Cranford Insurance Company v. Allwest Insurance Company*, 1986; *Zipkin v. Freeman*, 1968). In the case of *Roy v. Hartogs* (1976), a female patient successfully sued her psychiatrist for damages that occurred as a result of a 13-month sexual relationship while therapy was in progress. Since this New York Appellate Court case, the therapy relationship is viewed as a fiduciary one, with an implicit "warranty of good faith and care" for the patient's welfare (Jorgenson et al., 1991). Furthermore, Presiding Justice Markowitz recognized that from Freud to the present day, mental health practitioners agree that therapist-patient sex is harmful to patients (Pope & Vasquez, 1998).

The financial burden of losing a sexual misconduct civil suit can be enormous. By 1980, nearly 10% of the APA Insurance Trust's malpractice suits were for sexual misconduct allegations (Wright, 1981, cited in Hunsaker, 1998). Only one of the 726 claims of sexual malpractice filed from 1975 through 1984 with the Insurance Trust led to the therapist being exonerated (Cummings & Sobel, 1985). Of the total amount paid by the APA's insurance carrier between 1978 and 1988, 45% was for sexual misconduct cases (Seto, 1995). To overcome this financial drain, many insurance policies have placed limits on the amount of damages that can be awarded for cases involving sexual misconduct (Seto, 1995).

The gender differences found in the research as to which clinicians tend to engage in therapist-patient sex have been reflected in the insurance claims. The first malpractice suit filed against a female clinician was by a female patient in 1983 (Cummings & Sobel, 1985). By the end of 1984, there were 11 such claims filed, as well as two cases involving a male patient suing a female psychotherapist and one case with both parties being male (Cummings & Sobel, 1985).

In California, in response to the bevy of therapist sexual misconduct cases, civil and criminal statutes have been enacted to protect the public and the profession alike. Therapist sexual misconduct constitutes a criminal offense, punishable by imprisonment in a county jail for not more than six months, or a fine not to exceed $1000, or both.[1] If there is more than one victim involved, the jail time may be up to three years in a state prison with the fine as high as $10,000.[2] This law applies to sexual contact during therapy or when therapy is ended for the purpose of having sexual contact with a patient. " 'Sexual contact' is defined as sexual intercourse or the touching of an intimate part of a patient for the purpose of sexual arousal, gratification, or abuse."[3]

The California statute that creates a civil cause of action for therapist sexual exploitation eradicates the need for the patient to prove there was a breach of duty of care, provided it can be shown that there was sexual intimacy within the treatment relationship. After this is established, the patient must show that harm occurred as a result of the sexual contact.[4] There is no need to prove emotional dependence on the psychotherapist.[5]

Ethics complaints and administrative action. While the number of sexual misconduct complaints sharply increased during the 1970s and 1980s, there has since been a decline (E. Marine, American Professional Agency, personal communication, September 24, 1999). Of the 31 cases that the APA Ethics Committee opened in 1998 in response to loss of licensure, 58% of those were due to sexual misconduct (APA, 1999). Sexual misconduct accounted for 53% of cases that resulted in loss of APA membership in 1998, as compared with 57% in 1997; 67% in 1996; 58% in 1995; 58% in 1994; 43% in 1993; and 56% in 1992 (APA, 1999). In 1998, male psychologists and their female patients were the predominant gender combination in the sexual dual-relationship allegations (72% of cases). That same year, there were three female-female cases, one case with a female psychologist and a male patient, and none involving a male-male case (APA, 1999).

Psychologists must also face and be accountable to professional bodies and licensing boards for their behavior. Gottlieb, Sell, and Schoenfeld (1988) found that the rate of sexual misconduct complaints to state licensing boards and state ethics committees rose by 482.4% between 1982-1985. Statistics from the California Board of Psychology (1998) show that there were 12 decisions made regarding sexual misconduct violations out of a total 600 complaints in 1996-1997, and 9 out of 521 in 1997-1998. It is unclear what type of violations are listed as undecided or dismissed. Administrative action can range from fines to suspensions of practice and membership revocations. Unfortunately, there are some hurdles to overcome to file a complaint against a therapist. Due to the increase in complaints being lodged, delays in processing have risen (Gottlieb et al., 1988). In 1982, 17.6% of cases were left pending, and by 1985 this number rose to 56.1%. In addition, for a patient seeking some retribution, knowing that the therapist might be faced with a fine or temporary suspension can seem unsatisfying (Seto, 1995).

The courts did not uphold the action of state licensing boards dealing with sexual misconduct until the 1970s. In 1965, the Colorado Supreme Court in *Colorado State Board of Medical Examiners v. Weiler* impeded the board's attempts to revoke the license of a therapist who allegedly had prescribed sexual intercourse as part of the treatment plan. Only in 1973, in *Morra v. State Board of Examiners of Psychologists*, did the Kansas Supreme Court recognize the Kansas State Board's authority to take away the clinician's license for trying to convince two patients to have sex with him. Likewise, a California Appellate Court supported the California Board's power to revoke a license due to therapist sexual misconduct with three patients in *Cooper v. Board of Medical Examiners* (1975). There the sexual relationship constituted gross negligence (Ethics Committee of the APA, 1988).

The current California Business and Professions Code has attempted to stipulate what is inappropriate behavior and how that behavior is to be handled by the Board of Psychology. Sex with a patient constitutes a cause of action for license discipline in Section 2960(o), and this discipline must be followed by license revocation pursuant to Section 2960.1. If a therapist is told by a patient that he or she had sexual contact with a prior clinician, the treating therapist must hand the patient the booklet *Professional Therapy Never Includes Sex* (California Department of Consumer Affairs, 2002), which outlines and explains that such conduct is illegal and that there are remedies open to the patient to pursue. The therapist also needs to explain the option of reporting to the appropriate state licensing board that such conduct has taken place. The patient's decision not to lodge a complaint necessitates the therapist's maintaining this information as confidential. Failure to follow this procedure can be grounds for discipline for the treating therapist.[6]

PROFILE OF THERAPISTS INVOLVED

"The best single predictor of exploitation in therapy is a therapist who has exploited another patient in the past" (Bates & Brodsky, 1989, p. 141, cited in Wohlberg et al., 1997, p. 5). The profile that has consistently emerged is that of a middle-aged male who is often well-trained and who has undergone personal therapy (Gartrell et al., 1987; Pope, 1990b). Typically, he is approximately 16.5 years older than his female patients, whose average age when sexually intimate with him is 22 (Butler & Zelen, 1977, cited in Claman, 1987, p. 36). Added to this, he is professionally isolated and undergoing some situational stress or a crisis, such as a divorce. This stress paves the way for the slippery slope of boundary violations wherein he attempts to seek comfort from the patient by sharing his vulnerability with his typically much younger female patient (Gabbard, 1991; Olarte, 1991). Of these violating therapists, 80% could not recall what led to the sexual encounter (Zelen, 1985). Pope (1990b) suggested that these clinicians "are well represented among the most prominent and respected mental health professionals" (p. 233). He indicated that their high professional status has contributed to their lack of detection and to the profession's reluctance to explore the matter with greater rigor. Approximately 60% of these therapists saw themselves as having a father role for their patient-sexual partners, and 55% said they loved their patients and that the sexual involvement resulted from their completely being attracted to the client in every way, namely, physically, intellectually, and emotionally (Butler & Zelen, 1977, cited in Claman, 1987, p. 36).

Celenza (1998) obtained what she termed "preliminary findings" (p. 378) based on psychological testing, interviews, and consultations with 14 male and 3 female therapists who had engaged in sexual intimacies with patients. The common themes that emerged in these clinicians included: chronic low self-esteem, sexualization in early childhood, limited use of fantasy in their lives, and having experienced subtle boundary violations by a caretaker and so having unresolved hostility towards authority and not tolerating negative transference, instead converting countertransferential hate into love in a defensive manner. Celenza (1998) concluded that most often the sexual act was a means to bypass the patient's negative transference and simultaneously to allow the therapist to express hidden anger. Furthermore, the sexual act frequently took place when the therapists felt that the treatment was at an impasse, the patient was beginning to express anger or disappointment, and the therapist felt frustrated by the lack of success resulting from his/her efforts to help (Celenza, 1998).

Given these various themes that have been ascertained in therapists who have had sex with their patients, attempts have been made to provide a typology and classification of these clinicians. Keith-Spiegel and Koocher (1985) listed four profiles of offenders: the seducer, the sexpert, the hit-and-runner, and the love-bitten. In a paper presentation, Schoener (1984, cited in Coleman & Schaefer, 1986, p. 342) believed that there are five levels of disturbance possible in offending clinicians. From highest to lowest level of functioning, these are characterized as follows:

1. The higher functioning clinician may get embroiled in an episodic occurrence of therapist-patient sex as an isolated incident of poor judgment, loss of control, or due to situational factors. Remorse is often expressed and there is good prognosis for rehabilitation.
2. Neurotic disturbance in an isolated, lonely therapist who has unmet intimacy needs.
3. The most common level of disturbance found is that of compulsive character disordered therapists. Similar to other chronic sex offenders, they have poor impulse control, rationalize their actions, and are not good rehabilitation candidates.
4. Narcissistic character disordered clinicians who show no remorse and believe they are acting in the patient's best interest.

5. Psychotic disordered clinicians–the rarest category found.

Pope and Bouhoutsos (1986) presented ten prototypical scenarios by which therapist-patient sex takes place. These scenarios were derived from their study of the topic, from the literature at large, and from public records. They were summarized by Schoener (1987) as:

1. Role trading: therapist becomes the patient;
2. Sex therapy: sex fraudulently presented as 'sex therapy';
3. As if wherein therapist ignores that feelings are likely to be transference;
4. Svengali: therapist exploits dependent client;
5. Drugs and/or alcohol are used in seduction;
6. Rape: overt force or threats are used by the therapist;
7. True love: therapist rationalizes that it is 'true love';
8. It just got out of hand: loss of control due to the emotional closeness of therapy;
9. Time out: therapist rationalizes that contact outside of session is legitimate;
10. Hold me: therapist exploits client's need to be held or touched. (p. 9)

Objecting to categorizations of scenarios and offending clinicians, Gabbard (1994a) wrote:

All systematic studies of psychotherapists who have been involved in sexual boundary violations indicate that sexual misconduct occurs among a diverse group of clinicians who become involved with patients for a variety of reasons. Any attempt to lump all the transgressing therapists into one politically correct category is reductionistic and misguided. (p. 439)

However, Gabbard (1994a, 1995) does sort offenders into four groups: (1) the psychotic disordered clinician; (2) the predatory psychopathic and paraphilic clinician; (3) the self-destructive clinician; and (4) the "lovesick" clinician. The first two categories account for only a small number of therapist-patient sexual encounters (Gabbard, 1991). They tend to prey on any attractive patient, often having more than one patient as a sexual victim, and they often humiliate the patient in the process (Gabbard, 1991). The self-destructive therapists succumb to tougher patients in the hopes of placating them with looser boundaries. They typically have trouble dealing with their own aggression. For the "lovesick" clinician narcissistic themes prevail, whereby the therapist desperately needs to be validated by patients to regulate his/her own self-worth. The bulk of the research focuses on this category (Gabbard & Lester, 1996). The lovesick type therapist typically becomes sexually involved with a dependent patient who can incite tremendous guilt in an analyst that s/he is not doing enough in the treatment (Gabbard, 1991). The two latter categories are the focus of rehabilitation efforts, as the first two groups are considered to be poor candidates.

Based on their clinical experience at the Walk-In Counseling Center with over 1,000 therapists who had been sexually intimate with patients, Schoener and Gonsiorek (1990) formulated a rehabilitation model so that some of the offending clinicians could return to their practice. They classified the offending therapists in terms of appropriateness for such efforts. Those with impulse control problems, anti-social personality, or thought disorders were least suited for rehabilitation. Some of their suggested interventions include psychotherapy, supervision, training, and restricted practices. At the time of their writing, no therapist who had undergone the rehabilitation model had incurred either a complaint or charge of sexual misconduct subsequently. Yet, this avenue has come under fire and sparked controversy. Pope (1989, 1990b) contended that rehabilitation has not proven to be effective, and compared it to allowing a teacher convicted of child sexual molestation to return to the classroom.

Sexual Contact Between Therapists and Former Patients

The most recent *Ethical Principles of Psychologist and Code of Conduct* published by the APA (2002) explicitly states in Standard 10.08:

> (a) Psychologists do not engage in sexual intimacies with a former clients/patients for at least two years after cessation or termination of therapy.
> (b) Psychologists do not engage in sexual intimacies with former clients/patients even after a two-year interval except in the most unusual cirumstances. Psychologists who engage in such activity after the two years following cessation or termination of therapy and of having no sexual contact with the former client/patient bear the burden of demonstrating that there has been no exploitation, in light of all relevant factors, including (1) the amount of time that has passed since therapy terminated; (2) the nature, duration, and

intensity of the therapy; (3) the circumstances of termination; (4) the client/patient's personal history; (5) the client/patient's current mental status; (6) the likelihood of adverse impact on the client/patient; and (7) any statements or actions made by the therapist during the course of therapy suggesting or inviting the possibility of a posttermination sexual or romantic relationship with the client/patient. (p. 15)

The 1992 revision of the APA ethics code included for the first time since its inception in 1953 a prohibition against sexual intimacies with former patients within the two-year period following termination. Even after this period, except "in the most unusual circumstances," this behavior is still labeled as unethical. The 1999 NASW Code of Ethics states in Section 1.09(c) that social workers should not have any sexual contact with former clients unless there are "extraordinary circumstances" and it can be demonstrated that no exploitation, coercion, or manipulation took place. The AAMFT Code (1998) allows for no such discretion within the two-year period since the termination of the therapy (Section 1.2).

Much debate had occurred as a precursor to the 1992 APA Ethics Code's Standard 4.07 (Standard 10.08 in the 2002 Code). In fact, all 15 earlier drafts of the 1992 APA Code included a complete ban on all post-termination sex (Gabbard, 1994a), in contrast with the new guidelines. There remains a great deal of controversy related to the question of sex with former patients (e.g., Bersoff, 1994, 1995; Gabbard, 1994a) and specifically whether the 'once a patient always a patient' ideology should be codified. Bersoff (1994) wrote an article about the 1992 code, entitled "Explicit Ambiguity: The 1992 Ethics Code as an Oxymoron," referring to the debate on establishing an absolute prohibition on post-termination sexual involvement. In contrast with the APA's 1992 position, the American Psychiatric Association reacted two months later by imposing an absolute ban on sexual contact with former patients (Gabbard, 1994a).

Attitudes Regarding Therapist-Former Patient Sexual Contact

While research in the field has consistently shown that professionals view sexual contact with current patients as unethical (e.g., Borys & Pope, 1989; Pope et al., 1987), there is much less consensus in attitudes about the acceptability and appropriateness of post-termination sexual involvement (Thorenson et al., 1995). Borys and Pope's (1989) study revealed that engaging in sexual activity with a current patient was thought by 98.3% of the psychologists surveyed to never be ethical, and only 0.4% were not sure. By comparison, 68.4% of clinicians said that it was "never ethical" to engage in sexual activity with a patient after termination, 23.2% said it was ethical "under rare circumstances," with 2.6% not sure.

The results of a study by Holroyd and Bouhoutsos (1985) suggested that therapists who have been sexually involved with patients differ in their attitudes about how harmful such practices are, compared with therapists who have not engaged in such behavior. Respondents who had been involved with former patients considered such relationships to be significantly less unethical and significantly more different from relationships with current patients than the other respondents.

In the 1987 survey conducted by Pope and colleagues, where 1,000 questionnaires were sent out to psychologists from APA's Division 29 (Psychotherapy), 84.6% of the 456 respondents indicated that they believed sex with former patients was "unquestionably not" ethical or ethical "only under rare circumstances." Of the remaining respondents, 3.9% thought this behavior was ethical "under many circumstances," 3.3% thought it was "unquestionably" ethical, and 7.2% endorsed "don't know/unsure." The reasons given for these discrepancies were the potential harmful consequences, the position of the law whereby even in malpractice cases when the sexual involvement began after termination, general and punitive damages were awarded (e.g., *Whitesell v. Green*, 1973), and the position of state licensing boards and state ethics committees as examined in Sell, Gottlieb, and Schoenfeld's (1986) study (Pope et al., 1987).

Herman et al. (1987) surveyed 1,423 practicing psychiatrists regarding sexual contact with patients; of the 26% completed questionnaires, 29.6% said that sexual contact after therapy ends might sometimes be acceptable. An additional 8.5% who returned their questionnaires (116 of 1370) had no opinion on this question. Of those who had had sexual contact with patients, 74% reported that such contact could be appropriate after termination, which was in marked contrast to only 27.4% of psychiatrists who had not done so. Not only did 241 psychiatrists wrongly believe that sexual intimacies with patients were allowed by the ethics code, they felt this way especially about intimacies after termination. The many written opinions provided by the respondents indicated much confusion about the matter. Although no exact data were provided, a few commented that sex with a patient is always prohibited regardless of whether therapy was in progress or completed: "A 32-year-old divorced man wrote, "Once someone walks through the door as a patient, they can *never* be a friend or lover, etc. This still leaves me about 5 billion other people to be involved with" (p. 165).

Akamatsu (1988) conducted a survey of APA members, which produced results consistent with those of Herman et al. (1987). He found that 44.7% of the respondents believed that intimate relationships, which he defined as sexually intimate relationships, with former patients were highly unethical; 23.9% felt that they were somewhat unethical; and 22.9% rated them as "neither ethical nor unethical." The researcher asked about an appropriate time interval between termination of therapy and beginning an intimate relationship; 37% said that no time limit is appropriate, with 18.7% indicating that time had to be considered with other factors. Among those who proposed a specific interval, 7.5% supported a two-year waiting period.

Conte et al. (1989) surveyed 101 practicing outpatient psychotherapists in the Department of Psychiatry of an urban medical school regarding various ethical issues in clinical practice. The sample consisted of 74% psychiatrists, 22% psychologists, and 4% social workers. When asked to rate their attitudes about sex during therapy and after treatment ends, 80.2% felt that having sexual contact with a patient while he or she is still in treatment was grounds for malpractice and 19.8% felt that it was unethical. In comparison, sexual contact with a patient after proper termination of long-term or brief therapy was considered to be grounds for malpractice by 14% of respondents and unethical by about 50% of respondents. Marrying a patient after termination of therapy, brief or long-term, or after consultation, was rated by the psychoanalysts in the sample as either inappropriate or unethical behavior. This finding was in contrast with the other therapists who considered this behavior to fall somewhere between acceptable practice and inappropriate conduct.

Thoreson et al. (1995) studied the attitudes and behaviors of female counselors regarding sexual contact during and after professional relationships, broadening the scope to include relationships with supervisees and students as well as with patients. They found that of the 377 in the sample, 85% to 95% indicated that sexual contact constitutes misconduct and is harmful when it occurs during a professional relationship. Opinions were more varied regarding sexual contact that occurs following professional relationships. Specifically, less than half (31% to 45%)

of the sample rated these behaviors as definitely misconduct or as definitely harmful. Using comparison data from Thoreson et al. (1993), male counselors were significantly more likely than female counselors to have sexual contact with patients, either current or former.

Lamb, Strand, Woodburn, Buchko, Lewis, and Kang (1994) studied the incidence and attitudes of sexual contact with former patients via a sample of 1,000 APA members. Of the 334 respondents (33.4%), 48% were female and 52% were male. The sexual relationship was defined to include both physical and nonphysical expressions of sexual intent or desire. The males were four times more likely than the females to admit to having had a post-termination sexual relationship, with 6.5% of the total sample reporting this activity. Those involved with former patients tended to be single, older men with more years of clinical experience.

A dissertation by Collins (1999) sampled 1,000 psychologists using self-report data. From the 200 (20%) who responded, "[s]exual contact with clients within a year of termination was viewed to be significantly less unethical than sexual contact with current clients and more unethical than sexual contact more than two years post-termination" (p. 262). Her hypothesis about gender differences, with male psychologists more likely than their female counterparts to rate sexual contact with patients after termination as more ethical, was borne out in the data. The differences between gender rose as the time increased from one to two years post-termination. Female psychologists thought that the impact of sexual contact at both one and two years post-termination was more harmful than did the male psychologists. Both male and female psychologists rated sexual contact with former patients more than two years after termination as less harmful than after one year since the end of the treatment (Collins, 1999).

A qualitative study investigating the opinions of psychoanalytic psychologists regarding sexual contact between therapists and former patients suggested great disparity of opinion about what might constitute acceptable, ethical behavior in this domain (Shavit, 2001). Nonetheless, all the clinicians agreed that the potential for harm resulting from post-termination sexual involvement was great. It was concluded that transference did not resolve with termination, that professional responsibilities continued after treatment ended, and that power differentials between therapist and patient lingered perhaps in perpetuity. For the most part, the participants felt that the ethical standards in this area needed to be more rigorous where psychoanalytic psychotherapy was concerned (Shavit, 2001).

Reported Prevalence of Therapist-Former Patient Sexual Contact

In one of the first studies examining the prevalence of therapist-former patient sexual contact, Holroyd and Brodsky (1977) surveyed 1,000 licensed psychologists and found that 5.5% of the male therapists and 0.6% of the female therapists of the 657 who responded admitted to having had sexual intercourse with their patients. An additional 2.6% of the males and 0.3% of the females said they had had sexual intercourse with former patients within three months after termination of the therapy relationship. Gartrell et al.'s (1987) large self-report survey of psychiatrists found that of the respondents who acknowledged sexual contact with their own patients (6.4% of a sample of 1,316), 69% admitted to having had sex with patients after termination, with 18% of these occurring within a month and 63% within six months post-therapy. They found no differences in demographic characteristics, number of repeat offenders, or the characteristics of their most recent sexual relationship with a patient between those who began sexual contact during treatment as compared with those who did after treatment ended. However, 81% of the respondents who entered into sexual relations after termination stated that they were in love with the patient, which was almost twice the number of those who became sexually involved prior to termination. Pope et al. (1987) surveyed 456 members of Division 29 (Psychotherapy) of the APA. Among their findings, 88.2% claimed that they had never had sex with a former patient, while 10.5% said it happened "rarely," 0.4% "sometimes," and 0.2%, "very often." The Akamatsu (1988) study of the same sample size from Division 29 found that 11% of the 395 respondents reported having had sex with former patients; 14.2% of these were male therapists and 4.7% were female therapists (Schoener, 1990).

Finally, in a survey of the male members of a counseling association, 7% of the respondents reported sexual contact with former patients (Thoreson et al., 1993). A similar study was conducted with 377 female counselors, with 4.6% reporting having engaged in sexual contact with either a patient, student, or supervisee after a professional relationship (Thoreson et al., 1995). Self-reported rates of sexual contact with patients before or after termination did not differ between social workers, psychiatrists, and psychologists (Borys & Pope, 1989).

Overall, the estimates of the prevalence of post-termination sexual involvement based on self-report surveys of therapists prior to the 1992 Ethics Code revision are relatively consistent, sitting somewhere between 5-15% for males and 0.6-8% for females (Akamatsu, 1988; Borys & Pope, 1989; Holroyd & Brodsky, 1977). Realistically, however, the true base rate of such therapist former-patient sexual contact is unknown. It is difficult to ascertain the reliability of such incidence data. There is every reason to believe that even the higher numbers of incidence reported represent a small percentage of the total number of occurrence of sexual involvement between psychologists and ex-patients. Inferences from reported incidence rates and the extent of harm from survey respondent data to the general population are limited because of the self-selecting nature of patients who choose to make formal complaints and therapists who are motivated to respond to surveys gathering information. Some therapists who engage in such behavior will not acknowledge it, even if assured of anonymity. On the other hand, it is unlikely that therapists would report sexual contact that did not occur (Seto, 1995).

Marriage Between Therapists and Former Patients

A potential outcome of sexual relationships between therapists and former patients is that of marriage between the two parties. Gonsiorek and Brown (1990) contended that mental health professionals are uncomfortable with this union and consequently it is not given much press either in professional circles or in the ethics literature. The issue has not been empirically researched despite being anecdotally known to occur, with some prominent figures in psychology implicated. A leading example is Frieda Fromm-Reichmann, whose husband, Erich Fromm, was her patient when they became romantically involved. The two married after the therapy was terminated for that reason (Schoener, 1997).

When the purpose of sexual contact with a former patient is said to be for marriage, clinicians seem to think of the behavior as more acceptable (Conte et al., 1989). This was reflected in the study of psychiatrists done by Herman et al. (1987):

> Many respondents . . . indicated a belief that, while casual sexual contacts with a patient could not be condoned even after termination, such contacts could be countenanced if both patient and therapist were seeking marriage or a serious love relationship . . .

Written comments from a number of their respondents indicated that they were disposed to allow exceptions to the code of professional ethics in the name of romantic love. (p. 165)

Gabbard (1994a), in his formulations on the need for a complete prohibition on post-termination therapist-patient sexual involvement, held marriage as a result does not answer the question of harm done: "Certainly abuse occurs in numerous marriages, and marriage as an institution does not–or at least should not–legitimate that abuse. For many years, marriage has been used as a rationalization to protect husbands from the legal consequences of rape and battering" (p. 333).

Clinical Consequences of Sexual Contact Between Therapists and Former Patients

The professional relationship between therapist and patient exists beyond termination. Ryan and Anderson (1996) used the principles surrounding confidentiality as a model to argue against post-termination sexual contact. They stated that just as people will not reveal key information if they know such information could be broadcast two years after the last appointment, patients may be deterred from the emotional intimacy demands of treatment if they know it could be a prequel to sexual intimacy after termination. Even if it were possible to determine with some confidence that a particular relationship between the patient and the therapist has terminated both legally and clinically, there is always the possibility that the patient may need to return to the therapist for future therapy (Gonsiorek & Brown, 1990).

Prior to the 1992 APA Ethics Code's introduction of a two-year waiting period, Herman et al. (1987) rejected the concept of any waiting period, holding that it "disregards both the continued inequality of the roles of the therapist and former patient and the timelessness of unconscious processes, including transference" (p. 168). Similarly, Gabbard and Pope (1989) argued that by virtue of distorted transference responses and the internalized representations of the therapist by the patient, the significant power differential that exists between therapists and patients does not end with the end of treatment.

Harm to the patient is a very serious reason for therapists to abstain from post-termination sexual contact. Brown (1988) tried to examine the impact such relationships have on the former patients, the community of other past, current, and potential patients of the therapist in question, and on the therapist. She offered anecdotal and observational information about those effects in the contextual framework of a lesbian community. On learning that their therapist had become lovers with a former patient, the women interviewed reported feeling jealousy, an over-generalized sense of unsafety, as well as grief and loss. Many of them spoke of the death of their idealized image of their therapist and in some cases, therapists as a group. The author also interviewed two women who had been involved in long term relationships with their former therapists. Both described their relationships as "isolated" and "enmeshed," and displayed a range of symptoms and complaints that greatly resembled those of patients whose overt sexual contact with the therapist had begun prior to termination, that is, comparable to 'therapist-patient sex syndrome' (Pope, 1988). Brown concluded that "it seems highly likely that some aspect of post-termination romantic relationships between therapists and patients carries potential for grave harm to all parties involved" (p. 255). However, Appelbaum and Jorgenson (1992) disqualified Brown's data because it was derived from a highly selected sample who engaged in post-termination sexual involvement and then sought subsequent therapy. She did not indicate when after termination the sexual involvement began, and it is of note that in both cases she used the relationships had already ended.

Much of the debate regarding the harm is based on the sexual activity that occurs within the first two years post treatment. Pope and Vetter (1992) showed that 80% of therapist-patient sex cases involved harm even when the involvement began after termination. In this research, the waiting period was less than two years after termination.

Professional Consequences of Therapist-Former Patient Sexual Contact

Ethics complaints and administrative action. Post-termination sexual involvement is not supported by the courts, licensing boards, or ethics committees. A complaint by a former patient or third party may result in a financial loss, suspension, revocation of license, censure or expulsion from a professional association (Gabbard & Pope, 1989). Of the 198 cases alleging sexual impropriety handled by state association ethics committees and state psychology boards between 1982 and 1985, no psychologist was exonerated by virtue of the sexual contact occurring only after a reasonable time had elapsed since termination (Gottlieb et al., 1988). In one instance, a four-year wait between therapy ending and the sexual relationship beginning was still insufficient (Gottlieb et al., 1988). The psychologist involved was found to be guilty of an ethics violation. Gottlieb et al. (1988) concluded that "there is no statute of limitation regarding sexual relations with former clients" (p. 461). State boards may find a psychologist to be liable regardless of the time passed since termination and "in such matters, the therapeutic relationship may be assumed to never end" (p. 462). Moreover, the $25,000 cap on coverage in regard to sexual intimacies in the APA's professional liability policy follows the same vein owing to the cap on any settlement amount paid for sexual boundary violations with patients, whether current or former (Gottlieb et al., 1988).

Post-termination sex with former patients exposes the psychologists involved to potentially serious disciplinary action. The California Board of Psychology firmly advises against ever engaging in sex with a former patient, saying that regardless of the two year rule it is unacceptable at any time. "The fact is that sex with former patients is often, if not always, extremely harmful to patients" (p. 4). The Board also commented that it would be a sorry reflection for the entire profession if a clinician's dating prospects need to include previous patients (California Board of Psychology, 1998).

Legal sanctions. A recent Supreme Court case, *Poliak v. Board of Psychology* (1997), questioned the California Board's authority to discipline a psychologist for sex with a former patient. In this case, a heterosexual female psychologist was treating a lesbian patient for approximately two years, over the course of which therapeutic boundaries gradually began to blur. After the therapy concluded, the therapist accepted an all-expense paid trip to France with the patient and at this time, approximately seven months after termination, they became sexually involved. The Administrative Law Judge concluded that the psychologist had been grossly negligent for having sex with a patient and recommended three years of probation. The Board of Psychology decided not to adopt this recommendation and instead revoked her license. On Appeal, the Court concurred with the therapist that she did not have sexual contact with a current patient and that the Board had abused its discretion in revoking her license. The Board took the case to the Supreme Court where the same determination was reached.

Although the decision found that when the therapy has been terminated, there can be no accusation of "sexual relations with a patient" as necessary in Section 726 and 2960(o), other statutes can still be called upon to discipline a licensee. Section 2960(o) of the Business and Professions Code prohibits sexual misconduct "substantially related to the qualifications, functions and duties of a psychologist or psychological assistant." Alternatively, Section 2960(j) could be used with the help of expert testimony to establish that sex with a former patient amounts to gross negligence in the practice of psychology, or that it is "unprofessional conduct" under Section 2960. In 1999, Section 2960(p) was amended to include sexual relations or sexual abuse with a "patient or former patient within two years following termination of therapy" as grounds for action under the auspices of unprofessional conduct.[7]

For there to be grounds for criminal prosecution, the state must prove that the therapist terminated the treatment relationship primarily to engage in a sexual one.[8] It constitutes a felony which is punishable by imprisonment in a county jail for a maximum of six months or a fine of not more than $1000, or both.[9] The patient or former patient's consent can never amount to an adequate defense of this violation.[10] However, there is a loophole in this law. If the therapist refers the patient to an impartial, independent therapist before the sexual involvement is commenced, whatever the reason for ending the treatment, the termination is a satisfactory one. This referral requirement can be fulfilled with a phone call (Haspel et al., 1997).

A civil statute was enacted in California effective January 1, 1988, creating a cause of action by former patients against their psychotherapists for alleged sexual relationships: "A cause of action against a psychotherapist for sexual contact exists for patient or former patient for injury caused by sexual contact with the psychotherapist, if the sexual contact occurred . . . within 2 years following termination of therapy."[11] It eradicates the need to prove that the contact constituted malpractice, being actionable as long as the victim proves it occurred within the time frame listed and that it caused damages for which restitution is sought (Haspel et al., 1997). While some major amendments were made in the legislation regarding misconduct effective January 1, 1994, the administrative regulations that specifically target post-termination relationships have never been revised (Caudill & Pope, 1995). Furthermore, it is unclear whether sex between a psychotherapist and a former patient is unethical and/or illegal following the two year civil liability period (Conte et al., 1989).

Even in the absence of an express statutory imposition of civil or criminal liability, the case law finds sexual contact between therapist and a former patient to constitute harm (Madden, 1998). By 1984, the APA Insurance Trust had an unnamed number of malpractice cases filed where the sexual relationship began after the treatment had been terminated. The courts ruled in favor of the former patients, claiming that regardless of the termination, the emotional transference was still in operation (Cummings & Sobel, 1985).

The case of *Noto v. St. Vincent Hospital and Medical Center* (1988) addressed the matter of sexual relations after termination in common law. In that case, the patient entered the hospital specifically for treatment of drug abuse and "seductive behavior." After the treatment ended and the patient had been out of the hospital for approximately three weeks, her treating therapist began a sexual relationship with her and re-introduced her to drugs. The court found that the therapist was not insulated from liability since the sexual relationship stemmed from, and was a product of, the original treatment.

The legal system also rejected the argument that therapy had ended before a sexual relationship began in *Whitesell v. Green* (1973). This involved marital counseling whereby two weeks after the treatment was over, the therapist began a sexual involvement with the wife. When the husband sued for breach of duty, the psychologist attempted to argue as a defense that the professional relationship was over before the sexual relationship with his former patient had begun. The court found in favor of the husband, and he was awarded $18,000 in damages (Simon, 1985).

Clearly, case law does not validate the post-termination argument, typically basing its rationale on its violating the standard of care that psychotherapists owe to their patients. The law perceives that power differentials remain even after the treatment, which enable undue influence and exploitation on the part of the clinician. A 1996 case, *Clausen v. New York State Department of Health*, concerned a state administrative board's decision to suspend a psychiatrist's license for three years because of sexual misconduct. The psychiatrist argued that his relationship with his former patient began after treatment had ended and after he had found her a new clinician to work with. The appellate court, concurring with the board, found that the doctor's actions confused the patient and furthered her continued dependence on him (Madden, 1998).

CONCLUSION

While sex with current patients is clearly prohibited by law and the Ethics Code (AAMFT, 1998; APA, 2002; NASW, 1999), the ethics of engaging in sexual contact with former therapy patients remains controversial and confusing, especially as time passes after termination. Gabbard (1994a) believed that the APA's permitting this behavior to be deemed ethical under some circumstances was premature. Investigation of current professional opinions regarding the psychodynamics and potential ramifications of such sexual involvements needs to be conducted so that theories, policies, and standards of care can be tested and solidified. By so doing, increased confidence, support, and protection against harm will be gained, to the benefit of all mental health professionals engaged in the delivery of psychotherapy, but more importantly, to the benefit of all their consumers.

NOTES

1. Cal. Bus. & Prof. Code § 729(a)(1).
2. Cal. Bus. & Prof. Code § 729(a)(3).
3. *Id..* at § 729(c)(3).
4. Cal. Civ. Code § 43.93 (West 1993).
5. Cal. Civ. Code §43.94(a)(2) (West Supp. 1991).
6. Cal. Bus. & Prof. Code § 728.
7. Cal. Bus. & Prof. Code § 2960.
8. Cal. Bus. & Prof. Code § 729(a).
9. Cal. Bus. & Prof. Code § 729(b)(1).
10. Cal. Bus. & Prof. Code § 729.
11. Cal. Civil Code § 43.93.

REFERENCES

Akamatsu, T. J. (1988). Intimate relationships with former clients: National survey of attitudes and behavior among practitioners. *Professional Psychology, 19,* 454-458.

American Association for Marriage and Family Therapy. (1998). *AAMFT Code of Ethics.* Retrieved March 15, 2002 from, www.aamft.org/about/ethics.htm

American Psychological Association. (1992). Ethical principles of psychologists and code of conduct. *American Psychologist, 47,* 1597-1611.

American Psychological Association. (2002). *Ethical principles of psychologists and code of conduct.* Washington DC: Author.

American Psychological Association. (1999). Report of the Ethics Committee. *American Psychologist, 54*(8), 701-710.

Appelbaum, P. S., & Jorgenson, L. (1992). Letters to the editor. *American Journal of Psychiatry, 149*(7), 987-989.

Benowitz, M. (1994). Comparing the experience of women clients sexually exploited by female versus male psychotherapists. *Women and Therapy, 15*(1), 69-83.

Bersoff, D. N. (1994). Explicit ambiguity: The 1992 Ethics Code as an oxymoron. *Professional Psychology: Research and Practice, 25,* 382-387.

Bersoff, D. N. (1995). *Ethical conflicts in psychology*. Washington DC: American Psychological Association.

Bouhoutsos, J., Holroyd, J., Lerman, H., Forer, B. R., & Greenberg, M. (1983). Sexual intimacy between psychotherapists and patients. *Professional Psychology: Research and Practice, 14*(2), 185-196.

Borys, D. S., & Pope, K. S. (1989). Dual relationships between therapist and client: A national study of psychologists, psychiatrists and social workers. *Professional Psychology: Research and Practice, 20*(5), 283-293.

Brodsky, A. M. (1986). The distressed psychologist: Sexual intimacies and exploitation. In R. R. Kilburg, P. E. Nathan, & R. W. Thoreson (Eds.), *Professionals in distress: Issues, syndromes, and solutions in psychology* (pp. 153-171). Washington DC: American Psychological Association.

Brodsky, A. M. (1989). Sex between patient and therapist: Psychology's data and response. In G. O. Gabbard (Ed.), *Sexual exploitation in professional relationships* (pp. 15-25). Washington DC: American Psychiatric Press.

Brown, L. S. (1988). Harmful effects of post-termination sexual and romantic relationships between therapists and their former clients. *Psychotherapy, 25*(2), 249-255.

California Board of Psychology. (1998, July). Message from the chairperson. *Board of Psychology Update*, p. 4.

California Department of Consumer Affairs. (2002). *Professional therapy never includes sex*. Sacramento, CA: Author.

Canter, M. B., Bennett, B. E., Jones, S., E., & Nagy, T. F. (1994). *Ethics for psychologists: A commentary on the APA ethics code*. Washington, DC: American Psychological Association.

Caudill, O. B., & Pope, K. S. (1995). *Law and mental health professionals: California*. Washington, DC: American Psychological Association.

Celenza, A. (1998). Precursors to therapist sexual misconduct: Preliminary findings. *Psychoanalytic Psychology, 15*(3), 378-395.

Claman, J. M. (1987). Mirror hunger in the psychodynamics of sexually abusing therapists. *American Journal of Psychoanalysis, 47*(1), 35-40.

Clausen v. New York State Department of Health, 232 AD. 2d 917; 648 N.Y.S. 2d 842 (N.Y. App. Div. 1996).

Coleman, E., & Schaefer, S. (1986). Boundaries of sex and intimacy between client and counselor. *Journal of Counseling and Development, 64*, 341-344.

Collins, P. L. (1999). *Psychologists' attitudes regarding sexual contact with pre- and post-termination clients: An examination of ethicality, harm, moral judgment and empathy*. Unpublished doctoral dissertation, Seton Hall University, New Jersey.

Colorado State Board of Medical Examiners v. Weiler, 157 Colo. 244, 402 P.2d 606 (Colo. 1965).

Conte, H. R., Plutchik, R., Picard, S., & Karasu, T. B. (1989). Ethics in the practice of psychotherapy: A survey. *American Journal of Psychotherapy, 43*(1), 32-42.

Cooper v. Board of Medical Examiners, 49 Cal. App. 3d 931, 123 Cal. Rptr. 563 (1975).

Corey, G., Corey, M. S., & Callahan, P. (1995). *Issues and ethics in the helping professions*. Pacific Grove, CA: Brooks/Cole Publishing Company.

Cranford Insurance Company v. Allwest Insurance Company, 645 F. Supp. 1440 (N.D. Cal. 1986).

Cummings, N. A., & Sobel, S. B. (1985). Malpractice insurance: Update on sex claims. *Psychotherapy, 22*(2), 186-188.

D'Addario, L. (1977). *Sexual relationships between female clients and male therapists.* Unpublished doctoral dissertation, California School of Professional Psychology, San Diego.

Ethics Committee of the American Psychological Association. (1988). Trends in ethics cases, common pitfalls, and published resources. *American Psychologist, 43*(7), 564-572.

Feldman-Summers, S., & Jones, G. (1984). Psychological impacts of sexual contact between therapists or other health care practitioners and their clients. *Journal of Consulting and Clinical Psychology, 52*(6), 1054-1061.

Finkelhor, D. (1984). *Child sexual abuse: New theory and research.* New York: Free Press.

Freud, S. (1958). Observations on transference-love (Further recommendations on the technique of psychoanalysis). In J. Strachey (Ed)., *The standard edition of the complete psychological works* (Vol. 12, pp. 158-171). London: Hogarth Press. Original work published in 1915.

Gabbard, G. O. (1991). Psychodynamics of sexual boundary violations. *Psychiatric Annals, 21*(11), 651-655.

Gabbard, G. O. (1994a). Reconsidering the American Psychological Association's policy on sex with former patients: Is it justifiable? *Professional Psychology: Research and Practice, 25*(4), 329-335.

Gabbard, G. O. (1995). Transference and countertransference in the psychotherapy of therapists charged with sexual misconduct. *Psychiatric Annals, 25*(2), 100-105.

Gabbard, G. O., & Lester, E. P. (1996). *Boundaries and boundary violations in psychoanalysis.* New York: Basic Books.

Gabbard, G. O., & Pope, K. S. (1989). Sexual intimacies after termination: Clinical, ethical and legal aspects. In G. O. Gabbard (Ed.), *Sexual exploitation in professional relationships* (pp. 115-127). Washington, DC: American Psychiatric Press.

Gartrell, N., Herman, J., Olarte, S., Feldstein, M., & Localia, R. (1987). Psychiatrist-patient sexual contact: Results of a national survey. I: Prevalence. *American Journal of Psychiatry, 143*, 1126-1131.

Gonsiorek, J. C., & Brown, L. S. (1990). Post therapy sexual relationships with clients. In G. R. Schoener, J. H. Milgram, J. C. Gonsiorek, E. Luepker, & R. Conroe (Eds.), *Psychotherapists' sexual involvement with clients: Intervention and prevention* (pp. 289-302). Minneapolis: Walk-In Counseling Center.

Gottlieb, M. C., Sell, J. M., & Schoenfeld, L. S. (1988). Social/romantic relationships with present and former clients: State licensing board actions. *Professional Psychology: Research and Practice, 19*(4), 459-462.

Grosso, F. C. (1998, August). The ethical therapeutic duty and clinical implications of secrets policy. *San Diego Therapist.* Retrieved February 20, 2000 from, www.camft-sandiego.org

Haspel, K. C., Jorgenson, L. M., Wincze, J. P., & Parsons, J. P. (1997). Legislative intervention regarding therapist sexual misconduct: An overview. *Professional Psychology: Research and Practice, 28*(1), 63-72.

Herman, J. L., Gartrell, N., Olarte, S., Feldstein, M., & Localio, R. (1987). Psychia-trist-patient sexual contact: Results of a national survey, II: Psychiatrists' attitudes. *American Journal of Psychiatry, 144*(2), 164-169.

Holroyd, J. C., & Bouhoutsos, J. C. (1985). Biased reporting of therapist-patient sexual intimacy. *Professional Psychology: Research and Practice, 16*(5), 701-709.

Holroyd, J. C., & Brodsky, A. M. (1977). Psychologists' attitudes and practices regarding erotic and non-erotic physical contact with patients. *American Psychologist, 32,* 843-849.

Hunsaker, E. (1998). *Erotic transference/countertransference and facilitating discussion of sexual feelings in supervision.* Unpublished doctoral dissertation, California School of Professional Psychology, San Diego, CA.

Jorgenson, L., & Appelbaum, P. S. (1991). For whom the statute tolls: Extending the time during which patients can sue. *Hospital and Community Psychiatry, 42*(7), 683-684.

Kardener, S. H. (1974). Sex and the physician-patient relationship. *American Journal of Psychiatry, 131,* 1134-1136.

Keith-Spiegel, P., & Koocher, G. P. (1985). *Ethics in psychology: Professional standards and cases.* Hillsdale, NJ: Lawrence Erlbaum Associates, Inc.

Lamb, D. H., Strand, K. K., Woodburn, J. R., Buchko, K. J., Lewis, J. T., & Kang, J. R. (1994). Sexual and business relationships between therapists and former clients. *Psychotherapy, 31*(2), 270-278.

Madden, R. G. (1998). *Legal issues in social work, counseling, and mental health: Guidelines for clinical practice in psychotherapy.* Thousand Oaks, CA: Sage Publications.

Masters, W. H., & Johnson, V. E. (1976). Principles of the new sex therapy. *American Journal of Psychiatry, 110,* 3370-3373.

Morra v. State Board of Examiners of Psychologists, 212 Kan. 103, 510 P.2d 614 (Kan. 1973).

National Association of Social Workers. (1999). *Code of ethics of the National Association of Social Workers.* Retrieved March 15, 2002 from, www.naswdc.org/code/ethics.htm

Noto v. St. Vincent Hospital and Medical Center, 537 N.Y.S.2d 446 (Sup. Ct. 1988), *aff'd,* 559 N.Y.S. 2d 510 (App. Div. 1990).

Olarte, S. W. (1991). Characteristics of therapists who become involved in sexual boundary violations. *Psychiatric Annals, 21*(11), 657-660.

Poliak v. Board of Psychology, S062012 Supreme Court of California, 1997 Cal. LEXIS 4486; 55 Cal. App. 4th 342, 63 Cal. Rptr 2d 866 (2nd Dist. 1997).

Pope, K. S. (1988). How clients are harmed by sexual contact with mental health professionals: The syndrome and its prevalence. *Journal of Counseling and Development, 67,* 222-226.

Pope, K. S. (1989). Therapists who became sexually intimate with a patient: Classifications, dynamics, recidivism and rehabilitation. *Independent Practitioner, 9,* 28-34.

Pope, K. S. (1990b). Therapist-patient sex as sex abuse: Six scientific, professional, and practical dilemmas in addressing victimization and rehabilitation. *Professional Psychology: Research and Practice, 21*(4), 227-239.

Pope, K. S., & Bouhoutsos, J. (1986). *Sexual intimacy between therapists and patients.* New York: Praeger.

Pope, K. S., Keith-Spiegel, P., & Tabachnick, B. G. (1986). Sexual attraction to clients: The human therapist and the (sometimes) inhuman training system. *American Psychologist, 41*(2), 147-158.

Pope, K. S., Levenson, H., & Schover, L. R. (1979). Sexual intimacy in psychology training: Results and implications of a national survey. *American Psychologist, 34,* 682-689.

Pope, K. S., Tabachnick, B. G., & Keith-Spiegel, P. (1987). Ethics of practice: The beliefs and behaviors of psychologists as therapists. *American Psychologist, 42,* 993-1006.

Pope, K. S., & Vasquez, M. J. T. (1998). *Ethics in psychotherapy and counseling: A practical guide* (2nd ed.). San Francisco, CA: Jossey-Bass Publishers.

Pope, K. S., & Vetter, V. A. (1992). Ethical dilemmas encountered by members of the American Psychological Association: A national survey. *American Psychologist, 47*(3), 397-411.

Roy v. Hartogs, 381 N.Y.S.2d 587 (N.Y. App. Term.1976).

Ryan, C. J., & Anderson, J. (1996). Sleeping with the past: The ethics of post termination patient therapist-sexual contact. *Australian and New Zealand Journal of Psychiatry, 30,* 171-178.

Schoener, G. R. (1997, September). *Assessment and rehabilitation of psychotherapists who violate boundaries with clients.* Paper presented at the Norwegian Psychological Association Conference, Oslo, Norway.

Schoener, G. R. (1990). Sexual involvement of therapists with clients after therapy ends: Some observations. In G. R. Schoener, J. H. Milgram, J. C. Gonsiorek, E. Luepker, & R. Conroe (Eds.), *Psychotherapists' sexual involvement with clients: Intervention and prevention* (pp. 265-287). Minneapolis: Walk-In Counseling Center.

Schoener, G. R., & Gonsiorek, J. C. (1990). Assessment and development of rehabilitation plans for the therapist. In G. R. Schoener, J. H. Milgram, J. C. Gonsiorek, E. Luepker, & R. Conroe (Eds.), *Psychotherapists' sexual involvement with clients: Intervention and prevention* (pp. 401-420). Minneapolis: Walk-In Counseling Center.

Searles, H. F. (1959). Oedipal love in the countertransference. *International Journal of Psychoanalysis, 40,* 180-190.

Sell, J. M., Gottlieb, M. C., & Schoenfeld, L. (1986). Ethical considerations of social/romantic relationships with present and former clients. *Professional Psychology: Research & Practice, 17*(6), 504-508.

Seto, M. C. (1995). Sex with therapy clients: Its prevalence, potential consequences, and implications for psychology training. *Canadian Psychology, 36*(1), 70-86.

Shavit, N. R. (2001). *Sexual involvements between psychotherapists and their former therapy patients:Psychoanalytic perspectives and professional implications.* Unpublished doctoral dissertation, California School of Professional Psychology-San Diego.

Simon, R. I. (1985). Sexual misconduct of therapists: A cause of civil and criminal action. *Trial, 21*(5), 47-50.

Simon, R. I. (1998). Therapist-patient sex: From boundary violations to sexual misconduct. *Psychiatric Clinics of North America, 22*(1), 31-47.

Smith, D., & Fitzpatrick, M. (1995). Patient-therapist boundary issues: An integrative review of theory and research. *Professional Psychology: Research and Practice*, *26*(5), 499-506.

Stake, J. E., & Oliver, J. (1991). Sexual contact and touching between the therapist and client: A survey of psychologists' attitudes and behavior. *Professional Psychology*, *22*, 297-307.

Steres, L. (1992). *Therapist/patient sexual abuse and sexual attraction in therapy: A professional training intervention.* Unpublished doctoral dissertation, California School of Professional Psychology-San Diego.

Taylor, B. J., & Wagner, N. N. (1976). Sex between therapists and clients: A review and analysis. *Professional Psychology: Research & Practice*, *7*(4), 593-601.

Thoreson, R. W., Shaughnessy, P., & Frazier, P. A. (1995). Sexual contact during and after professional relationships: Practices and attitudes of female counselors. *Journal of Counseling and Development*, *74*, 84-89.

Thoreson, R. W., Shaughnessy, P., Heppner, P. P., & Cook, S. W. (1993). Sexual contact during and after the professional relationship: Attitudes and practices of male counselors. *Journal of Counseling and Development*, *71*, 429-434.

Whitesell v. Green, No. 38745 (D. Hawaii Nov. 19, 1973).

Wohlberg, J. W., McGraith, D. B., & Thomas, D. R. (1997). *Sexual misconduct and the victim/survivor: A look from the inside out.* Retrieved February 20, 2000 from, www.advocateweb.com

Zelen, S. L. (1985). Sexualization of therapeutic relationships: The dual vulnerability of patient and therapist. *Psychotherapy*, *22*(2), 178-185.

Zipkin v. Freeman, 436 S.W.2d 753 (Mo. 1968).

Bartering

Ronald Gandolfo

SUMMARY. This article examines issues related to bartering arrangements in the context of providing professional mental health services. The risks associated with significant conflict of interest in the professional-client relationship and the potential for exploitation of the client are analyzed by examining the interplay of personal, business, and clinical interests in bartering relationships. Professional practice guidelines are suggested. *[Article copies available for a fee from The Haworth Document Delivery Service: 1-800-HAWORTH. E-mail address: <docdelivery@haworthpress.com> Website: <http://www.HaworthPress.com> © 2005 by The Haworth Press, Inc. All rights reserved.]*

KEYWORDS. Bartering, dual relationship, conflict of interest, exploitation

Bartering is the trading or exchanging of goods and services. In the context of providing professional services, it may at times be viewed as a practical solution when a client is unable or is hard-put to make mone-

---

Address correspondence to: Ronald Gandolfo, PhD, ABPP, Alliant International University, 5130 East Clinton Way, Fresno, CA 93727.

[Haworth co-indexing entry note]: "Bartering." Gandolfo, Ronald. Co-published simultaneously in *Journal of Aggression, Maltreatment & Trauma* (The Haworth Maltreatment & Trauma Press, an imprint of The Haworth Press, Inc.) Vol. 11, No. 1/2, 2005, pp. 241-248; and: *Ethical and Legal Issues for Mental Health Professionals: A Comprehensive Handbook of Principles and Standards* (ed: Steven F. Bucky, Joanne E. Callan, and George Stricker) The Haworth Maltreatment & Trauma Press, an imprint of The Haworth Press, Inc., 2005, pp. 241-248. Single or multiple copies of this article are available for a fee from The Haworth Document Delivery Service [1-800-HAWORTH, 9:00 a.m. - 5:00 p.m. (EST). E-mail address: docdelivery@haworth press.com].

tary remuneration for services received. Because mental health professionals are often involved in providing services that are predicated on a high level of trust and are of an emotional and sensitive nature, bartering arrangements can have a high potential for creating conflict and thereby compromise the professional relationship.

The ethics codes of the American Psychological Association (APA; 1992, 2002), National Association of Social Workers (NASW; 1999), and the American Association for Marriage and Family Therapy (AAMFT; 1998) caution against the establishment of dual relationships between mental health providers and the clients they serve because of the danger for exploitation of clients. Examples of dual relationships include business or personal relationships with clients. The ethics codes do not absolutely prohibit dual relationships if there is minimal or no risk of exploitation (for a complete discussion of multiple relationships, see Clipson, this volume).

The APA ethics code makes specific reference to the bartering of goods and services, and its treatment of the subject has been inconsistent. During its February 1982 Ethics Committee Meeting, the APA adopted a formal policy on bartering that held that the bartering of personal services constituted an unethical dual relationship (Sonne, 1994). In the 2002 APA ethics code, the APA Ethics Committee altered its policy on bartering from that of its 1982 meeting and appeared more permissive on the subject. It now allows that bartering is permissible if it is not clinically contraindicated and the relationship is not exploitative. The rationale for APA's reversal of policy on the subject of bartering was predicated on the notion that in difficult economic times certain client populations may find it difficult to pay in cash for mental health services. It was apparently felt that bartering is "a normal and inevitable practice" within populations in small, rural communities" (Sonne, 1994, p. 341). The 2002 APA Code of Ethics continued to support this position.

PROVIDERS' VIEWS ON BARTERING

There have been two studies that surveyed psychologists' views of bartering arrangements. Haas, Malouf, and Mayerson (1986) obtained completed questionnaires containing vignettes describing ethical dilemmas from 294 psychologists who were members of the Psychotherapy Division of APA. Ninety-three percent of the respondents felt that a psychologist should decline an offer from a certified public accountant client who offers to prepare part of the psychologist's tax return as a partial payment for services. Respondents also rated conflicting interests to be a serious concern. Pope, Tabachnick, and Keith-Spiegel (1987) received responses from 456 psychologists who were also members of the Psychotherapy Division of APA regarding the rate of occurrence and their judgment as to the ethical propriety of behaviors that may occur in a therapeutic context. Only 3.7% and 0.6 % of the respondents reported that they respectively often accepted services or goods from a client in lieu of money. Over 22% felt that accepting bartered services was ethical, and 14.5% reported that they were unsure. A slightly higher percentage of the respondents (27.8%) felt that accepting goods was ethical, with 21.3% reporting that they were uncertain.

The above findings indicate that slightly more psychologists find it appropriate to barter for goods rather than services, although at least one-half of the psychologists surveyed viewed any type of bartering as unethical. Bartering for services was reported as occurring rarely, and bartering for goods as occurring very infrequently, in actual practice.

ETHICAL ISSUES

An ethical risk in a bartering arrangement is the potential creation of a conflict of interest that might compromise the professional services afforded the client. In general, the greater the complexity of a bartered arrangement, the greater the risk of conflict. Because of the potential for impairment to an established professional relationship, consideration should be given to the establishment of the market value of goods or services and the complexity of the multiple relationship that is created.

Market value. Unlike a monetary standard for which there is a consensus regarding the value of a unit of currency, the market value of goods or services may not easily be established. Generally it is easier to establish the value of a commodity than a service because the quality or quantity is easier to determine. Hence, if a client with a thriving vegetable garden pays for a psychotherapy visit with a dozen oranges, it is usually not difficult to agree whether the oranges look reasonably healthy and ripe. In the same way, if a client were to pay for completed services by delivering the provider a cord of wood, the amount and quality of wood can usually be reasonably determined. However, conflict may later occur if there is disappointment with the sweetness of the oranges or the degree of dryness and burning quality of the wood. Likewise, the value of some goods may be hard to determine, such as a work of art or an antique. The value of these types of goods change over time, possibly rendering what was considered a fair deal initially as unfair at a later time.

The value of a service is usually harder to determine. Many of the same types of services in the market place are attributed varying worth according to the perceived value of the service provider. Some gardeners are more knowledgeable than others; not all entertainers command the same ticket prices; not all mental health professionals charge the same fee for like services. The value of a particular service may not be immediately known or may be initially perceived to be greater than is justified with the passage of time. A person may find after a tax audit that her accountant did a poor job or that his car continues to have transmission problems one month after it is rebuilt.

Dual relationships. In a sense, all professional services are delivered in the context of a dual or multiple relationship in that for any service rendered a provider has both a service delivery interest and an economic interest. As long as provider and client adhere to their respective responsibilities of reasonable quality of service delivery and payment for services, little conflict is likely. However, a client who reneges on payment for no acceptable reason may raise the ire of the provider and the professional relationship may be compromised. The bartering of goods most clearly resembles monetary payment and may only minimally raise the risk of conflict beyond that which is already inherent in the usual cash for services fee arrangement.

Bartering services is more complex and raises the risk that a conflict will ensue. Consideration should be given to the type of services exchanged, time frame of the transactions, and the potential of the compromise of appropriate boundaries of the professional client relationship.

Type of services. Mental health services most often are therapeutic, evaluative, or consultative in nature and these generally respectively entail the highest to the lowest risks. Bartering for therapeutic services is particularly problematic because therapy is an ongoing process during which interpersonally sensitive issues are dealt with in a special relationship. This should occur in the context of trust and a feeling of safety for the client. Clients come to therapy with personal issues and personality traits that are expressed in the interaction between therapist and client. The particulars of a bartering arrangement can become part of this expression in a manner that can make it difficult for the provider to maintain an objective attitude. For example, consider the passive-aggressive client who continually compromises the quality of bartered services to the therapist. The therapist now has a conflict between maintaining a therapeutic approach in dealing with the passive-aggressive behavior, or a business approach wherein he attempts to get his service needs met. Consider the overly dependent client who goes well beyond the bartered service agreement in hopes that his efforts will be recognized and he will get the special attention and reassurance that he feels he needs and deserves. The therapist has a conflict between expressions of gratefulness and the proper therapeutic handling of the dependency issues. The risk for problems is greater in more interpersonally intensive and psychodynamic therapies than in behaviorally oriented or brief solution-focused therapies. Longer and more in-depth therapies will more strongly foster transference in the client and counter transference for the therapist. Borys and Pope (1989) found that psychodynamically oriented practitioners viewed multiple relationships as less ethical than practitioners from other theoretical orientations.

Evaluation services pose less of a problem because there is less demand on issues of trust and interpersonal sensitivity. Although therapeutic services are rendered in the best interests of a client, the same does not necessarily hold true in assessment in the absence of a treatment relationship. For example, custody evaluations are generally conducted in the best interest of the child rather than those of the parents. An evaluation in a forensic context may invalidate the emotional stress claims of the examinee and not be in the examinee's financial interest. Evaluations are expected to render objective information without observance of the sensitivities, as would be the case in a therapeutic context. Consultative services have the least interpersonal sensitivity because they typically do not focus on the personal characteristics of the client.

Time frame. The time frame under which the bartering arrangement occurs is an important consideration. There is less risk of conflict if the client's obligation under the bartering arrangement is satisfied after the termination of the professional services. However, this may be problematic in the case of a client involved in ongoing psychotherapy. Even after termination of services, a client may have a need for future consultations, and the nature of the relationship with the therapist can remain important long after therapeutic contact has ended. Evaluation or assessment services pose less of a problem because of the limited time frame during which services are usually provided.

Provider-client boundaries. There is a danger that appropriate boundaries between the provider and the client will become ambiguous or compromised to the degree that the bartering arrangement inappropriately exposes the provider's personal life to the client. When a client makes payment by way of a service, it is difficult to avoid some personal exposure. The most problematic situation occurs when a bartered service from the client is delivered in a context in or around the provider's home, when the provider's personal possessions are involved, or when the arrangement relates to matters that are of significant personal importance to the provider. Services provided in a context less personal to the provider preserves more of a business relationship and more likely will maintain a modicum of personal distance as long as there is little contact between the provider and the client.

Risks for the provider. A provider in a bartering arrangement raises the risk of a malpractice action or ethical complaint. A malpractice suit may be brought against a provider if the client feels the provider did not maintain a proper standard of care and as a consequence the client was harmed (Stromberg et al., 1988). A client may feel exploited in the case where the quality or quantity of services provided by the client is perceived as not reciprocated by the provider. Even if the provider maintains a proper standard of care, an overly dependent client may go to extreme lengths to satisfy a provider and expect special treatment in return. The standard of care may be violated because a situation was created that interfered with the client's trust in the provider; that is, the standard of care is more likely to be violated when the provider is disappointed with the quality or quantity of bartered goods or services and responds by compromising the quality of his or her treatment. The provider may feel exploited if the quality of goods or services is below expectations.

Disagreements arising from bartering may be viewed as a business dispute and not covered by the provider's professional liability insurance policy. To help mitigate these risks careful records should be kept and the criteria for determining the value of goods and services should be clearly and carefully documented (Koocher, 1994). There may be a liability and insurance problem if a client is injured while providing work for the provider on the provider's premises.

A provider needs to be knowledgeable about the position of his/her state's licensing board regarding bartering. For example, Sonne (1994) reported that in California a mental health licensing board has stated that hiring a client or a bartering arrangement is inappropriate and viewed as a misuse of power. The provider should also recognize that bartered goods or services are viewed as taxable under the federal and state tax codes and thus carry a monetary consequence.

GUIDELINES FOR CONSIDERING
A BARTERING ARRANGEMENT

1. Generally, bartering relationships should be avoided. The provider's first consideration in a circumstance that a client has no

monetary resources for payment of services should be to offer services on a pro bono basis or for a nominal fee, or to make an appropriate referral.

2. In the case of a client who finds it important to pay for services and is uncomfortable in accepting services on a pro bono or nominal payment basis, a bartering arrangement where payment is made in the form of goods may be desirable. The nature of the goods should be clear to all parties and their value be reasonably agreed upon.

3. Avoid service bartering because of the potential for misunderstanding and exploitation. If service bartering is entered into, the service should be relatively simple, of little personal concern or importance to the provider, and the nature of the service should preserve the boundaries of the provider-client relationship.

4. Generally, payment by goods or services is best consummated after professional service is terminated. Bartering arrangements should be avoided when professional services are ongoing, such as in psychotherapy, because of the greater potential that the relationship will be interfered with by conflict.

5. Be prepared to accept disappointment in the nature of the goods or services received and accept them as payment regardless of quality or quantity. Arrangements that include goods or services of high monetary value should be avoided to minimize the degree of disappointment.

6. Avoid a bartering arrangement when the personality dynamics of the client raise the potential for conflict or dissatisfaction.

7. Routinely consult with colleagues before entering into bartering arrangements, especially if uneasy or uncertain over a proposed bartering arrangement.

8. Keep careful records of the goods or services exchanged and the method of determining their value.

9. Consider state licensing laws pertaining to professional practice as well as limitations of professional malpractice liability policies and other insurance concerns when entering into a bartering arrangement.

REFERENCES

American Association for Marriage and Family Therapy. (1998). *AAMFT Code of Ethics*. Washington, DC: Author.

American Psychological Association. (1992). Ethical principles of psychologists and code of conduct. *American Psychologist, 47*, 1597-1611.

American Psychological Association. (2002). *Ethical principles of psychologists and code of conduct.* Washington DC: Author.

Borys, D. S., & Pope, K. S. (1989). Dual relationships between therapist and client: A national study of psychologists, psychiatrists, and social workers. *Professional Psychology: Research and Practice, 20,* 283-293.

Clipson, C. R. (2005). Misuse of psychologist influence: Multiple relationships. *Journal of Aggression, Maltreatment & Trauma,* 11(1/2), 169-203.

Haas, L. J., Malouf, J. L., & Mayerson, N. H. (1986). Ethical dilemmas in psychological practice: Results of a national survey. *Professional Psychology: Research and Practice, 17*(4), 316-321.

Koocher, G. P. (1994). The commerce of professional psychology and the new ethics code. *Professional Psychology: Research and Practice, 25,* 355-361.

National Association for Social Workers. (1999). *Code of ethics of the National Association of Social Workers.* Washington, DC: NASW Press.

Pope, K. S., Tabachnick, B. G., & Keith-Spiegel, P. (1987). Ethics of practice: The beliefs and behaviors of psychologists as therapists. *American Psychologist, 42,* 993-1006.

Sonne, J. L. (1994). Multiple relationships: Does the new ethics code answer the right questions? *Professional Psychology: Research and Practice, 25,* 336-343.

Stromberg, C. D., Haggarty, D. J., Leibenluft, R. F., McMillian, M. H., Mishkin, B., Rubin, B. L., & Trilling, H. R. (1988). The psychologists legal handbook. Washington, DC: The Council for the National Register of Health Service Providers in Psychology.

Requirements and Implementation of Maintaining Patient Records: The Mental Health Professional's Best Protection

O. Brandt Caudill, Jr.

SUMMARY. This article will discuss the need for psychotherapists to document the statements of patients, the techniques they use, and other aspects of their work to avoid ethical and legal problems. Elements of session notes and written informed consent will be identified. No informed consent can legitimize some actions and they will be addressed. *[Article copies available for a fee from The Haworth Document Delivery Service: 1-800-HAWORTH. E-mail address: <docdelivery@haworthpress.com> Website: <http://www.HaworthPress.com> © 2005 by The Haworth Press, Inc. All rights reserved.]*

KEYWORDS. Patient records, informed consent, controversial, fees, ethical issues, legal issues

---

Address correspondence to: O. Brandt Caudill, Jr., JD, 111 Fashion Lane, Tustin, CA 92780 (E-mail: brandt_caudill@cmwlaw.net).

[Haworth co-indexing entry note]: "Requirements and Implementation of Maintaining Patient Records: The Mental Health Professional's Best Protection." Caudill, Jr., O. Brandt. Co-published simultaneously in *Journal of Aggression, Maltreatment & Trauma* (The Haworth Maltreatment & Trauma Press, an imprint of The Haworth Press, Inc.) Vol. 11, No. 1/2, 2005, pp. 249-262; and: *Ethical and Legal Issues for Mental Health Professionals: A Comprehensive Handbook of Principles and Standards* (ed: Steven F. Bucky, Joanne E. Callan, and George Stricker) The Haworth Maltreatment & Trauma Press, an imprint of The Haworth Press, Inc., 2005, pp. 249-262. Single or multiple copies of this article are available for a fee from The Haworth Document Delivery Service [1-800-HAWORTH, 9:00 a.m. - 5:00 p.m. (EST). E-mail address: docdelivery@haworthpress.com].

Record keeping is one of the major areas of conflict between what the law requires and what psychotherapists actually practice. It is not uncommon for a defense lawyer in a malpractice case to discover that a psychologist has no records, other than billing records, to describe a patient's care. In several instances, the author has defended cases of 10 to 20 years of therapy with no notes whatsoever. This practice presented extreme problems in the defense of the psychotherapists in question.

It is essential for psychotherapists to understand the origin of the requirement of record keeping, the technical requirements, and the situations in which record keeping is a practical necessity, even if not called for by statute or rule. This article deals with: (1) the circumstances in which records are mandated by statute, licensing board regulation, or ethical principles; (2) what records must contain; (3) some problems with the use of modern electronic technology in maintaining records; and (4) confidentiality. This article will not deal with the issue of access to records. The issue of access to records will be governed by state statutes, except where the Health Insurance Portability and Accountability Act of 1996 (HIPAA) is more restrictive and therefore takes precedence.

THE REQUIREMENT OF RECORD KEEPING

Contrary to the perception of many psychologists and other mental health professionals, the question of whether to keep records is not one for their individual judgment. The requirement of keeping records can be imposed by state or federal statute, regulation of a licensing board, or rule of an ethics committee. In addition, litigation has defined certain areas where record keeping is a practical necessity, although it may not be required by a statute or regulation. Further, there are certain areas of litigation where standards of care are currently unsettled, such as the repressed memory controversy, where part of the debate has involved the extent to which records are kept.

It is important to understand that there are four separate time frames in which record keeping comes into play: (1) the inception of the relationship; (2) the course of therapy; (3) the termination of the relationship; and (4) post-termination contacts, whether positive or negative. Of these four areas, the two that have been most critical in terms of litigation, and in which the practice of therapists have been woefully inadequate, are the inception of the relationship and the course of therapy.

The Inception of the Relationship

The issue of informed consent for therapy techniques to be utilized is raised any time a psychotherapeutic relationship arises (see Golub, this volume). In recent years, this has become a particularly critical issue because of contentions that therapists who engage in memory recovery work are not giving patients adequate informed consent about the possibility that false memories might be developed. In addition, certain books that have been used for years in the profession, such as Courage to Heal (Bass & Davis, 1988) and Secret Survivors (Blume, 1990), are now sufficiently controversial that prudence dictates an informed consent being rendered about the reference or utilization of them.[1] In short, particularly in the area of memory retrieval work, there is substantial professional controversy of which patients must be advised.

Each state has its own laws relating to informed consent. California was one of the states to first pioneer the informed consent doctrine, and an area that has generated a number of court cases that can be looked to for instruction. The California Supreme Court has discussed the informed consent doctrine in several cases. The most significant are *Truman v. Thomas* (1980), *Cobbs v. Grant* (1972), and *Moore v. Regents of the University of California* (1990).

The *Truman* and *Cobbs* cases articulate the doctrine of informed consent and stress the importance that a patient be given all material information to make informed decisions about whether particular treatment is necessary, and what specific techniques should be used. The patient must also be given adequate information about the risks of not proceeding with the treatment recommended by the medical or mental health professional.

In *Truman*, the Supreme Court defined material information as "that which a physician knows or should know would be regarded as significant by a reasonable person in the patient's position when deciding to accept or reject the recommended procedure."[2] The court also noted that to "be material a fact must also be one which is not commonly appreciated."[3] To be meaningful, such an informed consent must be explained in terms that a layperson can understand, and should not just be a rote recitation of a laundry list of risks that is so all-encompassing that it covers everything from disappointment to death. *Truman* and *Cobbs* both arose in the context of specific medical techniques that had risks that were not disclosed to the patient, or were inadequately disclosed to the patient and the patient suffered a resulting injury that was in the scope of reasonable risk.

The *Moore* case was somewhat unusual because it involved the utilization of tissue from biopsies taken from a patient for the doctor's research purposes. The Supreme Court saw this as a conflict of interest, which was required to be disclosed before the biopsies were taken so that the patient could make an informed decision about whether the biopsies should be used.

A series of lower court cases has clarified that not every risk must be disclosed, only those that are substantial. Further, a medical or mental health professional is not required to disclose the existence of alternate schools of thought about treatment that the doctor or mental health professional does not actually subscribe to, unless that information is material to the patient's decision.[4] The American Psychological Association (APA), American Association of Marriage Family Therapists (AAMFT), and National Association of Social Workers (NASW) all require informed consent in their ethical principles (see Appendices to this volume for each of these codes). These ethical principles typically require disclosure of the risks and benefits of therapy, and any significant information regarding treatment techniques (such as the lack of supporting research).

From these cases we can draw the conclusion that at the inception of therapy a psychotherapist should disclose to a patient the treatment techniques that will be used, the likely course of therapy, the risks, if any, of the procedures being used, the limitations on confidentiality, and whether or not a particular technique is controversial. Because of the inherent difference between medical and mental health treatments, it is somewhat harder to identify the risks of an unsuccessful therapy. For example, it would be ludicrous to list depression as a risk for unsuccessful psychotherapy (e.g., that the patient might commit suicide). A more realistic disclosure would include the fact that no particular technique is guaranteed to produce the results that the patient is seeking and that the particular technique being used is one that may or may not be successful.

Currently, the larger issue in terms of informed consent is whether a particular therapy or treatment is controversial. The controversy is the most heated in regard to areas that have impact on memories, particularly memories of sexual abuse. Among the techniques that have been specifically attacked in lawsuits are hypnosis, guided imagery, anatomically correct dolls, psychodrama, re-parenting, abreaction work, past life regressions, use of spirit guides, entity releasement work, channeling, any technique involving nudity, use of books such as *Courage to Heal* (Bass & Davis, 1988) and *Secret Survivors* (Blume, 1990), and use of symptom checklists in the area of child sexual abuse and repressed memories.

When using any of these techniques, a psychotherapist must disclose to the patient the existence of the controversy and provide a succinct but fair recitation of the controversy. As an example, the use of hypnosis to recover memories of child sexual abuse that have been repressed should involve a statement of the following type:

> In the course of our therapy we will be using hypnosis to try and reach memories to which you do not have conscious access. There is currently a controversy in the profession about the extent to which the memories recovered in hypnosis are accurate or inaccurate. The courts have previously determined that memories recovered through the use of hypnosis are sufficiently questionable that certain steps must be taken before hypnosis is used, or you will not be able to be a witness in a criminal or civil case. The hypnosis process has a tendency to make memories seem real and concrete, even when they are not accurate. However, I believe that the technique is appropriate for use in your case and will provide the following benefit . . . (the benefit of the procedure should be listed).

However, the law is also clear that in some areas no consent will ever be adequate, no matter how broadly it is phrased. For example, in *Rains v. Superior Court* (1984) the court held that therapists could be sued for assault and battery even though the patients had consented to be beaten as part of therapy. This unusual approach was referred to in the court decision as "sluggo therapy."[5] In a case before the California Medical Board, an appellate court commented on consents that had been obtained by an unlicensed practitioner to provide certain types of holistic services. The Court of Appeal stated that it was not possible for a patient to give an informed consent to treatment by an unlicensed practitioner.[6]

Thus, the informed consent is a critical piece of evidence at the initial stages of the relationship. The question then becomes what other documents are necessary at the inception of the relationship. The APA specifically requires that there be a written statement to the patient identifying how the fee will be calculated and obtaining the patient's consent to the fee. The APA has found psychologists to be in violation of ethical principles where the fee agreement is not spelled out. The AAMFT has a similar requirement. In addition, it is also important to spell out any policy of charging patients for missed sessions.

The California Board of Psychology has a specific requirement that if the patient is going to be treated by a psychological assistant, the supervisor must notify the patient in writing that the therapist who will be doing the treatment is a psychological assistant.[7] If a patient did not receive the written notification required by this regulation, and a dispute arose, the patient could argue that he or she was mislead as to the psychological assistant's qualifications. Regardless of which state a therapist practices in, it is sound practice to always have a written acknowledgement by the patient that services are being provided by a psychological assistant, intern, or trainee who is under supervision.

The limitations on confidentiality must also be identified (see Caudill & Kaplan, this volume). Thus, a therapist must inform the patient that disclosure may be required in the following circumstances:

1. if the patient discloses information that is required to be reported under the Child Abuse Reporting Law;
2. if the patient makes a serious threat of violence against a readily ascertainable third party;
3. to protect the patient from harming him/herself or others;
4. where the patient is a party to a lawsuit and tenders his or her mental condition; and
5. in any subsequent action between the therapist and the patient where breach of a duty is an issue.

A consistent theme in recent malpractice litigation has been the failure of psychotherapists to obtain an adequate history at the inception of the therapeutic relationship. The author's experience is that the failure to take an adequate history has been a significant issue in almost every malpractice suit and board discipline case seen in the last three years. Traditionally, history-taking has been an area where more psychiatrists and medical doctors have been focused than in non-M.D. psychotherapists. The taking of the history should be accomplished both by a verbal interview of the patient, and by having the patient fill out a detailed history form containing significant factual information. The importance of having the patient fill out the history form is that in subsequent litigation it quite frequently develops that the patient has either lied on the history form, or omitted extremely significant information that would have put the facts in a different light.

It is particularly critical to inquire about past psychotherapy, significant diseases with mental health consequences, the mental health history of other family members, current and past stressors, and whether any litigation is ongoing. The fact that a patient is in litigation or has been in litigation in the recent past may be a significant distorting factor. By the same token, there are some signs of mental illness that may be misread if it is not known that the patient has a significant family history of mental illness. If the patient does disclose treatment by prior mental health professionals, then the psychotherapist must obtain releases and attempt to obtain those records.

In the case of *Jablonski by Pahls v. United States* (1963), the 9th Circuit Court of Appeal held that where mental health professionals working at a veteran's hospital had failed to obtain prior records of mental health treatment, they withheld the knowledge of whatever information was contained in those records. In that case, the prior records contained references to extreme violent behavior on the part of Jablonski, which would have put the therapist on notice that he was extremely dangerous to the woman that he ultimately killed.

At the inception of the relationship, the psychotherapist must consider whether to use an arbitration clause. There is a strong public policy in California favoring arbitration, and psychotherapists can use such clauses provided they comply with the number of extremely detailed and technical requirements.[8] The code section requires, among other things, special typeface that brings the arbitration clause clearly to the patient's attention, and contains key language.

Records Regarding the Course of Therapy

The California Health and Safety Code[9] articulates what the contents of various records should be in certain circumstances. That statute requires records to contain, at a minimum, the diagnosis of treatment, medications prescribed, etc.

Where a patient requests records, a psychotherapist may under certain specific circumstances provide a written summary in lieu of the actual records. The statute that permits a summary lists what the summary must contain.[10] This is a useful guide to what information psychotherapy records should contain. Table 1 lists the information the statute identifies that should be included. Therapists should note that where a

TABLE 1. Information to Include in a Written Summary of Patient Records[12]

1.	the chief complaint and pertinent history;
2.	any findings from consultations on referrals to other health care providers;
3.	the diagnosis where one has been determined;
4.	the treatment plan;
5.	the progress of treatment;
6.	the prognosis, including any significant continuing problems or conditions;
7.	reports of diagnostic procedures and tests;
8.	all discharge summaries; and
9.	a list of medications prescribed by the provider.

request for access to records under this statute is made, a refusal to produce the records because of an unpaid bill can subject the therapist to a fine and disciplinary action by his or her licensing board.[11]

Aside from statutory considerations, experience with malpractice litigation suggests that the following areas should be addressed in psychologist's notes:

1. any reference by a patient of sexual interest in the therapist should be noted as well as what the therapist did about the patient's conduct;
2. any feelings of countertransference the therapist has should be noted along with whatever the therapist did about it; and
3. any expressions by the patient of desires to harm themselves or others should be noted and, if necessary, the provisions of Civil Code Section 43.92 should be complied with.

Even if the patient is not expressing a specific threat to harm anyone, recurrent violent themes should be noted.

Obviously, any mention of child abuse that would require reporting under the Child Abuse Reporting Act should be noted, and what the therapist did about the information as well. In addition, if the therapist figures prominently in the patient's dreams, those dreams should be recorded along with whatever discussion occurred about them. If there are any gifts that the patient gives to the psychologist or the psychologist gives to the patient, they should be identified in the notes along with the rationale for accepting or giving the gift. By the same token, a refusal to give a gift or accept a gift should be noted along with an explanation.

The diagnosis must appear in the notes and must be consistent with the diagnosis given to insurance carriers. *Psychotherapists cannot use one diagnosis for insurance purposes and another diagnosis for other purposes*; that is fraud. Many therapists offer the rationale that they use a less severe diagnosis in billing insurance companies for fear of stigmatizing the patient. However, if an inaccurate diagnosis is submitted, this is below the standard of care and it will be difficult for a psychologist to justify if called on in a civil suit or administrative hearing.

The notes should document and explain any contact between therapist and patient outside the office or outside the therapy context. Referrals to other medical or mental health professionals should also be documented. The notes should include any books, articles, or videos that the patient is referred to, as well as the reason for the referral. Any tests that are administered should be noted along with the results.

Psychotherapists should be aware that there is a continuing problem with the lack of consistency between billing records and the dates of notes in the chart. Generally, this is due to the fact that in most therapy offices, the psychologist writes the notes and someone else does the billing. It is extremely important to ensure that the dates for which therapy is billed are the actual dates sessions occurred. The notes should be consistent with the billing.

A complete note has two parts: first, what the patient said or did in the session; and second, what the therapist said or did in response. It can be problematic for the therapist to note only what the patient said. For example, if the patient expresses suicidal ideation and the notes do not reflect what the therapist said or did about it, it can appear as if the therapist did not respond at all, much less respond appropriately.

The psychotherapist should keep all documents given to him or her by the patient, of any nature whatsoever. This includes greeting cards, poetry, articles from mental health publications, and journal entries. If these documents are discarded, destroyed, or returned uncopied, then it will be difficult to prove in subsequent litigation or administrative hearings that such documents ever existed. It is a common experience for the author, in representing psychologists, to have the psychologist indicate that the patient had submitted key documents in their own handwriting, either laudatory of the psychologist's efforts or contradictory of assertions in a subsequent suit or complaint, only to have those documents be unavailable.

Once these determinations are made as to what should be kept in terms of contents of notes, the question arises as to the technology of notes taken. Most psychotherapists continue to write notes by hand, and that is within the standard of care. However, as technology advances, psychotherapists have to adjust their practice to reflect that technology. For example, more psychotherapists are now using computers to keep their notes. This raises special problems because those notes can be more readily altered than handwritten notes. For example, if the psychotherapist's practice is to go back and review the notes and make changes over time, an attorney would contend that the records had been altered to put the psychotherapist in a better light. Attorneys are trained to be skeptical about documents and often suspect alteration, even when notes are genuine. The ease with which computer records can be changed creates an inherent potential for a credibility issue. A more serious problem, however, is what happens if the computer breaks down. This is illustrated by the deposition of an expert that was taken by the author in a malpractice case. There was no question that the expert was a reputable individual. On the day of the deposition, the expert went to print out his notes and the disk crashed. As a result, what was produced was random words, question marks, and exclamation points. Although computer technology is of great assistance, there has to be back-up documentation to avoid this type of result. Computer malfunctions are sufficiently common that a psychologist has to take into account electing to use a computerized note taking system. The best way to avoid a problem is to periodically print out notes that are computer generated, sign and date them, and put them in the patient's file. Because of computer security issues it is a better practice to not use email for substantive communications with patients. Where email is used, copies should be printed off and saved in the file.

If the sessions are audio- or videotaped, then the cassettes need to be stored in a fashion where they are not likely to be erased or altered, either deliberately or inadvertently. Thus, the manner and place of storing audio and video cassettes is important. The use of audio-and videotapes seems to be a growing practice, particularly in cases involving patients with multiple personality disorders and/or repressed memories. Psychotherapists should also be aware that if hypnosis is going to be used on a patient and there is any potential for litigation, that the Evidence Code requires that records be made of the patient's recollection prior to the hypnosis, and that the hypnotic sessions be recorded on audio tape, or the patient's testimony in a criminal proceeding may be inadmissible.[13] This rule has just been extended to civil cases. Finally, the contents of the file should include all requisite consent forms in writing and signed by the patient, including consent to have the sessions audio- or video-taped.

Technology issues also affect the system of receiving and maintaining telephone messages. Many psychologists use a service that allows them to be contacted as needed. The author had a case in which a psychiatrist was using an answering machine only, without a service or paging system. A patient called in to report that she had taken a drug overdose, and had changed her mind about committing suicide. She wanted the psychiatrist to call her and assist her in getting emergency help. By the time the psychiatrist received the message, the patient was already dead. In the litigation that ensued over the patient's death, one contention was that it was below the standard of care to have only an answering machine. While no case law requires more than an answering machine, if the technology is available it is readily foreseeable that an answering machine may be inadequate to meet the standard of care.

Another issue that arises with regard to paging and answering systems is the illusion that some psychologists have about the nature of their practice. At a presentation the author made to the Arizona Psychological Association, a psychologist stated that he did not need an answering service or paging system because he did not have a crisis practice for patients who would have emergencies requiring such a service. The reality is that any patient can potentially need to contact a psychologist in an urgent situation involving possible suicidality, child abuse, homicidal impulses, or any number of serious and substantial concerns. If a psychologist is treating patients, he or she must assume that the potential for such emergency contact exists.

Records Regarding Termination of the Relationship

All too frequently therapy ends when patients simply do not return, and there is no attempt made to document for the record how the relationship terminates. It is particularly a problem where the patient has been seeing an intern or psychological assistant who leaves the clinic or practice setting. As a general rule, although it is not required by any ethical or legal standard, a sound practice would be for a supervisor of an intern or psychological assistant to have an exit interview with the patient. To ensure that the patients are willing to provide such interviews, the necessity for the exit interview should be disclosed at the inception of the relationship as part of the contract that the patient normally signs. Since the purpose of the exit interview is to see how the patient is satisfied with the course of therapy and the services rendered, it is better practice to not bill the patient for such a session. In undertaking such an exit interview, the supervisor is attempting to guard against possible patient dissatisfaction that could lead to litigation. Further, the patient may in fact reveal some comments by the intern or psychological assistant that will suggest a possible problem of greater dimension that should be considered.

Frequently, supervisors do not understand that because interns and psychological assistants are not allowed by law to practice independently, in the eyes of the law the patient is the patient of the supervisor, at least for the purposes of liability. This potential liability also raises the necessity of taking and keeping supervision notes. As most psychotherapists currently practice, the supervisor may never see a patient that an intern or assistant is treating. Further, the supervisor generally does not keep notes of supervision. This is a situation that has led to numerous suits where supervisors are charged with negligence for their assistant's or intern's acts, and have little knowledge of the patient and no documentation of the date supervision was provided. Thus, better practice would be to have either the supervisor or a licensed person evaluate each patient at the inception of treatment if the patient is going to be seen subsequently by an intern or assistant. Further, the supervision sessions should be documented as to what issues were discussed and what cases were discussed. Generally, in many supervision sessions the patient's name is not even mentioned. This is sometimes due to a misplaced belief that the patient has some type of confidentiality precluding the intern or assistant from discussing matters with the supervisor, which is clearly a misunderstanding of the law. As the California Board of Psychology regulation states, it is incumbent upon the supervisor to ensure not only the quality of care provided by the assistant, but that the assistant does not exceed the statutory limits on his or her authority.[14]

Thus, better practice would be to have the supervision notes specifically reflect which patients and what issues were discussed. Where an intern or assistant is required to be registered with a licensing board, the supervisor must, in his or her own self interest, personally assure the requisite paper work is filed and accepted. *No matter how long a psychological assistant or intern has been working for a supervisor, the statutory requirement of supervision cannot be waived or diluted, and a failure to provide supervision at the frequency set by statute is negligence.*

Records Regarding Post-Termination Contracts

Post-termination contacts are particularly significant because such contacts may be the first warning that a possible board complaint or civil suit is on the horizon. It is unfortunate that in many instances psychotherapists do not see these signs coming from such contacts, or ignore the patient's request for contact in general. As a practical matter, all post-therapy written communications with a patient must be preserved, whether they are favorable or unfavorable. It is particularly distressing to have a suit filed and have the defendant therapist explaining that there were multiple friendly and laudatory communications that were destroyed because they were not deemed important. *Every post-therapy communication with a patient is significant and must be preserved.* This necessity is particularly true of positive communications that reflect a state of mind that the patient may not be willing to admit to at a later date. It also takes on particular added significance if the patient subsequently becomes suicidal or homicidal, and the nature of the communications with the therapist become critical.

CONCLUSION

While maintaining detailed notes and files can be burdensome, not to do so creates an unacceptable risk of being found liable in civil litigation, or being subjected to discipline in a licensing board action. It is incumbent on the therapist to be sure the records accurately reflect the course of treatment, from the initial informed consent to the termination.

NOTES

1. The author has defended therapists in two cases where the authors of *Courage to Heal* were sued for the asserted impact of the book on the plaintiffs. In both cases the claims against the authors were dismissed on First Amendment grounds.
2. *Truman v. Thomas*, at 27 Cal 3d 291.
3. *Supra* at 27 Cal 3d.291.
4. *Mathis v. Morrissey*, 11 Cal.App.4th 332 (1992).
5. *Rains v. Superior Court*, at 150 Cal. App. 3d 936-937.
6. *Board of Medical Quality Assurance v. Andrews*, 211 Cal.App.3d 1346 (1989).
7. Cal. Code Regs. tit. 16, § 1391.6(b).
8. See Cal. Civil Code § 129.
9. Cal. Health & Safety Code § 123100.
10. Cal. Health & Safety Code § 123130.

11. Cal. Health & Safety Code § 1795.12(f) and (g).
12. Cal. Health & Safety Code § 1795.20.
13. *People v. Shirley*, 31 Cal.3d 18 (1992); *People v. Guerra* 27 Cal.3d 385 (1984); ? Cal. Evid. Code § 795.
14. Cal. Code Regs. tit. 16, § 1387.1.

REFERENCES

Bass, E., & Davis, L. (1988). *Courage to heal.* New York: Harper & Row.

Blume, E. S. (1990). *Secret survivors.* New York: John Wiley & Sons.

Caudill, O. B., & Kaplan, A. (2005). Protecting privacy and confidentiality. *Journal of Aggression, Maltreatment & Trauma,* 11(1/2), 117-134.

Cobbs v. Grant, 8 Cal.3d 229 (1972).

Golub, M. (2005). Informed consent. *Journal of Aggression, Maltreatment & Trauma,* 11(1/2), 101-115.

Health Insurance Portability and Accountability Act of 1996, Pub. L. No. 104-191 (1996).

Jablonski by Pahls v. United States, 712 F.2d 391 (1963).

Moore v. Regents of the University of California, 51 Cal.3d 120 *cert. den.* 499 U.S. 936 (1990).

Rains v. Superior Court, 150 Cal.App.3d 933 (1984).

Truman v. Thomas, 27 Cal.3d 285 (1980).

How a Mental Health Professional
Handles Referrals and Fees

Alan I. Kaplan

SUMMARY. The choice of referral and the relationship between referral sources can pose clinical and ethical dilemmas, due to the potential
that the relationship between the psychologist and the referral source
will interfere with the treatment relationship. Once the referral has been
made, the referring psychologist must be sensitive to a second, and often
a more problematic level of risk: conflicts that occur between the patient
and the referral recipient. The situation becomes even more problematic
when a psychologist is giving or receiving any form of compensation in
connection with the referral. In addition to clouding the clinical relationship, the giving or receiving of such compensation, whether it is characterized as "referral fees" or otherwise, has important legal consequences,
and may well result in license revocation proceedings or even criminal
liability. *[Article copies available for a fee from The Haworth Document Delivery
Service: 1-800-HAWORTH. E-mail address: <docdelivery@haworthpress.com>
Website: <http://www.HaworthPress.com> © 2005 by The Haworth Press, Inc.
All rights reserved.]*

Address correspondence to: Alan I. Kaplan, JD, Law Offices of Alan I. Kaplan,
1925 Century Park East, Suite 500, Los Angeles, CA 90067-2706 (E-mail: Aikaplan1@
aol.com).

[Haworth co-indexing entry note]: "How a Mental Health Professional Handles Referrals and Fees."
Kaplan, Alan I. Co-published simultaneously in *Journal of Aggression, Maltreatment & Trauma* (The Haworth
Maltreatment & Trauma Press, an imprint of The Haworth Press, Inc.) Vol. 11, No. 1/2, 2005, pp. 263-270;
and: *Ethical and Legal Issues for Mental Health Professionals: A Comprehensive Handbook of Principles and Standards* (ed: Steven F. Bucky, Joanne E. Callan, and George Stricker) The Haworth Maltreatment & Trauma Press, an imprint of The Haworth Press, Inc., 2005, pp. 263-270. Single or multiple
copies of this article are available for a fee from The Haworth Document Delivery Service
[1-800-HAWORTH, 9:00 a.m. - 5:00 p.m. (EST). E-mail address: docdelivery@haworthpress.com].

Digital Object Identifier: 10.1300/J146v11n01_17   *263*

KEYWORDS. Referrals, fees, confidentiality, consultations, patient needs, APA Ethics Code, aspirational principles, risk, compensation, kick-back, contracts, federal/state law

For many psychologists, patient referrals constitute the lifeblood of their professional practice. The cultivation of productive referral relationships with other mental health colleagues, physicians, educators, and associates of all kinds is often indispensable to a psychologist's economic survival. On the other hand, the choice of referral and the relationship between referral sources can pose clinical and ethical dilemmas, due to the potential that the relationship between the psychologist and the referral source will interfere with the treatment relationship. For example, where husband and wife are both psychologists and share an office together, can they refer patients to each other? What if the psychologists who share the office are brother and sister? What if they are father and daughter? What if they are close friends?

The American Psychological Association's (APA; 2002) Ethics Code provides, "When indicated and professionally appropriate, psychologists cooperate with other professionals in order to serve their patients or clients effectively and appropriately" (Standard 3.09). The 2002 Ethics Code has deleted prior provisions that specifically deal with the appropriateness of referrals, leaving in place only a requirement for cooperation and collaboration between psychologists and other professionals. Notwithstanding the comparative silence of the Ethics Code on this topic, an essential consideration of any psychologist should be the issue of whether the referral is made objectively and is reasonably calculated to meet the patient's needs. Initially, a psychologist who makes or receives a referral must give careful consideration to the issue of whether the referral is truly designed to meet the patient's needs or whether it is being made because the psychologist feels friendship for, or a desire to benefit, the psychologist who will be treating the patient. Along these lines, one could argue that the closer the relationship between the referral recipient and the psychologist, the more care must be taken to ensure that the patient's needs are being met and that the referral is truly the most appropriate one. Additionally, when there is a close relationship between the psychologist and the referral recipient, it is crucial to clarify with the patient what confidential information, if any, will be shared between the psychologist and the referral source.

The situation becomes even more problematic when the referral is made between a psychologist and a non-psychologist, such as from a psychologist to an attorney, dentist, auto mechanic, etc. Is the psychologist making the referral primarily because he has received business from the referral recipient? Is the psychologist truly aware of the risks that the patient will be encountering in their new relationship with the person they are being referred to? The psychologist really has no way of assessing the risk that these sorts of referrals will prove to the patient and should inform the patient of this in advance.

Two aspirational principles of the 2002 APA Ethics Code may prove helpful in analyzing a referral decision. Principle B provides, in part, that "Psychologists consult with, refer to, or cooperate with other professionals and institutions to the extent needed to serve the best interests of those with whom they work." Principle A of the Code addresses concern for others' welfare, and provides, "Because psychologists' scientific and professional judgments and actions may affect the lives of others, they are alert to and guard against personal, financial, social, organizational, or political factors that might lead to misuse of their influence." The foregoing aspirational principles suggest that in making a referral, psychologists should ask themselves the following questions:

a. Is there a substantial conflict of interest?
b. Is the referral in the best interest of the patient?
c. Does the referral stem from a treatment call that is well documented?
d. Will the objectivity of the psychologist be diminished by the new role?
e. How vulnerable is the patient?
f. Will the secondary relationship prevent the patient from continuing therapy?

The answers to these questions should help the psychologist in determining whether to make a referral, and then assessing the degree of caution to exercise if the referral is made.

Once the referral has been made, the referring psychologist must be sensitive to a second, and often a more problematical level of risk: conflicts that occur between the patient and the referral recipient (e.g., fee disputes and problems arising out of the services performed by the referral recipient). Such problems will commonly be brought into the therapy session or otherwise communicated to the psychologist, who will then have to determine whether to side with the patient or the referral recipient.

While such conflicts clearly present a "no-win" situation for the psychologist, it is very important to avoid the appearance of taking sides against the patient. This would clearly encourage the patient to feel betrayed by the psychologist and take steps to treat the psychologist as an adversary, including complaints to the Licensing Board and possible malpractice litigation. In any event, it is extraordinarily important for psychologists to realize the sensitive position that they are in if such a conflict erupts, and to do everything possible to avoid exacerbating the situation. Sometimes, it may be the best policy to acknowledge the conflict of interest and to encourage the patient to seek advice and support from an independent third party.

In summary, there is a host of clinical and ethical risk factors associated with any referral, whether the psychologist is on the sending or the receiving end. The risk will be greater if the relationship between practitioner and the referral source is closer. The risk is accentuated where the psychologist is referring outside of his or her profession, and is further accentuated where the psychologist is referring (or receiving referrals) from outside of the mental health field entirely. The most significant risk to be aware of is that factors outside of the incipient therapeutic relationship, such as the closeness between the psychologist and the referral source or other factors intrinsic to the referral relationship, may cloud or interfere with the dynamics of the incipient clinical relationship.

Of course, a referring or receiving psychologist's objectivity can always be clouded if he or she is giving or receiving any form of compensation in connection with the referral. In addition to clouding the clinical relationship, the giving or receiving of such compensation, whether it is characterized as "referral fees" or otherwise, has important legal consequences, and may well result in license revocation proceedings or even criminal liability. The next section of this article discusses these issues.

LEGAL ISSUES

California law. California Business and Professions Code Section 2960(f) provides that a psychologist's license may be revoked for "paying, or offering to pay, or accepting or soliciting any consideration, compensation, or remuneration, whether monetary or otherwise, for the referral of clients." For all health care practitioners, the payment or receipt of anything of value for the referral of patients, including worker's compensation patients, is a crime punishable by imprisonment, or a fine up to $10,000, or both.[1] The payment of fees for the referral of patients is commonly referred to as "kick-back scheme," and participation in such kick-back schemes by psychologists or by *anyone else* is expressly prohibited by California Insurance Code Sections 750 and 754 (for insurance claims), California Labor Code Section 139.3, Labor Code Sections 3215 and 3820 (which prohibits anyone from participating in kick-back schemes regarding worker's compensation claims) and 3219 (which prohibits giving kick-backs to worker's compensation claims adjusters).

In the case of *Beck v. American Health Group International*,[2] the plaintiff's psychiatrist was tentatively hired to serve as the medical director for Mental Health Services at Palmdale Hospital Medical Center. The psychiatrist was to prepare clinical psychologists for hospital practice at the center, help formulate mental health policies and participate in the Mental Health Committee, and maintain active admitting privileges, allowing him to admit his psychiatric patients along with other psychiatrists and clinical psychologists. The hospital agreed to pay him 10% of the room and board charges of all general psychiatric patients, for each month of the agreement. The court held that such a formula linked the psychiatrist's compensation to the number of the psychiatric inpatients at the hospital, thereby providing an inducement for the psychiatrist to refer (admit) these patients to the hospital. Accordingly, the Court refused to enforce the contract.

Seemingly in response to this ruling, the California Legislature enacted the following amendment to Business and Professions Code Section 650 in 1990:

> the payment or receipt of consideration for services other than the referral of patients which is based on a percentage of gross revenue or similar type of contractual arrangement shall not be unlawful if a consideration is commensurate with the value of the services furnished, or with a fair rental value of any premises or equipment leased or provided by the recipient to the payor.

In light of this amendment, it is safe to say that in California, while gross percentage arrangements can be legally acceptable, the courts will scrutinize them closely to determine whether the amount of consideration received by the referring practitioner is in line with the value of services he actually furnishes. It is therefore important before entering into such a contract to have independent verification of the value of the services that one is about to render, and then compare that value to the amount one would receive under the contemplated arrangement. The value of specific services may often be obtained through state, local, or national professional associations as well as hospital associations and publications of all these entities. Additionally, there are many consultants that specialize in medical and hospital management, and who tabulate and maintain various forms of compensation data. Acquiring such data before entering into a percentage type contract is an important defense, not only to protect ones right to enforce the contract but also to protect one's licensure status and to avoid possible criminal liability for violation of Business and Professions Code Section 650. Taking the right defensive steps will assure that a percentage compensation contract is legal and enforceable.

In summary, compensation can, and does, legally change hands in connection with the referral of patients. Business and Professions Code Section 650 has been generally interpreted not to prohibit the following actions:

a. The payment of reasonable compensation for services rendered;
b. A return on investment based on the amount of the investment that is not tied to the number or value of patients referred.

It is legal and appropriate to pay for advertising services, secretarial work, general promotional work, and other services rendered in connection with the promotion of patient traffic. A percentage compensation formula is defensible where the percentage is truly equivalent to the fair market value of the services being rendered.

Federal law. Similarly, federal Medicare and Medical law[3] provides that anyone who knowingly solicits or receives compensation of any kind in return for referring an individual to any federal or state funded health care program is guilty of a felony and shall be fined not more than $25,000 or imprisoned for not more than five years, or both. In the case of the *United States v. Lipkis,*[4] a physician group that owned a management company referred clinical patients to a laboratory. The laboratory returned 20% of its revenues to the physician's management company. The defendant physicians alleged that these payments by the laboratory represented fair compensation for "specimen collection and handling services"[5] performed by the management company. The court rejected this defense, noting that: "the fair market value of these services was substantially less than the (amount paid), and there is no question that (the laboratory) was paying for referrals as well as the described services."[6]

In *United States v. Kats,*[7] the court held that it is not a defense that there might have been reasons other than referral of patients for a payment. According to *Kats,* criminal conviction is justified unless a payment is "wholly attributable to the delivery of goods or services."[8]

The most recent California ruling clarifying the laws in this area may be found in *The Hanlester Network v. Shalala,*[9] holding that for a violation of the federal anti-kickback statute to occur, the government must prove that the conduct at issue was both "knowing and willful," which means:

1. Knowing that the anti-kick-back statute prohibits the offering or paying of enumeration to induce referrals, and
2. Engaging in the unlawful conduct with the "specific intent to disobey the law."

Notwithstanding the level of comfort that this decision may induce, any psychologist who wishes to avoid criminal liability for the payment of referral fees should take careful steps to ensure that the fees being paid match the market value of the services being rendered as closely as possible.

Additionally, as fee-sharing and economically motivated referral systems are much more prevalent in the medical community, psychologists must exercise special care when entering into referral relationships with physicians and medical groups. The cash flow of these entities is often far greater, their overhead is much higher, and they are prone to operate in an environment of greater financial pressure than many psychologists are used to. The ethical standards that are applied to physicians by the Medical Board will often result in a different, often less severe outcome than the same facts will if adjudicated by the Board of Psychology.

CONCLUSION

Because the payment of compensation for the referral of patients carries with it risks to the integrity of the clinical relationship, the psychologist's licensure status, as well as the risk of criminal penalties that could result in the deprivation of the psychologist's personal freedom, great care must be taken to avoid circumstances where a psychologist can be seen as paying or receiving compensation for the referral of patients.

NOTES

1. Cal. Bus. & Prof. Code § 650 (1990).
2. 211 Cal.App. 3d 1555 (1989).
3. 42 U.S.C. § 1320a-7b(b) (As of September 23, 1997).
4. 770 F.2d 1447, 1449 (9th Cir. 1985).
5. 770 F.2d 1447, 1449 (9th Cir. 1985).
6. 770 F.2d 1447, 1449 (9th Cir. 1985).
7. 871 F.2d 105, 108 (9th Cir. 1989).
8. 871 F.2d 105, 108 (9th Cir. 1989).
9. 51 F.3d 1390 (9th Cir. 1995).

REFERENCE

American Psychological Association. (2002). *Ethical principles of psychologists and code of conduct.* Washington DC: Author.

ETHICS IN TEACHING

Ethical and Legal Considerations in the Training of Mental Health Professionals

Thomas McGee

SUMMARY. A discussion is provided regarding ethical and legal considerations that relate to the training of mental health professionals. A training program which emphasizes a proactive approach to identifying and resolving potential ethical and legal problems, and their close connection with clinical issues is described, as are the responsibilities of supervisors and supervisees in such a program. For illustrative purposes, a training vignette and a clinical vignette conclude the article. *[Article copies available for a fee from The Haworth Document Delivery Service: 1-800-HAWORTH. E-mail address: <docdelivery@haworthpress.com> Website: <http://www.HaworthPress.com> © 2005 by The Haworth Press, Inc. All rights reserved.]*

Address correspondence to: Thomas F. McGee, PhD, ABPP, Alliant International University, Daley Hall 105, 10455 Pomerado Road, San Diego, CA 92131-1799 (E-mail: tmcgee@alliant.edu).

[Haworth co-indexing entry note]: "Ethical and Legal Considerations in the Training of Mental Health Professionals." McGee, Thomas. Co-published simultaneously in *Journal of Aggression, Maltreatment & Trauma* (The Haworth Maltreatment & Trauma Press, an imprint of The Haworth Press, Inc.) Vol. 11, No. 3, 2005, pp. 271-285; and: *Ethical and Legal Issues for Mental Health Professionals: A Comprehensive Handbook of Principles and Standards* (ed: Steven F. Bucky, Joanne E. Callan, and George Stricker) The Haworth Maltreatment & Trauma Press, an imprint of The Haworth Press, Inc., 2005, pp. 271-285. Single or multiple copies of this article are available for a fee from The Haworth Document Delivery Service [1-800-HAWORTH, 9:00 a.m. - 5:00 p.m. (EST). E-mail address: docdelivery@haworthpress.com].

KEYWORDS. Training, supervision, supervisor, supervisee, ethical and legal considerations

The mental health professions have continued to register phenomenal growth during the past 50 years. The development of ethical standards and legislative statutes governing and regulating the practice of the mental health professions has tended to parallel this growth. As a consequence, ethical standards and legislative statutes have become both more comprehensive and more complex, reflecting the continued development of the mental health professions. As an illustration, the first Code of Ethics of the American Psychological Association (APA) appeared in 1953. It has been followed by revised and expanded codes of ethics in 1958, 1963, 1968, 1977, 1979, 1981, 1990, and 1992, culminating in the present code, which became effective in June 2003; thus between 1953 and 2003, a span of 50 years, ten different codes of ethics have been adopted by the APA. Despite their increasing comprehensiveness and complexity, ethical codes and legal statutes governing and regulating the mental health professions are currently regarded not only as indispensable in practice and training, but also as a vital and positive force in the continued development of these professions.

BACKGROUND

Originally fostered by the Veterans Administration following World War II, training in clinical psychology has been advancing in comprehensiveness and complexity since that time. As a partial consequence, ethical and legal standards have come not only to govern and regulate many details of the practice of clinical psychology, but also training and supervision in clinical psychology. For example, ethical and legal considerations now guide the definition of terms such as "training," "supervision," "supervisor," "intern," and "practicum student," among others. From an ethical viewpoint, such definitions and usage serve to assure that the training and supervision of future psychologists is guided by clear ethical standards, while embodying a thorough, first hand understanding of ethical considerations as they relate to the practice of psychology. The legal view concerning the definitions and usage of such terms serves to delineate the requisites and parameters of activities, such as training and supervision, which are oriented toward assuring competence in the training of psychologists. Laws regulating psychology and training in psychology serve not only to regulate most aspects of its practice, but ultimately to protect the public from practitioners who are less than competent.

Carefully supervised, sound, in-depth exposure to ethical and legal matters is essential to developing sound, balanced psychologists and to providing excellence in the delivery of clinical and other services, while avoiding potential harm to and exploitation of the recipients of services. Given this perspective, it becomes extremely important not to view ethical/legal issues as abstract ethical codes and remote sets of laws that the aspiring psychologist must somehow master, often through memory, in order to provide protection against the seemingly distant possibility that an ethical/legal problem might occur. Rather, as part of one's training it is essential to accept ethical and legal issues as potentially omnipresent, and as intimately interwoven with all aspects of clinical and other practice as well as all aspects of training and supervision. Such a perspective implies that a vigorous and consistent *in vivo* approach to identifying, assessing, and resolving potential ethical and/or legal problems as they occur constitutes an indispensable part of a training program. This perspective helps both supervisor and supervisee develop a deeper appreciation and understanding of ethical and legal values; it also tends to orient training toward sensitivity, responsiveness, and thoroughness with respect to identifying more fully, understanding and resolving potential ethical/legal problems as they arise. Ultimately, such an approach greatly strengthens training; it also contributes to quality and excellence in the services that are provided as part of the training.

THE TRAINING PROGRAM

Orientation Toward Potential Ethical and Legal Issues

A training program can provide a critically important context in which to develop a broad understanding of the extraordinary range and complexity of ethical and legal issues that confront psychologists. It is assumed that a primary goal of a strong, well-organized training program is to help psychologists-in-training to become knowledgeable, sensitive, and balanced with respect to ethical/legal matters. Accordingly, it is essential that the training program have a foundation that is ethically and legally sound, clear, and comprehensive. It is equally important that the training program have a commitment to a proactive posture toward the identification and resolution of potential ethical/legal problems as they arise. In its development and operation, the training program must adhere fully to the relevant sections of the APA (2002) ethical code and to relevant legal statutes of the state where the training site is located. For example, in California any psychology training program is required to conform to all relevant provisions of *Laws and Regulations Relating to the Practice of Psychology*, issued by the Board of Psychology (State of California Department of Consumer Affairs, 2003). In addition, a strong, well organized training program would probably emphasize that staff members and psychologists-in-training become thoroughly familiar with the *Guidelines for Providers of Psychological Services to Ethnic, Linguistic, and Culturally Diverse Populations* (APA, 1993), and the *General Guidelines for Providers of Psychological Services* (APA, 1987).

When such a foundation and orientation exists, the training program is able to set clear and consistent expectations and responsibilities regarding the identification and management of potential ethical and legal problems for both supervisors and supervisees. This type of foundation and orientation also tends to foster a rich atmosphere for learning to identify, understand, and address potential ethical and legal problems. Not only is a proactive posture toward potential ethical and legal problems enhanced, the inextricable linkage between ethical/legal issues and an extremely broad range of clinical phenomena is also underscored. Such an orientation to training has at least three possible outcomes: (1) it provides a particularly valuable training experience with respect to understanding, identifying, and resolving potential ethical and legal problems as they arise; it also heightens awareness that ethical and legal issues are inevitably deeply interwoven with clinical and practice issues; (2) the promotion of a proactive approach toward potential ethical/legal problems usually assists psychologists-in-training to learn that such an approach often serves to prevent the emergence of more serious ethical and legal problems; and (3) in addition to its positive effects on the quality of training, this orientation enhances the quality of clinical and other services provided. Not only is the quality of clinical services delivered at the training site strengthened, but it is quite likely that the quality of services delivered by those who have received training at such a site, once they have become licensed psychologists, are more sensitive, knowledgeable, and balanced in relation to understanding and managing potential ethical and legal problems.

Orientation Toward Ethical and Legal Considerations Specific to Training

The most recent APA Ethics Code (2002) contains twelve standards that relate directly to academic and training settings as well as to supervisors and supervisees. Ten of these standards have been strengthened and/or augmented from those in the 1992 Code of Ethics; additionally, the 2002 Code of Ethics contains two new standards. This strengthening and augmentation is most welcome, as until these most recent standards were promulgated, there were some gaps and imprecision regarding the role of ethics in areas specific to the graduate education and training of psychologists. As a partial result, ethical and legal standards tended to be applied more rigorously in the professional practice of psychology, and less rigorously in graduate education and training in psychology. This presented a rather serious shortcoming in the education and training of future psychologists. In light of recent developments in the ethical and legal arenas, this important dimension of training was strengthened appreciably as a result of the new APA Ethics Code (2002).

Specifically, the evolving ethical emphases related to education, training, and supervision in psychology can be illustrated by the invaluable development of the following new or augmented ethical standards in the 2002 Ethical Code. The two new ethical standards in the 2002 Ethical Code are: (1) Standard 7.04 Student Disclosure of Personal Information; and (2) Standard 7.05 Mandatory Individual or Group Therapy. The ten standards that have been strengthened or augmented in the 2002 Ethical Code are as follows: (1) Standard 2.05 Delegation of Work to Others; (2) Standard 3.02 Sexual Harassment; (3) Standard 3.03 Other Harassment; (4) Standard 3.04 Avoiding Harm; (5) Standard 3.05 Multiple Relationships; (6) Standard 3.08 Exploitive Relationships; (7) Standard 7.01 Design of Education and Training Programs; (8) Standard 7.02 Descriptions of Education and Training Programs; (9) Standard 7.06 Assessing Student and Supervisee Performance; and (10) Standard 7.07 Sexual Relationships with Students and Supervisees. (For further discussion on ethical issues in teaching, see Callan & Bucky, in this volume.)

The ethical and legal aspects of the training foundation become substantially strengthened when there is a sustained effort to value and integrate fully those ethical standards and legal codes that are specific to training. Such an orientation strengthens the possibility that ethical standards and legal codes specific to training constitute a clear and integral part of the training program. To illustrate, the following ethical standards constitute some of the more important ones that an ethically sensitive and sound training program must integrate in its day to day operation: Standard 2.05 Delegation of Work to Others; Standard 3.08 Exploitive Relationships; Standard 7.01 Design of Education and Training Programs; Standard 7.02 Descriptions of Education and Training Programs; Standard 7.04 Student Disclosure of Personal Information; Standard 7.05 Mandatory Individual or Group Therapy; and Standard 7.06 Assessing Student and Supervisee Performance.

With respect to legal statutes regulating psychology, they tend to be increasingly explicit with respect to training. If the training foundation is to be secure and stable, laws regulating psychology that pertain to training must also be carefully and systematically integrated into it. For example, in the state of California, aspects of the Psychology Licensing Law that relate to training and supervision in psychology are comprehensive, multifaceted, and extremely detailed. Specific and detailed legal provisions cover areas such as the regulation and limitations of psychologists-in-training, psychological assistants, and licensure requirements, among others. Similarly, legal statutes relating to training and supervision in psychology provide detailed descriptions of areas such as psychological assistants, requisite education and experience, and examination for licensure, among others.

Accordingly, any sound training program in psychology and other mental health professions will value the vital importance of ethical and legal guidelines and their indisputably positive contributions to training as well as to clinical activities provided at the training site.

ROLES AND RESPONSIBILITIES OF THE SUPERVISOR

Overview

Typically, the director of training and licensed, supervisory psychologists have responsibility for assuring that all relevant, current ethical standards and legal statutes and regulations are thoroughly integrated into the training program. Similarly, the training director and licensed supervisors are responsible for ensuring that ethical standards and legal statutes and regulations that relate to psychologists-in-training are followed sensitively and explicitly at all times. It is also critical for all supervisory individuals to review and monitor ethical standards and legal statutes and regulations regularly for applicability and for any changes. Specifically, there have been three different ethical codes since 1990, and in many states additions and revisions to laws and regulations pertinent to psychology appear frequently, often on an annual basis.

With respect to service delivery, a cornerstone of a sound training program is related to the necessity for the supervisor to assume ultimate responsibility for potential legal and ethical issues that may arise in relation to the clinical activities of psychologists-in-training that are being supervised. In addition to its ethical and legal soundness, the assumption of this responsibility tends to sensitize the supervisor toward scrupulosity and thoroughness in discussing, examining, and attempting to resolve potential ethical/legal issues as expeditiously as possible, often as a part of supervision. Such an approach to supervision also tends to reinforce the view that ethical and legal issues are usually inseparable from clinical and service issues. Rapport, openness, mutual respect, and trust are some of the more important attributes that characterize good supervision. A consistently articulated awareness of the supervisor's ultimate responsibility for potential ethical/legal matters, which may occur in relation to supervisees accompanied by a high degree of receptivity to the open discussion of such issues, is also indispensable in strengthening the supervisory relationship as well as in resolving incipient ethical/legal problems. This point of view is clearly articulated by Lakin (1991) who notes, "Just as the therapist should function to serve the legitimate needs of the client/patient, the supervisor should enable the trainee to develop the necessary skills to conduct therapy without denigrating or exploiting that person in their own relationship" (p. 119).

Issues Regarding Potential Trainee Impairment

Professional psychologists and psychologists-in-training are always subject to personal issues/conflicts that have the potential to affect their professional activities adversely. Some of the stresses that are often the precursors to the impairment of mental health professionals have been well documented by Sussman (1994). Moreover, when personal impairment appears to be affecting the functioning of a professional psychologist, his or her conduct and behavior as well as that of his or her colleagues should be guided by relevant ethical codes and legal statutes. The same is true for psychologists-in-training.

It is likely that the stress and competition associated with an intensive internship program, in addition to concurrent stresses and competition associated with a graduate program, contribute much to trainee impairment. This is augmented by preexisting personality conflicts the intern may bring to the training program. The prevalence of trainee impairment has been documented by Boxley, Drew, and Rangel (1986), who studied APA accredited psychology training programs and reported an average rate of 4.6% trainee impairment per program. The director of training and the supervisory staff play a most significant role in identifying and helping to resolve trainee impairment when it occurs, optimally, as early as possible.

Training Issues

Beyond the proactive stance of the training program *vis a vis* potential ethical/legal problems, it is imperative that individual supervisors have a detailed, well developed, comprehensive understanding of current ethical standards and legal codes specific to training and specific to the provision of services. Such a level of awareness strengthens the possibility that a supervisor will be highly sensitized to ethical and legal issues and their applicability to both training and clinical practice. Thus, the individual supervisor can be regarded as a prime individual in helping to educate psychologists-in-training about ethical and legal considerations by articulating a sensitive, comprehensive understanding of such issues and their critical role in daily supervisory activities and the ongoing clinical activities of his/her supervisee(s).

When supervision embodies a consistent and sound awareness of the vital importance of ethical and legal considerations, this greatly augments a foundation where ethical/legal considerations and their interrelationships with clinical work become incorporated in all aspects of the training program implicitly and explicitly, including during regular supervisory sessions and emergent supervisory consultations.

Clinical and Service Issues

As has been suggested, the supervisor plays a critically important role for psychologists-in-training, in at least three ways: (1) as a supervisor, (2) as a clinician, and (3) as a potentially valuable role model. A supervisor's skills, understanding, and utilization of supervision are enhanced not only by prior experiences in supervision, but also by his or her own clinical and professional experience. This blended type of experience is particularly valuable in providing supervision around ethical/legal matters.

In addition to these types of role modeling functions, the supervisor must consistently demonstrate in supervision, clinical understanding, and professional demeanor that ethical standards and legal statutes are not abstractions, but are usually closely interwoven with an extremely broad range of ongoing training and clinical activities. Thus, in day-to-day training and clinical activities the supervisor must consistently demonstrate a clear and comprehensive understanding of the complex, intimate relationships between ethical/legal issues and service issues. Central to the importance of the supervisor demonstrating and modeling ethical and legal understanding and behaviors is the view that training and clinical practice invariably possess potential ethical and legal uncertainties and problems. Likewise, there can be no doubt that clinical and other professional work is positively informed by a thorough understanding of ethical and legal issues. It is also important that the supervisor be comfortable with a posture that suggests that emergent ethical and legal issues are rarely clear cut, often fall into gray areas, and only occasionally lend themselves to unequivocal clarity and immediate resolution. When potential ethical or legal problems arise in relation to the work of a supervisee, it is advisable for the supervisor to cultivate an atmosphere where such potential problems can be thoroughly and sensitively reviewed and evaluated jointly by supervisor and supervisee before any definitive action is taken. It is extremely important that such a review and evaluation encompass potential service implications as well as potential ethical and/or legal problems.

As has been suggested, in a training setting it is also valuable to utilize an egalitarian approach regarding the assessment and resolution of potential ethical/legal problems. While it is true that the supervisor bears ultimate responsibility for all ethical and legal matters carried out by psychologists-in-training under her or his supervision, it is also likely that training will become strengthened when psychologists-in-training feel free to bring not only potential ethical/legal problems but also uncertainties and questions about ethical/legal matters to supervision so that they too may be understood and resolved more fully. An openness to this type of ethical/legal focus tends to promote the professional growth and ethical/legal understanding of clinicians-in-training; additionally, it often constitutes a powerful basis for the effective resolution of potential legal/ethical problems as they arise.

An invaluable tone is set in a training setting when it is made clear that the director of training and/or licensed professional supervisors bear ultimate responsibility for all ethical/legal matters, actions, and decisions carried out by those in training under their supervision. As suggested by Lakin (1991), the fact that this responsibility is basic to all aspects of the training situation must be underscored, and it is of great importance that all supervisees understand fully the scope of their supervisors' responsibility for any ethical/legal matters supervisees may encounter. Such clear and consistent identification and assumption of supervisory responsibility for ethical/legal matters is not without some drawbacks and risks, but it tends to enhance clarity and trust within the training setting. It also compels the supervisor to stay fully informed about the clinical activities of supervisees under her or his supervision. This is regarded as an indispensable aspect of an open training system where the identification, assessment, and resolution of potential ethical/legal matters is regularly identified and integrated in all aspects of supervision and training. The consistent assumption of these responsibilities also forces the supervisor to provide a knowledgeable, open, and proactive stance toward the identification, assessment, and resolution of any potential ethical/legal matters that may occur in the training setting.

It should be emphasized that many training settings have significant after-hours responsibilities that also contain important clinical and supervisorial elements. In maintaining appropriate standards of care, the program may operate a 24 hours per day, 7 days per week telephone response system for patients being seen under its auspices. Such systems are often managed by individuals in training, but it is ethically and legally essential and indispensable in their therapeutic effectiveness that supervisory back-up be readily available, usually by telephone. When crises are identified under such a system, they often have ethical and legal implications in addition to clinical ones. While a telephonic collaborative approach can contribute much to resolve such crises effectively, here too the supervisor is required to exercise ultimate clinical, ethical, and legal responsibility, although the supervisee is often left to carry out the supervisorial recommendations.

The integration and understanding of ethical/legal matters and complexities also tends to be enhanced if the supervisor takes the lead in routinely sharing with all clinicians-in-training any ethical/legal matters as they may arise in the training setting. Specifically, it is often quite fruitful to use a training seminar, psychotherapy seminar, etc., to focus discussion on any ethical/legal matters that have arisen in the training setting and to make the identification, understanding, and resolution of such matters, as well as their clinical implications, an ongoing part of such a seminar. Such an approach constitutes a powerful *in vivo* learning experience for both supervisors and supervisees regarding ethical/legal matters as they occur, as well as their complexities and clinical implications. This approach also tends to heighten sensitivity, openness, and supervisor/supervisee collaboration regarding the identification and resolution of potential ethical/legal problems.

ROLES AND RESPONSIBILITIES OF THE SUPERVISEE

Several factors are important in guiding the work of supervisees in a training setting with respect to ethical/legal matters. While all of their professional activities are subject to relevant ethical codes and legal statutes, no supervisee is expected to have "all the answers" regarding ethical/legal matters, though at times it would seem that some charge themselves with this level of knowledge at the outset of their training. At the same time, there is a reasonable expectation that a supervisee entering a training setting will have at least a rudimentary knowledge of the importance of ethical codes and legal regulations as well as their complexities. For example, the supervisee must come to understand the importance of readily identifying him or herself to all potential patients as being in training, providing the length of time that she or he will be in the training program, and clearly acknowledging that she or he is receiving supervision from a licensed mental health professional. This type of requisite ethical and legal disclosure is not without drawbacks as it can lead to complex questions (e.g., "exactly what will you tell your supervisor?"), and on occasion disparaging attitudes toward the supervisee.

Having a rudimentary knowledge of ethical/legal matters tends to constitute a foundation upon which an increasingly sophisticated understanding and broadened awareness of ethical and legal issues can be developed. Similarly, the psychologist-in-training must work toward realizing that he or she eventually will be experiencing ethical/legal matters in the real world of clinical practice. As such, the reactions of the clinician-in-training to potential ethical/legal matters obviously bears only a remote relationship to a graduate class and subsequent examination about ethical/legal matters. In the practice setting, training is oriented toward learning about understanding the critical importance of identifying and resolving potential ethical/legal problems as they arise. It is also oriented toward learning to understand the impact of these issues on the clinical enterprise as well as on the supervisees' professional development. Though sometimes difficult for supervisees in the early stages of training, it is extremely important that they learn to avoid "knee jerk" reactions to what seem to be potential ethical or legal problems. An extremely important facet of training is for the clinician-in-training to become more adept and more comfortable in learning to take adequate time to evaluate critically potential ethical/legal issues and their possible clinical ramifications before acting on them. Likewise, the supervisee is well advised to learn never to act on potential ethical/legal problems alone, not only because the supervisor bears ultimate responsibility for their management, but also because supervisory consultation generally leads to a clearer, deeper understanding and more adequate resolution. At the same time, it is important for the supervisee to learn to think critically and sensitively about the impact of potential ethical/legal issues on clinical and service issues, which can often be multifaceted.

It is also important for the supervisee to bring a sense of curiosity and openness to his or her training regarding potential ethical/legal matters, concerns, and questions. Adherence to two basic guidelines on the part of the supervisee can do much to enhance appropriate understanding of and response to potential ethical/legal problems as well as the supervisee's professional growth. These are as follows: (1) *when concerned* about any potential ethical/legal conflict, matter, or question, discuss it with a supervisor as soon as feasible; (2) *when in doubt* about any potential ethical/legal conflict, matter, or question, discuss it with a supervisor as soon as feasible. As suggested by Pope, Kieth-Speigel, and Tabachnik (1986), such ethical concerns might include feelings of sexual attraction toward clients/patients, among other things.

While a great deal can be learned about potential ethical/legal problems, concerns, and questions in regularly scheduled supervision, it is also important that all individuals in a training setting understand the value of immediate *in vivo* consultation between supervisee and supervisor regarding the clarification of potential ethical/legal problems and concerns *as they arise*. Due to the importance of such issues as well as the supervisor's ultimate responsibility for them, she or he will usually be very willing to provide emergent consultation to the trainee about such issues. As suggested earlier, at times these consultations may occur via telephone when a face-to-face meeting is not feasible.

TRAINING VIGNETTE

After approximately four months of training in a one-year program, an intern began taking an unusual number of sick days, apparently for seemingly minor complaints such as colds, headaches, etc. His professional activities also appeared to be suffering, and several patients he was seeing had abruptly dropped out of psychotherapy. When this behavior persisted for approximately one month, several fellow interns approached the training director, expressing concern about this intern's emotional well-being. The training director shared this information with the intern's primary individual supervisor, who discussed these concerns with the intern at their next regularly scheduled supervision. After some initial difficulty in discussing this matter, the intern began to express relief and acknowledged that he had become depressed over a recent romantic loss. His depression had begun to intensify, in part, due to fears that he would be discharged from the training program if he discussed his deepening sense of depression openly with his supervisors or fellow interns.

Following this discussion, the intern was informed that he would receive no new clinical assignments, and that he would receive additional individual supervision until he became less depressed, and until his professional performance improved. He was also encouraged to re-enter individual psychotherapy. After approximately six weeks, the intern's professional functioning had improved, and it was apparent that he was becoming considerably less depressed. On the recommendation of his supervisor, he again assumed a full workload. Eventually, he completed the internship in a good manner, and he was invited to remain in the training program for a post-doctoral year.

CLINICAL VIGNETTE

A seriously disturbed borderline patient with a long history of emotional problems, including intermittent alcoholism, had been in supportive psychotherapy with an intern for approximately two years. During the course of the two years, she made three suicidal gestures, numerous crisis telephone calls to the intern, and was placed in a crisis house as a result of two of her suicidal gestures. However, during the final six months of her therapy with the intern, she had not made any crisis calls and had been neither alcoholic nor suicidal.

At the conclusion of the intern's training period, the patient was transferred to an intern entering training. The patient readily expressed her displeasure and feelings of rejection and abandonment at the loss of her first therapist; however, she appeared to be making a seemingly smooth transfer to her new therapist. Approximately two months later, the new therapist received an evening phone call from the patient, indicating that she had been drinking and superficially cutting her arms. Despite this behavior, she told the intern that she was only seeking reassurance and that she was not suicidal. Following her intervention, the intern requested that the patient call her back within two hours. The intern then called her supervisor at home and they reviewed the situation in detail, with particular emphasis on clinical, ethical, and legal considerations.

The patient called the intern back at the designated time. She had continued to drink and cut herself superficially, but again denied that she was suicidal. Following this intervention, the intern again called her supervisor, and they again reviewed the situation in detail. During this review, the intern mentioned that the patient had said, "When I did something like this before, my previous therapist called the police." Accordingly, it was jointly decided by supervisor and intern that the intern was required to break confidentiality immediately and contact the police. The police intervened and took the patient to a crisis facility where she remained for approximately one week. She resumed therapy with the intern within the week. During the next session, the patient freely acknowledged that her behavior had constituted "a test" to see if the new therapist cared enough about her to take drastic, but ultimately therapeutic, actions. She indicated that she had relied on her former therapist to take such actions, when indicated.

CONCLUSION

A well-developed clinical training program in psychology and other mental health professions will include a strong, sensitive focus on ethical and legal issues in addition to clinical ones. An invaluable way to actualize this comprehensive, integrated focus is found in consistent, thorough, and open supervision between supervisor and supervisee. Such an approach to clinical training and supervision strengthens the possibility that ultimately, the quality of the clinical training and the clinical services provided will be enhanced.

REFERENCES

American Psychological Association. (1987). General guidelines for providers of psychological services. *American Psychologist, 42,* 712-723.

American Psychological Association. (1993). Guidelines for providers of psychological services to ethnic, linguistic, and culturally diverse populations. *American Psychologist, 48,* 45-48.

American Psychological Association. (2002). Ethical principles of psychologists and code of conduct. *American Psychologist, 57,* 1060-1073.

Boxley, R., Drew, C. R., & Rangel, D. M. (1986). Clinical trainee impairment in APA approved internship programs. *Clinical Psychologist, 39,* 49-52.

Callan, J. E., & Bucky, S. F. (2005). Ethics in the teaching of mental health professionals. *Journal of Aggression, Maltreatment & Trauma,* 11(1/2), 287-309.

Lakin, M. (1991). *Coping with ethical dilemmas in psychotherapy.* New York: Pergamon Press.

Pope, K. S., Keith-Spiegel, P., & Tabachnick, G. G. (1986). Sexual attraction to clients: The human therapist and the (sometimes) inhuman training system. *American Psychologist, 41,* 147-158.

State of California, Department of Consumer Affairs. (2003). *Laws and regulations relating to the practice of psychology.* Sacramento, California: Board of Psychology, Department of Consumer Affairs.

Sussman, M. B. (1994). *The perilous profession: The hazards of psychotherapy practice.* New York, John Wiley.

Ethics in the Teaching
of Mental Health Professionals

Joanne E. Callan
Steven F. Bucky

SUMMARY. It is the position of the authors that mental health professionals-in-training must be well versed in the ethical/legal matters of clinical practice. Indeed, most graduate programs in the field of mental health require formal training in Ethics. The California School of Professional Psychology (Alliant International University) San Diego campus has developed a model that requires (a) an ethics course integrated with the student's on-campus supervision in the Fall and Spring semesters at the practicum level, focusing on the American Psychological Association's Ethics Code (2002) and California's Licensing Laws; and (b) an advanced ethics course (in the fourth year of training) that focuses on the integration of ethical and legal issues in clinical practice and providing a knowledge base of sound ethical judgment. Syllabi for these two courses are included. *[Article copies available for a fee from The Haworth Document Delivery Service: 1-800-HAWORTH. E-mail address: <docdelivery@haworthpress.com> Website: <http://www.HaworthPress.com> © 2005 by The Haworth Press, Inc. All rights reserved.]*

Address correspondence to: Steven F. Bucky, PhD, 10455 Pomerado Road, San Diego, CA 92131-1799.

[Haworth co-indexing entry note]: "Ethics in the Teaching of Mental Health Professionals." Callan, Joanne E., and Steven F. Bucky. Co-published simultaneously in *Journal of Aggression, Maltreatment & Trauma* (The Haworth Maltreatment & Trauma Press, an imprint of The Haworth Press, Inc.) Vol. 11, No. 3, 2005, pp. 287-309; and: *Ethical and Legal Issues for Mental Health Professionals: A Comprehensive Handbook of Principles and Standards* (ed: Steven F. Bucky, Joanne E. Callan, and George Stricker) The Haworth Maltreatment & Trauma Press, an imprint of The Haworth Press, Inc., 2005, pp. 287-309. Single or multiple copies of this article are available for a fee from The Haworth Document Delivery Service [1-800-HAWORTH, 9:00 a.m. - 5:00 p.m. (EST). E-mail address: docdelivery@haworthpress.com].

Digital Object Identifier: 10.1300/J146v11n03_02

KEYWORDS. Ethics in academia, teaching ethics, syllabus, ethics in academic settings, multiple relationships

ETHICS IN EDUCATION AND TRAINING

Psychologist-educators and trainers have been guided on the appropriate conduct of research, practice, and teaching by each edition or revision of the American Psychological Association's (APA) ethical code since the emergence of the first version in 1953, through the most recent version in 2002. Because they are involved in the education and training of future psychologists, they have particular interest in assuring that psychology students be informed on each current code; beyond codes, they have also emphasized the study of state laws and encouraged debate on various challenging professional issues and situations as actually experienced by psychologists in different settings. In the last several decades, not only has there been a trend toward more intensive instruction on professional ethics, especially in graduate programs preparing students to enter professional practice, there has also been increasing dialogue around the individual psychologist's responsibility for ethical practices in academia (i.e., in the teaching of psychology at all levels; Vanek, 1990). This article focuses on these two emphases, with initial attention to the teaching of ethics as a part of education and training in psychology at all levels, followed by attention to ethical considerations more generally relevant to all academic settings and relationships therein. In support of both of these concerns, but particularly the former (the teaching of ethics as a part of education and training in psychology), an example of one curricular model, as developed for educating future professional psychologists during their doctoral training, is described.

Ethics Education and Training in Psychology

Nature and extent of current curricula and teaching activities. Because psychology is paying more attention to professional ethics than in the past, it is understandable that psychologist-educators are curious about the current status of ethics education in psychology. Indeed, in the last decade or so a number of psychologists have been studying the nature and extent of ethics education in psychology. For example, Welfel (1992), after reviewing relevant literature of the preceding thirty to forty years, found several areas in which she thought there were gaps in student competencies. Following on several prior independent surveys on ethics education (see Table 1), she then conducted a national survey of 101 internship directors, seeking information regarding their views on the ethical capabilities of predoctoral psychology interns. Welfel's discussion on her survey findings included results consistent with those from the surveys listed in Table 1, but as just described, discrepant with empirical research findings. Points she identified as relevant to improving ethics education focused on: (a) the need for more attention to clinical applications of the APA's Ethical Code; (b) interns' understandings of competence; and (c) the need for more formal evaluations regarding the outcomes of ethics education.

Graduate Education and Training: Emphases and Resources

Currently, graduate psychology programs, in particular those in clinical and counseling psychology, typically offer one or more required courses focusing primarily on ethics and the responsible practice of psychology; this contrasts with earlier approaches that were characterized by an occasional ethics seminar or colloquium. Indeed, as indicated above, surveys on what kind of ethics instruction are offered and how they are offered (one of the most complete being Vanek's [1990] dissertation research) suggest that attention to ethics education is increasing. As an example, whereas earlier approaches sometimes involved the integration of ethics education with other topics in professional issues classes, includ-

TABLE 1.Surveys of Ethics Education Prior to Welfel (1992)

Survey	Results
DePalma & Drake (1956)	Found, as the first published survey, that only 6% of the graduate programs included a separate required ethics course.
Jorgensen & Weigil (1973)	Found that there were ethics courses in 14% of the programs, although 80% had some exposure.
Tymchek et al. (1979)	Found that 55% of clinical psychology programs required an ethics course, and 96% gave some attention to ethics instruction (although only 67% of them employed a formal structure for doing so).
Vanek (1990)	Found that all 209 respondents from APA-approved clinical and counseling programs indicated ethics education to be a part of the graduate curriculum, with 69% requiring a formal course.

ing matters of professional practice in psychology along with that in other disciplines, today's educators have come to see the necessity for more intensive exposure and detailed instruction on ethics in practice. Educators today are aware that those whom they teach are preparing for this new century when they are sure to be confronted with increasingly complex human and societal matters, including heightened consumer scrutiny and related legal challenges. Indeed, some educators have come to advocate curricular revision in two key directions: (a) to provide for greater exposure to applied issues; and (b) to offer courses on the philosophy of ethics, the purpose being to encourage an attitude of respect and caring for those with whom one works beyond the inculcation of ethical considerations that relate more directly to professional skills and practices.

With regard to content and preferred ways of teaching, Vanek (1990), in her doctoral dissertation focusing on clinical and counseling programs, found that lecture, discussion, and case studies were the dominant methods. She reported at that time that the text of choice was *Ethics in Psychology* (Keith-Spiegel & Koocher, 1985), and found that the goals of ethics education most espoused by faculty for their students were: (a) to become sensitive to ethical issues in research and counseling; (b) to execute ethically appropriate behavior; (c) to facilitate ethical decision-making; and (d) to apply the APA's (1992) *Ethical Principles of Psychologists and Code of Conduct.* Vanek also found that among the topics most stressed were the 1992 Ethics Code (the extant code at the time of her study); confidentiality; informed consent; sexual intimacy and exploitation; and professional responsibility.

Another reference that has been used often in graduate education is Pope and Vasquez's (1991) book *Ethics in Psychotherapy and Counseling*, which according to the subtitle provided a "practical guide" to major issues faced in the teaching and practice of psychotherapy and counseling. Although published prior to the adoption of the 1992 Code, the twelve chapters in this book cover philosophical, attitudinal, and applied matters critical in the education and training of those who plan to practice as professional psychologists. In a subsequent publication, one written and compiled since the adoption of the 1992 Code, Bersoff (1995) introduced eleven different topics related to the conduct of therapy and other forms of intervention, all of which are relevant in the education and training of professional psychologists (e.g., the rights of clients or patients and the various responsibilities of therapists, including attention to key considerations in working with special client populations).

Regarding the teaching of ethics in psychotherapy, Greene (1994) advocated the use of training exercises to develop trainees' appreciation of the complexity of ethical issues and dilemmas in conducting psychotherapy. Among the many important principles that she said must be addressed are four frequently encountered problem areas: basic service contract, professional competence, confidentiality, and conflicts of interest. She cautioned that these principles are only guidelines, underscoring her "assumption that psychotherapists will behave in ways that do not misuse or exploit their power or influence, promote the general welfare of the client, and generally display respect for the rights of others" (p. 25).

Also focusing on ethics in psychotherapy, Vasquez and Eldridge (1994) noted the impact of major demographic changes in our society (e.g., that by 2000 one-third of the US population would consist of ethnic minorities, and the dramatic increase in the number of women in the workforce) and the importance of addressing these substantively in the education of future psychologists. These authors also pointed out the related demographic shifts within the field of psychology (e.g., the increase in the number of women entering graduate applied programs). Their overall message stressed the responsibility of psychologist-educators to include information in the academic curriculum on "gender, ethnicity, and sexual orientation, with basis in psychological knowledge, theory, and research" since such information is "not only legitimate, important, and central to human behavior, but is an ethical responsibility" (p. 4). The authors related this responsibility of psychologists to Principle 6.03, Accuracy and Objectivity in Teaching, in the 1992 version of the APA Ethics Code, and they suggested two documents as useful guidelines in learning about principles related to the provision of services to diverse populations: (a) *Principles Concerning the Counseling and Therapy of Women* (APA, 1978); and (b) "Guidelines for Providers of Psychological Services to Ethnic, Linguistic, and Culturally Diverse Populations" (APA, 1993).

APA Codes of Ethics as Guides: Some Comparisons for Learning

Although the APA's 1992 revision of the Ethics Code received mixed reviews among psychologists, its division into two parts (principles and standards) generally received high marks.[1] On the other hand, its aspirational tone and less restrictive nature were examples of what some psychologists saw as a weakening of the prior Code. The 1992 code provides stimulating and informative study for psychologists and for graduate students. For example, future professional psychologists can gain from comparisons of the 1990 and 1992 revisions (e.g., those on Standard 4, focused on Therapy, and on Standard 5, focused on Privacy and Confidentiality, as reviewed by Vasquez [1994]).

With regard to assessment, Dana (1994) noted an improvement in the 1992 Code, specifically as related to testing and assessment content. He advocated strongly the responsibility of each psychologist to demonstrate cultural competency with respect to conducting psychological assessments, even though he indicated that the process of doing so may involve both effort and distress, given the intense self-scrutiny required. He recommended the work of Mio and Iwamasa (1993) as helpful in appreciating the need for, and the pursuit of, such sensitivity. Chapter 6 of Bersoff's (1995) book, *Ethical Conflicts in Psychology*, is focused also on psychological assessment, providing "an introduction to the complex ethical issues inherent to gathering, storing, interpreting, and disseminating information about test takers that is gleaned from assessment" (p. 249).

Because teaching future psychologists about establishing and maintaining appropriate boundaries with clients or patients as well as any others with whom they work professionally is seen as a major responsibility by most faculty, Gabbard's (1994) comparative review of the 1981 Code with the 1992 revision regarding acceptability of sex with former patients offers students an opportunity to explore various views on this matter, one which has certainly received wide attention among the several health care disciplines in the last several decades. Gabbard's five major concerns, as related to detrimental effects of post-termination sexual relationships and the suggestion that they deserve further consideration among our profession, provide rich material for student discussion and for their gaining a more informed understanding on such issues as (a) transference, (b) internalized therapist, (c) continuing professional responsibilities, (d) unequal power, and (e) harm to patients and the therapeutic process. Gabbard presents nine countering arguments that support some kinds of post-termination sexual relationships, which not only enriches dialogue and debate, but also promotes critical thinking among students. Gabbard's concluding statements outlining difficulties in actually enforcing a permanent, or "forever," prohibition challenge practitioners as well as students to consider the complexities and difficulties in implementing and imposing ethical "policy."

The consideration of issues having to do with multiple relationships, as raised by Sonne (1994), points out to students various difficulties experienced in defining just what a multiple relationship is. Although

Sonne acknowledged the importance of careful thought regarding consecutive relationships as well, her emphasis on problems that arise with concurrent relationships suggested a range of behaviors among therapists that can constitute multiple or dual relationship situations. She noted that most relevant research has focused on multiple relationships involving sexual roles and added that other therapist-patient and educator-student roles deserve further attention. It should be noted that the acceptability of dual relationships is considered differently in the 2002 Code from how it was in the 1992 Code.

Slimp and Burian (1994) dealt more specifically with multiple role relationships that occur during the internship experience, noting problems and consequences that can develop in sexual, social, therapy, and business relationships. They stated, "the working relationship between the individuals in multiple role relationships is always affected, regardless of the form or outcome" (p. 42). Even so, they acknowledged that, given the developmental nature of the internship experience, the potential for harmful outcomes lessens, as does the power differential between student and supervisor. These authors suggested several recommendations to internship programs for advancing ethics education and ethical practices, among which are: establishing an ethics committee; making available an outside ethics consultant; having access to and consulting with the APA Ethics Committee and state psychology boards; establishing and observing written standards for delivering consumer services; establishing policies and procedures regarding the handling of ethics questions and issues, congruent with existing professional standards and codes; and providing applied training in ethics.

The necessity for practicing psychologists to develop "a sophisticated understanding of commercial issues" is emphasized by Koocher (1994), who asserted that most graduate training does not "routinely address" such matters (p. 355). His review of the 1992 Code stressed that specific client contracts were the ethical responsibility of practicing psychologists, and he provided discussion on such possible contractual components as informed consent, terminations, workplace issues, harassment issues, records, and advertising fees and financial arrangements.

Perrin and Sales (1994) considered the 1992 Code with respect to forensic standards, noting that for the first time, in this revision a section focusing on forensic issues was included. Although positive about that focus, these authors expressed concern regarding what they identified as routine forensic practices and then reviewed the Code toward identifying how effectively it dealt with such issues. Bersoff (1996) introduced a series of discussions on forensic settings, noting the complexity of the American legal system and also cautioning that all psychologists, not just forensic psychologists, are likely to find themselves involved with legal issues. Psychologists are encouraged to consider these comments on forensic standards and related issues and are encouraged to note the changes made on these matters in the 2002 Code.

Research

Sieber (1994) reviewed and critiqued the APA's 1992 Code with regard to its guidance on research ethics. Acknowledging that a "Herculean task" (p. 375) was undertaken by the APA in this revisionary effort, with attention to such matters as "research planning, consulting with one's institutional review board, compliance with laws, informed consent, data sharing, and serving as a reviewer" (p. 369), she nonetheless viewed the document as insufficient for fully informing, and thus for guiding, students and researchers. She referred those seeking fuller information to the *Ethical Principles in the Conduct of Research with Human Participants* (APA, 1982). Further, she emphasized that more work is needed to effectively guide the ethical conduct of research, noting in particular the following issues: limited autonomy, privacy and confidentiality, research on marginal populations, and research conducted in organizations or institutions (p. 375).

Being alert to ways of enhancing research procedures and methodology is encouraged by such works as that of Bell-Dolan and Wessler (1994). Through a survey, they sought information on how researchers' sociometric procedures compared with the APA Ethical Code (1992) and how to best use such measures for maximizing benefits and minimizing risk. Adding to the minimal literature on the supervision of student research is a study reported by Goodyear, Crego, and Johnston (1992), which focused on incidents seen by the professional psychologists who were surveyed as ones that presented ethical problems. Among the categories identified were: incompetent supervision; inadequate supervision; supervision abandonment; intrusion of supervisor values; abusive supervision; exploitive supervision; dual relationships; and encouragement to fraud. In addition to encouraging further study on this topic, the authors point to the advisability of developing faculty-student contracts in advance of conducting supervised research.

Undergraduate Ethics Education

Matthews (1991) pointed to some particular needs with respect to ethical considerations in the teaching of undergraduate students. As examples, and focusing on both the teaching of ethics and the ethics of teaching, she noted the probable lack of comprehensiveness among introductory psychology as well as social psychology textbooks in addressing ethical issues and, in particular, the APA's Principles. She also identified ethical issues involved in the selection of textbooks, advising that further consideration be given this topic.

Beyond these undergraduate education matters is ethics related to research. One approach to the teaching of ethics specifically related to the conduct of psychological research at the undergraduate level involves role-playing exercises. Rosnow (1990), for example, described a classroom exercise involving undergraduate research methods students in a sequence of activities beginning with a lecture on research ethics and ending with a role-playing exercise. Findings reported from a validation study by Strohmetz and Skleder (1992) supported the effectiveness of Rosnow's exercise "in sensitizing students to the complexity of research ethics" (p. 109).

Ethics in Academia and Teaching

As indicated above, psychologist-educators have long been interested in assuring the observance of ethical guidelines and practices by future psychologists; thus, ethics classes at the graduate level have given attention to existing codes as well as to national and state laws that pertain to the practice of psychology. As in other disciplines, they have focused as well on ethics in academia; that is, how teachers and students function and relate to one another in responsible and respectful ways. Curricular offerings are revised and updated to keep abreast of (a) current events related to or affecting psychology as a profession and (b) ethical guidelines and regulatory changes. For example, as psychologists, and more formally the APA, have become more sensitive to diversity issues and as laws were enacted and the APA's ethical code was revised to respond to and reflect the increasing diversity within the United States, course outlines have been changed. These changes reflect psychology's commitment to keeping its ethical guidelines both current and relevant. Yet, there are critical areas where psychologists arguably have not been as diligent as would be helpful, and ethical issues more specifically related to education and teaching have been identified as constituting one such area.

On this matter, Welfel and Kitchener (1992) stated that there has been insufficient attention to ethics in education, or more precisely to "ethical issues that faculty and supervisors ought to consider in training students for practice and research" (p. 179). A set of articles presented in the journal *Professional Psychology: Research and Practice* in 1992 (as authored by Canon; Goodyear, Crego, & Johnston; Kitchener; Vasquez; Welfel; and Welfel & Kitchener) was developed to address these under-attended issues. Readers have the good fortune to be introduced to these articles, then guided through them, by Welfel and Kitchener's (1992) use of the writings of two psychologists: Rest (1983) and Kitchener (1984). In the lead article, they pointed out that, whereas Rest's work provides a model for understanding moral behavior that is helpful in organizing empirical literature, Kitchener's work is more useful in relating ethical issues in education and training in psychology to views of ethics scholars.

This entire set of articles is recommended to the psychologist-educator. Summary remarks on Rest's and Kitchener's writings, with reliance on Welfel's and Kitchener's (1992) review, are included here to present a framework regarding morality and moral behavior relevant to psychology and its practice, one which undergirds education ethics.

Rest (1983). Rest identifies four components that he views as essential to the enactment of behaviors that are moral in the sense of balancing one's individual welfare and intrinsic values with those of others: (a) interpreting the situation as a moral one, which Kitchener (1992) relates to moral sensitivity; (b) deciding which course of action is "just, right, and fair" (p. 179), which Kitchener relates to moral reasoning; (c) deciding what one intends to do; and (d) implementing the moral action. As Welfel and Kitchener (1992) asserted, "this model is particularly useful in pointing out to psychologist-educators the importance of being concerned with 'students' moral sensitivity, moral reasoning, their ability to sort the moral from the nonmoral issues, and their ego strength" (p. 180).

Kitchener (1984). Kitchener, and also Steere (1984), applied Beauchamp and Childress' (1983, 1989) work on biomedical ethics to psychology, focusing more on principles than did Rest (1983). Kitchener observed that although professionals often turn to a code of ethics or to some formal statement regarding ethical standards as a first resource for guiding and informing their professional behaviors, there are limitations that can exist with such usage or reliance, as, for example, in the emergence of new, thus uncovered, areas. In accord with Beauchamp and Childress's view that such limitations can be handled by taking into account ethical principles, Kitchener identified five ethical principles that seem to related to psychology: benefit others; do no harm; respect autonomy of others; be just or fair; and be faithful.

Writing on ethical values as they relate to psychologists as teachers and mentors, Kitchener (1992) identified two "extracurricular issues" (p. 190) that, in her view, must receive further attention: (a) faculty must be ethical in their own interactions with students; and (b) faculty must deal responsibly with students when they engage in unethical or unprofessional conduct. Her essential point is that effective training of ethical professionals goes beyond the curriculum. Indeed, she encourages faculty to examine together the ethical dilemmas they confront and also to develop ethically appropriate courses of action.

Ethics Instruction in Professional Training

In 1993, the California School of Professional Psychology (CSPP)-San Diego Campus (now a college within Alliant International University) implemented a two-pronged formal ethics curriculum that included required ethics courses in the second and fourth years of the clinical psychology doctoral programs (PhD & PsyD). Prior to 1993, the only formal ethics training had been an Advanced Ethics course offered during the fourth year of the clinical doctoral programs. Although students evaluated that class favorably, they took the position that it came "too late" in their training (e.g., too late to assist them with practicum and internship training experiences). In response, CSPP's Professional Training Faculty developed a course for second-year students (those at the practicum level), in which ethics, legal, and clinical issues are integrated with a combination of joint ethics lectures and discussions with the clinical consultation supervision groups on campus. This class was designed to meet weekly throughout the second year of the doctoral programs (for a total of 30 sessions, 15 each semester). Each faculty member meets for one hour with two supervision groups of approximately eight students per group, separated by an hour-long discussion of legal/ethical issues with the combined 16 students (see Appendix A for course outline and requirements). The topics of focus in these groups are listed in Table 2.

The Advanced Ethics class has been taught by the co-editor of this volume and co-author of this article, Steven Bucky, for approximately 30 years (see Appendix B for course outline and requirements). The

TABLE 2. Focus Topics of CSPP Practicum-level Law and Ethics Course

1.	Competence
2.	Welfare
3.	Integrity
4.	Responsibility
5.	Maintaining Expertise
6.	Respect for People's Dignity
7.	Concern for Others
8.	Human Differences
9.	Respecting Others
10.	Nondiscrimination
11.	Confidentiality

course is team-taught, with the first half of the class focusing on the integration of the Code of Ethics, licensing laws, and legal and clinical issues in the form of mock oral exams. Students are asked to submit a question that focuses on ethical, legal, and clinical issues. One student asks his/her question to another student (randomly selected). After the latter has had an opportunity to answer the question, the entire class and instructor discuss the issues and complexities within each vignette in considerable detail. The issues tend to focus on child custody, child and elder abuse, Tarasoff, cultural/gender/sexual preference issues, involuntary confinement, suicide prevention, sexual attraction in therapy, sexual misconduct, confidentiality, informed consent, and the integration of assessment, diagnosis, and treatment planning issues. The second half of the course focuses primarily on legal and ethical issues and is organized in the following manner: introduction to ethics; treatment issues; the business of therapy; relationship issues; assessment; and academic and research issues.

It has been necessary to teach this class with a focus on changes emerging within the profession. Among the most recent changes have been issues related to technology, such as confidentiality, structuring the therapeutic relationship, informed consent, the use of the Internet, record keeping, licensing, assessment, and avoiding harm.

The 2002 Code speaks to new issues that are particularly relevant to students: for example, Principle 7 states that psychological programs must provide: (a) "appropriate knowledge and proper experiences" for its students (7.01); (b) a "current and accurate description of the program content" (7.02); and (c) "ensure that the course syllabi are accurate" (7.03). Psychologists do not require students or supervisees to disclose personal information regarding sexual history, history of abuse and neglect, psychological treatment, and relationships with parents, peers and spouses or significant others in course or program-related activities, either orally or in writing, except if: (a) the program or training facility has identified this requirement in its admissions and program materials; or (b) the information is necessary to evaluate or obtain assistance for students whose personal problems could reasonably be judged to be preventing them from performing their training or professionally related activities in a competent manner or posing a threat to the students or others (7.06). Other ethical principles relevant to students are quoted in Table 3.

TABLE 3. Ethical Principles Relevant to Students (APA, 2002)

- "When individual or group therapy is a program or course requirement, psychologists responsible for that program allow students in undergraduate and graduate programs the option of selecting such therapy from practitioners unaffiliated with the program" (7.05). Faculty who are "responsible for evaluating students' academic performance" do not provide such therapy.

- "A timely and specific process for providing feedback to students and supervisees. Information regarding the process is provided to the student at the beginning of supervision." Psychologists evaluate students and supervisees on the basis of their "actual performance on relevant and established program requirements" (7.06).

- "Psychologists do not engage in sexual relationships with students or supervisees who are in their department, training center or over whom psychologists have or are likely to have evaluative authority" (7.07).

- "Psychologists protect prospective research participants from adverse consequences of declining to participate in research" (8.04).

- Psychologists take (a) credit, including authorship credit only for work they have actually performed which they have substantially contributed; (b) principal authorship and other publication credits accurately reflect the relative scientific or professional contributions; (c) except under exceptional circumstances. A student is listed as the principal author on any multiple authored article that is substantially based on the student's doctoral dissertation. "Faculty advisors discuss publication credit with students as early as feasible and throughout the research and publication process as appropriate" (8.12).

- Psychologists are cautious about providing therapy to those served by others "due to the potential risk and confusion" (10.04).

- Psychologists avoid sexual intimacies with (a) current therapy clients/patients (10.05); (b) relatives or significant others or current therapy clients/patients (10.06); (c) therapy with former sexual partners (10.07); and (d) sexual intimacies with former therapy clients/patients for at least two years and even then in the most unusual circumstances due to the likelihood of the potential harm to the patient (10.08).

CONCLUSION

This article discusses the teaching of ethics to mental health professionals using CSPP-San Diego (Alliant International University) as a model. The authors stress the importance of thoroughly teaching mental health professionals-in-training how to integrate clinical, legal, and ethical issues in an organized, systematic fashion.

NOTE

1. Note that the 2002 Code remains divided into these two major parts.

REFERENCES

American Psychological Association. (1978). *Principles concerning the counseling and therapy of women.* Washington, DC: Author.

American Psychological Association. (1982). *Ethical principles in the conduct of research with human participants.* Washington DC: Author.

American Psychological Association. (1992). Ethical principles of psychologists and code of conduct. *American Psychologist, 47,* 1597-1611.

American Psychological Association. (1993). Guidelines for providers of psychological services to ethnic, linguistic, and culturally diverse populations. *American Psychologist, 48*(1), 45-48.

American Psychological Association. (2002). *Ethical principles of psychologists and code of conduct.* Washington DC: Author.

Beauchamp, T. L., & Childress, J. F. (1983). *Principles of biomedical ethics* (2nd ed.). Oxford, England: Oxford University Press.

Beauchamp, T. L., & Childress, J. F. (1989). *Principles of biomedical ethics* (3rd ed.). Oxford, England: Oxford University Press.

Bell-Dolan, D., & Wessler, A. E. (1994). Ethical administration of sociometric measures: Procedures in use and suggestions for improvement. *Professional Psychology: Research and Practice, 25*(1), 23-32.

Bersoff, D. N. (1995). *Ethical conflicts in psychology.* Washington, DC: American Psychological Association.

Bersoff, D. N. (1996). *Ethical conflicts in psychology.* Washington, DC: American Psychological Association.

Canon, H. J. (1992). Psychologist as university administrator: Visible standard bearer. *Professional Psychology: Research and Practice, 23,* 211-215.

Dana, R. N. (1994). Testing and assessment ethics for all persons: Beginning and agenda. *Professional Psychology: Research and Practice, 24*(4), 349-354.

DePalma, N., & Drake, R. (1956). Professional ethics for graduate students in psychology. *American Psychologist, 11,* 554-557.

Gabbard, G. O. (1994). Reconsidering the American Psychological Association's policy on sex with former patients: Is it justifiable? *Professional Psychology: Research and Practice, 25*(4), 329-335.

Goodyear, R. K., Crego, C. A., & Johnston, M. W. (1992). Ethical issues in the supervision of student research: A study of critical incidents. *Professional Psychology: Research and Practice, 23*, 203-210.

Greene, B. (1994). Teaching ethics in psychotherapy. *Women and Therapy, 15*(1), 17-27.

Jorgensen, G. T., & Weigil, R. G. (1973). Training psychotherapists: Practices regarding ethics, personal growth, and locus of responsibility. *Professional Psychology: Research and Practice, 4*, 23-2.

Keith-Spiegel, P., & Koocher, G. (1985). *Ethics in psychology: Professional ethics and cases.* Hillsdale, NJ: Erlbaum.

Kitchener, K. S. (1984). Intuition, critical evaluation and ethical principles: The foundation for ethical decisions in counseling psychology. *Counseling Psychologist, 12*, 43-56.

Kitchener, K. S. (1992). Psychologist as teacher and mentor: Affirming ethical values throughout the curriculum. *Professional Psychology: Research and Practice, 23*, 190-195.

Koocher, G. P. (1994). The commerce of professional psychology and the new ethics code. *Professional Psychology: Research and Practice, 25*(4), 355-361.

Matthews, J. (1991). The teaching of ethics and the ethics of teaching. *Teaching of Psychology, 18*(2), 80-85.

Mio, J. S., & Iwamasa, G. (1993). To do or not to do: That is the question for white cross-cultural researchers. *The Counseling Psychologist, 21*, 197-212.

Payton, C. (1994). Implications of the 1992 ethics code for diverse groups. *Professional Psychology: Research and Practice, 25*(4), 317-320.

Perrin, G. I., & Sales, B. D. (1994) Forensic standards in the new ethics code. *Professional Psychology: Research and Practice, 25*(4), 376-381.

Pope, K. S., & Vasquez, M. J. T. (1991). *Ethics in psychotherapy and counseling: A practical guide for psychologists.* San Francisco: Jossey-Bass Publishers.

Rest, J. R. (1983). Morality. In. P. Mussen (Series Ed.), J. Flavell & E. Markham (Vol. Eds.), *Handbook of child psychology: Vol. 3 Cognitive development* (4th ed., pp. 520-629). New York: Wiley.

Rosnow, R. L. (1990). Teaching research through role-play and discussion. *Teaching of Psychology, 17*, 179-181.

Sieber, J. E. (1994) Will the new code help researchers to be more ethical? *Professional Psychology: Research and Practice, 25*(4), 369-375.

Slimp, P. A., & Burian, B. K. (1994). Multiple role relationships during internship: Consequences and recommendations. *Professional Psychology: Research and Practice, 25*(1), 39-45.

Sonne, J. L. (1994). Multiple relationships: Does the new ethics code answer the right questions? *Professional Psychology: Research and Practice, 25*(4), 336-343.

Steere, J. (1984). *Ethics in clinical practice.* Cape Town: Oxford University Press.

Strohmetz, D. B., & Skleder, A. A. (1992). The use of role-play in teaching research ethics. A validation study. *Teaching of Psychology, 19*(2), 106-108.

Tymchek, A. J., Drapkin, R. S., Ackerman, A. B., Major, S. M., Coffman, E. W., & Baum, M. S. (1979). Psychology in action: Survey of training in ethics in APA-approved clinical psychology programs. *American Psychologist, 34,* 1168-1170.

Vanek, C. (1990). Survey of ethics education in clinical and counseling psychology. *Dissertation Abstracts International, 52,* 5797B. (UMI No. 99-14, 449).

Vasquez, M. J. T. (1992). Psychologist as clinical supervisor: Promoting ethical practice. *Professional Psychology: Research and Practice, 23,* 196-202.

Vasquez, M. J. T. (1994). Implications of the 1992 ethics code for the practice of psychology. *Professional Psychology: Research and Practice, 25*(4), 321-328.

Vasquez, M. J. T., & Eldridge, N. S. (1994). Bringing ethics alive: Training practitioners about gender, ethnicity, and sexual orientation issues. *Women and Therapy, 15*(1), 1-16.

Welfel, E. R. (1992). Psychologist as ethics educator: Successes, failures, and unanswered questions. *Professional Psychology: Research and Practice, 23*(3), 182-189.

Welfel, E. R., & Kitchener, K. S. (1992). Introduction to the special section: Ethics education-An agenda for the 90's. *Professional Psychology: Research and Practice, 23*(3), 179-181.

APPENDIX A
CSPP Practicum Consultation and Ethics Course Outline

FALL SEMESTER

I. RATIONALE:

"The role of education is to train the student how to become a responsible handler of power."
John Henrik Clarke

This course is designed to provide students with a general overview of and exposure to the ethical and legal issues, as well as potential dilemmas, inherent in the practice of professional psychology. With suggested guidelines and discussion, students will have an opportunity to apply ethical principles and legal requirements to clinical material presented in class.

II. ORGANIZATION:

A. Objectives

1. Students will develop a basic and practical understanding of ethical and legal parameters in professional psychology.
2. Students will approach clinical material with enhanced ability to apply ethics principles and legal requirements.
3. Students will become aware of how personal biases may be reflected in their clinical interventions and how to deal with them.
4. The likelihood of unethical conduct will be reduced, as responsible decision making and clinical judgment in the frequently encountered "gray" areas are enhanced.
5. In the consultation groups, students will begin to develop competency in understanding the whole person by evaluating, organizing and conceptualizing psychological data in the context of a theoretical orientation from which appropriately identified problems and goals may be derived.

B. Method

This course will consist of two components:
1. A Clinical Consultation Group in which:
   (a) Students will discuss general issues related to their Practicum experiences; and,
   (b) Each student will make at least one brief case presentation during the semester.
2. A Basic Ethics class in which:
   (a) Students will be asked to present a brief summary of readings and key issues raised in the Syllabus; and,
   (b) Students will discuss case vignettes and the clinical application of these issues.

C. Course Credit

Pass/Fail based on demonstrated competence in or compliance with regard to the following requirements:
1. A true/false, multiple choice exam based on assigned readings and the instructor's summary. Passed at 75%.
2. The student's case presentation in the consultation group as outlined in Objective 5.
3. Participation in group discussion in both components.
4. **Due to the interactive nature of the course, attendance is required at all classes. Students with more than 2 absences may receive a No Credit.**

D. Assigned Texts

    1. *APA Code of Ethics, December 2002 (APA)*
    2. *Course Handbook*
Optional: Keith-Spiegel, P. and Koocher, G. *Ethics in Psychology.* McGraw-Hill, 1985 (KK)
On reserve: Lakin, Martin. *Coping with Ethical Dilemmas in Psychotherapy.* Pergammon
Press, 1991 (ML)

III. SYLLABUS:

Session

1. Pre-Test
    Overview and Structure of Course
    General Concepts
    A. History and Structure (*APA, CPA, SDPA, Board of Psychology*)
    B. Differences Among Values, Morals, Ethics, Laws and Regulations

2. General Principles (*APA Introduction, Preamble and General Principles; Vignettes*)
    A. Competence
    B. Integrity
    C. Professional and Scientific Responsibility
    D. Respect for People's Rights and Dignity
    E. Concern for Other's Welfare
    F. Social Responsibility

3. Ethical Standards-General (*APA #1; Readings; Vignettes*)
    A. Ethics and Law
    B. Competence
    C. Describing Psychological Services
    D. Non-Discrimination and Harassment
    E. Personal Problems and Conflicts
    F. Misuse of Psychologist's Influence
    G. Multiple Relationships

4. Ethical Standards-General (cont'd); (*APA Record Keeping Guidelines, 1993; Vignettes*)
    H. Barter
    I. Exploitative Relationships
    J. Consultations and Referral
    K. Third Party Requests
    L. Delegation and Supervision
    M. Documentation, Records and Data
    N. Fees and Financial Arrangements

5. Evaluation, Assessment, or Intervention (*APA #2; Readings;Vignettes*)

6. Advertising and Other Public Statements (*APA #3; Readings; Vignettes*)

7. Therapy (*APA #4; Readings; Forms; Vignettes*)
    A. Structuring the Relationship
    B. Informed Consent
    C. Couple and Family Relationships
    D. Providing Services to Those Served by Others
    E. Sexual Intimacies
    F. Interruption and Termination

8. Privacy, Confidentiality and Psychotherapist-Patient Privilege (*APA #1 & #5; Provisions
    of Evidence Code Relating to P-P Privilege; Readings; Forms; Vignettes*)
    A. Maintenance and Limitations of Confidentiality
    B. Records and Disclosure

   C. Privilege
      1. Definitions
      2. Control
      3. Exceptions

9. Reporting Requirements (*APA #5; Summaries–Tarasoff, Child Abuse, Elder Abuse, Spousal Abuse; Readings; Forms; Vignettes*)
   A. Tarasoff v. UC Regents, 1976
      1. The Duty to Warn
      2. Exceptions to Warn
      3. Headlund Case (Failure to Diagnose Dangerousness)
   B. Child and Elder Abuse
      1. Definitions
      2. Reporting Laws
      3. Behavioral Indications of Abuse
      4. Child Custody
   C. Spousal Abuse
      1. Definitions
      2. Conditions of Reporting

10. Treatment of Adolescents (*APA #4 & #5; Readings; Vignettes*)
   A. Laws Relating to Treatment
   B. Parental Consent and Confidentiality
   C. Family Therapy

11. Teaching, Training Supervisors, Research and Publishing (*APA #6; Vignettes*)
   A. Descriptions of Education and Training Programs
   B. Accuracy and Objectivity in Teaching
   C. Assessing Student and Supervisee Performance
   D. Research Responsibilities
   E. Informed Consent
   F. Plagiarism and Publication Credit

12. Forensic Activities (*APA #7; Readings; Vignettes*)
   A. Assessments
   B. Clarification of Role
   C. Compliance with Law and Rules

13. Resolving Ethical Issues (*APA #8; Readings; Vignettes*)
   A. Familiarity with Ethics Code
   B. Confronting Ethical Issues
   C. Conflicts between Ethics and Organizational Demands
   D. Who is at risk?

14. Post-Test and Test Review

15. Summary and Feedback

SPRING SEMESTER

I. RATIONALE:

This course is designed to expand students' grasp of the ethical and legal issues in psychology, particularly as they are delineated in the "Laws and Regulations Relating to the Practice of Psychology," and the specific Codes relating to their implementation. Such knowledge is expected to help students not only in their clinical work, but also in planning their training, licensing and practice experiences. Specific segments relating to cultural diversity, sexual attraction and business practice are intended to address those areas in which problems of ethics and professionalism are most likely to occur. Discussion of clinical vignettes, selected readings and current Practicum experiences will offer an opportunity to further enhance the students' familiarity with ethical issues in practice.

II. ORGANIZATION:

A. Objectives

1. Students will develop a basic understanding of the licensing laws and regulations.
2. Students will become aware of issues of cultural diversity and be better able to deal with them in treatment planning and therapy.
3. Students will approach clinical material with better understanding and ability to deal with sexual attraction in therapy, as well as related issues of boundaries, risks and vulnerabilities for sexual impropriety.
4. Students will be better prepared to apply for licensure, and to make decisions involving legal issues related to training and professional liability.
5. In the consultation groups, students will continue to develop competency in evaluating, organizing and conceptualizing psychological data in the context of a theoretical orientation from which appropriately identified problems and goals may be derived.

B. Method

This course will consist of two segments:
1. A Clinical Consultation Group in which:
   A. Students will discuss general issues related to their Practicum experience and,
   B. Each student will make a least one case presentation with audiotape, videotape and/or psychological test battery during the semester.
2. A class on the Psychology Licensing Laws and Regulations, as well as issues related to sexual attraction, diversity and clinical practice, in which:
   A. The instructor will present a brief summary of the key issues raised in the Syllabus, and
   B. Students will discuss case vignettes and readings related to the clinical application of these issues.

C. Course Credit

Pass/Fail based on demonstrated competence in:
1. A True/False, Multiple Choice exam based on assigned readings and the Instructor's summary.
2. The student's case presentation in the consultation group.
3. Participation in group discussion in both segments.
4. **Due to the interactive nature of the course, attendance is required at all classes. Students with more than 2 absences may receive a No Credit.**

D. Assigned Texts

1. Lakin, Martin. *Coping with Ethical Dilemmas in Psychotherapy*. Pergamon Press 1991 (ML)
2. "Laws and Regulations Relating to the Practice of Psychology."
3. Course Handbook.

(Optional)   Keith-Spiegel, P. and Koocher, G. *Ethics in Psychology*. McGraw-Hill, 1985.

III. SYLLABUS

Session

1. Pretest
   Overview and Structure of Course (*Organizational Chart; BOP Newsletter, 11/94*)
   A. Diversity
   B. Sexual attraction in therapy
   C. Laws, regulations and codes
   D. Clinical practice

APPENDIX B
CSPP Advanced Ethics and Professional Issues Course Outline

I. **RATIONALE:** It is essential for graduate students in clinical psychology to develop their identity as psychologists and as responsible members of an organized profession. Towards this end, this course will provide knowledge about psychological organizations, standards and regulations. Familiarization with the APA Code of Ethics will take place in such a manner that utilization of these guidelines will occur in student's everyday practice as professional psychologists.

II. **ORGANIZATION OF COURSE:** The course will focus on professional, ethical and legal issues which affect the day-to-day work of psychologists. It will also attempt to clarify the interplay of these in practice. With this as background, the foremost contemporary professional issues will be discussed and placed in perspective and their implications for the future of the profession will be considered. These issues will be examined in such a manner as to facilitate the development in the student of an organized method for not only understanding the issues from all relevant perspectives, but facilitating the students assuming a responsible stand on the issues.

III. **INSTRUCTIONAL METHODS:** The course will be team taught by two (2) instructors. While one instructor is focusing on professional and licensing issues with one-half of the class, the other will focus on legal and ethical issues with the other half of the class.
   A. The section which focuses primarily on legal and ethical issues is organized in the following manner: introduction to ethics; treatment issues; the business of therapy; relationship issues; assessment; academic and research issues.
   B. The section which focuses on the licensing laws and the integration of the APA Code of Ethics with every day clinical practice will be organized as follows:
   Session 1–Application for Licensure;
   Session 2–Review of the California State Licensing Laws;
   Session 3–Review of the California State Regulations;
   Sessions 4-6–Mock oral examination with the instructor and student feedback integrating the APA Code of Ethics, laws that relate to Psychologists with legal issues and sound clinical practice.

IV. Two sessions of the Advanced Ethics Class will be devoted to addressing sexual attraction and therapist/patient sexual abuse in psychotherapy. This topic is currently the subject of intense discussions among psychologists. Training in this area is being called for by our profession, experts in the field and the state legislature.
   Session 1 will focus on education regarding the facts of therapist/patient sexual attraction and sexual intimacies including:
   a. Definition of terms
   b. Prevalence
   c. Therapists at risk
   d. Characteristics of victims
   e. Consequences to the victim
   f. Consequences to the therapist
   g. Ethics Code
   h. Insurance

Also included will be a discussion of what behaviors by a therapist are acceptable, as well as a group discussion regarding the similarities and differences between romantic and therapeutic relationships. First session readings: *Sexual Feelings in Psychotherapy*, pp. 3-77, 205-261.
Session 2 will include discussion of therapeutic use and alternative responses to sexual attraction between therapist and patient. The students will be given an opportunity to practice different responses and hear other student's responses through the use of a video presentation of patient vignettes that contain sexual overtones. Second session readings: *Sexual Feelings in Psychotherapy*, pp. 79-190.

V. EVALUATION: Each instructor will evaluate performance in his segment of the course as follows:
A. Participation & contribution to class discussion.
B. Quality of written & oral reports.
C. Final examination.

VI. GRADING: Passing grade = 75% of combined scores from the two (2) instructors.
Vignettes–10%
Oral Exam–10%
Paper–20%
Final Exam–60%

VII. READINGS:

Pope, Kenneth S., Sonne, Janet L. and Holroyd, Jean. *Sexual feelings in psychotherapy*. Washington, D.C.: American Psychological Association, 1993.

Pope, Kenneth S. and Vasquez, Melba J.T. *Ethics in Psychotherapy and Counseling*. San Francisco: Jossey-Bass, Inc., 1991.

Course Handbook includes:
Ethical Principles of Psychologists, American Psychological Association, Washington, D.C., 1992.
Ethical Principles of Psychologists, American Psychological Association, Washington, D.C., 2002.
Laws and Regulations Relating to the Practice of Psychology, California Board of Psychology, 1998.
Specialty Guidelines for Forensic Psychologists, American Psychological Association, Washington, D.C., 1991.
Pope, K.S., Keith-Spiegel, P. & Tabachnick, B.G. (1986). Sexual attraction to clients: The human therapist and the (sometimes) inhuman training system. *American Psychologist, 41*(2), 147-157.
California Department of Consumer Affairs. (1990). *Professional Therapy Never Includes Sex.*
Guidelines for Providers of Psychological Services to Ethnic, Linguistic, and Culturally Diverse Populations, American Psychologist, American Psychological Association, Washington, D.C., January 1993.
Specialty Guidelines for the Delivery of Services by Clinical Psychologists, American Psychological Association, Washington, D.C., 1981.
Ebert, Bruce. *Dual-relationship prohibition: A concept whose time never should have come*. Applied & Preventative Psychology, Cambridge University Press, 1997.
Winner, Karen. *Expertise, ethics of court psychologists come under fire*. The San Diego Union Tribune, November 11, 1997.
Medical Board of California. *The Hot Sheet-Monthly Disciplinary Summary*, State of California Department of Consumer Affairs, October 1997.

OTHER SUGGESTED READING:

Pope, Kenneth S. & Bouhoutsos, Jacqueline C. *Sexual Intimacy Between Therapists and Patients*. New York: Praeger Publishers, 1986.

VIII. A TA is required for this course.

IX. Course is not challengeable. Required of G-4 students.

X. Course may not be waived.

Ethics in Research

Julian Meltzoff

SUMMARY. This article presents an overview of the history of efforts to protect human subjects in research. It discusses the establishment of international, national, organizational, and institutional procedures designed to protect human participants. The article provides a detailed summary of the principal ethical codes for research and their origins. It includes discussions of the most frequently encountered ethical issues ranging from the initial decision to undertake the project, through the selection and application of the various research procedures, to the analysis and interpretation of the data. *[Article copies available for a fee from The Haworth Document Delivery Service: 1-800-HAWORTH. E-mail address: <docdelivery@haworthpress.com> Website: <http://www.HaworthPress. com> © 2005 by The Haworth Press, Inc. All rights reserved.]*

KEYWORDS. Research ethics, protection of human subjects, ethical codes, research design, research procedures, informed consent, privacy, biases in research, deception and debriefing, experimenter demand characteristics, data analysis, falsification and fabrication of data

---

Address correspondence to: Julian Meltzoff, PhD, 7056 Vista Del Mar Avenue, La Jolla, CA 92037.

[Haworth co-indexing entry note]: "Ethics in Research." Meltzoff, Julian. Co-published simultaneously in *Journal of Aggression, Maltreatment & Trauma* (The Haworth Maltreatment & Trauma Press, an imprint of The Haworth Press, Inc.) Vol. 11, No. 3, 2005, pp. 311-336; and: *Ethical and Legal Issues for Mental Health Professionals: A Comprehensive Handbook of Principles and Standards* (ed: Steven F. Bucky, Joanne E. Callan, and George Stricker) The Haworth Maltreatment & Trauma Press, an imprint of The Haworth Press, Inc., 2005, pp. 311-336. Single or multiple copies of this article are available for a fee from The Haworth Document Delivery Service [1-800-HAWORTH, 9:00 a.m. - 5:00 p.m. (EST). E-mail address: docdelivery@haworthpress.com].

Digital Object Identifier: 10.1300/J146v11n03_03

Ethical decisions must be made throughout the research process, beginning with the decision about whether or not to conduct the study in the first place. There are ethical issues in the various aspects of the design of the research, in soliciting and in dealing with the participants, and in analyzing and reporting the data. Finally there is the author's ethical responsibility in deciding whether or not to submit the completed research for publication, the editor's in deciding whether or not to publish it, and those citing the findings of the study to buttress their own points of view.

PROTECTION OF HUMAN SUBJECTS

Increased societal sensitivity to human rights and reactions to egregious violations in the name of research spawned the codification of ethical principles and their widespread adoption. Medical "experiments" in Nazi concentration camps, albeit embedded in the context of a larger miasma of horrors, raised the consciousness of the world scientific community to ethical issues. Ethically dubious research practices neither started in the concentration camps nor did they end at Nuremberg. In fact, some of the most celebrated triumphs of medical research used human subjects in ways that today would be considered as unconscionable. Walter Reed led a group of U.S. Army medical officers who were appointed to the Yellow Fever Commission in Havana in the aftermath of the Spanish-American War. In 1900, they conducted a famous experiment that proved that yellow fever was transmitted from infected persons to victims by the Aedes mosquito rather than via direct person-to-person contact, or by contact with bedding and clothing of infected persons. First, James Carroll, one of the Commission members, subjected himself to the mosquito bite and contracted a severe case of yellow fever from which he recovered. A bacteriologist on the Commission, Jesse W. Lazear, was less fortunate and succumbed to the disease after having been bitten by a mosquito. A controlled experiment on soldier volunteers then revealed that subjects who were bitten, those who were injected with infected blood, and those who were given serum filtered from infected blood, all contracted yellow fever. Those who were exposed only to clothes and bedding remained free of the disease (The New Encyclopaedia Britannica, 2002).

In 1932, a study under the aegis of the United States Public Health Service was launched in Alabama for the purpose of following the course of untreated syphilis. The participants were all poor African-American males who had syphilis. They were falsely told that they were to undergo a course of treatment. Instead, they were merely examined periodically and autopsies were performed when they died. Now commonly referred to as the Tuskegee Experiment, the study was still going on in 1972, long after the discovery of treatments that were never offered to participants (Jones, 1981).

Contemporary reports in the press of the results of Federal inquiries have brought the issue of abuse of human subjects in studies of radiation exposure to widespread public attention. Whether or not they are totally accurate, public perception of the dangers of research is being shaped by such alarming reports, as evidenced by the newspaper editorial "Experiments on humans" (1994):

> Retarded teen-agers in a Massachusetts school in the 1940s and '50s were given radioactive milk with their cereal to see how radiation affects the digestive system. In the late 1940s, 751 pregnant women were fed pills containing radioactive iron to determine its effect on fetal development. In the 1950s more than 240 babies were injected with radioactive iodine in attempts to find a test for thyroid disease. From 1945 to 1957, 18 terminally ill people were injected with highly radioactive plutonium to track its effect on the body. In the 1960s, the testicles of 131 inmates in Washington and Oregon prisons were exposed to X-rays to study sperm production and sterility. And radiation-contaminated fish were fed to 11 people near the Hanford nuclear weapons facility to see if radioactivity accumulated in humans. (p. B-6)

Although not as lethal, psychological experiments can easily bring about unacceptable harm to participants by creating marked distress, by causing embarrassment, by provoking anxiety, and by damaging self-esteem. When deception and concealment are involved, at the very least they give psychological research an undeservedly unsavory reputation. For example, fear of death was created in soldiers by simulating an imminent airplane crash and by other contrived situations (Berkun, Bialek, Kern, & Yagi, 1962). Schuler (1982) points to a number of other examples of potentially damaging studies, such as one in which subjects were falsely informed that they had homosexual tendencies, another in which reactions to stress were examined by injecting quantities of smoke under a door into a room, and one in which hypnotized subjects were persuaded to sell heroin. Perhaps most poignant is Schuler's excerpt from

Argyle's report to the British Psychological Society in June of 1960 on his dealings with the APA Committee on Scientific and Professional Ethics, describing an experiment reported at the West Coast Conference for Small Groups Research held in San Francisco in 1959:

> In this experiment, young G.I.'s, who were not volunteers had a sample of blood drawn by an allegedly inexperienced medical orderly. In the middle of the operation, the orderly quickly withdrew the syringe, dropped it, and ran cursing and screaming from the bunker. Immediately afterwards the experimenter rushed in, told the subject that the untrained orderly had accidentally injected a bubble of air, and that the subject would shortly die as a result. The subject was left alone but kept under observation for a period, later claimed to be half an hour. It was reported that all subjects tested had sat apathetically waiting for the end. (Argyle, cited in Schuler, 1982, pp. 73-74)

A few years later, Stanley Milgram's study of obedience attracted a great deal more attention (Milgram, 1963). His study, commended by some and criticized by others, continues to be debated more than four decades later. It served as one of the stimuli, along with other studies, for thinking about and for codifying psychological research ethics (Milgram, 1963). Studies of far lesser note may present ethical problems. Investigators who are excited about their experiments, and who are narrowly focused on the potential benefits to themselves and society, are sometimes inclined to overlook or to underestimate the risks to participants.

Codes of ethics that were sparked, first by medical research and then by research in the social and behavioral sciences, include the Nuremberg Code ("Trials of War," 1949), The Helsinki Declaration (World Medical Association, 1964), The Belmont Report (National Commission for the Protection of Human Subjects of Biomedical and Behavioral Research, 1979), the American Psychological Association (APA) Ethical Principles in the Conduct of Research with Human Participants (APA, 1973, 1982), and the APA Ethical Principles of Psychologists and Code of Conduct (APA, 2002). Schuler (1982) also presents codes of ethics from national psychological associations in Great Britain, the Federal Republic of Germany, Netherlands, Austria, Poland, Sweden, Switzerland, and France.

The Nuremberg Code (1949)

A code of ethics governing research was prepared in the aftermath of the war crimes trials that followed the Second World War. The code stressed that informed voluntary consent is essential, that experiments are to be planned "for the good of society," that "unnecessary physical and mental suffering and injury" is to be avoided and steps are to be taken to protect participants from any harm, that the importance of the study to humanity outweighs any risks, and that the study "should be conducted only by scientifically qualified persons" ("Trials of War," 1949, pp. 181-182). It further specifies that the participants have a right to withdraw from participating in a study and that the scientist has an obligation to terminate the experiment if it becomes apparent that continuation is apt to place subjects in harm's way. These central principles formed the core of all subsequent ethical codes.

Helsinki Declaration (1964)

The World Medical Association Declaration of Helsinki (1964) reaffirmed and elaborated on the Nuremberg Code. The Declaration added the requirement that an investigator should submit a detailed research proposal to an independent committee for review. This formed the basis for the establishment of Institutional Review Boards (IRB) in research centers.

Belmont Report (1979)

The 1979 Belmont Report was prepared under the auspices of the National Commission for the Protection of Human Subjects of Biomedical and Behavioral Research of the then Department of Health Education and Welfare. The Commission was created by the *National Research Act* (1974). The Belmont Report incorporates the principles of the Nuremberg and Helsinki codes under three metacategories: Respect for Persons, Beneficence, and Justice. Respect for Persons calls for recognition of the autonomy of each individual and "the requirement to protect those with diminished autonomy" (p. 4). Here they are referring to people such as children, prisoners, and hospitalized mental patients who have reduced autonomy. The principle of Beneficence calls for the maximization of potential benefits and the minimization of potential harms. Justice concerns fairness in subject selection, and mandates review to assure that certain classes of people are not being selected "because of their easy availability, their compromised position, or their manipulability" (p. 5).

APA Ethical Principles in the Conduct of Research with Human Participants (1973, 1982)

In 1966, the APA began to develop a code of research ethics. Extensive member participation and several years of committee work culminated in the *Ethical Principles in the Conduct of Research with Human Participants* (EPR), which appeared in 1973 and was revised in 1982. Like the Nuremberg Code, it consists of 10 principles, and it incorporates most of the principles and the spirit of its progenitor.

Principle A calls for "a careful evaluation of its ethical acceptability" and a "weighing of scientific and human values" (p. 5) when an investigator plans a research study. According to Principle B, the investigator has the ethical obligation to consider the level of risk for the participants in the planned study. These risks are to be weighed against potential benefits when considering the scientific and human values in Principle A. Principle C places the responsibility for the ethical treatment of participants on the investigator, who may not pass the responsibility on to others. All others who collaborate in the research, whether they are assistants, students, or employees, however, share the responsibility.

Principle D addresses the need to obtain fully-informed consent from prospective research participants except when there is minimal risk, and to introduce special safeguards when participants are children or others who have limited or impaired ability to understand the information transmitted. Principle E involves studies that require concealment or deception. Here the code exhorts investigators to ascertain whether these conditions are really justified in the light of potential benefits, and whether alternative procedures could be used. If concealment or deception are to be employed, as soon thereafter as possible investigators should debrief participants, should tell them that they were deceived, and should explain the reasons for it.

Principle F is concerned with "the individual's freedom to decline to participate in or to withdraw from the research at any time" (p. 6). Special consideration is to be given to protect the individual's freedom when the investigator is in a position of authority over the participant. Principle G mandates the protection of participants "from physical and mental discomfort, harm, and danger that may arise from research procedures" (p. 6). In accord with Principle H, information about the study is to be provided to participants following the collection of the data, and "misconceptions" are to be removed. Principle I establishes the investigator's responsibility "to detect and remove or correct" (p. 6) any undesirable consequences for research participation. Finally, Principle J stresses the confidentiality of information obtained about individuals during the research unless there has been an advance agreement to the contrary. The manual contains extensive elaboration on each of these principles.

It should be noted that this code, by title and by intent, is limited to the conduct of research with *human* participants. It also does not deal with other issues of research ethics besides those that have to do with the protection of human subjects. The present chapter, although it is also restricted to ethical issues in research with humans, goes beyond protection of human subject matters, which have been well-treated in all of the existing codifications of ethical principles, and focuses primarily on ethical implications of intentionally faulty research design, research practices in executing the design, and in the analysis and interpretation of the data.

In a broad sense, research that is intentionally biased in any of the ways to be discussed below does violate the existing ethical code. Research whose internal validity has been compromised cannot justify *any* risk or inconvenience to participants, and even when risk-free, wastes participants' time, squanders funds, and is a loss to "the general investment that society has made in supporting science and its practitioners" (Rosenthal, 1994, p. 127). Rosenthal argues that the higher the quality of research, the more that it is apt to be ethically defensible.

APA Ethical Principles of Psychologists and Code of Conduct (2002)

Beginning with 1953, the APA has published and frequently updated a set of ethical standards for psychologists. Both professional and scientific behaviors are covered. The ethical principles for research with human participants are folded into the Ethical Code (EC) in the form of concise standards.

DECISION TO CONDUCT RESEARCH

The initial decision about whether or not to do a study is usually thought to be an ethical decision when the research poses a risk to participants that exceed the anticipated benefits. As is correctly pointed out in the APA's (1973) EPR, deciding *not* to do a study because it is judged to be too risky is also an ethical issue if failure to do the study may deprive the world of important information that could bring about benefits that, in the long run, would far outweigh the immediate risks. As stated, "Moreover, the decision not to act is itself an ethical choice that can be as reprehensible as deciding to act" (p. 26). There are times when refraining from doing or sponsoring research borders on irresponsibility. A scientist-practitioner who devises a test and offers it for use by the professional community has an ethical obligation to do a research evaluation of its validity and reliability. The same would hold if one were to devise and to promulgate a new mode of clinical intervention before taking the trouble to do the research to establish its effectiveness.

There is another sensitive and debatable issue that arises when deciding whether or not to do research whose findings could potentially reflect negatively upon some segment of the population. This is especially the case for research that is designed to compare ethnic groups, cultural groups, genders, or sexual preference groups on aptitudes, mental abilities, or personality characteristics. Some people maintain that studies of this kind ought not be done because they have the potential for being divisive and for being used malevolently. Others maintain that unpleasant truths are not inherently evil, but that the lack of beneficence is created by the way that the truths are employed. One is saying, "Don't open a can of worms." The other is countering, "Open the can. Worms may be unfit for human consumption, but they are beneficial for loosening compact soil, and for feeding birds. It all comes down to how you use them." Principle J of the EPR begins to grapple with this issue:

> Sometimes a problem of confidentiality involves the individual participant's valued groups. The concept of betraying confidentiality "by category" arises when research reveals things that may be seen as degrading these groups. This issue presents the investigator with a severe value conflict. On one side is an obligation to research participants who may not wish to see derogatory information (in whose validity they will probably not believe) published about their valued groups. On the other side is an obligation to publish findings one believes relevant to scientific progress, an objective that in the investigator's view will contribute to the eventual understanding and amelioration of social and personal problems. To make this suggestion is not to diminish the magnitude of the dilemma under consideration. The investigator must be constantly aware that many potential topics of study are emotionally and politically explosive. Just as investigators are sensitive to their scientific responsibilities, they must also be sensitive to the social, political, and human implications of the interpretations that others

might place upon this research once the findings have been published. (p. 74)

The partial resolution of the dilemma in the APA guidelines is for the investigator to provide participants with information about the potential uses of the data so that their decision about whether or not to participate will be more fully informed. As the investigator can only speculate about how the ultimate data will be interpreted, and how they possibly might be malevolently misused, it may not be possible to inform participants fully or to be sure that they understand the implications of various hypothetical outcome scenarios. Collegial review is helpful in the sense that impartial reviewers do not have the same vested interest as does the investigator in seeing that a study gets done. On the other hand, the judgments of the investigator and the reviewers are likely to be shaped by the same politically and socially-correct attitudes and values that prevail in that time, place, and context. Dr. Mengele's research probably would have been approved by a hypothetical pre-Nuremberg Code Institutional Review Board at Buchenwald on the grounds that the benefits to the state would have been judged to outweigh the risks to the participants, who were considered to be non-persons anyway. They would have ruled that the studies were good for their society, and that pain, suffering, and injury to the participants were necessary and therefore justified.

The 1993 *Protecting Human Research Subjects: Institutional Review Board Guidebook*, prepared by the Office for Protection from Research Risks of the National Institutes of Health, advises IRBs in this manner:

Other researchers believe that IRBs sometimes perceive research on controversial topics, such as deviant sexual behavior or fraud in science, as presenting ethical problems because of the nature of the activity being studied, rather than because of research methods, risks, or rights of subjects. . . . Some behavioral research involves human subjects in studies of heredity and human behavior, genetics, race and IQ, psychobiology, or sociobiology. Vigorous ethical debates about these studies arise out of the fear that scientific data may be used to justify social stratification and prejudice, or that certain groups will appear to be genetically inferior. The possible use–or misuse–of research findings, however, should not be a matter for IRB review, despite the importance of this question. . . . IRBs should resist placing restrictions on research because of its subject matter; IRBs must differentiate disapproving a research proposal because of qualms about the subject being explored or its possible findings, such as genetic differences in intelligence, from disapproving research involving the performance of illegal or unethical acts. The former raises serious issues of academic freedom; the latter is quite different and appropriate. Whatever the propriety of institutional administrators prohibiting research to protect the institutions from being associated with controversial or sensitive subjects, it is generally agreed that this is not an appropriate concern for an IRB, whose function is to protect human subjects. (5-4)

In addition to the risks/benefit ratio, Rosenthal and Rosnow (1984) and Rosenthal (1994) have proposed a cost/utility ratio in appraising whether or not to do a study. In their view, when costs clearly exceed utility a study is ethically flawed on the grounds that it is improper to waste scarce resources. In his critique of this position, Sears (1994) takes issue with this point of view. He states, "Specifically, I do not believe that decisions about resource allocations should be moralized. Wasting one's own time and money is unfortunate, but it is not unethical" (p. 237).

Judgments of benefits and costs are, of course, subjective. There are, however, predictors of these judgments that are based on group membership. In a survey of 259 psychologists asked to do a costs/benefits analysis and to rate their approval of a hypothetical study, Kimmel (1991) reported that people who were more approving in their ethical evaluations, and who placed greater emphasis on *benefits*, were those who were male, held a degree in a basic psychology area, were further away in years from the receipt of their terminal degree, and who worked in "research-oriented contexts." Respondents who were more disapproving and placed more emphasis on research *costs* were women, those whose degree had been held for a shorter time, those whose degrees were in an applied area, and those who were employed in contexts that were service-oriented.

A provocative corollary of the scientist's responsibility to do research has been observed by Veatch (1975): "It has been argued that the researcher has an obligation to society or to a patient to conduct research. Now, potential subjects are beginning to claim a right to have experimental treatment" (p. 57). This is clearly evidenced in requests for experimental treatments by AIDS patients, just as it has been for victims of cancer in the past.

RESEARCH DESIGN

Ethical research requires objectivity on the part of the investigator. That is not to say that people who do research do not have strongly held positions and care not how the study turns out. On the contrary, they usually have a vital interest in the outcome and hold strong expectations about what the findings will be. It is precisely for this reason that the research must be designed in a way that rules out the effects of experimenter bias. The investigator's biases are generally pronounced in advance in the form of hypotheses. Procedures, too, are planned step-by-step and are described in detail and in advance. Nothing in the procedures should favor one outcome over another. Ideally, anyone who is skeptical about the truth of the hypotheses, or anyone who holds an opposing point of view, should be able to agree that the research is designed in a way that will provide a fair and objective test of the hypotheses, would agree that the proposed method for selecting subjects and for assigning them to treatment groups is free of bias, would concur that appropriate steps will be taken to control experimenter bias and experimenter demand characteristics, and would endorse the validity and reliability of the criterion measures to be used. Should there be any surprises in the results, the critic who is satisfied with the way the study was designed can only fault the way in which it has been carried out.

A study that is intentionally designed so as to favor a particular outcome, for whatever reason, is ethically deficient. Sometimes the stakes are very high, and the higher the dividend the greater the temptation to tilt the odds in one's favor. Such considerations as sales of a product or continuation of a funded program may rest on the outcome and strain the researcher's objectivity. One hopes that deeply incorporated values about scientific integrity and the discipline that comes with the perception of responsibility to society will prevail (see APA, 2002, Principle B: Fidelity and Responsibility and Principle C: Integrity).

Sponsored research (e.g., research that is specifically contracted to an investigator by a company, agency, or institution with a vested interest in obtaining a particular answer to a question about a product, program, or procedure) is unusually vulnerable to ethical violations of commission or omission. Bias could come from the researcher or from the sponsor. Bias could arise because of the conditions, limitations, or arrangements required by the sponsor. Or, with the collusion of the investigator, the design itself could be rigged so as to favor some anticipated outcome. There might be no control group where one was essential, or a non-equivalent control group that favored one outcome. Demand characteristics in a market research study on product preference could markedly affect the results. In addition, protection of human subject issues could be introduced. As noted in the EPR (APA, 1982), "In such instances, the investigator should ensure that the scientific integrity of the research process is not compromised by such influences and that the research process, if so influenced, does not endanger the well-being of participants. . . . The possibility also exists that an organization will apply the research in a way detrimental to the participants or to society in general" (p. 23).

Using "Ethics" to Mask Inadequate Design

Let us look at some examples of design flaws that are unethical because they bias the study in favor of the hypotheses before any data have been collected.

An investigator omits an untreated control group, a standard treatment contrast group, or a placebo control group in a treatment outcome study on the grounds that it is unethical to deprive subjects of treatment. If any improvements are shown, the investigator then proceeds to make causal inferences about the benefits of the treatment, even though there is no basis for such conclusions. If treatment benefits are so certain that withholding of the treatment is thought to be unethical, then there is no point whatsoever to doing the research in the first place. If there are sufficient doubts to warrant systematic study, there is no ethical problem about withholding a dubious treatment, providing an alternative treatment, or giving a placebo for contrast purposes. The history of medicine is littered with instances of research showing the worthlessness, and sometimes the outright danger, of treatments that had been routinely applied by practitioners who had great confidence in their efficacy. For example, Hill (1963) cites various medical studies employing controlled trials showing (a) no reduction in post-operative chest infections by routine prophylactic use of antibiotics, (b) no benefits of aspirin and antibiotics in the treatment of minor respiratory infections, and (c) no protection from recurrence of cerebrovascular accident with anticoagulant therapy. In reference to the latter, Hill raises the question about the ethical decision to withhold treatment when beginning the study; and the ethical implications at the end of the trial of having subjected participants to an ineffective treatment regimen.

A distinction must be made between the use of placebo controls in studies on drugs that are intended to be beneficial, and the use of attention placebo controls in the assessment of psychological treatments. Rothman and Michels (1994) argue that the use of placebo controls in drug studies is unethical. They base their position on the clause in the Declaration of Helsinki that asserts the right of every research participant, including controls, to the best-proven method. They state, in effect, that the efficacy of a new treatment should be judged in comparison to the best existing treatment available. They decry the fact that the Food and Drug Administration favors the use of placebo controls in drug studies, and believe that it is unethical to hold back "proven" drugs from anyone when testing new drugs. The placebo effect in psychological therapies is comprised of two components: (a) expectancies of improvement from treatment, and (b) the benefits that accrue to the client merely from spending time with and receiving attention from the therapist (attention placebo). Drugs are relatively constant in the sense that all measured doses are expected to be as identical as quality controls in manufacture permit. In psychotherapy, there is a two-part equivalent to the drug: (a) the psychological intervention (the applied therapeutic method), which is never as constant and standardized as a drug dose, and (b) the therapist who administers, and is indeed a part of, the treatment. Unlike the uniformity within a sample of pills, therapists are variable. "Proven" psychological treatments are not assuredly consistent, for they vary not only with what is done, but also with how it is done and by whom. One resolution of the dilemma has been to inform the participants in advance that various competing treatments are being studied and to assure them that, at the end of the study, they will be offered the treatment that proves to be the most effective if they have not already been in the group that has received it. Such a commitment would of course have to be honored.

Subject Selection

Biased subject selection can compromise the internal validity of the study and lead to false conclusions. For example, a researcher proposes that members of a particular minority group are intellectually inferior to Caucasians. The design describes selection of the minority group subjects from a population of poor, uneducated, migrant farmers, whereas the majority group is to be selected from among affluent, private college students. The biased sample confounds SES, education, occupation, and minority group status.

Criterion Measure

In the above example of biased subject selection, the study is further compromised by the use of a paper and pencil test of IQ, knowing in advance that many of the migrant farmers are not fluent in English. The situation does not have to be that flagrant and obvious in favoring one group.

It could be something as simple as using vocabulary that is not likely to be understood equally by two groups who are to respond to a questionnaire. Standard 2.01 (c) of the APA ethics code (APA, 2002) advises psychologists who are planning to ". . . conduct research involving populations, areas' techniques or technologies new to them to undertake relevant education, training, supervised experience, consultation or study."

Informed Consent

The EPR and the ethics code provide detailed guidelines for obtaining informed consent, the circumstances in which it is not necessary to obtain consent, and the use of inducement to entice people to participate. In their eagerness to obtain participants, some investigators err in the interpretation and application of these principles.

By way of illustration, an investigator in a study with children in a primary school located in a neighborhood that is heavily populated with foreign-born parents sends a highly technical consent form printed in English to parents. This procedure potentially violates Standard 3.10(a) of the ethics code because it fails to use ". . . language that is reasonably understandable . . ." (APA, 2002). The language is not understandable because the parents lack fluency in English and because they are unfamiliar with the technical language. Furthermore, an official document from a school to a parent may be perceived as a requirement with consequences for noncompliance. Compliance would then be an outgrowth of an exploitative relationship (Standard 3.08) unless the parents fully understood the situation and truly believed that there would be no negative consequences for themselves or their children were they to decline to give consent.

Ethical codes are especially attentive to the potential for taking advantage of some of the most vulnerable in our society, such as children, hospitalized and institutionalized individuals, prisoners, and soldiers (EPR, Principle F). As Wertz (1973) has noted, "The subject, diminished in his autonomy by illness, confinement or conscription, confronts the experiments in an environment dominated by the economics and ambitions of research" (p. 13). Title 45 of the Code of Federal Regulations, §46.408 specifies the requirements for permission by parents and guardians, and for assent by children: ". . . The IRB shall determine that adequate provisions are made for soliciting the assent of the children, when in the judgment of the IRB the children are capable of providing assent" (Department of Health and Human Services, National

Institutes of Health, & Office for Protection from Research Risks, 1991, p. 16). The child's age, maturity, and psychological state must be taken into consideration. When consent ought not reasonably be required, as in the case of abused or neglected children, consent requirements can be waived. Title 45 mandates special precautions for prisoners, as incarceration could affect the ability of prisoners "to make a truly voluntary and uncoerced decision whether to not to participate as subjects in research" (p. 13).

Diener and Crandall (1978) point to a potential negative effect stemming from ". . . overreliance on informed consent" in that "unscrupulous investigators will shift responsibility from themselves to the subjects" (p. 58). No matter what happens, some investigators are likely to defend themselves by an exculpatory claim of having obtained informed consent, even though they might have known that some of the subjects would not have elected to participate had they been fully capable of comprehending the attendant risks.

Confidentiality and Privacy

One of the tenets of most ethical codes in research as well as in clinical work is the protection of confidentiality and privacy of research participants (cf. APA, 1982, Principle J; APA, 2002, Standard 4). In some studies the participants are protected because they can remain completely anonymous. In others, the researcher must takes steps to assure confidentiality and incorporates this into the informed consent procedures. Researchers have found it helpful to promote confidentiality by giving participants code numbers (e.g., S#1, S#2, etc.) in place of names. The question has arisen of whether or not the *Tarasoff v. Regents of the University of California* (1976) decision applies to researchers as well as to psychotherapists, making it necessary to violate confidentiality in the interest of protecting potential victims from violence (for a discussion of the clinical application of *Tarasoff*, see Simone & Fulero, this volume). In their review of this issue, Applebaum and Rosenbaum (1989) noted, "The statutes adopted to date invariably frame the duty in terms of a 'patient's' or 'client's' potential violence" (p. 890), and note that it is unclear how this applies in nontherapeutic research settings (i.e., studies not involving psychotherapy procedures). They state, "In fact, relatively few obligations have been placed on researchers by the courts, which rarely have been called in to adjudicate issues in the research setting" (p. 890). Applebaum and Rosenbaum speculate on the conditions that might heighten the probability of the duty to report being imposed. They observe that "Research on sensitive topics, such as violence, child maltreatment, substance abuse, AIDS, and sexuality, might seriously be compromised by such obligations" (p. 893).

Subject Assignment

To illustrate how subject assignment to treatments could bias results, consider a therapy outcome study in which an investigator wants to demonstrate the superiority of Treatment A over Treatment B. Instead of random assignment, the subjects for Treatment B are drawn from a group of cases known to be exceptionally difficult, whereas those to be assigned to Treatment A are to come from a group that is believed to have a good prognosis.

Judging and Rating

In the therapy outcome study cited above, the investigator is to be the therapist for the groups receiving both Treatment A and Treatment B, and is to be the judge of therapy outcome. Special precautions must be taken whenever human judgments serve as the yardstick. Obviously it would not do to have the investigator who wrote the hypotheses serve as judge or rater in situations where the group membership of the participants is known at the time of rating. The same would hold for any associate or supposedly "impartial" judge who was not blind to the hypotheses and group membership of the participants. Bias can result by inattention to the qualifications of the raters, inadequate numbers of raters, failure to plan for rater independence from each other in making judgments, failure to keep them free of experimenter influence, and inattention to the need for planning for the establishment of inter-rater reliability. Any intentional variation in rating procedures could give an unfair edge in shaping the results in the desired direction.

Filming and Recording

Invasion of privacy is a major ethical concern in research. With the accessibility and ease of use of camcorders, videotaping of behavior for research purposes merits renewed emphasis on the guidelines that cover filming and tape recording. Because of its potential for misuse to embarrass easily identified participants, special care must be taken to obtain consent (see APA, 2002, Standard 8.03).

Deception and Debriefing

One of the issues of greatest sensitivity is that of deception in research. Some studies require temporary deception, but it is difficult to justify any procedure that causes physical harm or psychological damage (APA, 2002, Standard 8.07). Any time that deception is used, full explanation of the nature of and reasons for the deception should be given as soon after the experience as possible. The likelihood of communication among subjects in some research may rule out immediate debriefing, but in such cases particular care must be given to assessing the risk/benefit ratio in deciding whether or not to proceed with the study.

Timely debriefing is essential, particularly when harboring false beliefs about oneself could inflict psychological harm. For example, an investigator deceives college freshmen by falsely informing them of poor performance on scholastic aptitude tests in relation to the college's norms. The participants are left to carry the anguish of this false revelation for several months until the study is completed (APA, 2002, Standard 8.08).

Both Principle E of the EPR and Standard 8.07 of the ethics code are directly concerned with deception in research and stress the special precautions that should be taken before, during, and after research that uses intentional deception. Deception is considered to be acceptable only if benefits are judged to outweigh risks, participants are debriefed as soon as feasible, and no alternative way can be found to get answers to the research question without deception. Concealment is a kind of deception if information that might influence subjects' willingness to participate is withheld. One of the substitutes for deception that are applicable in some research designs is to find real-life parallels of contrived deceptions. In a study of stress effects, for example, instead of stressing participants by using deceptive instructions, the researcher studies people who are experiencing genuine life stressors.

Arguments in the literature over the use of deception have been long and vigorous. Aguinis and Handelsman (1997) and others citing important information gained from some studies using deception, maintain that the effects of deception in research are usually not profound and are far outweighed by the potential benefits. Others, such as Baumrind

(1985), argue that deception harms the subject, the profession, and society. She states, "Full disclosure of everything that could possibly affect a given subject's decision to participate is not possible, and therefore cannot be ethically required" (p. 165). She goes on to say that the researcher has a fiduciary obligation to the subject, and that "The overriding duty of the fiduciary is loyalty and trustworthiness" (p. 167). She regards the violation of this trust as immoral, and especially so when the subject is also a student.

Inducements

Inducements to participate should never become so coercive as to lead participants to consent to doing things that they would not ordinarily be willing to do, and will probably later regret having done. For example, an investigator doing research in an economically deprived area offers a sum of money that participants cannot bring themselves to refuse even though they must overcome their own resistance to being in the study. In this case, the size of the offer could be seen as coercive (APA, 2002, Standard 8.06).

DATA COLLECTION

Once the study has been designed, the investigator bears an ethical responsibility to assure that it is carried out without compromise. If random assignment is dictated by the design, there should be no deviation in order to cater to anyone and thereby favor any group. Unforeseen events that crop up during the course of research require decisions. The more complete and detailed the planning, the less likely this is to happen. Some problems are nevertheless unavoidable. The researcher should anticipate them and have contingency plans and decision rules at hand. If these decision rules for types of eventualities are made in advance and are public, the chances of biases coming from on-the-spot decisions will be reduced.

Experimenter Demand Characteristics

Most delicate is protection against any biasing influence of the investigator on the behavior of the participants. The experimenter, by facial expressions, demeanor, postures, or verbal comments, encourages and reinforces certain classes of response while discouraging others. The encouraged responses are those that support the hypotheses. These are commonly referred to as demand characteristics. Orne (1962) has asserted that subjects try to figure out what the study is all about and attempt to please the researcher by performing in ways that are consistent with expectations. Schuler (1982) noted, "In order to discover what is expected, the subject presumably draws upon all available information: instructions and explanations of the experiment, rumors about the purpose of the research, the personality of the experimenter, the other subjects, the experimental setting, etc." (p. 21). This is not to say that researchers should avoid collecting their own data. There is every good reason for the investigator to remain directly involved except where there is a reasonable potential for bias that would not be present were someone else to collect the data. If, for example, the researcher merely has to hand participants a packet of paper and pencil psychological tests with printed instructions about how to proceed, no experimenter influence on response is plausible, and there would be no reason for the investigator to avoid participation. Any foreknowledge on the part of participants would exist whoever were to serve as data collector.

Subject Attrition

Loss of subjects, for any number of reasons, is an ever-present potential source of bias. Selective dropping of people who perform in ways that do not support the hypotheses is a clear-cut ethical violation. Decisions to drop participants must be made on sound technical grounds without any consideration given to whether it will help or hurt the chances for obtaining positive results. This holds for the dropping of outliers as well. Preferably, the investigator should state in advance the criteria for dropping participants. As an example of how selective dropping of people can bias a study, consider the case of a pretest posttest design comparing two methods of treating depression, with 50 participants per group. Treatment A is predicted to be superior to Treatment B. During the course of the study, 10 people receiving Treatment A commit suicide. All 50 participants complete Treatment B. The researcher seriously biases the sample in favor of Treatment A by deciding to drop the 10 lost patients on the grounds that they were not available for the posttest measure. The most telling data against Treatment A do not enter into the analysis.

PROCEDURE

An investigator, in a comparison of favored Treatment A vs. Treatment B, treats both groups. The investigator, in the role of therapist, exerts maximal effort when working with Group 1, but does listless, slipshod, inept work with Group 2 and transmits lack of confidence in the procedures to the participants. Clearly, this willful effort to influence outcomes represents an ethical transgression, not an accidental design error (APA, 2002, Principles B and C).

The experimenter, who favors Treatment 1 over Treatment 2 but has properly designed a study with random assignment, deviates from this procedure to place in Treatment 1 some people who appear to be particularly good candidates. Correspondingly, some poor candidates are placed in Treatment 2. The act of placing someone who looks like a sure loser in favored Treatment 1, although mandatory, calls for personal discipline and scientific integrity. Psychologists have a responsibility under Standard 2 of the ethics code (APA, 2002) to "conduct research competently" and, in accord with Principle C of the ethics code, "Psychologists seek to promote integrity in the science, teaching, and practice of psychology" (APA, 2002).

Records

Researchers have an ethical obligation to record data with an acceptable degree of precision, and to maintain records that are open to external scrutiny but which protect confidentiality (APA, 2002, Standards 4.01, 6.01). Recording of data should be done in a manner that allows ". . . for replication of research design and analyses" (Standard 6.01 [2]). When research has been federally funded by the Public Health Service (PHS; U.S. Dept. Health and Human Services, 1994), the data are ". . . owned by the grantee institution, not the principal investigator or the researcher producing the data." Institutions are obliged to retain records for "specific lengths of time and to provide records on request" (p. 2). These records can be crucial in the event of an allegation of scientific misconduct. The *Publication Manual* (APA, 1994) recommends the retention of "data, instructions, details of procedure, and analyses so that copies may be made available in response to inquiries from interested readers . . . for a minimum of 5 years after your article has been published" (p. 283).

ANALYSIS OF THE DATA

A statistical design is part of the overall research plan. Alternatives are generally available. The researcher is expected to select the most appropriate statistical test rather than one that is less suitable but which appears to yield more favorable results. The unethical researcher will try out various statistics on the data and will select the one that provides the "best" results. This is especially the case when more precise and refined techniques do not yield significant results but when cruder tests of the data are reported because they make the results look more favorable. The ethical breach is extended when the experimenter suppresses the less favorable analysis. Transgressions in data processing may also be evident when investigators ignore the assumptions of statistical techniques employed (e.g., normality, homogeneity of variance) when it suits them, but are attentive to the assumptions when it is favorable to do so.

'Massaging' or 'milking' data are questionable practices. Here the hypotheses are not supported up to expectations, and the researcher resorts to gyrations in the effort to squeeze something that looks favorable out of the data. This is then featured at the expense of the legitimate failure to get expected results. 'Data snooping' involves searching the data for unplanned relationships in the hope of finding something of interest. Nobody likes to see hard-earned data go to waste, and nothing seems wrong with mining for nuggets. We cannot gainsay the inductive use of data to inform subsequent studies. Data snooping becomes a problem, however, when an investigator makes no effort to control Type I error arising from multiple unplanned post hoc tests, and then draws conclusions as though they were confirmations of predictions. "See, I told you so" statements are easy to come by when the question is posed while staring at the answer. The information gained may be biased and selective if the researcher disregards other relationships that have been looked at but found *not* to be supportive of the researcher's viewpoint, while those that do offer support are highlighted.

Premature Termination

An investigator does a power analysis when designing the study, and is informed by this and other rationale considerations when selecting the sample size before starting the study. When only a portion of the target sample has been obtained, a preliminary statistical analysis is very supportive of the hypothesis. The investigator decides to quit while ahead and claim victory. This is analogous to stopping a coin-toss experiment on psychokinesis aimed at producing "heads" after 10 tosses when the number of heads happens to exceed chance. The related scenario is quitting while behind and abandoning the experiment to avoid having to acknowledge defeat. Even worse is starting up again as if it were a new experiment, and hoping for a better run on the next trial.

Ignoring Negative Data

Plunging headlong towards proving a point, some investigators have been known to ignore their own main findings and to feature some minor portions of the data analysis when drawing conclusions. This process supports hypotheses but distorts the facts. Scientists have an obligation to respect good data and to accept what the data say, regardless of their own pre-suppositions and whatever the consequences of their having to admit that they were wrong.

Fabricating and Falsifying Data

Fabricating and falsifying data are the most flagrant ethical transgressions (APA, 2002, Standard 8.10). Sadly enough, cases are reported every year to the Office of Research Integrity. According to the U.S. Department of Health and Human Services (DHHS; 1993), "Scientific misconduct became a public issue in the United States in 1981 when then Representative Albert Gore Jr., Chairman of the Investigations and Oversight Subcommittee of the House Science and Technology Committee, held the first hearing on the emerging problem" (p. 1). In 1985, Congress established a process to review and to report cases of scientific fraud to the Secretary of Health and Human Services. In 1989, the Public Health Service established an Office of Scientific Integrity and an Office of Scientific Integrity Review. These were merged in 1992 to become the Office of Research Integrity (ORI), which became an independent body within DHHS and separate from funding agencies. The ORI has responsibility for (a) developing policies, procedures, and regulations; (b) administering an Assurance Program whereby applicants for PHS research support agree to comply with relevant Federal regulations; (c) reviewing institutional investigations of alleged misconduct; (d) conducting its own investigations of misconduct in PHS intramural research and presents its findings; and (e) "promoting research integrity in collaboration with universities, medical schools, and scientific and professional societies" (p. 5). Institutional investigations that confirm scientific misconduct may bring about sanctions by the institution and by the Federal agency.

Some cases receive a great deal of notoriety in the press, but others no doubt go undetected and unreported. Diener and Crandall (1978) cite reports of cheating in the social sciences and state, "These findings suggest that falsification of data may be more widespread than is usually believed, particularly among students and hired assistants" (p. 156). Established researchers are not exempt, as in the case of an internationally-known figure, Sir Cyril Burt, and his suspect data from his studies of identical twins reared apart. The well-known Director of the Institute for Parapsychology at Duke University was found to have altered data by unplugging an electronic recording device at strategic times (Asher, 1974). Contemporary reports from the Office of Research Integrity indicate that incidents of fabrication and falsification continue to occur and to be uncovered. Sanctions are applied at several levels. Independent of Federal penalties, the academic or research institution may take punitive action that affects tenure, promotion, or retention in the organization. The DHHS exacts penalties and withdraws privileges, and professional associations may expel or penalize the unethical investigator (U.S. Dept. of Health and Human Services, 1993). The ORI Newsletter (U.S. Dept. of Health and Human Services, 1994) reported the first settlement for ". . . alleged scientific misconduct under the False Claims Act" (p. 1). The investigator carried out his research under NIH grants at the University of Utah and the University of California, San Diego, in the field of immunosuppression. The settlement included the repayment by the universities for the grants in the amount of $1,575,000. The "whistleblower," a former lab assistant of the investigator, was awarded $311,000 plus $255,000 for his legal fees. Letters of retraction for five scientific articles and letters of correction for four other articles were required. The ORI Newsletter (U.S. Dept. of Health and Human Services, 1994) states, "ORI believes that it is crucial that whistleblowers are protected from reprisal by their colleagues and from those that they have accused of misconduct" (p. 4), and "Institutions that permit retaliation against good faith complainants are in violation of their Federal assurance and may have their assurance of compliance reviewed as a result" (p. 4). The operative phrase here is "good faith" to distinguish it from "witch hunt." It means that the accusation was made when honestly believing the charge to be true.

There have been cases of major fines and even of incarceration in cases where the research was supported by Federal funds. Worst of all, false data have misled clinical practitioners, and have thereby brought great potential harm to innocent victims. Exposed fabrications have unjustly aroused public skepticism about the forthright and legitimate research efforts of the large majority of researchers.

CONCLUSION

In so far as research findings inform clinical practice and potentially influence the welfare of multitudes of people, researchers have a particularly profound responsibility. In addition to protecting the welfare of participants, stringent adherence to ethical standards is necessary in all phases of research beginning with its conceptualization and design, and continuing through the collection and analysis of data, and through the process of interpreting and reporting the results.

REFERENCES

Aguinis, H. & Handelsman, M. M. (1997). Ethical issues in the use of the bogus pipeline. *Journal of Applied Social Psychology, 27*, 557-573.

American Psychological Association. (1973). *Ethical principles in the conduct of research with human participants.* Washington, DC: Author.

American Psychological Association. (1982). *Ethical principles in the conduct of research with human participants* (2nd ed.). Washington, DC: Author.

American Psychological Association. (2002). *Ethical principles of psychologists and code of conduct.* Washington, DC: Author.

American Psychological Association. (1994). *Publication manual of the American Psychological Association* (4th ed.). Washington, DC: Author.

Applebaum, P. S., & Rosenbaum, A. (1989). Tarasoff and the researcher: Does the duty to protect apply in the research setting? *American Psychologist, 44*, 885-894.

Asher, J. (1974). Can parapsychology weather the Levy affair? *APA Monitor, 5*, 4.

Baumrind, D. (1985). Research using ethical deception: Ethical issues revisited. *American Psychologist, 40*, 165-174.

Berkun, M. M., Bialek, H. M., Kern, R. P., & Yagi, K. (1962). Experimental studies of psychological stress in man. *Psychological Monographs, 76*(15, Whole No. 534).

Department of Health and Human Services, National Institutes of Health, Office for Protection from Research Risks. (1991). *Code of Federal Regulations, Title 45, Public Welfare, Part 46*, 4-16.

Diener, E., & Crandall, R. (1978). *Ethics in social and behavioral research.* Chicago: The University of Chicago Press.

Experiments on humans. (1994, January 5). *The San Diego Union-Tribune*, p. B-6.

Hill, A. B. (1963). Medical ethics and controlled trials. *British Medical Journal, 1,* 1043-1049.

Jones, J. H. (1981). *Bad blood.* New York: The Free Press.

Kimmel, A. J. (1991). Predictable biases in the ethical decision making of American psychologists. *American Psychologist, 46,* 786-788.

Milgram, S. (1963). Behavioral study of obedience. *Journal of Abnormal and Social Psychology, 67,* 371-378.

National Commission for the Protection of Human Subjects of Biomedical and Behavioral Research. (1979). *The Belmont Report: Ethical principles and guidelines for the protection of human subjects,* Vol. II, DHEW No. (OS), 78-0014. Washington, DC: U.S. Government Printing Office.

National Research Act, Pub. L. No. 93-348, §474(b) (1974).

Office for Protection from Research Risks. (1993). *Protecting human research subjects: Institutional review board guidebook.* Washington, DC: U.S. Government Printing Office.

Orne, M. T. (1962). On the social psychology of the psychological experiment: With particular reference to demand characteristics and their implication. *American Psychologist, 17,* 776-783.

Rosenthal, R. (1994). Science and ethics in conducting, analyzing, and reporting psychological research. *Psychological Science, 5,* 127-134.

Rosenthal, R., & Rosnow, R. (1984). Applying Hamlet's question to the ethical conduct of research: A conceptual addendum. *American Psychologist, 39,* 561-563.

Rothman, K. J., & Michels, K. B. (1994). The continuing unethical use of placebo controls. *The New England Journal of Medicine, 331*(6), 331-398.

Schuler, H. (1982). *Ethical problems in psychological research.* New York: Academic Press.

Sears, D. O. (1994). On separating church and lab. *Psychological Science, 5,* 237-239.

Simone, S., & Fulero, S. (2005). Tarasoff and the duty to protect. *Journal of Aggression, Maltreatment & Trauma,* 11(1/2), 145-168.

Tarasoff v. Regents of the University of California, 17 Cal.3d 425, 131 Cal.Rptr. 14. 551 P.2d 334 (1976).

The New Encyclopaedia Britannica. (2002). Walter Reed. In *The New Encyclopaedia Britannica* (Vol. 9, pp. 991-992). Chicago: Encyclopaedia Britannica.

Trials of war criminals before the Nuremberg Military Tribunals under Control Council Law. (1949). No.10, vol. 2, pp. 181-182. Washington, DC: U.S. Government Printing Office.

U.S. Department of Health and Human Services. (1993). *ORI: An introduction.* Rockville, MD: Author.

U.S. Department of Health and Human Services. (1994). *ORI Newsletter, 2,* 1-8. Washington, DC: Author.

Veatch, R. M. (1975). Ethical principles in medical experimentation. In A. M. Rivlin, & P. M. Timpane (Eds.), *Ethical and legal issues of social experimentation* (pp. 21-78). Washington, DC: The Brookings Institution.

Wertz, R. W. (1973). *Readings on ethical and social issues in biomedicine.* Englewood Cliffs, NJ: Prentice-Hall.

World Medical Association. (1964). *Declaration of Helsinki: Ethical principles for medical research involving human subjects.*

Ethics in Publication

Julian Meltzoff

SUMMARY. This article highlights ethical issues in publication. It addresses the provenance of ideas, problems with joint authorship, plagiarism, and the practice of duplicate submission of material for publication. Confidentiality and privacy matters, and the protection of human subjects in publication of research and clinical case studies are also discussed. The article further examines biases in literature reviews, and in the biased selection of one's best results for publication, intentional misinterpretation of data and the slanting of discussion, summary, and conclusions. Finally, the article deals with ethical problems that can arise in the publication of sponsored research, and the ethical responsibilities of editors and readers. *[Article copies available for a fee from The Haworth Document Delivery Service: 1-800-HAWORTH. E-mail address: <docdelivery@haworthpress.com> Website: <http://www.HaworthPress.com> © 2005 by The Haworth Press, Inc. All rights reserved.]*

KEYWORDS. Ethics in publication, provenance of ideas, joint authorship, plagiarism, duplicate submissions, protection of human subjects, confidentiality, privacy, clinical case studies, research, sponsored research, data analysis, data presentation biases, bias in literature review, editorial ethics, reader responsibility

---

Address correspondence to: Julian Meltzoff, PhD, 7056 Vista Del Mar Avenue, La Jolla, CA, 92037.

[Haworth co-indexing entry note]: "Ethics in Publication." Meltzoff, Julian. Co-published simultaneously in *Journal of Aggression, Maltreatment & Trauma* (The Haworth Maltreatment & Trauma Press, an imprint of The Haworth Press, Inc.) Vol. 11, No. 3, 2005, pp. 337-355; and: *Ethical and Legal Issues for Mental Health Professionals: A Comprehensive Handbook of Principles and Standards* (ed: Steven F. Bucky, Joanne E. Callan, and George Stricker) The Haworth Maltreatment & Trauma Press, an imprint of The Haworth Press, Inc., 2005, pp. 337-355. Single or multiple copies of this article are available for a fee from The Haworth Document Delivery Service [1-800-HAWORTH, 9:00 a.m. - 5:00 p.m. (EST). E-mail address: docdelivery@haworthpress.com].

Available online at http://www.haworthpress.com/web/JAMT
Digital Object Identifier: 10.1300/J146v11n03_04

In its more restricted sense, publication means bringing written matter such as a book or periodical before the public. The act of bringing private knowledge into the public domain can be expanded to include orally delivered papers, audio taped and videotaped lectures, and writings for computer display. Psychologists are bound by the same ethical standards when producing these types of materials, and when referring to sources that originated in these media. The goal of this article is to highlight some of the principal ethical themes that are encountered when making scholarly information public.

PROVENANCE OF IDEAS

Ideas are not as tangible as objects, but they are nonetheless regarded as the intellectual properties of the originators. When a number of people are all working in the same field and are thinking about the same things in parallel ways, it is not always possible to determine who was the first to think about something. There is justification in claiming ownership if there has been a clear trail of the ideas from the originator to someone else. It is not justified to say, "I thought of that. Therefore Dr. X must have gotten it from me." Once someone has been the first to go public with an idea or body of thought, claims of provenance can be made unless it can be demonstrated that the work was pirated from someone else. The person who makes a scientific discovery has to do more than to announce it to the press as a way of going public. First, it should be presented to a scientific society or published in writing in an appropriate periodical so that it can be scrutinized and evaluated by other scientists. In a case that attracted international attention in 1989, Pons and Fleishmann ran into difficulty on just this issue by prematurely announcing the incorrect discovery of a cheap process to create energy by producing cold atomic fusion in a test tube. However, announcements had been made to the general public before the scientific community had examined their work.

The ethical thing to do is to acknowledge the source when expressing an idea that is known to have originated elsewhere. This acknowledgement cannot be made if one does not know that one's own private ruminations have already been spoken publicly by someone else's voice. It becomes a problem when people who are in a working relationship marked by differential power, such as professor/student, head of laboratory/laboratory assistant, or employer/employee, share ideas. The professor claims ownership of ideas that have been conveyed to the student for educational purposes or that have been transmitted as a blueprint for further development. Subsequently, the student claims to be the originator of the ideas that were presented to the professor who then appropriated them. A leading scientist achieved world fame for the discovery of an important new drug. Two research assistants claimed that they had discovered the drug while working in his laboratory, but had not received credit for or share of the profits. The scientist countered that their work was assigned to them as a part of his established research program, and that they were merely following through on his work under his direction. One way to diminish the likelihood of misunderstanding about the provenance of intellectual products is to make a clear, fair, and explicit agreement in advance about the shared or exclusive ownership of any intellectual products or joint work efforts.

AUTHORSHIP

Related to the issue of provenance is that of joint authorship of publications. Results of a national survey on ethical dilemmas by Pope and Vetter (1992) revealed that, "Dilemmas in the area of publishing tended to focus on giving publication credit to those who do not deserve it, denying publication credit to those who deserve it, and teachers plagiarizing students' papers for their own articles" (pp. 406-407). Based on rankings by respondents on a survey, Spiegel and Keith-Spiegel (1970) assert that designing the research and writing the final report should be the main determinants of publication credit. Diener and Crandall (1978) advocate acknowledging in a footnote ". . . those who contribute to the study in ways that have no direct influence on its design or content" (p. 164). In their opinion, routine data collection from subjects, clerical work, and computer work do not merit author credit. Various collaborative relationships have to be examined.

Colleague/Co-Worker

When two or more colleagues or co-workers voluntarily collaborate on a research project and decide to publish the results, or when they agree to write a non-research paper together, they are guided by the *Ethical Principles of Psychologists and Code of Conduct*, Standard 8.12 (American Psychological Association [APA], 2002). This standard states that credit for shared authorship is decided on the basis of the extent of each author's contribution to the joint effort. The major contributor (and the one who usually writes the first draft) becomes the principal author. Successive places in the listing of authors are determined by contribution. In cases where contributions are more or less equal, authors decide position by alphabetical order, a coin flip, or by taking turns being first on subsequent joint publications. It is obviously unethical for one person to claim sole authorship rights to what has been a collaborative effort. It is also unethical for an author who was not the primary contributor but who is more senior in the field or in the organization to gain first authorship by "pulling rank."

Professor/Student

Some people who are in positions of authority take it as their prerogatives to exploit those over whom they exercise power. Professors are clearly in this position with students. The unethical professor's attitude is, "I opened up your mind to this topic. I taught you all that you know about it. Therefore, any of your intellectual products belong to me." Thus a student writes a term paper and the professor edits it and publishes it without giving the student credit. Or a group of students in a class write term papers on assigned topics, and the professor combines them and publishes them. Standard 3.08 of the Ethical Code (hereafter referred to as EC) states, "Psychologists do not exploit persons over whom they have supervisory, evaluative, or other authority such as clients/patients, students, supervisees, research participants, and employees" (APA, 2002, p. 1065). Also relevant here, EC Standard 8.12 (a) states, "Psychologists take responsibility and credit, including authorship credit, only for work they have actually performed or to which they have substantially contributed" (APA, 2002, p. 1070).

Researcher/Research Assistant

In one hypothetical case, a paid research assistant participates in collecting data exactly as assigned and under the supervision of the researcher. The researcher designed the study, planned the procedures, and writes the paper. Here, a footnote that recognizes the assistant's work would be sufficient. In another case, the research assistant is given the role of collaborator in the formulation, design, and execution of the project, and in the analysis and interpretation of the data. Here co-authorship is warranted [EC, Standard 8.12 (b)].

Theses and Dissertations

Theses and dissertations are regarded as the primary intellectual property of the student. Joint publication that is substantially based on the dissertation is at the discretion of the student. The student is the first author [EC, Standard 8.12 (c)]. Professors sometimes advise students of the low acceptance rate for journal article submissions and imply that if their name is attached to the paper it has a far better chance of being accepted for publication. This implication is meant as an inducement to urge the student to grant co-authorship to someone who may actually have had little to do with the study. In view of the fact that the professor knows that the manuscript will be blind-refereed with the authors' names deleted, the intent is to deceive and to pressure the student (EC, Standard 3.08).

Department Chair or Chief of Service/Staff

Some administrators, such as Chiefs of Service in medical settings, insist on being included as co-author on all of the products of their fiefdom, whether or not they personally have made any direct contribution. In other cases, the staff member as a way of currying favor initiates the offer of co-authorship. In either case it is an exploitative use of a power relationship (EC, Standard 3.08). Standard 8.12 (b) (APA, 2002) indicates, "Principal authorship and other publication credits accurately reflect the relative scientific or professional contributions of the individuals involved, regardless of their relative status. Mere possession of an institutional position, such as department chair, does not justify authorship credit" (p. 1070).

Reviewer

Reviewers and referees have a very special trust. They are supposed to be fair and non-prejudicial in their critical evaluation and recommendations about pre-publication material, and they are expected to refrain from quoting or referring to the material before it is published (EC, Standard 8.15). In view of the fact that referees are selected because of the interests and specialized knowledge that they share with the author, it may be difficult to maintain a neutral stance. This possibility is especially likely if the referee's own work and ideas are antagonistic to those of the author. Even though the names of the author(s) are deleted with the intent of making the review blind, there are times when the reviewer has no difficulty recognizing the topic, the content, and the style of the author. If one feels that this compromises fairness and objectivity, the ethical thing to do would be to excuse oneself from the assignment.

Most nefarious is the usurpation of an author's work by a confidential reviewer. Here, someone entrusted with the responsibility of refereeing an article for publication or a proposal for a research grant, excerpts and publishes these confidential materials. The Office of Research Integrity has reported several such cases. In one such instance (U.S. Department of Health and Human Services [USDHHS], 1993a), "The complainant, a reviewer on an NIH study section, noted that one of the applications he was reviewing contained material identical to that in an application he had submitted himself to NIH about two years earlier. The principal investigator (respondent) of the application under review had served as chairman of the NIH group that had reviewed the complainant's application" (p. 7).

PLAGIARISM

The prohibition against plagiarism is known to all students, and is presumed to be comprehended by all advanced scholars and professionals. The mystery is why it ever happens in publication. When it is uncovered, plagiarists often deny intentional copying and plead sloppiness, carelessness, hasty proofreading, or misplaced trust in others on whom they relied to carry out certain tasks. Of course these events can happen. Someone carelessly omits quote marks on original note cards or when transcribing from note cards, thereby confusing quoted material with one's own original commentary. Or, when there is more than one writer, the notes of one may be shared with the co-authors, who may mis-identify quotes as original thoughts. Or a writer relies upon an assistant to retrieve material from published works, and does not personally check the original material. All of these kinds of errors may "inadvertently" happen on a small scale. However, when substantial sections are lifted verbatim from someone else's manuscript, it becomes implausible to accept it as inadvertent or due to simple carelessness. Some outstanding scholars and well-known public figures have been acutely embarrassed and besmirched by charges of plagiarism.

Plagiarism involves the direct use of the words of others without the use of quotation marks, giving the impression that someone else's work is one's own (EC Standard 8.11). This applies to unpublished as well as to published manuscripts. According to the *APA Publication Manual* (APA, 2001), "Under the Copyright Act of 1976 (title 17 of the *United States Code*), an unpublished work is copyrighted from the moment it is fixed in tangible form–for example, typed on a page. Copyright protection is 'an incident of the process of authorship' (U.S. Copyright Office, 1981, p. 3). Until the author formally transfers copyright (see section 7.01), the author owns the copyright on an unpublished manuscript, and all exclusive rights due the owner of the copyright of a published work are also due the author of an unpublished work" (p. 355). Oral presentations are even more subject to plagiarism than are written documents. Quotation marks cannot be seen in verbal presentations, but the presenter is no less obliged to acknowledge the sources of quoted material and to verify the accuracy of the quotes. Audiovisual materials, including motion picture films, television productions, and tape recordings, must be referenced; this also holds for on-line journals, CD-ROM, computer software, and electronic data tapes or files.

Occasional citation of the source does not relieve the writer from the requirement of demarcating quoted words. When the act is intentional, plagiarists sometimes go to relatively obscure sources in the hope of not being detected. Employers, sponsoring organizations, and the USDHHS in the case of federally-funded work, deal with such cases when they are discovered and reported. Sanctions can be severe, including withholding of academic degree if plagiarism is discovered in a dissertation, and even rescission of a degree if it is discovered after the degree has been awarded. As described by the Office of Research Integrity (USDHHS, 1993b), possible consequences of scientific misconduct, including plagiarism, are:

> In some cases the researcher resigns or is dismissed. Institutions also may deny or revoke tenure, withdraw principal investigator status, issue letters of reprimand, review applications more stringently, or require withdrawal of manuscripts and correction of the literature. Government actions may included (sic) debarment from Federal funding, prohibition from service on PHS advisory committees, institutional certification of accuracy of the respondent's applications, and supervision of the respondent's research. (p. 6)

DUPLICATE SUBMISSIONS AND PUBLICATIONS

Attempting to publish the same article as original material in more than one journal is ethically unacceptable (EC, Standard 8.13). Despite the uncertainty of gaining acceptance of an article in a periodical of choice, the author who submits it to more than one journal at the same time is in ethical violation. Duplicate publication of part or of all of an already published manuscript is clearly prohibited by APA policy (see APA, 2001, pp. 351-354). In as much as journals are copyrighted, duplication would violate copyright laws as well. Additionally, when submitting an article in the form of a Brief Report, authors agree not to submit a longer version to another journal.

PROTECTION OF HUMAN SUBJECTS (CONFIDENTIALITY)

After the study has been completed, breaching assurances of confidentiality in publication can do harm. Authors of publications of clinical case studies, theoretical pieces that are illustrated with real-life case examples, or reports of research must vigilantly avoid revealing confidential information about people (EC, Standards 4, 4.01, 4.02, 4.03). Case details and names must be skillfully disguised so as to make individuals unidentifiable. The smaller the sample and the more easily identified the source, the greater the risk of loss of confidentiality.

In accordance with Principle J of the 1982 version of the APA's *Ethical Principles for the Conduct of Research with Human Participants* (EPR), in addition to protecting the confidentiality of individuals, valued groups and organizations must be shielded from public revelation of potentially injurious research or clinical findings. For example, a researcher finds that citizens of Town A have a lower mean IQ than those in Town B. The results could be misinterpreted as reflecting poorly on all of the residents of Town A. An ethical dilemma presents itself when investigators struggle with the decision about whether or not to publish information that could be perceived as derogatory and damaging. This sensitive issue has been discussed in the article "Ethics in Research" (Meltzoff, in this volume). There, the dilemma was about whether or not to undertake the research in the first place. Here, the dilemma concerns if, and how, to make the results public.

CLINICAL CASE STUDIES

There are two ethical issues in the publication of clinical case studies: accuracy and confidentiality/privacy.

Accuracy

Unless they are labeled as hypothetical, clinical case studies require recollection and reproduction of what actually happened, precisely what was said, how and in what order it was said, and in what context and what time frame. Accuracy in reporting what the therapist said (or did not say) is equally as important as accuracy in reproducing the remarks and behavior of the client. Even when aided by notes, mis-emphases, mis-recollections, omissions, additions, exaggerations, minimizations, distortions, and even fabrications can be inadvertently or intentionally introduced to make a case and its outcome fit a pet theory. So many hours of material and years of life experiences have to be organized, condensed, encapsulated, and characterized that the case study, unlike a research report, becomes a literary endeavor. It is a non-fiction short story that no two people would write exactly the same way. The writer is free to draw all kinds of causal inferences within this study of a portion of someone's life. The literary effort can be charming and compelling and can generate great interest. The product is often too pat and too tidy. The ethics of the case study lie in the accuracy, the balance, the objectivity, the truthfulness, and the comprehensiveness of the facts and formulations. Unlike a psychological experiment, the case cannot be replicated and the data cannot be checked. The reader simply has to take the writer's word for everything, and trust the writer's judgment about what actually happened and how it happened. They can disagree only with the author's formulation of the *why* of things, and can challenge the theory to which it is all linked. Mistakes, misperceptions, and misjudgments that the therapist/author may have made are not typically featured or even acknowledged. Because case studies inform clinical practice and influence theory, there is a great deal of reliance on the ethical integrity of the author/therapist. Exaggerating or falsifying case facts is the same kind of ethical violation as fabricating research data. However, it is not subject to the same open scrutiny, review, and independent verification. The individual case cannot be replicated by anyone else.

Privacy and Confidentiality

The pledge to hold a client's or a research participant's revelations as privileged and confidential must not be violated by publication. Publication showcases confidences and publicizes the private. In order to avoid harm, clinicians and researchers need either to withhold publication or presentation, or to follow rigid guidelines for disguise to prevent recognition. Although this might seem to be a contradiction of earlier statements about the need for accuracy of reporting, it can be done without making substantive concessions if done with care. Clifft (1986) presents hypothetical "real" and disguised versions as examples. EC Standard 4.07 concerns the use of confidential information for didactic and other purposes.

Selection Bias

Clinical case studies that are selected for publication are not apt to be picked if they do not illustrate the particular point that the author wants to make. If meant to illustrate the success of a method of treatment, authors are unlikely to publish and thereby to advertise their failures. This is also true of reports of single case research designs. Two of the leading advocates of single case experimental designs (Hersen & Barlow, 1992) observe, "Unfortunately, however, failures in a single case are seldomly published in journals. Among the numerous successful reports contained in the differential attention series, none reported a failure, although it is our guess that differential attention has failed on many occasions and these failures simply have not been reported" (p. 354). It does not take much imagination to realize the effect that this could have on our "knowledge" base if the reports in the literature were restricted to successes. This danger is compounded, as we shall see below, by the biases of editors, reviewers, and information consumers.

BIASED RESEARCH DATA PRESENTATION

Distortion of Scale

Enlarging or shrinking when presenting illustrative figures achieves this distortion. A mountain can be made to look like an anthill, or an anthill a mountain, depending on the scale. Figures are meant to illumi-

nate and to give an accurate visual picture of certain results and relationships. For example, Figure 1 depicts the portrayal of a 2-point difference
in the means of Group A and Group B. Here, even though the abscissa is
correctly broken to indicate that the full scale is not drawn, the visual
image is deceptive to the hasty reader, making it falsely appear that the
mean of Group B is twice that of Group A.

Selection of Best Results

Presentation of one's best results and burying one's worst results in
publication is tempting to an author with a mission, but is ethically un-
sound (EC, Principle C: Integrity). This practice includes dipping into a
distribution of scores to illustrate a point by singling out the most extreme scores in one's favor.

As previously noted in the biased selection of case studies for publication, there may be selective reporting of only those portions of a study that
support the investigator's position. Another approach that has been subject
to criticism is the practice of applying many statistical tests but only reporting the ones that yield the most favorable results. Further, entire studies
may be suppressed if found to challenge one's cherished beliefs. As Diener
and Crandall (1978) state, "An investigator may complete several studies
whose results do not substantiate his hypothesis and finally report only the
one study that does support his theory" (p. 160). This mis-selection is precisely what happened in a case of falsification that was adjudicated by the
Office of Research Integrity (USDHHS, 1994b), in which the research investigator "selectively suppressed data that did not support his hypothesis,

FIGURE 1. The IQ Results of Two Groups as Represented by a Distorted Scale
(on the left) and a more Accurate Scale (on the right).

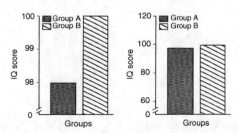

From *Critical Thinking about Research: Psychology and Related Fields* (Meltzoff, 1998). Reprinted with permission.

and reported consistently positive data whereas only one of four experiments had produced positive results" (p. 9).

Publication of Errors

From time to time, errata appear in numerical table entries and data analyses due to transcribing mistakes, faulty proofreading, or printing errors. Such errors, once discovered, should be flagged and corrected as soon as possible; EC Standard 8.10 (b) states, "If psychologists discover significant errors in their published data, they take reasonable steps to correct such errors in a correction, retraction, erratum, or other appropriate publication means" (APA, 2002, p. 1070). Intentional errors, which are introduced for purposes of deception, come under the category of falsification.

As a check on the accuracy of reported data, Wolins (1962) set out to re-examine original data from a number of published studies. Errors were found in data analysis and/or reporting of studies reviewed, but the majority of authors declined to forward data on the grounds of having destroyed or misplaced them. This practice has now been codified as an ethical issue. EC Standard 8.14 states, ". . . psychologists do not withhold the data on which their conclusions are based from other competent professionals who seek to verify the substantive claims through reanalysis and who intend to use such data for that purpose . . ." (APA, 2002, p. 1071).

Misinterpretation for Effect

In order to create a desired effect that is not unequivocally supported by the data, authors may intentionally distort the significance of the findings. For example, an investigator reports $p = .10$, and observes that this "just missed significance." Thereafter in the manuscript, and in the conclusions and the abstract, the relationship is discussed as if it were an established fact (EC Principle C: Integrity). For a discussion of Principle C, see "Professional and Scientific Responsibility: Integrity" (Lowman, in this volume).

Conclusions and Abstract

As some hurried readers turn directly to the conclusions or restrict their reading to the abstract, which embeds the conclusions, it is of ethical concern to know whether or not the conclusions are fairly drawn from the data. Conclusions that echo the hypotheses, but which ignore or contradict the actual data, are especially troublesome. Researchers have an ethical responsibility to maintain enough scientific objectivity, and to display sufficient integrity, to be able to admit that their own data contradict their hypotheses, and to be honest enough to draw conclusions that follow from their data instead of from their pre-judgments (EC Principle C: Integrity).

Discussion Section

Authors of scientific papers are responsible for differentiating fact from fiction. Results sections present readers with "findings" accompanied by probability levels that indicate the confidence that can be placed in the results. When writing Discussion sections, writers sometimes slip over into a science fiction mode. Their writing features speculations, formulations, and pronouncements that go far beyond the data in the study. Readers have to be vigilant if they wish to separate the science from the fiction. The two frequently become so intertwined that it takes a good deal of effort to sort them out. The ethical writer will clearly label statements that are data-based, and will identify speculations, weak inferences, and hypotheses for future studies for what they are instead of implying that they are factual.

REVIEWING LITERATURE

Authors of scientific publications usually refer to existing theoretical and research literature in establishing their theses. The tendency when marshaling one's polemical forces is to be less critical and more supportive of work that is in harmony with one's own beliefs. Nonetheless, some weighing of pros and cons, and some even-handedness of presentation, is desirable. This issue becomes an ethical one when a psychologist knowingly disregards all countervailing literature and gives an intentionally skewed presentation. Publication is meant to inform and to illuminate, not to conceal and to deceive. While the Ethical Code does not directly refer to literature reviews, the spirit of the issue is reflected in Principle C: Integrity.

FABRICATION AND FALSIFICATION

EC Standard 8.10 (a) (APA, 2002) states, "Psychologists do not fabricate or falsify results in their publications" (p. 1070). This standard applies to the description of details of clinical cases, and to observations and evaluations of outcomes of such cases, as well as to research. Fabrication and falsification of clinical material may never be discovered, but it is through the process of publication that scientific misconduct in research is usually laid bare. The fact that the Office of Research Integrity (USDHHS, 1994a) tells us that most of the cases under investigation have taken place in medical schools may merely reflect a predominance of research awards to these setting by the USDHHS. It does not provide evidence that psychologists function on a higher ethical plane. Most complainants in the ORI report came from within the same institution as the respondent, and occupied a higher position in the organization. It takes considerable courage to complain about someone in a superordinate position. A survey of psychology interns, faculty, and licensing boards by Holaday and Yost (1993) revealed that 84.3% of the interns failed to report violations that they suspected. Fear of reprisal was one of the main reasons. It is noteworthy that the American Institute of Chemists gave its 1993 ethics award to Dr. Margot O'Toole, who held a junior post at M.I.T. but who reported a flaw in a paper by an internationally-known Nobel Laureate at that university. Her audacious act cost her her job and she was obliged to work as a telephone operator until able to find suitable employment in her field (USDHHS, 1993c). She won vindication, recognition, and high plaudits in the end.

Some who are charged with scientific misconduct are blatant and unabashed, and show a pattern of repeated offenses. For example, one case cited in the Biennial Report of ORI (USDHHS, 1993a) is that of an Associate Professor who was reported by the Department Chair. "The committee concluded that the respondent falsified data in two studies reported in a published manuscript, plagiarized the unpublished method of other investigators, and improperly attributed authorship in an abstract" (p. 7).

EDITORIAL ETHICS

According to Caelleigh (1993), we cannot hold editors responsible for the accuracy of the materials that they publish, but they are responsible for publishing and enforcing policies and standards, and are obliged to publish corrections and retractions if appropriate. Editors of journals are in a position to influence the shape of the literature by selective acceptance and rejection of submitted manuscripts. Presumably, a fair and unbiased process is one in which the soundest studies within the journal's content domain are selected following peer review. Fortunately, editors are usually outstanding scholars in their own right and can make the necessary decisions with integrity. Ceci, Peters, and Plotkin (1985) assert that the "true gatekeepers may not be journal editors and reviewers but rather funding agencies, review panels and study groups" (p. 994), and also Institutional Review Boards (IRB's) that may "employ sociopolitical considerations in their judgments in ways that are explicitly prohibited by federal mandate" (pp. 994-995). They maintain that studies that are "socially sensitive" or have "social agendas" may be turned down because of "the nature of its sociopolitical impact," even though the *Code of Federal Regulations* (USDHHS, 1991, part 46.111) states that "The IRB should not consider possible long-range effects of applying knowledge gained in the research (for example, the possible effects of the research on public policy) as among those research risks that fall within the purview of its responsibility" (p. 8). Arguments have been raised in support of both sides of the issue of whether or not it is desirable to have gatekeepers of science to control possible misapplications of knowledge.

To the extent that there is any tendency for editors to reject studies with null or negative results because they are less interesting to read, and to the extent that there is any proclivity on the part of researchers not to submit such studies as readily as they submit studies that have robust positive findings, our knowledge base is in danger of becoming distorted. This problem holds for the publication of clinical case studies as well. Those who are in the chain of producing and communicating knowledge, whether they be researchers, writers of technical literature, editors, or teachers, have an ethical responsibility for monitoring what they choose to study, what they elect to submit for publication, what they select to print in their journals, and how they summarize published materials for their colleagues, their students, and the laity. As Rosenthal (1994) has observed, "Failing to report data that contradict one's earlier research, or one's theory or one's values, is poor science and poor ethics . . . Censoring or suppressing results we do not like or do not believe to have high prior probability is bad science and bad ethics" (p. 133).

SPONSORED RESEARCH

As discussed in the article "Ethical Considerations in Professional Research" (Meltzoff, in this volume), studies that have been done under the auspices of an organization or by individuals who have a vested interest in the outcome can be biased at the level of design and execution or at the level of publication. Setting aside incidents of outright fabrication and falsification of data, an honest investigator can encounter ethical problems when the study has been completed and the time has come for public dissemination of the findings. Some organizations sponsor research for internal purposes. Thus, the findings are proprietary and not for general distribution or publication. The investigator fully understands the conditions in advance, as in classified research for the military or research on the internal affairs or morale within a private company. Then there is research that, without any advance restrictions, is expected to produce generalizable knowledge with social value. Take the hypothetical case of research sponsored by a grant from a tobacco company for the purpose of determining if smoking is addictive and to find out if there is any real danger from second-hand smoke. What would be the likelihood of the sponsor's giving widespread publicity to favorable findings, but suppressing the results if unfavorable? The *Ethical Practices in the Conduct of Research with Human Participants* (APA, 1982) observes, "Conflicts between the scientist's commitment to advance knowledge and the organization's commitment to its own mission can arise when research results are contrary to the interests of the organization. The investigator should explore with the organization the possibility of delayed publication or of censorship of results before undertaking the research" (p. 23). Furthermore, EC Standard 1.01 states, "If psychologist, learn of misuse or misrepresentation of their work, they take reasonable steps to correct or minimize the misuse or misrepresentation" (p. 1063).

Psychologists who make their thoughts public under the auspices of a sponsor who has vested interests place themselves in a potential ethical dilemma of having to pronounce against their best scientific judgment in order to fulfill their obligations to their sponsor. For example, a psychologist who is employed by or hired to give a testimonial for a toy company, for an encyclopedia, or for a company that produces TV learning software pronounces psychological benefits of these products without any research support for such claims. In their national survey of ethical dilemmas, Pope and Vetter (1992) quoted one of their respondents as saying,

> I design, analyze and write up research reports that identify the advantages of one medium over the other media. Yet with large ex-

penditures for research, I feel constrained to report *something* . . .
But there is a limit to how many unpleasant findings I come up
with. Finally, I have to find some truthful positives, or I start look-
ing for another job. (p. 403)

EC Standard 2.04 (APA, 2002) on Basis for Scientific and Professional
Judgments states, "Psychologists' work is based upon established scientific and professional knowledge of the discipline" (p. 5). Pronouncements that are not data-based should be identified as speculation or
opinion. Consumers of information may be less able than are experts to
differentiate fact from opinion in a specialized domain of knowledge.
Pope and Vetter (1992) provided the following report by a respondent,
". . . A particular company . . . has been citing my research conclusions
. . . without considering my stated cautions, qualifications, and so
forth. That is, my work is cited out of the context of conflicting research
and the conclusions are uncritically overgeneralized or overstated. I am
concerned that my name or my research may be associated with a kind
of deceit" (p. 403).

CONSUMER ETHICS: THE ETHICAL READER

So far, all of the ethical responsibility has been placed on the authors,
reviewers, and editors. The reader shares the final responsibility, at least
to some small extent. Professionals have an obligation to keep themselves informed and to read critically and intelligently. Until an article is
read, its influence parallels the noise of a tree falling in an un-peopled
forest. Publication initiates an interaction with a host of readers who are
information consumers. One article opens as many dialogues as there
are readers. Readers, and replies by the author make some of these dialogues public in the form of responses, critiques, and rebuttals. Most remain at the level of two monologues—one by the author in the form of
the published word, and another by the reader in the form of self-messages. Self-messages can be thought of as unethical if one tries to deceive
oneself, not just by reading without understanding, but by intentionally
distorting or misinterpreting the printed matter. The closed mind "ex-
cludes the light," "turns a deaf ear," or "shoots the messenger" of ill-fa-
vored information. People who deceive themselves by the way they
receive information and ideas are apt to deceive others when discussing

these ideas. Nearly as bad as distorting what has been presented is the uncritical and thoughtless acceptance of the printed word. Just as a safe and nourishing food can be consumed in unhealthful ways, a written article that is "swallowed whole" can be injurious. When it works at its best, a coven of scholars, including the author, editor, referees, reviewers, and reader, gather symbolically around a table and discuss the ideas that form the centerpiece.

REFERENCES

American Psychological Association. (1982). *Ethical principles in the conduct of research with human participants.* Washington, DC: Author.

American Psychological Association. (2001). *Publication manual of the American Psychological Association* (5th ed.). Washington, DC: Author.

American Psychological Association. (2002). *Ethical principles of psychologists and code of conduct.* Washington DC: Author.

Caelleigh, A. S. (1993). Role of the journal editor in sustaining integrity in research. *Academic Medicine, 68,* Suppl. 523-529.

Ceci, S. J., Peters, D., & Plotkin, J. (1985). Human subjects review, personal values and the regulation of social science research. *American Psychologist, 40,* 994-1002.

Clifft, M. A. (1986). Writing about psychiatric patients: Guidelines for disguising case material. *Bulletin of the Menninger Clinic, 50,* 511-524.

Diener, E., & Crandall, R. (1978). *Ethics in social and behavioral research.* Chicago, IL: The University of Chicago Press.

Hersen, M., & Barlow, D. H. (1992). *Single case experimental designs: Strategies for studying behavior change* (2nd ed.). New York: Pergamon Press.

Holaday, M., & Yost, T. E. (1993). Publication ethics. *Journal of Social Behavior and Personality, 8,* 557-566.

Lowman, R. (2005). Professional and scientific responsibility: Integrity. *Journal of Aggression, Maltreatment & Trauma,* 11(1/2), 63-70.

Meltzoff, J. (1998). *Critical thinking about research: Psychology and related fields.* Washington DC: American Psychological Association.

Meltzoff, J. (2005). Ethics in research. *Journal of Aggression, Maltreatment & Trauma,* 11(3), 311-336.

Pope, K. S., & Vetter, V. A. (1992). Ethical dilemmas encountered by members of the American Psychological Association: A national survey. *American Psychologist, 47,* 397-411.

Rosenthal, R. (1994). Science and ethics in conducting, analyzing, and reporting psychological research. *Psychological Science, 5,* 127-134.

Spiegel, D., & Keith-Spiegel, P. (1970). Assignment of publication credits: Ethics and practices of psychologists. *American Psychologist, 25,* 738-747.

U.S. Department of Health and Human Services. (1991). *Code of Federal Regulations, Title 45, Part 46.* Washington, DC: U.S. Government Printing Office.

U.S. Department of Health and Human Services. (1993a). *Office of Research Integrity Biennial Report, 1991-1992*. Rockville, MD: Author.

U.S. Department of Health and Human Services. (1993b). *ORI: An introduction*. Rockville, MD: Author.

U.S. Department of Health and Human Services. (1993c). *ORI Newsletter, 1*, No.3, 1-8.

U.S. Department of Health and Human Services. (1994a). *Office of Research Integrity Annual Report 1993* (PHS Publication). Rockville, MD: Author.

U.S. Department of Health and Human Services. (1994b). *ORI Newsletter, 2*, No.4, 1-8.

Wolins, L. (1962). Responsibility for raw data. *American Psychologist, 17*, 657-658.

APPENDICES

Ethics Codes of Major Mental Health Professional Associations

A.1: *Ethical Principles of Psychologists and Code of Conduct* (Copyright © 2002 by the American Psychological Association. Reprinted with permission. *American Psychologist, 57,* 1060-1073, 2002).

A.2: *Code of Ethics of the National Association of Social Workers* (Copyright © 1999, National Association of Social Workers, Inc., NASW Code of Ethics. Reprinted with permission.)

The reader is also referred to the Ethics Codes of the American Association of Marriage and Family Therapy and the American Psychiatric Association. Internet URLs are provided below.

AAMFT Code of Ethics (American Association of Marriage and Family Therapy, 2001). Available online from, http://www.aamft.org/resources/LRMPlan/Ethics/ethicscode2001.asp

The Principles of Medical Ethics with Annotations Especially Applicable to Psychiatry (American Psychiatric Association, 2001).

[Haworth co-indexing entry note]: "Ethics Codes of Major Mental Health Professional Associations." Co-published simultaneously in *Journal of Aggression, Maltreatment & Trauma* (The Haworth Maltreatment & Trauma Press, an imprint of The Haworth Press, Inc.) Vol. 11, No. 3, 2005, pp. 357-394; and: *Ethical and Legal Issues for Mental Health Professionals: A Comprehensive Handbook of Principles and Standards* (ed: Steven F. Bucky, Joanne E. Callan, and George Stricker) The Haworth Maltreatment & Trauma Press, an imprint of The Haworth Press, Inc., 2005, pp. 357-394. Single or multiple copies of this article are available for a fee from The Haworth Document Delivery Service [1-800-HAWORTH, 9:00 a.m. - 5:00 p.m. (EST). E-mail address: docdelivery@haworthpress.com].

Available online from, http://www.psych.org/psych_pract/ethics/ppaethics.cfm

ETHICAL PRINCIPLES OF PSYCHOLOGISTS AND CODE OF CONDUCT

CONTENTS

INTRODUCTION AND APPLICABILITY

PREAMBLE

GENERAL PRINCIPLES

Principle A: Beneficence and Nonmaleficence
Principle B: Fidelity and Responsibility
Principle C: Integrity
Principle D: Justice
Principle E: Respect for People's Rights and Dignity

ETHICAL STANDARDS

1. Resolving Ethical Issues
1.01   Misuse of Psychologists' Work
1.02   Conflicts Between Ethics and Law, Regulations, or Other Governing Legal Authority
1.03   Conflicts Between Ethics and Organizational Demands
1.04   Informal Resolution of Ethical Violations
1.05   Reporting Ethical Violations
1.06   Cooperating With Ethics Committees
1.07   Improper Complaints
1.08   Unfair Discrimination Against Complainants and Respondents

2. Competence
2.01   Boundaries of Competence
2.02   Providing Services in Emergencies
2.03   Maintaining Competence
2.04   Bases for Scientific and Professional Judgments

6.03   Withholding Records for Nonpayment
6.04   Fees and Financial Arrangements
6.05   Barter with Clients/Patients
6.06   Accuracy in Reports to Payors and Funding Sources
6.07   Referrals and Fees

7. Education and Training

7.01   Design of Education and Training Programs
7.02   Descriptions of Education and Training Programs
7.03   Accuracy in Teaching
7.04   Student Disclosure of Personal Information
7.05   Mandatory Individual or Group Therapy
7.06   Assessing Student and Supervisee Performance
7.07   Sexual Relationships with Students and Supervisees

8. Research and Publication

8.01   Institutional Approval
8.02   Informed Consent to Research
8.03   Informed Consent for Recording Voices and Images in Research
8.04   Client/Patient, Student, and Subordinate Research Participants
8.05   Dispensing with Informed Consent for Research
8.06   Offering Inducements for Research Participation
8.07   Deception in Research
8.08   Debriefing
8.09   Humane Care and Use of Animals in Research
8.10   Reporting Research Results
8.11   Plagiarism
8.12   Publication Credit
8.13   Duplicate Publication of Data
8.14   Sharing Research Data for Verification
8.15   Reviewers

9. Assessment

9.01   Bases for Assessments
9.02   Use of Assessments
9.03   Informed Consent in Assessments
9.04   Release of Test Data
9.05   Test Construction
9.06   Interpreting Assessment Results
9.07   Assessment by Unqualified Persons
9.08   Obsolete Tests and Outdated Test Results

INTRODUCTION AND APPLICABILITY

The American Psychological Association's (APA's) Ethical Principles of Psychologists and Code of Conduct (hereinafter referred to as the Ethics Code) consists of an Introduction, a Preamble, five General Principles (A-E), and specific Ethical Standards. The Introduction discusses the intent, organization, procedural considerations, and scope of application of the Ethics Code. The Preamble and General Principles are aspirational goals to guide psychologists toward the highest ideals of psychology. Although the Preamble and General Principles are not themselves enforceable rules, they should be considered by psychologists in arriving at an ethical course of action. The Ethical Standards set forth enforceable rules for conduct as psychologists. Most of the Ethical Standards are written broadly, in order to apply to psychologists in varied roles, although the application of an Ethical Standard may vary depending on the context. The Ethical Standards are not exhaustive. The fact that a given conduct is not specifically addressed by an Ethical Standard does not mean that it is necessarily either ethical or unethical.

This Ethics Code applies only to psychologists' activities that are part of their scientific, educational, or professional roles as psychologists. Areas covered include but are not limited to the clinical, counseling, and school practice of psychology; research; teaching; supervision of trainees; public service; policy development; social intervention; development of assessment instruments; conducting assessments; educational counseling; organizational consulting; forensic activities; program design and evaluation; and administration. This Ethics Code applies to these activities across a variety of contexts, such as in person, postal, telephone, Internet, and other electronic transmissions. These activities shall be distinguished from the purely private conduct of psychologists, which is not within the purview of the Ethics Code.

Membership in the APA commits members and student affiliates to comply with the standards of the APA Ethics Code and to the rules and procedures used to enforce them. Lack of awareness or misunderstanding of an Ethical Standard is not itself a defense to a charge of unethical conduct.

The procedures for filing, investigating, and resolving complaints of unethical conduct are described in the current Rules and Procedures of the APA Ethics Committee. APA may impose sanctions on its members for violations of the standards of the Ethics Code, including termination of APA membership, and may notify other bodies and individuals of its actions. Actions that violate the standards of the Ethics Code may also lead to the imposition of sanctions on psychologists or students whether or not they are APA members by bodies other than APA, including state psychological associations, other professional groups, psychology boards, other state or federal agencies, and payors for health services. In addition, APA may take action against a member after his or her conviction of a felony, expulsion or suspension from an affiliated state psychological association, or suspension or loss of licensure. When the sanction to be imposed by APA is less than expulsion, the 2001 Rules and Procedures do not guarantee an opportunity for an in-person hearing, but generally provide that complaints will be resolved only on the basis of a submitted record.

The Ethics Code is intended to provide guidance for psychologists and standards of professional conduct that can be applied by the APA and by other bodies that choose to adopt them. The Ethics Code is not intended to be a basis of civil liability. Whether a psychologist has violated the Ethics Code standards does not by itself determine whether the psychologist is legally liable in a court action, whether a contract is enforceable, or whether other legal consequences occur.

The modifiers used in some of the standards of this Ethics Code (e.g., *reasonably, appropriate, potentially*) are included in the standards when they would (1) allow professional judgment on the part of psychologists, (2) eliminate injustice or inequality that would occur without the modifier, (3) ensure applicability across the broad range of activities conducted by psychologists, or (4) guard against a set of rigid rules that might be quickly outdated. As used in this Ethics Code, the term *reasonable* means the prevailing professional judgment of psychologists engaged in similar activities in similar circumstances, given the knowledge the psychologist had or should have had at the time.

In the process of making decisions regarding their professional behavior, psychologists must consider this Ethics Code in addition to applicable laws and psychology board regulations. In applying the Ethics Code to their professional work, psychologists may consider other materials and guidelines that have been adopted or endorsed by scientific and professional psychological organizations and the dictates of their own conscience, as well as consult with others within the field. If this Ethics Code establishes a higher standard of conduct than is required by law, psychologists must meet the higher ethical standard. If psychologists' ethical responsibilities conflict with law, regulations, or other governing legal authority, psychologists make known their commitment to this Ethics Code and take steps to resolve the conflict in a responsible manner. If the conflict is unresolvable via such means, psychologists may adhere to the requirements of the law, regulations, or other governing authority in keeping with basic principles of human rights.

PREAMBLE

Psychologists are committed to increasing scientific and professional knowledge of behavior and people's understanding of themselves and others and to the use of such knowledge to improve the condition of individuals, organizations, and society. Psychologists respect and protect civil and human rights and the central importance of freedom of inquiry and expression in research, teaching, and publication. They strive to help the public in developing informed judgments and choices concerning human behavior. In doing so, they perform many roles, such as researcher, educator, diagnostician, therapist, supervisor, consultant, administrator, social interventionist, and expert witness. This Ethics Code provides a common set of principles and standards upon which psychologists build their professional and scientific work.

This Ethics Code is intended to provide specific standards to cover most situations encountered by psychologists. It has as its goals the welfare and protection of the individuals and groups with whom psychologists work and the education of members, students, and the public regarding ethical standards of the discipline.

The development of a dynamic set of ethical standards for psychologists' work-related conduct requires a personal commitment and life-long effort to act ethically; to encourage ethical behavior by students, supervisees, employees, and colleagues; and to consult with others concerning ethical problems.

GENERAL PRINCIPLES

This section consists of General Principles. General Principles, as opposed to Ethical Standards, are aspirational in nature. Their intent is to guide and inspire psychologists toward the very highest ethical ideals of the profession. General Principles, in contrast to Ethical Standards, do not represent obligations and should not form the basis for imposing sanctions. Relying upon General Principles for either of these reasons distorts both their meaning and purpose.

Principle A: Beneficence and Nonmaleficence

Psychologists strive to benefit those with whom they work and take care to do no harm. In their professional actions, psychologists seek to safeguard the welfare and rights of those with whom they interact professionally and other affected persons, and the welfare of animal subjects of research. When conflicts occur among psychologists' obligations or concerns, they attempt to resolve these conflicts in a responsible fashion that avoids or minimizes harm. Because psychologists' scientific and professional judgments and actions may affect the lives of others, they are alert to and guard against personal, financial, social, organizational, or political factors that might lead to misuse of their influence. Psychologists strive to be aware of the possible effect of their own physical and mental health on their ability to help those with whom they work.

Principle B: Fidelity and Responsibility

Psychologists establish relationships of trust with those with whom they work. They are aware of their professional and scientific responsibilities to society and to the specific communities in which they work. Psychologists uphold professional standards of conduct, clarify their professional roles and obligations, accept appropriate responsibility for their behavior, and seek to manage conflicts of interest that could lead to exploitation or harm. Psychologists consult with, refer to, or cooperate with other professionals and institutions to the extent needed to serve the best interests of those with whom they work. They are concerned about the ethical compliance of their colleagues' scientific and professional conduct. Psychologists strive to contribute a portion of their professional time for little or no compensation or personal advantage.

Principle C: Integrity

Psychologists seek to promote accuracy, honesty, and truthfulness in the science, teaching, and practice of psychology. In these activities psychologists do not steal, cheat, or engage in fraud, subterfuge, or intentional misrepresentation of fact. Psychologists strive to keep their promises and to avoid unwise or unclear commitments. In situations in which deception may be ethically justifiable to maximize benefits and minimize harm, psychologists have a serious obligation to consider the need for, the possible consequences of, and their responsibility to correct any resulting mistrust or other harmful effects that arise from the use of such techniques.

Principle D: Justice

Psychologists recognize that fairness and justice entitle all persons to access to and benefit from the contributions of psychology and to equal quality in the processes, procedures, and services being conducted by psychologists. Psychologists exercise reasonable judgment and take precautions to ensure that their potential biases, the boundaries of their competence, and the limitations of their expertise do not lead to or condone unjust practices.

Principle E: Respect for People's Rights and Dignity

Psychologists respect the dignity and worth of all people, and the rights of individuals to privacy, confidentiality, and self-determination.

Psychologists are aware that special safeguards may be necessary to protect the rights and welfare of persons or communities whose vulnerabilities impair autonomous decision making. Psychologists are aware of and respect cultural, individual, and role differences, including those based on age, gender, gender identity, race, ethnicity, culture, national origin, religion, sexual orientation, disability, language, and socioeconomic status and consider these factors when working with members of such groups. Psychologists try to eliminate the effect on their work of biases based on those factors, and they do not knowingly participate in or condone activities of others based upon such prejudices.

ETHICAL STANDARDS

1. Resolving Ethical Issues

1.01 Misuse of Psychologists' Work

If psychologists learn of misuse or misrepresentation of their work, they take reasonable steps to correct or minimize the misuse or misrepresentation.

1.02 Conflicts Between Ethics and Law, Regulations, or Other Governing Legal Authority

If psychologists' ethical responsibilities conflict with law, regulations, or other governing legal authority, psychologists make known their commitment to the Ethics Code and take steps to resolve the conflict. If the conflict is unresolvable via such means, psychologists may adhere to the requirements of the law, regulations, or other governing legal authority.

1.03 Conflicts Between Ethics and Organizational Demands

If the demands of an organization with which psychologists are affiliated or for whom they are working conflict with this Ethics Code, psychologists clarify the nature of the conflict, make known their commitment to the Ethics Code, and to the extent feasible, resolve the conflict in a way that permits adherence to the Ethics Code.

1.04 Informal Resolution of Ethical Violations

When psychologists believe that there may have been an ethical violation by another psychologist, they attempt to resolve the issue by bringing it to the attention of that individual, if an informal resolution appears appropriate and the intervention does not violate any confidentiality rights that may be involved. (See also Standards 1.02, Conflicts Between Ethics and Law, Regulations, or Other Governing Legal Authority, and 1.03, Conflicts Between Ethics and Organizational Demands.)

1.05 Reporting Ethical Violations

If an apparent ethical violation has substantially harmed or is likely to substantially harm a person or organization and is not appropriate for informal resolution under Standard 1.04, Informal Resolution of Ethical Violations, or is not resolved properly in that fashion, psychologists take further action appropriate to the situation. Such action might include referral to state or national committees on professional ethics, to state licensing boards, or to the appropriate institutional authorities. This standard does not apply when an intervention would violate confidentiality rights or when psychologists have been retained to review the work of another psychologist whose professional conduct is in question. (See also Standard 1.02, Conflicts Between Ethics and Law, Regulations, or Other Governing Legal Authority.)

1.06 Cooperating with Ethics Committees

Psychologists cooperate in ethics investigations, proceedings, and resulting requirements of the APA or any affiliated state psychological association to which they belong. In doing so, they address any confidentiality issues. Failure to cooperate is itself an ethics violation. However, making a request for deferment of adjudication of an ethics complaint pending the outcome of litigation does not alone constitute noncooperation.

1.07 Improper Complaints

Psychologists do not file or encourage the filing of ethics complaints that are made with reckless disregard for or willful ignorance of facts that would disprove the allegation.

1.08 Unfair Discrimination Against Complainants and Respondents

Psychologists do not deny persons employment, advancement, admissions to academic or other programs, tenure, or promotion, based solely upon their having made or their being the subject of an ethics complaint. This does not preclude taking action based upon the outcome of such proceedings or considering other appropriate information.

2. Competence

2.01 Boundaries of Competence

a. Psychologists provide services, teach, and conduct research with populations and in areas only within the boundaries of their competence, based on their education, training, supervised experience, consultation, study, or professional experience.

b. Where scientific or professional knowledge in the discipline of psychology establishes that an understanding of factors associated with age, gender, gender identity, race, ethnicity, culture, national origin, religion, sexual orientation, disability, language, or socioeconomic status is essential for effective implementation of their services or research, psychologists have or obtain the training, experience, consultation, or supervision necessary to ensure the competence of their services, or they make appropriate referrals, except as provided in Standard 2.02, Providing Services in Emergencies.

c. Psychologists planning to provide services, teach, or conduct research involving populations, areas, techniques, or technologies new to them undertake relevant education, training, supervised experience, consultation, or study.

d. When psychologists are asked to provide services to individuals for whom appropriate mental health services are not available and for which psychologists have not obtained the competence necessary, psychologists with closely related prior training or experience may provide such services in order to ensure that services are not denied if they make a reasonable effort to obtain the competence required by using relevant research, training, consultation, or study.

e. In those emerging areas in which generally recognized standards for preparatory training do not yet exist, psychologists nevertheless take reasonable steps to ensure the competence of their work and to protect clients/patients, students, supervisees, research participants, organizational clients, and others from harm.

f. When assuming forensic roles, psychologists are or become reasonably familiar with the judicial or administrative rules governing their roles.

2.02 Providing Services in Emergencies

In emergencies, when psychologists provide services to individuals for whom other mental health services are not available and for which psychologists have not obtained the necessary training, psychologists may provide such services in order to ensure that services are not denied. The services are discontinued as soon as the emergency has ended or appropriate services are available.

2.03 Maintaining Competence

Psychologists undertake ongoing efforts to develop and maintain their competence.

2.04 Bases for Scientific and Professional Judgments

Psychologists' work is based upon established scientific and professional knowledge of the discipline. (See also Standards 2.01e, Boundaries of Competence, and 10.01b, Informed Consent to Therapy.)

2.05 Delegation of Work to Others

Psychologists who delegate work to employees, supervisees, or research or teaching assistants or who use the services of others, such as interpreters, take reasonable steps to (1) avoid delegating such work to persons who have a multiple relationship with those being served that would likely lead to exploitation or loss of objectivity; (2) authorize only those responsibilities that such persons can be expected to perform competently on the basis of their education, training, or experience, either independently or with the level of supervision being provided; and (3) see that such persons perform these services competently. (See also Standards 2.02, Providing Services in Emergencies; 3.05, Multiple Relationships; 4.01, Maintaining Confidentiality; 9.01, Bases for Assessments; 9.02, Use of Assessments; 9.03, Informed Consent in Assessments; and 9.07, Assessment by Unqualified Persons.)

2.06 Personal Problems and Conflicts

(a) Psychologists refrain from initiating an activity when they know or should know that there is a substantial likelihood that their personal problems will prevent them from performing their work-related activities in a competent manner.

(b) When psychologists become aware of personal problems that may interfere with their performing work-related duties adequately, they take appropriate measures, such as obtaining professional consultation or assistance, and determine whether they should limit, suspend, or terminate their work-related duties. (See also Standard 10.10, Terminating Therapy.)

3. Human Relations

3.01 Unfair Discrimination

In their work-related activities, psychologists do not engage in unfair discrimination based on age, gender, gender identity, race, ethnicity, culture, national origin, religion, sexual orientation, disability, socioeconomic status, or any basis proscribed by law.

3.02 Sexual Harassment

Psychologists do not engage in sexual harassment. Sexual harassment is sexual solicitation, physical advances, or verbal or nonverbal conduct that is sexual in nature, that occurs in connection with the psychologist's activities or roles as a psychologist, and that either (1) is unwelcome, is offensive, or creates a hostile workplace or educational environment, and the psychologist knows or is told this or (2) is sufficiently severe or intense to be abusive to a reasonable person in the context. Sexual harassment can consist of a single intense or severe act or of multiple persistent or pervasive acts. (See also Standard 1.08, Unfair Discrimination Against Complainants and Respondents.)

3.03 Other Harassment

Psychologists do not knowingly engage in behavior that is harassing or demeaning to persons with whom they interact in their work based on factors such as those persons' age, gender, gender identity, race, ethnicity, culture, national origin, religion, sexual orientation, disability, language, or socioeconomic status.

3.04 Avoiding Harm

Psychologists take reasonable steps to avoid harming their clients/patients, students, supervisees, research participants, organizational clients, and others with whom they work, and to minimize harm where it is foreseeable and unavoidable.

3.05 Multiple Relationships

(a) A multiple relationship occurs when a psychologist is in a professional role with a person and (1) at the same time is in another role with the same person, (2) at the same time is in a relationship with a person closely associated with or related to the person with whom the psychologist has the professional relationship, or (3) promises to enter into another relationship in the future with the person or a person closely associated with or related to the person.

A psychologist refrains from entering into a multiple relationship if the multiple relationship could reasonably be expected to impair the psychologist's objectivity, competence, or effectiveness in performing his or her functions as a psychologist, or otherwise risks exploitation or harm to the person with whom the professional relationship exists.

Multiple relationships that would not reasonably be expected to cause impairment or risk exploitation or harm are not unethical.

(b) If a psychologist finds that, due to unforeseen factors, a potentially harmful multiple relationship has arisen, the psychologist takes reasonable steps to resolve it with due regard for the best interests of the affected person and maximal compliance with the Ethics Code.

(c) When psychologists are required by law, institutional policy, or extraordinary circumstances to serve in more than one role in judicial or administrative proceedings, at the outset they clarify role expectations and the extent of confidentiality and thereafter as changes occur. (See also Standards 3.04, Avoiding Harm, and 3.07, Third-Party Requests for Services.)

3.06 Conflict of Interest

Psychologists refrain from taking on a professional role when personal, scientific, professional, legal, financial, or other interests or relationships could reasonably be expected to (1) impair their objectivity, competence, or effectiveness in performing their functions as psychologists or (2) expose the person or organization with whom the professional relationship exists to harm or exploitation.

3.07 Third-Party Requests for Services

When psychologists agree to provide services to a person or entity at the request of a third party, psychologists attempt to clarify at the outset of the service the nature of the relationship with all individuals or organizations involved. This clarification includes the role of the psychologist (e.g., therapist, consultant, diagnostician, or expert witness), an identification of who is the client, the probable uses of the services provided or the information obtained, and the fact that there may be limits to confidentiality. (See also Standards 3.05, Multiple Relationships, and 4.02, Discussing the Limits of Confidentiality.)

3.08 Exploitative Relationships

Psychologists do not exploit persons over whom they have supervisory, evaluative, or other authority such as clients/patients, students, supervisees, research participants, and employees. (See also Standards 3.05, Multiple Relationships; 6.04, Fees and Financial Arrangements; 6.05, Barter with Clients/Patients; 7.07, Sexual Relationships with Students and Supervisees; 10.05, Sexual Intimacies With Current Therapy Clients/Patients; 10.06, Sexual Intimacies with Relatives or Significant Others of Current Therapy Clients/Patients; 10.07, Therapy with Former Sexual Partners; and 10.08, Sexual Intimacies with Former Therapy Clients/Patients.)

3.09 Cooperation with Other Professionals

When indicated and professionally appropriate, psychologists cooperate with other professionals in order to serve their clients/patients effectively and appropriately. (See also Standard 4.05, Disclosures.)

3.10 Informed Consent

(a) When psychologists conduct research or provide assessment, therapy, counseling, or consulting services in person or via electronic transmission or other forms of communication, they obtain the informed consent of the individual or individuals using language that is reasonably understandable to that person or persons except when conducting such activities without consent is mandated by law or governmental regulation or as otherwise provided in this Ethics Code. (See also Standards 8.02, Informed Consent to Research; 9.03, Informed Consent in Assessments; and 10.01, Informed Consent to Therapy.)

(b) For persons who are legally incapable of giving informed consent, psychologists nevertheless (1) provide an appropriate explanation, (2) seek the individual's assent, (3) consider such persons' preferences and best interests, and (4) obtain appropriate permission from a legally authorized person, if such substitute consent is permitted or required by law. When consent by a legally authorized person is not permitted or required by law, psychologists take reasonable steps to protect the individual's rights and welfare.

(c) When psychological services are court ordered or otherwise mandated, psychologists inform the individual of the nature of the anticipated services, including whether the services are court ordered or mandated and any limits of confidentiality, before proceeding.

(d) Psychologists appropriately document written or oral consent, permission, and assent. (See also Standards 8.02, Informed Consent to Research; 9.03, Informed Consent in Assessments; and 10.01, Informed Consent to Therapy.)

3.11 Psychological Services Delivered to or Through Organizations

(a) Psychologists delivering services to or through organizations provide information beforehand to clients and when appropriate those directly affected by the services about (1) the nature and objectives of the services, (2) the intended recipients, (3) which of the individuals are clients, (4) the relationship the psychologist will have with each person and the organization, (5) the probable uses of services provided and information obtained, (6) who will have access to the information, and (7) limits of confidentiality. As soon as feasible, they provide information about the results and conclusions of such services to appropriate persons.

(b) If psychologists will be precluded by law or by organizational roles from providing such information to particular individuals or groups, they so inform those individuals or groups at the outset of the service.

3.12 Interruption of Psychological Services

Unless otherwise covered by contract, psychologists make reasonable efforts to plan for facilitating services in the event that psychological services are interrupted by factors such as the psychologist's illness, death, unavailability, relocation, or retirement or by the client's/patient's relocation or financial limitations. (See also Standard 6.02c, Maintenance, Dissemination, and Disposal of Confidential Records of Professional and Scientific Work.)

4. Privacy and Confidentiality

4.01 Maintaining Confidentiality

Psychologists have a primary obligation and take reasonable precautions to protect confidential information obtained through or stored in any medium, recognizing that the extent and limits of confidentiality may be regulated by law or established by institutional rules or professional or scientific relationship. (See also Standard 2.05, Delegation of Work to Others.)

4.02 Discussing the Limits of Confidentiality

(a) Psychologists discuss with persons (including, to the extent feasible, persons who are legally incapable of giving informed consent and their legal representatives) and organizations with whom they establish a scientific or professional relationship (1) the relevant limits of confidentiality and (2) the foreseeable uses of the information generated through their psychological activities. (See also Standard 3.10, Informed Consent.)

(b) Unless it is not feasible or is contraindicated, the discussion of confidentiality occurs at the outset of the relationship and thereafter as new circumstances may warrant.

(c) Psychologists who offer services, products, or information via electronic transmission inform clients/patients of the risks to privacy and limits of confidentiality.

4.03 Recording

Before recording the voices or images of individuals to whom they provide services, psychologists obtain permission from all such persons or their legal representatives. (See also Standards 8.03, Informed Consent for Recording Voices and Images in Research; 8.05, Dispensing with Informed Consent for Research; and 8.07, Deception in Research.)

4.04 Minimizing Intrusions on Privacy

(a) Psychologists include in written and oral reports and consultations, only information germane to the purpose for which the communication is made.
(b) Psychologists discuss confidential information obtained in their work only for appropriate scientific or professional purposes and only with persons clearly concerned with such matters.

4.05 Disclosures

(a) Psychologists may disclose confidential information with the appropriate consent of the organizational client, the individual client/patient, or another legally authorized person on behalf of the client/patient unless prohibited by law.
(b) Psychologists disclose confidential information without the consent of the individual only as mandated by law, or where permitted by law for a valid purpose such as to (1) provide needed professional services; (2) obtain appropriate professional consultations; (3) protect the client/patient, psychologist, or others from harm; or (4) obtain payment for services from a client/patient, in which instance disclosure is limited to the minimum that is necessary to achieve the purpose. (See also Standard 6.04e, Fees and Financial Arrangements.)

4.06 Consultations

When consulting with colleagues, (1) psychologists do not disclose confidential information that reasonably could lead to the identification of a client/patient, research participant, or other person or organization with whom they have a confidential relationship unless they have obtained the prior consent of the person or organization or the disclosure cannot be avoided, and (2) they disclose information only to the extent necessary to achieve the purposes of the consultation. (See also Standard 4.01, Maintaining Confidentiality.)

4.07 Use of Confidential Information for Didactic or Other Purposes

Psychologists do not disclose in their writings, lectures, or other public media, confidential, personally identifiable information concerning their clients/patients, students, research participants, organizational clients, or other recipients of their services that they obtained during the course of their work, unless (1) they take reasonable steps to disguise the person or organization, (2) the person or organization has consented in writing, or (3) there is legal authorization for doing so.

5. Advertising and Other Public Statements

5.01 Avoidance of False or Deceptive Statements

(a) Public statements include but are not limited to paid or unpaid advertising, product endorsements, grant applications, licensing applications, other credentialing applications, brochures, printed matter, directory listings, personal resumes or curricula vitae, or comments for use in media such as print or electronic transmission, statements in legal proceedings, lectures and public oral presentations, and published materials. Psychologists do not knowingly make public statements that are false, deceptive, or fraudulent concerning their research, practice, or other work activities or those of persons or organizations with which they are affiliated.

(b) Psychologists do not make false, deceptive, or fraudulent statements concerning (1) their training, experience, or competence; (2) their academic degrees; (3) their credentials; (4) their institutional or association affiliations; (5) their services; (6) the scientific or clinical basis for, or results or degree of success of, their services; (7) their fees; or (8) their publications or research findings.

(c) Psychologists claim degrees as credentials for their health services only if those degrees (1) were earned from a regionally accredited educational institution or (2) were the basis for psychology licensure by the state in which they practice.

5.02 Statements by Others

(a) Psychologists who engage others to create or place public statements that promote their professional practice, products, or activities retain professional responsibility for such statements.

(b) Psychologists do not compensate employees of press, radio, television, or other communication media in return for publicity in a news item. (See also Standard 1.01, Misuse of Psychologists' Work.)

(c) A paid advertisement relating to psychologists' activities must be identified or clearly recognizable as such.

5.03 Descriptions of Workshops and Non-Degree-Granting Educational Programs

To the degree to which they exercise control, psychologists responsible for announcements, catalogs, brochures, or advertisements describing workshops, seminars, or other non-degree-granting educational programs ensure that they accurately describe the audience for which the program is intended, the educational objectives, the presenters, and the fees involved.

5.04 Media Presentations

When psychologists provide public advice or comment via print, internet, or other electronic transmission, they take precautions to ensure that statements (1) are based on their professional knowledge, training, or experience in accord with appropriate psychological literature and practice; (2) are otherwise consistent with this Ethics Code; and (3) do not indicate that a professional relationship has been established with the recipient. (See also Standard 2.04, Bases for Scientific and Professional Judgments.)

5.05 Testimonials

Psychologists do not solicit testimonials from current therapy clients/patients or other persons who because of their particular circumstances are vulnerable to undue influence.

5.06 In-Person Solicitation

Psychologists do not engage, directly or through agents, in uninvited in-person solicitation of business from actual or potential therapy clients/patients or other persons who because of their particular circumstances are vulnerable to undue influence. However, this prohibition does not preclude (1) attempting to implement appropriate collateral contacts for the purpose of benefiting an already engaged therapy client/patient or (2) providing disaster or community outreach services.

6. Record Keeping and Fees

6.01 Documentation of Professional and Scientific Work and Maintenance of Records

Psychologists create, and to the extent the records are under their control, maintain, disseminate, store, retain, and dispose of records and data relating to their professional and scientific work in order to (1) facilitate provision of services later by them or by other professionals, (2) allow for replication of research design and analyses, (3) meet institutional requirements, (4) ensure accuracy of billing and payments, and (5) ensure compliance with law. (See also Standard 4.01, Maintaining Confidentiality.)

6.02 Maintenance, Dissemination, and Disposal of Confidential Records of Professional and Scientific Work

 (a) Psychologists maintain confidentiality in creating, storing, accessing, transferring, and disposing of records under their control, whether these are written, automated, or in any other medium. (See also Standards 4.01, Maintaining Confidentiality, and 6.01, Documentation of Professional and Scientific Work and Maintenance of Records.)
 (b) If confidential information concerning recipients of psychological services is entered into databases or systems of records available to persons whose access has not been consented to by the recipient, psychologists use coding or other techniques to avoid the inclusion of personal identifiers.
 (c) Psychologists make plans in advance to facilitate the appropriate transfer and to protect the confidentiality of records and data in the event of psychologists' withdrawal from positions or practice. (See also Standards 3.12, Interruption of Psychological Services, and 10.09, Interruption of Therapy.)

6.03 Withholding Records for Nonpayment

Psychologists may not withhold records under their control that are requested and needed for a client's/patient's emergency treatment solely because payment has not been received.

6.04 Fees and Financial Arrangements

(a) As early as is feasible in a professional or scientific relationship, psychologists and recipients of psychological services reach an agreement specifying compensation and billing arrangements.
(b) Psychologists' fee practices are consistent with law.
(c) Psychologists do not misrepresent their fees.
(d) If limitations to services can be anticipated because of limitations in financing, this is discussed with the recipient of services as early as is feasible. (See also Standards 10.09, Interruption of Therapy, and 10.10, Terminating Therapy.)
(e) If the recipient of services does not pay for services as agreed, and if psychologists intend to use collection agencies or legal measures to collect the fees, psychologists first inform the person that such measures will be taken and provide that person an opportunity to make prompt payment. (See also Standards 4.05, Disclosures; 6.03, Withholding Records for Nonpayment; and 10.01, Informed Consent to Therapy.)

6.05 Barter With Clients/Patients

Barter is the acceptance of goods, services, or other nonmonetary remuneration from clients/patients in return for psychological services. Psychologists may barter only if (1) it is not clinically contraindicated, and (2) the resulting arrangement is not exploitative. (See also Standards 3.05, Multiple Relationships, and 6.04, Fees and Financial Arrangements.)

6.06 Accuracy in Reports to Payors and Funding Sources

In their reports to payors for services or sources of research funding, psychologists take reasonable steps to ensure the accurate reporting of the nature of the service provided or research conducted, the fees, charges, or payments, and where applicable, the identity of the provider, the findings, and the diagnosis. (See also Standards 4.01, Maintaining Confidentiality; 4.04, Minimizing Intrusions on Privacy; and 4.05, Disclosures.)

6.07 Referrals and Fees

When psychologists pay, receive payment from, or divide fees with another professional, other than in an employer-employee relationship, the payment to each is based on the services provided (clinical, consultative, administrative, or other) and is not based on the referral itself. (See also Standard 3.09, Cooperation With Other Professionals.)

7. Education and Training

7.01 Design of Education and Training Programs

Psychologists responsible for education and training programs take reasonable steps to ensure that the programs are designed to provide the appropriate knowledge and proper experiences, and to meet the requirements for licensure, certification, or other goals for which claims are made by the program. (See also Standard 5.03, Descriptions of Workshops and Non-Degree-Granting Educational Programs.)

7.02 Descriptions of Education and Training Programs

Psychologists responsible for education and training programs take reasonable steps to ensure that there is a current and accurate description of the program content (including participation in required course- or program-related counseling, psychotherapy, experiential groups, consulting projects, or community service), training goals and objectives, stipends and benefits, and requirements that must be met for satisfactory completion of the program. This information must be made readily available to all interested parties.

7.03 Accuracy in Teaching

(a) Psychologists take reasonable steps to ensure that course syllabi are accurate regarding the subject matter to be covered, bases for evaluating progress, and the nature of course experiences. This standard does not preclude an instructor from modifying course content or requirements when the instructor considers it pedagogically necessary or desirable, so long as students are made aware of these modifications in a manner that enables them to fulfill course requirements. (See also Standard 5.01, Avoidance of False or Deceptive Statements.)

(b) When engaged in teaching or training, psychologists present psychological information accurately. (See also Standard 2.03, Maintaining Competence.)

7.04 Student Disclosure of Personal Information

Psychologists do not require students or supervisees to disclose personal information in course- or program-related activities, either orally or in writing, regarding sexual history, history of abuse and neglect, psychological treatment, and relationships with parents, peers, and spouses or significant others except if (1) the program or training facility has clearly identified this requirement in its admissions and program materials or (2) the information is necessary to evaluate or obtain assistance for students whose personal problems could reasonably be judged to be preventing them from performing their training-or professionally related activities in a competent manner or posing a threat to the students or others.

7.05 Mandatory Individual or Group Therapy

(a) When individual or group therapy is a program or course requirement, psychologists responsible for that program allow students in undergraduate and graduate programs the option of selecting such therapy from practitioners unaffiliated with the program. (See also Standard 7.02, Descriptions of Education and Training Programs.)

(b) Faculty who are or are likely to be responsible for evaluating students' academic performance do not themselves provide that therapy. (See also Standard 3.05, Multiple Relationships.)

7.06 Assessing Student and Supervisee Performance

(a) In academic and supervisory relationships, psychologists establish a timely and specific process for providing feedback to students and supervisees. Information regarding the process is provided to the student at the beginning of supervision.

(b) Psychologists evaluate students and supervisees on the basis of their actual performance on relevant and established program requirements.

7.07 Sexual Relationships with Students and Supervisees

Psychologists do not engage in sexual relationships with students or supervisees who are in their department, agency, or training center or

over whom psychologists have or are likely to have evaluative authority. (See also Standard 3.05, Multiple Relationships.)

8. Research and Publication

8.01 Institutional Approval

When institutional approval is required, psychologists provide accurate information about their research proposals and obtain approval
prior to conducting the research. They conduct the research in accordance with the approved research protocol.

8.02 Informed Consent to Research

(a) When obtaining informed consent as required in Standard 3.10, Informed Consent, psychologists inform participants about (1) the purpose of the research, expected duration, and procedures; (2) their
right to decline to participate and to withdraw from the research once
participation has begun; (3) the foreseeable consequences of declining or withdrawing; (4) reasonably foreseeable factors that may be
expected to influence their willingness to participate such as potential
risks, discomfort, or adverse effects; (5) any prospective research
benefits; (6) limits of confidentiality; (7) incentives for participation;
and (8) whom to contact for questions about the research and research participants' rights. They provide opportunity for the prospective participants to ask questions and receive answers. (See also
Standards 8.03, Informed Consent for Recording Voices and Images
in Research; 8.05, Dispensing with Informed Consent for Research;
and 8.07, Deception in Research.)

(b) Psychologists conducting intervention research involving the use
of experimental treatments clarify to participants at the outset of
the research (1) the experimental nature of the treatment; (2) the
services that will or will not be available to the control group(s) if
appropriate; (3) the means by which assignment to treatment and
control groups will be made; (4) available treatment alternatives if
an individual does not wish to participate in the research or wishes
to withdraw once a study has begun; and (5) compensation for or
monetary costs of participating including, if appropriate, whether

reimbursement from the participant or a third-party payor will be sought. (See also Standard 8.02a, Informed Consent to Research.)

8.03 Informed Consent for Recording Voices and Images in Research

Psychologists obtain informed consent from research participants prior to recording their voices or images for data collection unless (1) the research consists solely of naturalistic observations in public places, and it is not anticipated that the recording will be used in a manner that could cause personal identification or harm, or (2) the research design includes deception, and consent for the use of the recording is obtained during debriefing. (See also Standard 8.07, Deception in Research.)

8.04 Client/Patient, Student, and Subordinate Research Participants

(a) When psychologists conduct research with clients/patients, students, or subordinates as participants, psychologists take steps to protect the prospective participants from adverse consequences of declining or withdrawing from participation.
(b) When research participation is a course requirement or an opportunity for extra credit, the prospective participant is given the choice of equitable alternative activities.

8.05 Dispensing with Informed Consent for Research

Psychologists may dispense with informed consent only (1) where research would not reasonably be assumed to create distress or harm and involves (a) the study of normal educational practices, curricula, or classroom management methods conducted in educational settings; (b) only anonymous questionnaires, naturalistic observations, or archival research for which disclosure of responses would not place participants at risk of criminal or civil liability or damage their financial standing, employability, or reputation, and confidentiality is protected; or (c) the study of factors related to job or organization effectiveness conducted in organizational settings for which there is no risk to participants' employability, and confidentiality is protected or (2) where otherwise permitted by law or federal or institutional regulations.

8.06 Offering Inducements for Research Participation

(a) Psychologists make reasonable efforts to avoid offering excessive or inappropriate financial or other inducements for research participation when such inducements are likely to coerce participation.

(b) When offering professional services as an inducement for research participation, psychologists clarify the nature of the services, as well as the risks, obligations, and limitations. (See also Standard 6.05, Barter with Clients/Patients.)

8.07 Deception in Research

(a) Psychologists do not conduct a study involving deception unless they have determined that the use of deceptive techniques is justified by the study's significant prospective scientific, educational, or applied value and that effective nondeceptive alternative procedures are not feasible.

(b) Psychologists do not deceive prospective participants about research that is reasonably expected to cause physical pain or severe emotional distress.

(c) Psychologists explain any deception that is an integral feature of the design and conduct of an experiment to participants as early as is feasible, preferably at the conclusion of their participation, but no later than at the conclusion of the data collection, and permit participants to withdraw their data. (See also Standard 8.08, Debriefing.)

8.08 Debriefing

(a) Psychologists provide a prompt opportunity for participants to obtain appropriate information about the nature, results, and conclusions of the research, and they take reasonable steps to correct any misconceptions that participants may have of which the psychologists are aware.

(b) If scientific or humane values justify delaying or withholding this information, psychologists take reasonable measures to reduce the risk of harm.

(c) When psychologists become aware that research procedures have harmed a participant, they take reasonable steps to minimize the harm.

8.09 Humane Care and Use of Animals in Research

(a) Psychologists acquire, care for, use, and dispose of animals in compliance with current federal, state, and local laws and regulations, and with professional standards.
(b) Psychologists trained in research methods and experienced in the care of laboratory animals supervise all procedures involving animals and are responsible for ensuring appropriate consideration of their comfort, health, and humane treatment.
(c) Psychologists ensure that all individuals under their supervision who are using animals have received instruction in research methods and in the care, maintenance, and handling of the species being used, to the extent appropriate to their role. (See also Standard 2.05, Delegation of Work to Others.)
(d) Psychologists make reasonable efforts to minimize the discomfort, infection, illness, and pain of animal subjects.
(e) Psychologists use a procedure subjecting animals to pain, stress, or privation only when an alternative procedure is unavailable and the goal is justified by its prospective scientific, educational, or applied value.
(f) Psychologists perform surgical procedures under appropriate anesthesia and follow techniques to avoid infection and minimize pain during and after surgery.
(g) When it is appropriate that an animal's life be terminated, psychologists proceed rapidly, with an effort to minimize pain and in accordance with accepted procedures.

8.10 Reporting Research Results

(a) Psychologists do not fabricate data. (See also Standard 5.01a, Avoidance of False or Deceptive Statements.)
(b) If psychologists discover significant errors in their published data, they take reasonable steps to correct such errors in a correction, retraction, erratum, or other appropriate publication means.

8.11 Plagiarism

Psychologists do not present portions of another's work or data as their own, even if the other work or data source is cited occasionally.

8.12 Publication Credit

(a) Psychologists take responsibility and credit, including authorship credit, only for work they have actually performed or to which they have substantially contributed. (See also Standard 8.12b, Publication Credit.)

(b) Principal authorship and other publication credits accurately reflect the relative scientific or professional contributions of the individuals involved, regardless of their relative status. Mere possession of an institutional position, such as department chair, does not justify authorship credit. Minor contributions to the research or to the writing for publications are acknowledged appropriately, such as in footnotes or in an introductory statement.

(c) Except under exceptional circumstances, a student is listed as principal author on any multiple-authored article that is substantially based on the student's doctoral dissertation. Faculty advisors discuss publication credit with students as early as feasible and throughout the research and publication process as appropriate. (See also Standard 8.12b, Publication Credit.)

8.13 Duplicate Publication of Data

Psychologists do not publish, as original data, data that have been previously published. This does not preclude republishing data when they are accompanied by proper acknowledgment.

8.14 Sharing Research Data for Verification

(a) After research results are published, psychologists do not withhold the data on which their conclusions are based from other competent professionals who seek to verify the substantive claims through reanalysis and who intend to use such data only for that purpose, provided that the confidentiality of the participants can be protected and unless legal rights concerning proprietary data preclude their release. This does not preclude psychologists from requiring that such individuals or groups be responsible for costs associated with the provision of such information.

(b) Psychologists who request data from other psychologists to verify the substantive claims through reanalysis may use shared data only for the declared purpose. Requesting psychologists obtain prior written agreement for all other uses of the data.

8.15 Reviewers

Psychologists who review material submitted for presentation, publication, grant, or research proposal review respect the confidentiality of and the proprietary rights in such information of those who submitted it.

9. Assessment

9.01 Bases for Assessments

(a) Psychologists base the opinions contained in their recommendations, reports, and diagnostic or evaluative statements, including forensic testimony, on information and techniques sufficient to substantiate their findings. (See also Standard 2.04, Bases for Scientific and Professional Judgments.)

(b) Except as noted in 9.01c, psychologists provide opinions of the psychological characteristics of individuals only after they have conducted an examination of the individuals adequate to support their statements or conclusions. When, despite reasonable efforts, such an examination is not practical, psychologists document the efforts they made and the result of those efforts, clarify the probable impact of their limited information on the reliability and validity of their opinions, and appropriately limit the nature and extent of their conclusions or recommendations. (See also Standards 2.01, Boundaries of Competence, and 9.06, Interpreting Assessment Results.)

(c) When psychologists conduct a record review or provide consultation or supervision and an individual examination is not warranted or necessary for the opinion, psychologists explain this and the sources of information on which they based their conclusions and recommendations.

9.02 Use of Assessments

(a) Psychologists administer, adapt, score, interpret, or use assessment techniques, interviews, tests, or instruments in a manner and for purposes that are appropriate in light of the research on or evidence of the usefulness and proper application of the techniques.

(b) Psychologists use assessment instruments whose validity and reliability have been established for use with members of the population tested. When such validity or reliability has not been established, psychologists describe the strengths and limitations of test results and interpretation.

(c) Psychologists use assessment methods that are appropriate to an individual's language preference and competence, unless the use of an alternative language is relevant to the assessment issues.

9.03 Informed Consent in Assessments

(a) Psychologists obtain informed consent for assessments, evaluations, or diagnostic services, as described in Standard 3.10, Informed Consent, except when (1) testing is mandated by law or governmental regulations; (2) informed consent is implied because testing is conducted as a routine educational, institutional, or organizational activity (e.g., when participants voluntarily agree to assessment when applying for a job); or (3) one purpose of the testing is to evaluate decisional capacity. Informed consent includes an explanation of the nature and purpose of the assessment, fees, involvement of third parties, and limits of confidentiality and sufficient opportunity for the client/patient to ask questions and receive answers.

(b) Psychologists inform persons with questionable capacity to consent or for whom testing is mandated by law or governmental regulations about the nature and purpose of the proposed assessment services, using language that is reasonably understandable to the person being assessed.

(c) Psychologists using the services of an interpreter obtain informed consent from the client/patient to use that interpreter, ensure that confidentiality of test results and test security are maintained, and include in their recommendations, reports, and diagnostic or evaluative statements, including forensic testimony, discussion of any limitations on the data obtained. (See also Standards 2.05, Delegation of Work to Others; 4.01, Maintaining Confidentiality; 9.01, Bases for Assessments; 9.06, Interpreting Assessment Results; and 9.07, Assessment by Unqualified Persons.)

9.04 Release of Test Data

(a) The term *test data* refers to raw and scaled scores, client/patient responses to test questions or stimuli, and psychologists' notes and recordings concerning client/patient statements and behavior during an examination. Those portions of test materials that include client/patient responses are included in the definition of *test data*. Pursuant to a client/patient release, psychologists provide test data to the client/patient or other persons identified in the release. Psychologists may refrain from releasing test data to protect a client/patient or others from substantial harm or misuse or misrepresentation of the data or the test, recognizing that in many instances release of confidential information under these circumstances is regulated by law. (See also Standard 9.11, Maintaining Test Security.)

(b) In the absence of a client/patient release, psychologists provide test data only as required by law or court order.

9.05 Test Construction

Psychologists who develop tests and other assessment techniques use appropriate psychometric procedures and current scientific or professional knowledge for test design, standardization, validation, reduction or elimination of bias, and recommendations for use.

9.06 Interpreting Assessment Results

When interpreting assessment results, including automated interpretations, psychologists take into account the purpose of the assessment as well as the various test factors, test-taking abilities, and other characteristics of the person being assessed, such as situational, personal, linguistic, and cultural differences, that might affect psychologists' judgments or reduce the accuracy of their interpretations. They indicate any significant limitations of their interpretations. (See also Standards 2.01b and c, Boundaries of Competence, and 3.01, Unfair Discrimination.)

9.07 Assessment by Unqualified Persons

Psychologists do not promote the use of psychological assessment techniques by unqualified persons, except when such use is conducted for training purposes with appropriate supervision. (See also Standard 2.05, Delegation of Work to Others.)

9.08 Obsolete Tests and Outdated Test Results

(a) Psychologists do not base their assessment or intervention decisions or recommendations on data or test results that are outdated for the current purpose.

(b) Psychologists do not base such decisions or recommendations on tests and measures that are obsolete and not useful for the current purpose.

9.09 Test Scoring and Interpretation Services

(a) Psychologists who offer assessment or scoring services to other professionals accurately describe the purpose, norms, validity, reliability, and applications of the procedures and any special qualifications applicable to their use.
(b) Psychologists select scoring and interpretation services (including automated services) on the basis of evidence of the validity of the program and procedures as well as on other appropriate considerations. (See also Standard 2.01b and c, Boundaries of Competence.)
(c) Psychologists retain responsibility for the appropriate application, interpretation, and use of assessment instruments, whether they score and interpret such tests themselves or use automated or other services.

9.10 Explaining Assessment Results

Regardless of whether the scoring and interpretation are done by psychologists, by employees or assistants, or by automated or other outside services, psychologists take reasonable steps to ensure that explanations of results are given to the individual or designated representative unless the nature of the relationship precludes provision of an explanation of results (such as in some organizational consulting, preemployment or security screenings, and forensic evaluations), and this fact has been clearly explained to the person being assessed in advance.

9.11. Maintaining Test Security

The term *test materials* refers to manuals, instruments, protocols, and test questions or stimuli and does not include *test data* as defined in Standard 9.04, Release of Test Data. Psychologists make reasonable efforts to maintain the integrity and security of test materials and other assessment techniques consistent with law and contractual obligations, and in a manner that permits adherence to this Ethics Code.

10. Therapy

10.01 Informed Consent to Therapy

(a) When obtaining informed consent to therapy as required in Standard 3.10, Informed Consent, psychologists inform clients/patients as early as is feasible in the therapeutic relationship about the nature and anticipated course of therapy, fees, involvement of third parties, and limits of confidentiality and provide sufficient opportunity for the client/patient to ask questions and receive answers. (See also Standards 4.02, Discussing the Limits of Confidentiality, and 6.04, Fees and Financial Arrangements.)

(b) When obtaining informed consent for treatment for which generally recognized techniques and procedures have not been established, psychologists inform their clients/patients of the developing nature of the treatment, the potential risks involved, alternative treatments that may be available, and the voluntary nature of their participation. (See also Standards 2.01e, Boundaries of Competence, and 3.10, Informed Consent.)

(c) When the therapist is a trainee and the legal responsibility for the treatment provided resides with the supervisor, the client/patient, as part of the informed consent procedure, is informed that the therapist is in training and is being supervised and is given the name of the supervisor.

10.02 Therapy Involving Couples or Families

(a) When psychologists agree to provide services to several persons who have a relationship (such as spouses, significant others, or parents and children), they take reasonable steps to clarify at the outset (1) which of the individuals are clients/patients and (2) the relationship the psychologist will have with each person. This clarification includes the psychologist's role and the probable uses of the services provided or the information obtained. (See also Standard 4.02, Discussing the Limits of Confidentiality.)

(b) If it becomes apparent that psychologists may be called on to perform potentially conflicting roles (such as family therapist and then witness for one party in divorce proceedings), psychologists take reasonable steps to clarify and modify, or withdraw from, roles appropriately. (See also Standard 3.05c, Multiple Relationships.)

10.03 Group Therapy

When psychologists provide services to several persons in a group setting, they describe at the outset the roles and responsibilities of all parties and the limits of confidentiality.

10.04 Providing Therapy to Those Served by Others

In deciding whether to offer or provide services to those already receiving mental health services elsewhere, psychologists carefully consider the treatment issues and the potential client's/patient's welfare. Psychologists discuss these issues with the client/patient or another legally authorized person on behalf of the client/patient in order to minimize the risk of confusion and conflict, consult with the other service providers when appropriate, and proceed with caution and sensitivity to the therapeutic issues.

10.05 Sexual Intimacies with Current Therapy Clients/Patients

Psychologists do not engage in sexual intimacies with current therapy clients/patients.

10.06 Sexual Intimacies with Relatives or Significant Others of Current Therapy Clients/Patients

Psychologists do not engage in sexual intimacies with individuals they know to be close relatives, guardians, or significant others of current clients/patients. Psychologists do not terminate therapy to circumvent this standard.

10.07 Therapy with Former Sexual Partners

Psychologists do not accept as therapy clients/patients persons with whom they have engaged in sexual intimacies.

10.08 Sexual Intimacies with Former Therapy Clients/Patients

(a) Psychologists do not engage in sexual intimacies with former clients/patients for at least two years after cessation or termination of therapy.

(b) Psychologists do not engage in sexual intimacies with former clients/patients even after a two-year interval except in the most unusual circumstances. Psychologists who engage in such activity after the two years following cessation or termination of therapy and of having no sexual contact with the former client/patient bear the burden of demonstrating that there has been no exploitation, in light of all relevant factors, including (1) the amount of time that has passed since therapy terminated; (2) the nature, duration, and intensity of the therapy; (3) the circumstances of termination; (4) the client's/patient's personal history; (5) the client's/patient's current mental status; (6) the likelihood of adverse impact on the client/patient; and (7) any statements or actions made by the therapist during the course of therapy suggesting or inviting the possibility of a posttermination sexual or romantic relationship with the client/patient. (See also Standard 3.05, Multiple Relationships.)

10.09 Interruption of Therapy

When entering into employment or contractual relationships, psychologists make reasonable efforts to provide for orderly and appropriate resolution of responsibility for client/patient care in the event that the employment or contractual relationship ends, with paramount consideration given to the welfare of the client/patient. (See also Standard 3.12, Interruption of Psychological Services.)

10.10 Terminating Therapy

(a) Psychologists terminate therapy when it becomes reasonably clear that the client/patient no longer needs the service, is not likely to benefit, or is being harmed by continued service.
(b) Psychologists may terminate therapy when threatened or otherwise endangered by the client/patient or another person with whom the client/patient has a relationship.
(c) Except where precluded by the actions of clients/patients or third-party payors, prior to termination psychologists provide pretermination counseling and suggest alternative service providers as appropriate.

History and Effective Date Footnote

This version of the APA Ethics Code was adopted by the American Psychological Association's Council of Representatives during its meeting, August 21, 2002, and is effective beginning June 1, 2003. Inquiries concerning the substance or interpretation of the APA Ethics Code should be addressed to the Director, Office of Ethics, American Psychological Association, 750 First Street, NE, Washington, DC 20002-4242. The Ethics Code and information regarding the Code can be found on the APA web site, *http://www.apa.org/ethics*. The standards in this Ethics Code will be used to adjudicate complaints brought concerning alleged conduct occurring on or after the effective date. Complaints regarding conduct occurring prior to the effective date will be adjudicated on the basis of the version of the Ethics Code that was in effect at the time the conduct occurred.

The APA has previously published its Ethics Code as follows:

American Psychological Association. (1953). Ethical standards of psychologists. Washington, DC: Author.

American Psychological Association. (1959). Ethical standards of psychologists. American Psychologist, 14, 279-282.

American Psychological Association. (1963). Ethical standards of psychologists. American Psychologist, 18, 56-60.

American Psychological Association. (1968). Ethical standards of psychologists. American Psychologist, 23, 357-361.

American Psychological Association. (1977, March). Ethical standards of psychologists. APA Monitor, 22-23.

American Psychological Association. (1979). Ethical standards of psychologists. Washington, DC: Author.

American Psychological Association. (1981). Ethical principles of psychologists. American Psychologist, 36, 633-638.

American Psychological Association. (1990). Ethical principles of psychologists (Amended June 2, 1989). American Psychologist, 45, 390-395.

American Psychological Association. (1992). Ethical principles of psychologists and code of conduct. American Psychologist, 47, 1597-1611.

Request copies of the APA's Ethical Principles of Psychologists and Code of Conduct from the APA Order Department, 750 First Street, NE, Washington, DC 20002-4242, or phone (202) 336-5510.

Code of Ethics
of the National Association of Social Workers

© 1999, National Association of Social Workers, Inc.

750 First Street, Ne Suite 700 Washington, DC 20002-4241

PREAMBLE

The primary mission of the social work profession is to enhance human well-being and help meet the basic human needs of all people, with particular attention to the needs and empowerment of people who are vulnerable, oppressed, and living in poverty. A historic and defining feature of social work is the profession's focus on individual well-being in a social context and the well-being of society. Fundamental to social work is attention to the environmental forces that create, contribute to, and address problems in living.

Social workers promote social justice and social change with and on behalf of clients. "Clients" is used inclusively to refer to individuals, families, groups, organizations, and communities. Social workers are sensitive to cultural and ethnic diversity and strive to end discrimina-

Approved by the 1996 NASW Delegate Assembly and revised by the 1999 NASW Delegate Assembly

[Haworth co-indexing entry note]: "Code of Ethics of the National Association of Social Workers." National Association of Social Workers, Inc. Co-published simultaneously in *Journal of Aggression, Maltreatment & Trauma* (The Haworth Maltreatment & Trauma Press, an imprint of The Haworth Press, Inc.) Vol. 11, No. 3, 2005, pp. 395-422; and: *Ethical and Legal Issues for Mental Health Professionals: A Comprehensive Handbook of Principles and Standards* (ed: Steven F. Bucky, Joanne E. Callan, and George Stricker) The Haworth Maltreatment & Trauma Press, an imprint of The Haworth Press, Inc., 2005, pp. 395-422. Single or multiple copies of this article are available for a fee from The Haworth Document Delivery Service [1-800-HAWORTH, 9:00 a.m. - 5:00 p.m. (EST). E-mail address: docdelivery@haworthpress.com].

Available online at http://www.haworthpress.com/web/JAMT
Digital Object Identifier: 10.1300/J146v011n03_06

tion, oppression, poverty, and other forms of social injustice. These activities may be in the form of direct practice, community organizing, supervision, consultation, administration, advocacy, social and political action, policy development and implementation, education, and research and evaluation. Social workers seek to enhance the capacity of people to address their own needs. Social workers also seek to promote the responsiveness of organizations, communities, and other social institutions to individuals' needs and social problems.

The mission of the social work profession is rooted in a set of core values. These core values, embraced by social workers throughout the profession's history, are the foundation of social work's unique purpose and perspective:

- service
- social justice
- dignity and worth of the person
- importance of human relationships
- integrity
- competence

This constellation of core values reflects what is unique to the social work profession. Core values, and the principles that flow from them, must be balanced within the context and complexity of the human experience.

PURPOSE OF THE NASW CODE OF ETHICS

Professional ethics are at the core of social work. The profession has an obligation to articulate its basic values, ethical principles, and ethical standards. The *NASW Code of Ethics* sets forth these values, principles, and standards to guide social workers' conduct. The *Code* is relevant to all social workers and social work students, regardless of their professional functions, the settings in which they work, or the populations they serve.

The *NASW Code of Ethics* serves six purposes:

1. The *Code* identifies core values on which social work's mission is based.
2. The *Code* summarizes broad ethical principles that reflect the profession's core values and establishes a set of specific ethical standards that should be used to guide social work practice.

3. The *Code* is designed to help social workers identify relevant considerations when professional obligations conflict or ethical uncertainties arise.
4. The *Code* provides ethical standards to which the general public can hold the social work profession accountable.
5. The *Code* socializes practitioners new to the field to social work's mission, values, ethical principles, and ethical standards.
6. The *Code* articulates standards that the social work profession itself can use to assess whether social workers have engaged in unethical conduct. NASW has formal procedures to adjudicate ethics complaints filed against its members.* In subscribing to this *Code*, social workers are required to cooperate in its implementation, participate in NASW adjudication proceedings, and abide by any NASW disciplinary rulings or sanctions based on it.

*For information on NASW adjudication procedures, see *NASW Procedures for the Adjudication of Grievances.*

The *Code* offers a set of values, principles, and standards to guide decision making and conduct when ethical issues arise. It does not provide a set of rules that prescribe how social workers should act in all situations. Specific applications of the *Code* must take into account the context in which it is being considered and the possibility of conflicts among the *Code*'s values, principles, and standards. Ethical responsibilities flow from all human relationships, from the personal and familial to the social and professional.

Further, the *NASW Code of Ethics* does not specify which values, principles, and standards are most important and ought to outweigh others in instances when they conflict. Reasonable differences of opinion can and do exist among social workers with respect to the ways in which values, ethical principles, and ethical standards should be rank ordered when they conflict. Ethical decision making in a given situation must apply the informed judgment of the individual social worker and should also consider how the issues would be judged in a peer review process where the ethical standards of the profession would be applied. Ethical decision making is a process. There are many instances in social work where simple answers are not available to resolve complex ethical issues. Social workers should take into consideration all the values, principles, and standards in this *Code* that are relevant to any situation in which ethical judgment is warranted. Social workers' decisions and actions should be consistent with the spirit as well as the letter of this *Code*.

In addition to this *Code*, there are many other sources of information about ethical thinking that may be useful. Social workers should consider ethical theory and principles generally, social work theory and research, laws, regulations, agency policies, and other relevant codes of ethics, recognizing that among codes of ethics, social workers should consider the *NASW Code of Ethics* as their primary source. Social workers also should be aware of the impact on ethical decision making of their clients' and their own personal values and cultural and religious beliefs and practices. They should be aware of any conflicts between personal and professional values and deal with them responsibly. For additional guidance social workers should consult the relevant literature on professional ethics and ethical decision making and seek appropriate consultation when faced with ethical dilemmas. This may involve consultation with an agency-based or social work organization's ethics committee, a regulatory body, knowledgeable colleagues, supervisors, or legal counsel.

Instances may arise when social workers' ethical obligations conflict with agency policies or relevant laws or regulations. When such conflicts occur, social workers must make a responsible effort to resolve the conflict in a manner that is consistent with the values, principles, and standards expressed in this *Code*. If a reasonable resolution of the conflict does not appear possible, social workers should seek proper consultation before making a decision.

The *NASW Code of Ethics* is to be used by NASW and by individuals, agencies, organizations, and bodies (such as licensing and regulatory boards, professional liability insurance providers, courts of law, agency boards of directors, government agencies, and other professional groups) that choose to adopt it or use it as a frame of reference. Violation of standards in this *Code* does not automatically imply legal liability or violation of the law. Such determination can only be made in the context of legal and judicial proceedings. Alleged violations of the *Code* would be subject to a peer review process. Such processes are generally separate from legal or administrative procedures and insulated from legal review or proceedings to allow the profession to counsel and discipline its own members.

A code of ethics cannot guarantee ethical behavior. Moreover, a code of ethics cannot resolve all ethical issues or disputes or capture the richness and complexity involved in striving to make responsible choices within a moral community. Rather, a code of ethics sets forth values, ethical principles, and ethical standards to which professionals aspire and by which their actions can be judged. Social workers' ethical behavior should result from their personal commitment to engage in ethical practice. *The NASW Code of Ethics* reflects the commitment of all social workers to uphold the profession's values and to act ethically.

Principles and standards must be applied by individuals of good character who discern moral questions and, in good faith, seek to make reliable ethical judgments.

ETHICAL PRINCIPLES

The following broad ethical principles are based on social work's core values of service, social justice, dignity and worth of the person, importance of human relationships, integrity, and competence. These principles set forth ideals to which all social workers should aspire.

Value: *Service*

Ethical Principle: *Social workers' primary goal is to help people in need and to address social problems.*

Social workers elevate service to others above self-interest. Social workers draw on their knowledge, values, and skills to help people in need and to address social problems. Social workers are encouraged to volunteer some portion of their professional skills with no expectation of significant financial return (pro bono service).

Value: *Social Justice*

Ethical Principle: *Social workers challenge social injustice.*

Social workers pursue social change, particularly with and on behalf of vulnerable and oppressed individuals and groups of people. Social workers' social change efforts are focused primarily on issues of poverty, unemployment, discrimination, and other forms of social injustice. These activities seek to promote sensitivity to and knowledge about oppression and cultural and ethnic diversity. Social workers strive to ensure access to needed information, services, and resources; equality of opportunity; and meaningful participation in decision making for all people.

Value: *Dignity and Worth of the Person*

Ethical Principle: *Social workers respect the inherent dignity and worth of the person.*

Social workers treat each person in a caring and respectful fashion, mindful of individual differences and cultural and ethnic diversity. Social workers promote clients' socially responsible self-determination. Social workers seek to enhance clients' capacity and opportunity to change and to address their own needs. Social workers are cognizant of their dual responsibility to clients and to the broader society. They seek to resolve conflicts between clients' interests and the broader society's interests in a socially responsible manner consistent with the values, ethical principles, and ethical standards of the profession.

Value: *Importance of Human Relationships*

Ethical Principle: *Social workers recognize the central importance of human relationships.*

Social workers understand that relationships between and among people are an important vehicle for change. Social workers engage people as partners in the helping process. Social workers seek to strengthen relationships among people in a purposeful effort to promote, restore, maintain, and enhance the well-being of individuals, families, social groups, organizations, and communities.

Value: *Integrity*

Ethical Principle: *Social workers behave in a trustworthy manner.*

Social workers are continually aware of the profession's mission, values, ethical principles, and ethical standards and practice in a manner consistent with them. Social workers act honestly and responsibly and promote ethical practices on the part of the organizations with which they are affiliated.

Value: *Competence*

Ethical Principle: *Social workers practice within their areas of competence and develop and enhance their professional expertise.*

Social workers continually strive to increase their professional knowledge and skills and to apply them in practice. Social workers should aspire to contribute to the knowledge base of the profession.

ETHICAL STANDARDS

The following ethical standards are relevant to the professional activities of all social workers. These standards concern (1) social workers' ethical responsibilities to clients, (2) social workers' ethical responsibilities to colleagues, (3) social workers' ethical responsibilities in practice settings, (4) social workers' ethical responsibilities as professionals, (5) social workers' ethical responsibilities to the social work profession, and (6) social workers' ethical responsibilities to the broader society.

Some of the standards that follow are enforceable guidelines for professional conduct, and some are aspirational. The extent to which each standard is enforceable is a matter of professional judgment to be exercised by those responsible for reviewing alleged violations of ethical standards.

1. Social Workers' Ethical Responsibilities to Clients

1.01 Commitment to Clients

Social workers' primary responsibility is to promote the well-being of clients. In general, clients' interests are primary. However, social workers' responsibility to the larger society or specific legal obligations may on limited occasions supersede the loyalty owed clients, and clients should be so advised. (Examples include when a social worker is required by law to report that a client has abused a child or has threatened to harm self or others.)

1.02 Self-Determination

Social workers respect and promote the right of clients to self-determination and assist clients in their efforts to identify and clarify their goals. Social workers may limit clients' right to self-determination when, in the social workers' professional judgment, clients' actions or potential actions pose a serious, foreseeable, and imminent risk to themselves or others.

1.03 Informed Consent

a. Social workers should provide services to clients only in the context of a professional relationship based, when appropriate, on valid informed consent. Social workers should use clear and understandable language to inform clients of the purpose of the services, risks related to the services, limits to services because of the requirements of a third-party payer, relevant costs, reasonable alternatives, clients' right to refuse or withdraw consent, and the time frame covered by the consent. Social workers should provide clients with an opportunity to ask questions.

b. In instances when clients are not literate or have difficulty understanding the primary language used in the practice setting, social workers should take steps to ensure clients' comprehension. This may include providing clients with a detailed verbal explanation or arranging for a qualified interpreter or translator whenever possible.

c. In instances when clients lack the capacity to provide informed consent, social workers should protect clients' interests by seeking permission from an appropriate third party, informing clients consistent with the clients' level of understanding. In such instances social workers should seek to ensure that the third party acts in a manner consistent with clients' wishes and interests. Social workers should take reasonable steps to enhance such clients' ability to give informed consent.

d. In instances when clients are receiving services involuntarily, social workers should provide information about the nature and extent of services and about the extent of clients' right to refuse service.

e. Social workers who provide services via electronic media (such as computer, telephone, radio, and television) should inform recipients of the limitations and risks associated with such services.

f. Social workers should obtain clients' informed consent before audiotaping or videotaping clients or permitting observation of services to clients by a third party.

1.04 Competence

a. Social workers should provide services and represent themselves as competent only within the boundaries of their education, training, license, certification, consultation received, supervised experience, or other relevant professional experience.

b. Social workers should provide services in substantive areas or use intervention techniques or approaches that are new to them only after engaging in appropriate study, training, consultation, and supervision from people who are competent in those interventions or techniques.

c. When generally recognized standards do not exist with respect to an emerging area of practice, social workers should exercise careful judgment and take responsible steps (including appropriate education, research, training, consultation, and supervision) to ensure the competence of their work and to protect clients from harm.

1.05 Cultural Competence and Social Diversity

a. Social workers should understand culture and its function in human behavior and society, recognizing the strengths that exist in all cultures.
b. Social workers should have a knowledge base of their clients' cultures and be able to demonstrate competence in the provision of services that are sensitive to clients' cultures and to differences among people and cultural groups.
c. Social workers should obtain education about and seek to understand the nature of social diversity and oppression with respect to race, ethnicity, national origin, color, sex, sexual orientation, age, marital status, political belief, religion, and mental or physical disability.

1.06 Conflicts of Interest

a. Social workers should be alert to and avoid conflicts of interest that interfere with the exercise of professional discretion and impartial judgment. Social workers should inform clients when a real or potential conflict of interest arises and take reasonable steps to resolve the issue in a manner that makes the clients' interests primary and protects clients' interests to the greatest extent possible. In some cases, protecting clients' interests may require termination of the professional relationship with proper referral of the client.
b. Social workers should not take unfair advantage of any professional relationship or exploit others to further their personal, religious, political, or business interests.
c. Social workers should not engage in dual or multiple relationships with clients or former clients in which there is a risk of exploitation or potential harm to the client. In instances when dual or multiple relationships are unavoidable, social workers should take steps to protect clients and are responsible for setting clear, appropriate, and culturally sensitive boundaries. (Dual or multiple relationships occur when social workers relate to clients in more than one relationship, whether professional, social, or business. Dual or multiple relationships can occur simultaneously or consecutively.)
d. When social workers provide services to two or more people who have a relationship with each other (for example, couples, family members), social workers should clarify with all parties which in-

dividuals will be considered clients and the nature of social work-ers' professional obligations to the various individuals who are receiving services. Social workers who anticipate a conflict of in-terest among the individuals receiving services or who anticipate having to perform in potentially conflicting roles (for example, when a social worker is asked to testify in a child custody dispute or divorce proceedings involving clients) should clarify their role with the parties involved and take appropriate action to minimize any conflict of interest.

1.07 Privacy and Confidentiality

a. Social workers should respect clients' right to privacy. Social workers should not solicit private information from clients unless it is essential to providing services or conducting social work evaluation or research. Once private information is shared, stan-dards of confidentiality apply.
b. Social workers may disclose confidential information when ap-propriate with valid consent from a client or a person legally au-thorized to consent on behalf of a client.
c. Social workers should protect the confidentiality of all informa-tion obtained in the course of professional service, except for compelling professional reasons. The general expectation that so-cial workers will keep information confidential does not apply when disclosure is necessary to prevent serious, foreseeable, and imminent harm to a client or other identifiable person. In all in-stances, social workers should disclose the least amount of confi-dential information necessary to achieve the desired purpose; only information that is directly relevant to the purpose for which the disclosure is made should be revealed.
d. Social workers should inform clients, to the extent possible, about the disclosure of confidential information and the potential conse-quences, when feasible before the disclosure is made. This applies whether social workers disclose confidential information on the basis of a legal requirement or client consent.
e. Social workers should discuss with clients and other interested parties the nature of confidentiality and limitations of clients' right to confidentiality. Social workers should review with clients circumstances where confidential information may be requested and where disclosure of confidential information may be legally required. This discussion should occur as soon as possible in the

social worker-client relationship and as needed throughout the course of the relationship.

f. When social workers provide counseling services to families, couples, or groups, social workers should seek agreement among the parties involved concerning each individual's right to confidentiality and obligation to preserve the confidentiality of information shared by others. Social workers should inform participants in family, couples, or group counseling that social workers cannot guarantee that all participants will honor such agreements.

g. Social workers should inform clients involved in family, couples, marital, or group counseling of the social worker's, employer's, and agency's policy concerning the social worker's disclosure of confidential information among the parties involved in the counseling.

h. Social workers should not disclose confidential information to third-party payers unless clients have authorized such disclosure.

i. Social workers should not discuss confidential information in any setting unless privacy can be ensured. Social workers should not discuss confidential information in public or semipublic areas such as hallways, waiting rooms, elevators, and restaurants.

j. Social workers should protect the confidentiality of clients during legal proceedings to the extent permitted by law. When a court of law or other legally authorized body orders social workers to disclose confidential or privileged information without a client's consent and such disclosure could cause harm to the client, social workers should request that the court withdraw the order or limit the order as narrowly as possible or maintain the records under seal, unavailable for public inspection.

k. Social workers should protect the confidentiality of clients when responding to requests from members of the media.

l. Social workers should protect the confidentiality of clients' written and electronic records and other sensitive information. Social workers should take reasonable steps to ensure that clients' records are stored in a secure location and that clients' records are not available to others who are not authorized to have access.

m. Social workers should take precautions to ensure and maintain the confidentiality of information transmitted to other parties through the use of computers, electronic mail, facsimile machines, telephones and telephone answering machines, and other electronic or computer technology. Disclosure of identifying information should be avoided whenever possible.

n. Social workers should transfer or dispose of clients' records in a manner that protects clients' confidentiality and is consistent with state statutes governing records and social work licensure.

o. Social workers should take reasonable precautions to protect client confidentiality in the event of the social worker's termination of practice, incapacitation, or death.

p. Social workers should not disclose identifying information when discussing clients for teaching or training purposes unless the client has consented to disclosure of confidential information.

q. Social workers should not disclose identifying information when discussing clients with consultants unless the client has consented to disclosure of confidential information or there is a compelling need for such disclosure.

r. Social workers should protect the confidentiality of deceased clients consistent with the preceding standards.

1.08 Access to Records

a. Social workers should provide clients with reasonable access to records concerning the clients. Social workers who are concerned that clients' access to their records could cause serious misunderstanding or harm to the client should provide assistance in interpreting the records and consultation with the client regarding the records. Social workers should limit clients' access to their records, or portions of their records, only in exceptional circumstances when there is compelling evidence that such access would cause serious harm to the client. Both clients' requests and the rationale for withholding some or all of the record should be documented in clients' files.

b. When providing clients with access to their records, social workers should take steps to protect the confidentiality of other individuals identified or discussed in such records.

1.09 Sexual Relationships

a. Social workers should under no circumstances engage in sexual activities or sexual contact with current clients, whether such contact is consensual or forced.

b. Social workers should not engage in sexual activities or sexual contact with clients' relatives or other individuals with whom clients maintain a close personal relationship when there is a risk of exploitation or potential harm to the client. Sexual activity or sexual contact with clients' relatives or other individuals with whom clients maintain a personal relationship has the potential to be harmful to the client and may make it difficult for the social worker and client to maintain appropriate professional boundaries. Social workers–not their clients, their clients' relatives, or other individuals with whom the client maintains a personal relationship–assume the full burden for setting clear, appropriate, and culturally sensitive boundaries.

c. Social workers should not engage in sexual activities or sexual contact with former clients because of the potential for harm to the client. If social workers engage in conduct contrary to this prohibition or claim that an exception to this prohibition is warranted because of extraordinary circumstances, it is social workers–not their clients–who assume the full burden of demonstrating that the former client has not been exploited, coerced, or manipulated, intentionally or unintentionally.

d. Social workers should not provide clinical services to individuals with whom they have had a prior sexual relationship. Providing clinical services to a former sexual partner has the potential to be harmful to the individual and is likely to make it difficult for the social worker and individual to maintain appropriate professional boundaries.

1.10 Physical Contact

Social workers should not engage in physical contact with clients when there is a possibility of psychological harm to the client as a result of the contact (such as cradling or caressing clients). Social workers who engage in appropriate physical contact with clients are responsible for setting clear, appropriate, and culturally sensitive boundaries that govern such physical contact.

1.11 Sexual Harassment

Social workers should not sexually harass clients. Sexual harassment includes sexual advances, sexual solicitation, requests for sexual favors, and other verbal or physical conduct of a sexual nature.

1.12 Derogatory Language

Social workers should not use derogatory language in their written or verbal communications to or about clients. Social workers should use accurate and respectful language in all communications to and about clients.

1.13 Payment for Services

a. When setting fees, social workers should ensure that the fees are fair, reasonable, and commensurate with the services performed. Consideration should be given to clients' ability to pay.
b. Social workers should avoid accepting goods or services from clients as payment for professional services. Bartering arrangements, particularly involving services, create the potential for conflicts of interest, exploitation, and inappropriate boundaries in social workers' relationships with clients. Social workers should explore and may participate in bartering only in very limited circumstances when it can be demonstrated that such arrangements are an accepted practice among professionals in the local community, considered to be essential for the provision of services, negotiated without coercion, and entered into at the client's initiative and with the client's informed consent. Social workers who accept goods or services from clients as payment for professional services assume the full burden of demonstrating that this arrangement will not be detrimental to the client or the professional relationship.
c. Social workers should not solicit a private fee or other remuneration for providing services to clients who are entitled to such available services through the social workers' employer or agency.

1.14 Clients Who Lack Decision-Making Capacity

When social workers act on behalf of clients who lack the capacity to make informed decisions, social workers should take reasonable steps to safeguard the interests and rights of those clients.

1.15 Interruption of Services

Social workers should make reasonable efforts to ensure continuity of services in the event that services are interrupted by factors such as unavailability, relocation, illness, disability, or death.

1.16 Termination of Services

a. Social workers should terminate services to clients and professional relationships with them when such services and relationships are no longer required or no longer serve the clients' needs or interests.

b. Social workers should take reasonable steps to avoid abandoning clients who are still in need of services. Social workers should withdraw services precipitously only under unusual circumstances, giving careful consideration to all factors in the situation and taking care to minimize possible adverse effects. Social workers should assist in making appropriate arrangements for continuation of services when necessary.

c. Social workers in fee-for-service settings may terminate services to clients who are not paying an overdue balance if the financial contractual arrangements have been made clear to the client, if the client does not pose an imminent danger to self or others, and if the clinical and other consequences of the current nonpayment have been addressed and discussed with the client.

d. Social workers should not terminate services to pursue a social, financial, or sexual relationship with a client.

e. Social workers who anticipate the termination or interruption of services to clients should notify clients promptly and seek the transfer, referral, or continuation of services in relation to the clients' needs and preferences.

f. Social workers who are leaving an employment setting should inform clients of appropriate options for the continuation of services and of the benefits and risks of the options.

2. Social Workers' Ethical Responsibilities to Colleagues

2.01 Respect

a. Social workers should treat colleagues with respect and should represent accurately and fairly the qualifications, views, and obligations of colleagues.

b. Social workers should avoid unwarranted negative criticism of colleagues in communications with clients or with other professionals. Unwarranted negative criticism may include demeaning comments that refer to colleagues' level of competence or to individuals' attributes such as race, ethnicity, national origin, color, sex, sexual orientation, age, marital status, political belief, religion, and mental or physical disability.

c. Social workers should cooperate with social work colleagues and with colleagues of other professions when such cooperation serves the well-being of clients.

2.02 Confidentiality

Social workers should respect confidential information shared by colleagues in the course of their professional relationships and transactions. Social workers should ensure that such colleagues understand social workers' obligation to respect confidentiality and any exceptions related to it.

2.03 Interdisciplinary Collaboration

a. Social workers who are members of an interdisciplinary team should participate in and contribute to decisions that affect the well-being of clients by drawing on the perspectives, values, and experiences of the social work profession. Professional and ethical obligations of the interdisciplinary team as a whole and of its individual members should be clearly established.
b. Social workers for whom a team decision raises ethical concerns should attempt to resolve the disagreement through appropriate channels. If the disagreement cannot be resolved, social workers should pursue other avenues to address their concerns consistent with client well-being.

2.04 Disputes Involving Colleagues

a. Social workers should not take advantage of a dispute between a colleague and an employer to obtain a position or otherwise advance the social workers' own interests.
b. Social workers should not exploit clients in disputes with colleagues or engage clients in any inappropriate discussion of conflicts between social workers and their colleagues.

2.05 Consultation

a. Social workers should seek the advice and counsel of colleagues whenever such consultation is in the best interests of clients.
b. Social workers should keep themselves informed about colleagues' areas of expertise and competencies. Social workers should seek

consultation only from colleagues who have demonstrated knowledge, expertise, and competence related to the subject of the consultation.

c. When consulting with colleagues about clients, social workers should disclose the least amount of information necessary to achieve the purposes of the consultation.

2.06 Referral for Services

a. Social workers should refer clients to other professionals when the other professionals' specialized knowledge or expertise is needed to serve clients fully or when social workers believe that they are not being effective or making reasonable progress with clients and that additional service is required.

b. Social workers who refer clients to other professionals should take appropriate steps to facilitate an orderly transfer of responsibility. Social workers who refer clients to other professionals should disclose, with clients' consent, all pertinent information to the new service providers.

c. Social workers are prohibited from giving or receiving payment for a referral when no professional service is provided by the referring social worker.

2.07 Sexual Relationships

a. Social workers who function as supervisors or educators should not engage in sexual activities or contact with supervisees, students, trainees, or other colleagues over whom they exercise professional authority.

b. Social workers should avoid engaging in sexual relationships with colleagues when there is potential for a conflict of interest. Social workers who become involved in, or anticipate becoming involved in, a sexual relationship with a colleague have a duty to transfer professional responsibilities, when necessary, to avoid a conflict of interest.

2.08 Sexual Harassment

Social workers should not sexually harass supervisees, students, trainees, or colleagues. Sexual harassment includes sexual advances, sexual solicitation, requests for sexual favors, and other verbal or physical conduct of a sexual nature.

2.09 Impairment of Colleagues

a. Social workers who have direct knowledge of a social work colleague's impairment that is due to personal problems, psychosocial distress, substance abuse, or mental health difficulties and that interferes with practice effectiveness should consult with that colleague when feasible and assist the colleague in taking remedial action.

b. Social workers who believe that a social work colleague's impairment interferes with practice effectiveness and that the colleague has not taken adequate steps to address the impairment should take action through appropriate channels established by employers, agencies, NASW, licensing and regulatory bodies, and other professional organizations.

2.10 Incompetence of Colleagues

a. Social workers who have direct knowledge of a social work colleague's incompetence should consult with that colleague when feasible and assist the colleague in taking remedial action.

b. Social workers who believe that a social work colleague is incompetent and has not taken adequate steps to address the incompetence should take action through appropriate channels established by employers, agencies, NASW, licensing and regulatory bodies, and other professional organizations.

2.11 Unethical Conduct of Colleagues

a. Social workers should take adequate measures to discourage, prevent, expose, and correct the unethical conduct of colleagues.

b. Social workers should be knowledgeable about established policies and procedures for handling concerns about colleagues' unethical behavior. Social workers should be familiar with national, state, and local procedures for handling ethics complaints. These include policies and procedures created by NASW, licensing and regulatory bodies, employers, agencies, and other professional organizations.

c. Social workers who believe that a colleague has acted unethically should seek resolution by discussing their concerns with the colleague when feasible and when such discussion is likely to be productive.

d. When necessary, social workers who believe that a colleague has acted unethically should take action through appropriate formal channels (such as contacting a state licensing board or regulatory body, an NASW committee on inquiry, or other professional ethics committees).

e. Social workers should defend and assist colleagues who are unjustly charged with unethical conduct.

3. Social Workers' Ethical Responsibilities in Practice Settings

3.01 Supervision and Consultation

a. Social workers who provide supervision or consultation should have the necessary knowledge and skill to supervise or consult appropriately and should do so only within their areas of knowledge and competence.

b. Social workers who provide supervision or consultation are responsible for setting clear, appropriate, and culturally sensitive boundaries.

c. Social workers should not engage in any dual or multiple relationships with supervisees in which there is a risk of exploitation of or potential harm to the supervisee.

d. Social workers who provide supervision should evaluate supervisees' performance in a manner that is fair and respectful.

3.02 Education and Training

a. Social workers who function as educators, field instructors for students, or trainers should provide instruction only within their areas of knowledge and competence and should provide instruction based on the most current information and knowledge available in the profession.

b. Social workers who function as educators or field instructors for students should evaluate students' performance in a manner that is fair and respectful.

c. Social workers who function as educators or field instructors for students should take reasonable steps to ensure that clients are routinely informed when services are being provided by students.

d. Social workers who function as educators or field instructors for students should not engage in any dual or multiple relationships with students in which there is a risk of exploitation or potential harm to the student. Social work educators and field instructors are responsible for setting clear, appropriate, and culturally sensitive boundaries.

3.03 Performance Evaluation

Social workers who have responsibility for evaluating the performance of others should fulfill such responsibility in a fair and considerate manner and on the basis of clearly stated criteria.

3.04 Client Records

a. Social workers should take reasonable steps to ensure that documentation in records is accurate and reflects the services provided.
b. Social workers should include sufficient and timely documentation in records to facilitate the delivery of services and to ensure continuity of services provided to clients in the future.
c. Social workers' documentation should protect clients' privacy to the extent that is possible and appropriate and should include only information that is directly relevant to the delivery of services.
d. Social workers should store records following the termination of services to ensure reasonable future access. Records should be maintained for the number of years required by state statutes or relevant contracts.

3.05 Billing

Social workers should establish and maintain billing practices that accurately reflect the nature and extent of services provided and that identify who provided the service in the practice setting.

3.06 Client Transfer

a. When an individual who is receiving services from another agency or colleague contacts a social worker for services, the social worker should carefully consider the client's needs before agreeing to provide services. To minimize possible confusion and conflict, social workers should discuss with potential clients the nature of the clients' current relationship with other service providers and the implications, including possible benefits or risks, of entering into a relationship with a new service provider.

b. If a new client has been served by another agency or colleague, social workers should discuss with the client whether consultation with the previous service provider is in the client's best interest.

3.07 Administration

a. Social work administrators should advocate within and outside their agencies for adequate resources to meet clients' needs.

b. Social workers should advocate for resource allocation procedures that are open and fair. When not all clients' needs can be met, an allocation procedure should be developed that is nondiscriminatory and based on appropriate and consistently applied principles.

c. Social workers who are administrators should take reasonable steps to ensure that adequate agency or organizational resources are available to provide appropriate staff supervision.

d. Social work administrators should take reasonable steps to ensure that the working environment for which they are responsible is consistent with and encourages compliance with the NASW Code of Ethics. Social work administrators should take reasonable steps to eliminate any conditions in their organizations that violate, interfere with, or discourage compliance with the Code.

3.08 Continuing Education and Staff Development

Social work administrators and supervisors should take reasonable steps to provide or arrange for continuing education and staff development for all staff for whom they are responsible. Continuing education and staff development should address current knowledge and emerging developments related to social work practice and ethics.

3.09 Commitments to Employers

a. Social workers generally should adhere to commitments made to employers and employing organizations.

b. Social workers should work to improve employing agencies' policies and procedures and the efficiency and effectiveness of their services.

   c. Social workers should take reasonable steps to ensure that employers are aware of social workers' ethical obligations as set forth in the NASW Code of Ethics and of the implications of those obligations for social work practice.

   d. Social workers should not allow an employing organization's policies, procedures, regulations, or administrative orders to interfere with their ethical practice of social work. Social workers should take reasonable steps to ensure that their employing organizations' practices are consistent with the NASW Code of Ethics.

   e. Social workers should act to prevent and eliminate discrimination in the employing organization's work assignments and in its employment policies and practices.

   f. Social workers should accept employment or arrange student field placements only in organizations that exercise fair personnel practices.

   g. Social workers should be diligent stewards of the resources of their employing organizations, wisely conserving funds where appropriate and never misappropriating funds or using them for unintended purposes.

3.10 Labor-Management Disputes

   a. Social workers may engage in organized action, including the formation of and participation in labor unions, to improve services to clients and working conditions.

   b. The actions of social workers who are involved in labor-management disputes, job actions, or labor strikes should be guided by the profession's values, ethical principles, and ethical standards. Reasonable differences of opinion exist among social workers concerning their primary obligation as professionals during an actual or threatened labor strike or job action. Social workers should carefully examine relevant issues and their possible impact on clients before deciding on a course of action.

4. Social Workers' Ethical Responsibilities as Professionals

4.01 Competence

   a. Social workers should accept responsibility or employment only on the basis of existing competence or the intention to acquire the necessary competence.

b. Social workers should strive to become and remain proficient in professional practice and the performance of professional functions. Social workers should critically examine and keep current with emerging knowledge relevant to social work. Social workers should routinely review the professional literature and participate in continuing education relevant to social work practice and social work ethics.

c. Social workers should base practice on recognized knowledge, including empirically based knowledge, relevant to social work and social work ethics.

4.02 Discrimination

Social workers should not practice, condone, facilitate, or collaborate with any form of discrimination on the basis of race, ethnicity, national origin, color, sex, sexual orientation, age, marital status, political belief, religion, or mental or physical disability.

4.03 Private Conduct

Social workers should not permit their private conduct to interfere with their ability to fulfill their professional responsibilities.

4.04 Dishonesty, Fraud, and Deception

Social workers should not participate in, condone, or be associated with dishonesty, fraud, or deception.

4.05 Impairment

a. Social workers should not allow their own personal problems, psychosocial distress, legal problems, substance abuse, or mental health difficulties to interfere with their professional judgment and performance or to jeopardize the best interests of people for whom they have a professional responsibility.

b. Social workers whose personal problems, psychosocial distress, legal problems, substance abuse, or mental health difficulties interfere with their professional judgment and performance should immediately seek consultation and take appropriate remedial action by seeking professional help, making adjustments in workload, terminating practice, or taking any other steps necessary to protect clients and others.

4.06 Misrepresentation

  a. Social workers should make clear distinctions between statements made and actions engaged in as a private individual and as a representative of the social work profession, a professional social work organization, or the social worker's employing agency.
  b. Social workers who speak on behalf of professional social work organizations should accurately represent the official and authorized positions of the organizations.
  c. Social workers should ensure that their representations to clients, agencies, and the public of professional qualifications, credentials, education, competence, affiliations, services provided, or results to be achieved are accurate. Social workers should claim only those relevant professional credentials they actually possess and take steps to correct any inaccuracies or misrepresentations of their credentials by others.

4.07 Solicitations

  a. Social workers should not engage in uninvited solicitation of potential clients who, because of their circumstances, are vulnerable to undue influence, manipulation, or coercion.
  b. Social workers should not engage in solicitation of testimonial endorsements (including solicitation of consent to use a client's prior statement as a testimonial endorsement) from current clients or from other people who, because of their particular circumstances, are vulnerable to undue influence.

4.08 Acknowledging Credit

  a. Social workers should take responsibility and credit, including authorship credit, only for work they have actually performed and to which they have contributed.
  b. Social workers should honestly acknowledge the work of and the contributions made by others.

5. *Social Workers' Ethical Responsibilities to the Social Work Profession*

5.01 Integrity of the Profession

  a. Social workers should work toward the maintenance and promotion of high standards of practice.

b. Social workers should uphold and advance the values, ethics, knowledge, and mission of the profession. Social workers should protect, enhance, and improve the integrity of the profession through appropriate study and research, active discussion, and responsible criticism of the profession.

c. Social workers should contribute time and professional expertise to activities that promote respect for the value, integrity, and competence of the social work profession. These activities may include teaching, research, consultation, service, legislative testimony, presentations in the community, and participation in their professional organizations.

d. Social workers should contribute to the knowledge base of social work and share with colleagues their knowledge related to practice, research, and ethics. Social workers should seek to contribute to the profession's literature and to share their knowledge at professional meetings and conferences.

e. Social workers should act to prevent the unauthorized and unqualified practice of social work.

5.02 Evaluation and Research

a. Social workers should monitor and evaluate policies, the implementation of programs, and practice interventions.

b. Social workers should promote and facilitate evaluation and research to contribute to the development of knowledge.

c. Social workers should critically examine and keep current with emerging knowledge relevant to social work and fully use evaluation and research evidence in their professional practice.

d. Social workers engaged in evaluation or research should carefully consider possible consequences and should follow guidelines developed for the protection of evaluation and research participants. Appropriate institutional review boards should be consulted.

e. Social workers engaged in evaluation or research should obtain voluntary and written informed consent from participants, when appropriate, without any implied or actual deprivation or penalty for refusal to participate; without undue inducement to participate; and with due regard for participants' well-being, privacy, and dignity. Informed consent should include information about the nature, extent, and duration of the participation requested and disclosure of the risks and benefits of participation in the research.

f. When evaluation or research participants are incapable of giving informed consent, social workers should provide an appropriate explanation to the participants, obtain the participants' assent to the extent they are able, and obtain written consent from an appropriate proxy.

g. Social workers should never design or conduct evaluation or research that does not use consent procedures, such as certain forms of naturalistic observation and archival research, unless rigorous and responsible review of the research has found it to be justified because of its prospective scientific, educational, or applied value and unless equally effective alternative procedures that do not involve waiver of consent are not feasible.

h. Social workers should inform participants of their right to withdraw from evaluation and research at any time without penalty.

i. Social workers should take appropriate steps to ensure that participants in evaluation and research have access to appropriate supportive services.

j. Social workers engaged in evaluation or research should protect participants from unwarranted physical or mental distress, harm, danger, or deprivation.

k. Social workers engaged in the evaluation of services should discuss collected information only for professional purposes and only with people professionally concerned with this information.

l. Social workers engaged in evaluation or research should ensure the anonymity or confidentiality of participants and of the data obtained from them. Social workers should inform participants of any limits of confidentiality, the measures that will be taken to ensure confidentiality, and when any records containing research data will be destroyed.

m. Social workers who report evaluation and research results should protect participants' confidentiality by omitting identifying information unless proper consent has been obtained authorizing disclosure.

n. Social workers should report evaluation and research findings accurately. They should not fabricate or falsify results and should take steps to correct any errors later found in published data using standard publication methods.

o. Social workers engaged in evaluation or research should be alert to and avoid conflicts of interest and dual relationships with participants, should inform participants when a real or potential conflict of interest arises, and should take steps to resolve the issue in a manner that makes participants' interests primary.

p. Social workers should educate themselves, their students, and their colleagues about responsible research practices.

6. Social Workers' Ethical Responsibilities to the Broader Society

6.01 Social Welfare

Social workers should promote the general welfare of society, from local to global levels, and the development of people, their communities, and their environments. Social workers should advocate for living conditions conducive to the fulfillment of basic human needs and should promote social, economic, political, and cultural values and institutions that are compatible with the realization of social justice.

6.02 Public Participation

Social workers should facilitate informed participation by the public in shaping social policies and institutions.

6.03 Public Emergencies

Social workers should provide appropriate professional services in public emergencies to the greatest extent possible.

6.04 Social and Political Action

a. Social workers should engage in social and political action that seeks to ensure that all people have equal access to the resources, employment, services, and opportunities they require to meet their basic human needs and to develop fully. Social workers should be aware of the impact of the political arena on practice and should advocate for changes in policy and legislation to improve social conditions in order to meet basic human needs and promote social justice.
b. Social workers should act to expand choice and opportunity for all people, with special regard for vulnerable, disadvantaged, oppressed, and exploited people and groups.
c. Social workers should promote conditions that encourage respect for cultural and social diversity within the United States and globally. Social workers should promote policies and practices that demonstrate respect for difference, support the expansion of cultural knowledge and resources, advocate for programs and institu-

tions that demonstrate cultural competence, and promote policies that safeguard the rights of and confirm equity and social justice for all people.

d. Social workers should act to prevent and eliminate domination of, exploitation of, and discrimination against any person, group, or class on the basis of race, ethnicity, national origin, color, sex, sexual orientation, age, marital status, political belief, religion, or mental or physical disability.

Index

423